Praise for Larry Chase's
Essential Business Tactics for the Net, Second Edition

"The Internet is chaos. All the other Internet books that I have seen on the topic only add to the chaos. *Essential Business Tactics for the Net* helps bring order to this ever-changing medium. It will be worth the time and money for you, too."
—Martin Edelston, Founder, Bottom LinePersonal & Bottom Line Business

"Chase successfully demonstrates which traditional marketing strategies apply to the Net and where new thinking begins."
—David S. Klein, Associate Publisher/Editor, *Advertising Age*

"Now that the Internet Revolution is separating out the survivors, one needs Larry Chase's perspective more than ever to make sure they are or their company is one of the survivors."
—Alan Meckler, CEO, Internet.com

"A great primer for anyone who wants to excel in e-marketing! Larry Chase covers all the basics in this 'must have' book for online marketers."
—Patricia Seybold, Author, *Customers.com* and *The Customer Revolution*

"I have to stay on top of all things e-commerce. One way I do that is by subscribing to Larry Chase's *Web Digest For Marketers* email newsletter. Larry's got an uncanny sense of what's real and what isn't. If you're looking for clear-headed and frank assessments of where the Net's going and what it means to you, buy this book and read it, cover to cover."
—Stratton Sclavos, CEO, Verisign

"Larry Chase is the Sgt. Friday of Internet marketing. He has a no nonsense, no BS approach that sticks to the facts, unlike many of the fancy pants new arrivals who define old concepts with new terms and claim that equates to insights. Whether you're a Big Dog or a Puppy in the world of e-commerce, this book contains information that you will find useful. So grab a couple of pints of Guinness and read it."
—John Audette, President, Audette Media

"Is there anything about Internet business Larry Chase doesn't know? I can't think of it."

—Dana Blankenhorn, Internet Analyst

"The story behind too many Internet marketing failures lies in a poor understanding of tactics. Larry Chase has been in this business longer than most and has a way of boiling it down to its essence like few others. Read this book."

—Ken Magil, Editor, *I-Marketing News*

"It was Larry Chase's insights and enthusiasm for Internet marketing back in 1994 that made me decide to step over from traditional marketing communications into the world of e-marketing."

—Ger Dreijer, E-Finance Consultant for IG&H Management Consultants, The Netherlands

"Essential Business Tactics for the Net is the best resource I've found for businesses of any size to truly succeed in marketing on the Net. I could hardly wait for this new edition since my old copy was so dog eared it was nearly worn out."

—Bob Serling, VP Marketing, Nforma

"Focus and perspective. That's what this book offers the reader. Whether you view the Net as a productivity tool or as a marketing tool to expand your market reach, you owe it to yourself to read *Essential Business Tactics for the Net* from cover to cover."

—Gary Morgenstern, Public Relations Director, AT&T

"Large or small, your enterprise needs to have a well-defined strategy that leverages the Internet into competitive marketing advantages. This book shows you how to view your company as part of a Business Eco-System in the Internet Economy. Chase's book is not about the latest e-buzz word but rather how to develop the winning marketing strategies that create value for your enterprise."

—C. Edward Brice, VP Strategic Marketing, SAP Corporation

"I'll admit it. . .I'm a Larry Chase fan. I've been reading his *Web Digest For Marketers* newsletter (http://wdfm.com), for years and pick it above anything as a MUST SUBSCRIBE if you're going to do business on the Net. But why buy the book? Well, what else would a FAN do? I thought a quick read would be interesting, not expecting to learn much and maybe pick up a title I could recommend to the "should I get on the Net?" crowd. Boy. . .did I underestimate Larry's talents. Not only are all the essential tactics there. . .but every page YELLS at me to put down the book and go implement an idea! There aren't any "magic bullets". . .just a solid, complete course on getting down to using the Net for business. As a veteran Net user, I found dozens of ideas to add to my business. . .yet a novice could follow Larry's easy going style. If you're on the Net . . .this book is ESSENTIAL!"

—Warren Whitlock, owner, HeadSpinner.com

Essential Business Tactics for the Net

Second Edition

Larry Chase
Eileen Shulock

with Nancy C. Hanger

Wiley Computer Publishing

John Wiley & Sons, Inc.

NEW YORK • CHICHESTER • WEINHEIM • BRISBANE • SINGAPORE • TORONTO

I dedicate this book to my coauthor, Eileen Shulock, who devoted herself to its quality, detail, and completion. She, in turn, dedicates this book to her most patient husband, Brian Dunleavy, who, at long last, finally gets her back. Thank you, Brian. :) But wait, I'm not finished. The extraordinary efforts of Rebecca Rich were integral to the making of the first edition of this book; so much so that she deserves to be mentioned here in this second edition.

Copyright © 2001 by Larry Chase. All rights reserved.
Published by John Wiley & Sons, Inc.

Published simultaneously in Canada.

Library of Congress Cataloging-in-Publication Data:

Chase, Larry, 1953-
    Essential business tactics for the Net / Larry Chase, Eileen Shulock—2nd ed.
      p. cm.
    "Wiley Computer Publishing."
    Includes index.
    ISBN 0-471-40397-0 (pbk. : alk. paper)
    1. Business enterprises—Computer networks. 2. Internet marketing—Cost effectiveness.
   3. Electronic commerce. 4. World Wide Web.   I. Shulock, Eileen. II. Title.

   HD30.37 .C37 2001
   658.8'00285'4678—dc21   2001017649

Printed in the United States of America

10 9 8 7 6 5 4 3 2 1

Contents

Acknowledgments

The best parts of authorship are the dedication and acknowledgment pages.

Much gratitude goes to Wiley's Christina Berry for her exacting and light editorial touch. The same to the editors of my *Web Digest For Marketers*, Mary Gillen, Gayle Kerley, and Karyn Zoldan, who allowed my coauthor Eileen Shulock and I to focus on this book. Deep and heartfelt gratitude must be publicly acknowledged here to my devoted assistant Richard Witt who deftly provided me with enough "bandwidth" to produce this second edition.

So many others have been supportive in the making of this book. An incomplete list is made up of Silvia (with an "i" not a "y") Rich, Mac (the DM Fox) Ross, Neil Raphan, Matt Lederman, Steve Glusband, and Don Abraham. Additionally, I offer gratitude to Cary Sullivan, Carmela DellaRipa, Ellen Reavis-Gerstein, Deborah Lilly, Dr. Ralph Wilson, Bob Thompson, Adam Boettiger, Sam Alfstad, Geoff Ramsey, Karen Lake, John Audette, Wally Bock, Dan Janal, Anne Holland, and John Kremer.

But wait! There's more. . .Nina Rich, Mark Stacks, Priska Von Beroldingen, Jay Abraham, *Chicken Soup* coauthor Mark Victor Hansen, Danny Cox, Gus Johnson, Chris Knight, Dr. Isis Medina, Kevin Gallagher, Patrick Hennessey, Mike and Joni Zito, Jean Duck, Dick Rich, Tony D'Amelio, Tony Alessandra, Helmut Krone, Joe Karbo, Marty Edelston, Lew Rothman, Dana Blankenhorn, John Verity, Richard G. Nixon, Ken Magil, Ronnie Mesznik, Steve Saka, Dave Townsend, Rush Limbaugh, and. . .

But wait! There's *still* more. . .in addition to the stellar group above, coauthor Eileen Shulock gratefully acknowledges the support of her colleagues at Knowledge Strategies Group, in particular Cynthia Hollen, Doug Carlson, Cheryl Brinker, Patty Garcia, and the "Estrogen Room." Much appreciation goes to the eMarketer team, especially John Mulfinger and Jennifer Marino, who generously supplied us with reports and critical data that validated key suppositions of this book. Thanks as well to Webgrrls New York City, and to Andrea Brown, Randy Epstein, and Sue Khazoyan, who kept the Webgrrls vision alive. Kudos to Wiley's Marnie Wielage, who shepherded this book to completion with patience and class. Special recognition goes to Melanie Gordon of ChatOverIP, who lent her expertise at the final hour. A heartfelt thank you goes to Lori Schwab and Martha Sears for all of their support.

This book reflects the insight and expertise of many people, and gratitude must be extended to Courtney Pulitzer, Kenneth Hein, Tony Laxa Jr., Emily Noble Pushman, Chad Sterns, Rachel Pine, Jack O'Dwyer, Brooke Schulz, Stacey Albin, Ellen Ullman, Mark Beckloff, John Simpson, Jeff Seacrist, Colleen Kerry, Eric Norlin, Mark Hurst, Declan Dunn, Alice O'Rourke, Ellen Auwarter, Alexis Bonnell, Kristie Hughes, Sharla Sponhauer, Nick Nyhan, Michael Carlon, Jody Dodson, Danny Sullivan, Bob Thompson, Nandita Jhaveri, Carolyn Love, Tina Murphy, and Tom Peters.

Acknowledgment is hereby given to Nancy C. Hanger who worked with me on the first edition of this book.

About the Authors

Larry Chase is an international Internet consultant, author, and speaker. He has consulted with Fortune 500 companies such as Con Edison, New York Life, 3Com, and EDS, as well as some of the Internet marketing pioneers themselves, like Hotel Discounts, Auto-By-Tel, and 1-800FLOWERS. Since Chase saw the potential of the Net early on, he was prominently featured in the pivotal *Business Week* cover story, "How the Internet Will Change the Way You Do Business," way back in November of 1994. The *New York Times*, *USA Today*, *Inc.* magazine, *Bottom Line Business*, CNNfn, CNBC, plus scores of trade magazines and newsletters regularly seek him out for his insights. Reviews from Larry Chase's *Web Digest For Marketers* newsletter, (http://wdfm.com), which is read by more than 150,000 people each month, have been syndicated to *Advertising Age, DM News* and *Business Marketing* magazines. His columns and seminars are seen worldwide.

Chase started one of the first of two commercial websites in New York City. Prior to that, he worked for New York's most celebrated ad agencies as an award-winning strategic copywriter. After working on consumer brands such as Heinz, Volkswagen, Polaroid, CBS, and Avis, he chose to focus on high-tech products and services, "since there are always new and unique selling propositions worth writing about." Chase worked for technology clients such as AT&T, Compaq, IBM, Digital Equipment Corporation, GTE, Xerox, NYNEX, and "just about anything that had an 'x' in it." He specialized in technology ten years before it was fashionable to do so: "Now, it's chic to be geek."

Chase lives and works in New York City, and can be reached via email at me@larrychase.com. For more information on Chase and his services, visit his firm's website at http://www.chaseonline.com. If you have questions thereafter, call 212-876-1096.

 Eileen Shulock is an Internet marketing, e-commerce, and merchandising expert. As Vice President of Retail Strategy for Knowledge Strategies Group, an omnitailing development company, she works with clients to generate maximum sales and establish meaningful and long-lasting customer relationships via the Web, kiosks, mobile and wireless applications. She has over ten years of real-world retail management experience with some of the world's most successful specialty retailers and manufacturers, and more than six years of experience in the Internet business, where she has worked in the areas of online marketing, public relations, business strategy, and e-commerce development. For over five years Shulock has also been the managing editor of *Web Digest For Marketers*, and is publisher of the newly launched eTrendWire. As the former director of Webgrrls International, she continues her role with the organization as the volunteer director of Webgrrls New York City, the founding chapter of the 40,000-member network. Shulock is a frequently published author and speaker. She lives and works in New York City and can be reached via email at eileens@wdfm.com.

Introduction

Much of what was written in the last edition of this book has come to pass. You could call it prescience, or you could simply agree that the Internet has fundamentally changed the way we do business. However, the addition of a .com or a .biz to your brand name does not make you bulletproof, as events since April 2000 have shown us. The fact is, the laws of human nature and sound business practices haven't been changed, only modified and augmented by this new medium.

That's what this book is about: integrating the Internet into your business so that it makes strategic and financial sense for you. Since it's written by two seasoned Internet authorities who have been around from the days of "http what?" to the issuing of dot com stock options not worth the paper they are printed on, you'll be learning from the front lines. Whether you're a two-man startup in 800 square feet of space, or a product manager in a multinational corporation, you'll find practical options and opportunities you need to know about.

This book is rooted in reality, giving you examples and anecdotes from our experiences and those of our clients. If you want frank, brutally honest assessments of what works and what doesn't, keep reading. My coauthor, Eileen Shulock, and I promise to deliver just that.

Practical. If we were to describe the Net in a single word, that would be it. For that reason, this book takes the exact same approach. We want you to know what practical things you can do right now, after you close this book. We also want you to see what is realistically possible in the near term, both financially and technologically. We will share with you rules of measure that we use to determine whether something new on the Net is worth paying attention to, or whether it's a fleeting fad. Knowing the difference isn't always easy. In Figure I.1, you see a letter written from Thomas Alva Edison to my great-grandfather, Edmond Gerson, who was a showman and promoter in the mid-nineteenth century. In that letter, Edison referred to the "musical telephone," which we might think of today as a type of cable radio. You see, the wizard of Menlo Park himself couldn't always predict just how a technology would ultimately be used, once put into motion.

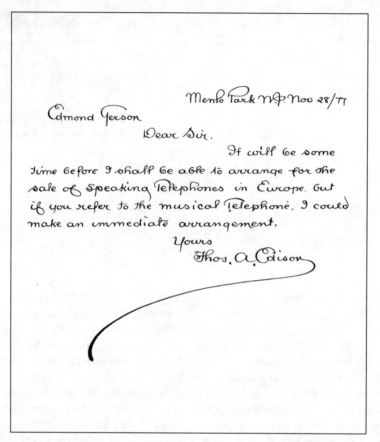

Menlo Park N.J. Nov 28/77

Edmond Gerson

    Dear Sir.

        It will be some time before I shall be able to arrange for the sale of speaking Telephones in Europe. But if you refer to the musical Telephone, I could make an immediate arrangement.

        Yours

        Thos. A. Edison

Figure I.1 Thomas Edison's letter to Larry Chase's great-grandfather shows not even Edison always knew how new technology would ultimately be employed.

This book is divided into two basic sections:

- Knowing how to use the Net for your company's "internal affairs," that is, how you can run faster, cheaper, and smarter.
- Employing the Internet for your company's "external affairs," whereby you use the Net as an effective communications tool for reaching those outside your firm.

Part One: Integrating the Internet Inside Your Company

Chapter 1, "Cutting Costs Across Your Enterprise: How to Run a Tighter, More Competitive Ship," shows you how the Net can do just that: bring down your faxing, phone, mailing, and other day-to-day costs to which you may hardly give a second thought. It also explores online auctions and business-to-business networks that have emerged to help the business owner work faster, smarter, and cheaper. The resulting newfound savings pour directly into profit margins, which are already being squeezed from every direction.

Chapter 2, "Using the Net as a Resource for Human Resources," outlines how you can tap into labor markets both near and far, and how to shape your company to appeal to potential employees. Taking advantage of the exploding fields of distance training and learning can also help you run a tighter ship and reduce costs.

Chapter 3, "Mining the Internet for All It's Worth," shows how you can have a field day digging up valuable information for free. Other information that used to be way beyond the budgets of many companies is now offered at bargain basement prices as well. We'll give you a road map to both.

Chapter 4, "http://007: Spying on Your Competitors and Yourself," demonstrates how to keep tabs on your competition, as well as on your own enterprise. You'll be able to get so close to what your competitors are thinking, you'll quite possibly be able to predict what their next move will be. Take advantage of your competition by learning from them. Let them show you what they're doing right and what they're doing wrong. After all, they may be your next business partners!

Part Two: Integrating the Internet into Your Marketing

Chapter 5, "Your Brand Image and the Internet," gives you proven guidelines to successfully represent yourself online, both as a person and as a company. We'll teach you that "branding is in the doing," and show you how to extend your brand every time you touch your customer.

Chapter 6, "Retail: Setting Up Shop on the Net," walks you through the different options you have to open up your online doors for business or build your e-commerce business so that it remains competitive with the current technical landscape. Written in plain English with whimsical asides, you'll see what to look for when figuring out the best approach for your given situation.

Chapter 7, "Online Events, Promotions, and Attractions: How to Make a "Scene" and Draw Them In," will help you breathe life into your website using both online and offline promotional techniques. Doing so will allow you to circulate key prospects through your online space on an ongoing basis.

Chapter 8, "Direct Marketing and Sales Support," shows you how the Internet employs tactics and practices similar to the disciplines of traditional Direct Marketing. It's also important to understand where these two disciplines diverge. This chapter not only shows you the differences, but demonstrates how you can develop instant, inbound leads on the Internet as well.

Chapter 9, "Public Relations, the Internet Way," demonstrates exactly why the Internet is proving to be the golden age of public relations. Learn some of the best-kept secrets of how to interact with the media and what will make you newsworthy—public relations tips and techniques that will serve you right now and in the future.

A Road Map for Readers

Should you read this book from front to back, or on an as-needed, "a la carte" basis? The answer is yes to both options. We wrote it both ways. We want you to benefit from the best practices and experiences used by the Internet cognoscente. If you're going to read Part Two primarily, we urge you to glean creative ideas from the first section. If you plan on primarily using Part One, consider reviewing the second half for a well-rounded look at the importance of marketing. After all, as Figure I.1 further underscores, Edison himself was keenly aware of how important marketing was to his business.

No matter which way you read this book, please be sure to check out the online resource sections that follow the chapters. These suggested URLs represent the best places for you to start exploring each subject online. We've waded through the noise to find the best of the best for you. In addition, most chapters in this book have an online resource center at http://www.wiley.com/compbooks/chase containing hyperlinked site reviews. These are the sites that we consider worthy of your valuable time. But by the time you read this, new sites will launch and old favorites may change. What's a reader to do? Go to http://wdfm.com to subscribe to my weekly *Web Digest For Marketers* newsletter, which brings you 15 mercifully short reviews of interest to marketers. Each edition is archived at my site (see Figure I.2), so you will also find over six years' worth of learning at your fingertips.

Finally, it is necessary to point out that any book written about the Internet is like taking a picture of a horse race, since the Internet is a dynamic and rapidly changing medium. Web addresses that are valid today may not be tomorrow. Things that are true this year may not be so next year. We want you, the reader, to know that we have put forth our best efforts in gathering together the information we think will benefit you most. We also urge you to do additional and continuous research in those specific areas that are germane to your pursuit.

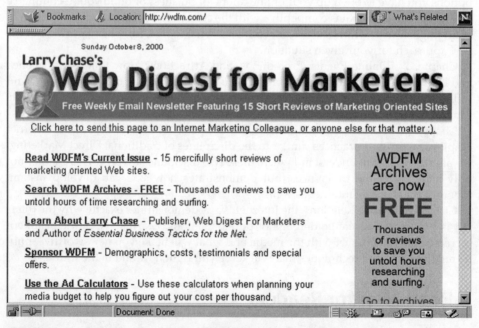

Figure I.2   Home page of Larry Chase's *Web Digest For Marketers.*

Integrating the Internet
Inside Your Company

Cutting Costs across Your Enterprise: How to Run a Tighter, More Competitive Ship

Several years back, the first edition of this book began with the question: "Skeptics of the Internet's influence on businesses often ask the question: 'How much money have you made on the Internet today?'"

The answer was, and still is: For most companies, that's the wrong question to ask at this time. A trailblazing few—such as Dell Computer, which manages to ring up web sales to the tune of $16 billion a year—have transformed their web operations into profit centers. A better question to ask companies right now would be: How has the Internet made your operation run faster, smarter, and cheaper? Whether you're a purchasing manager in a global enterprise or a two-man start-up in a basement, you will both have certain practices in common. Both companies buy office equipment, utilize communications networks and instruments, travel, employ personnel, and need to further exploit the Net to their respective ends in order to keep a competitive edge. This chapter will help you do this for your own company, as innumerable free or inexpensive web-based business tools and solutions created over the past few years have changed the way that we conduct business. You'll learn about the following:

- Application Service Providers (ASPs)
- Unified messaging
- Fax over IP
- Internet telephony
- B2B exchanges

■ Customer service savings

■ Intranets and Extranets

■ Distributed printing

Optimizing Your Purchasing Power

In geek-speak, the Internet is known as an open-computing environment. This openness has a monumental impact on the marketplace as well. Putting scores of competitors within one click of each other makes for a truly open, and often brutal, marketplace. According to Internet research firm Jupiter Communications, the nonservice business-to-business (B2B) e-commerce marketplace in the United States will be worth $6.3 trillion, or 42 percent of the market, by 2005—as compared to the 3 percent of nonservice B2B trade conducted online in year 2000.

Pretty impressive figures. In addition, about 92 percent of today's online B2B sales are now direct, or made by one seller to many buyers. Jupiter predicts that 35 percent of online B2B transactions will be made using a *net market* with many buyers and many sellers or a *coalition market* with a consortium of buyers and sellers. Jupiter advises companies to incorporate Internet strategies immediately throughout their procurement and sales processes. So do we. Let's begin.

Why Buy When You Can Rent?

You might recognize this reversal of the real estate adage, Why rent when you can buy? On the Internet, the opposite is true. As more and more web-supported products and services become available, it is increasingly common for businesses to "rent" the right to use a product or service from a particular company, and to manage that function over the Web (or incorporate it into their site). An *application service provider* (ASP) is a company that offers individuals or enterprises access over the Internet to applications and related services that would otherwise have to be located in their own personal or enterprise computers.

The ASP market is exploding, especially for the small to midsized business market. Why should you reinvent the wheel and build an application internally, when you can rent and manage the solution over the Web? If it's not part of your core business, then it makes perfect sense to tap into an ASP's expertise and constantly improve application functionality. You can either piece together various solutions for your computing or business from a number of ASPs, or there are complete business solutions that you can tap into to handle all of your business needs at once. Each approach has its pros and cons. You might want the convenience of managing all of your web-marketing activities from a small-business resource like bCentral. But what if you have very sophisticated needs for an email list, and bCentral does not provide them? You may need to tap into a special mailing list provider to meet that need. Throughout this chapter we will explore both single-service applications and integrated suites of services. The great thing about the ASP market is that its offerings are constantly improving. Even traditional software providers, such as Peachtree and Microsoft (see Figure 1.1) are moving to an ASP model so that you can pick and choose what works best for

Figure 1.1   Microsoft offers small businesses an ASP solution for Microsoft Office.

you. As a business owner, this is a business trend that will have a very direct and positive impact on your bottom line.

According to eMarketer's November 2000 *ASP Report*:

> Just over one year ago, there were fewer than 100 ASPs. As of May 2000, this number reached 500, and as of October 2000 the ASP Industry Consortium counted 650 members worldwide. Not unlike the mushrooming growth of B2B exchanges, new application service providers are launching at a spectacular rate.

A significant factor behind the growth of the ASP business model is the Internet and the success of network-based computing. In brief, the history of remote delivery of software applications began in the 1960s as businesses shared mainframe computer processing by remotely accessing their services on an as-needed basis.

In the 1980s, the development of desktop computing placed software applications on the personal computer at the fringes of the enterprise network. But as client-server computing grew during the last half of the 1990s, the cumbersome task of upgrading and maintaining software applications at the edge of the network was switched to a more centralized location at the server level.

The growing presence of the Internet, combined with increased and cheaper bandwidth, has further reasserted the vision of network-based computing in which the bulk of information is processed and stored at central locations on a network. Instead of returning to the dumb terminals of the past, however, so-called "thin-terminals" will be the personal computers of the future. Applications will be hosted and their data will be stored on central servers, while users will access the network from simple terminals equipped only with a browser and basic desktop software applications.

The five reasons cited for using an ASP are:

- Capital outlay is easier for small businesses that opt to use ASP services.

- Monthly subscription fee, rather than up-front installation charges.

- Upgrades and maintenance are handled by the ASP.

- Start-ups get up and running more quickly with the resources provided by an ASP.

- ASPs often have closer relationships with major software providers, thus speeding new product delivery and support. (Sources: Sun Microsystems 1999, eMarketer 1999.)

Even industry leader Microsoft has gone the ASP route. You might ask, Why wouldn't I just use Microsoft Office applications the old way, by installing the software? The answer is: time and money. Distributing and maintaining increasingly complex software applications on the customer's desktop has become increasingly expensive in terms of customer service for the software providers. Every time an upgrade is made, millions of customers must be supported and walked through changes and incompatibilities. On the user end, the headaches and downtime that result from technical installations (and reinstallations) can cost thousands of dollars in lost productivity and IT support, even for the small business. The ASP model eliminates the specialized IT infrastructure (and headcount) required to make sure that everything is running smoothly.

TIP If you'd like to start searching for ASPs for your particular needs right now, go to SearchASP.com, where you will find thousands to choose from (see Figure 1.2).

Deborah Lilly, my speaking agent, agrees. "Our biggest challenge was the need to coordinate everyone's schedules," she explains. Lilly reviewed five companies for a web-based solution. "We used to handle this on an intranet, and had people dial-in on a dial-up network. They would access their calendar, they could change, add, synchronize, and then everyone could access it," Lilly says. "But now there are too many of us to dial in." Lilly looked at calendar solutions, and she discovered that having what she needed custom made would cost about $300,000. "None of the companies I looked at had a quick and easy solution, which was to 'webify' our Intranet," she continues. "Finally, I said, Why reinvent the wheel?"

She visited the Microsoft site to find a local service that could set her up with an ASP version of Microsoft 2000 Exchange Server with Outlook. "Microsoft has the only solution now, today, that I could use," Lilly continues. "It's one that everybody already had, so there was no expense to go out and buy a $500 program for every employee. It made all the sense in the world to use the tools at hand" (see Figure 1.3). Lilly's solution runs $20 per user per month. "Best of all," concludes Lilly, "there is no learning curve. If someone doesn't know how to use Outlook, I send them out to get a tape at the local software store."

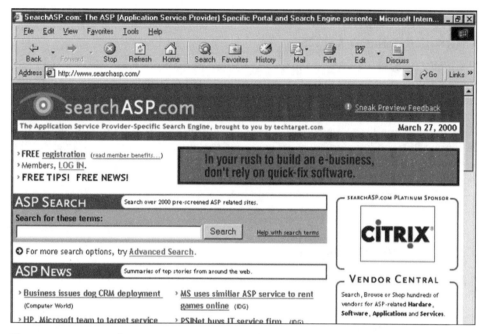

Figure 1.2   At SearchASP.com, you can review hundreds of ASP solutions.

SearchASP.com serves the needs of prospective and current users of Application Service Providers. It is part of TechTarget.com's network of industry-specific IT websites. All rights reserved. ©1999–2000 SearchASP.com.

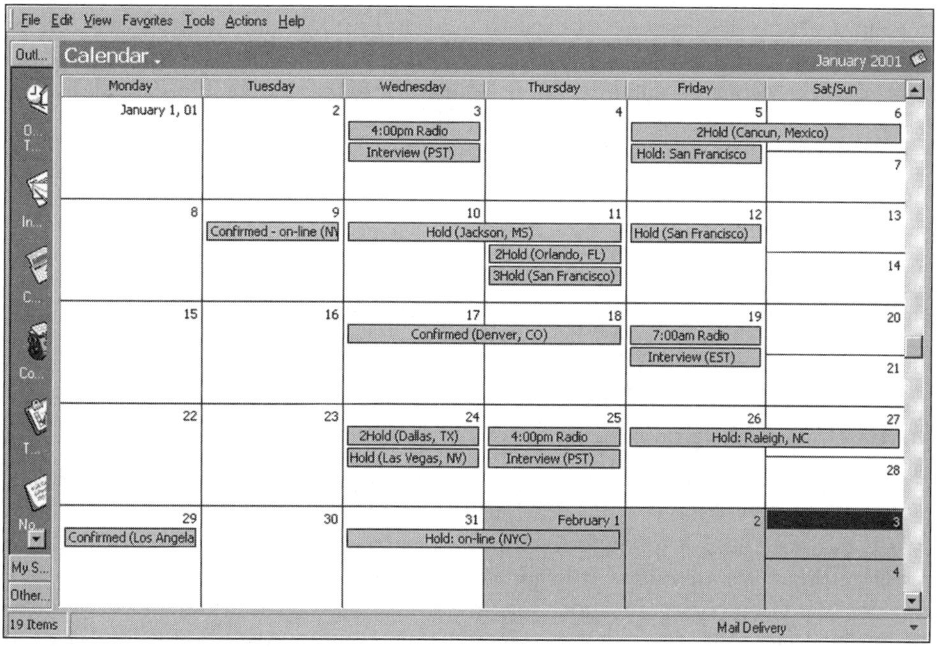

Figure 1.3   Deb Lilly, Larry Chase's speaking manager, uses an ASP solution to manage her speaker calendars.

Using the Internet to Cut Communication Costs

If you use the Internet to spend less on your communications costs, you'll have more money to spend on things that are core to building your business. When this book was first published, the concept of sending a fax over the Internet, thereby saving the cost of a local or long-distance phone call, was a very new and exciting concept. Today, we have moved from fax management to total communications integration systems. It is becoming less and less necessary for everyone to deliver the same message about the features and benefits of their products. These days, companies are not focusing on the benefits of a piece of their Fax over IP solution or their low prices to terminate minutes using Voice over IP; rather, the focus is on how to apply these solutions into corporate structure to decrease operational costs and improve work flow.

Communications Convergence

Communications integration is a trend to watch. Why? The Application Service Provider (ASP) model has been around for awhile, and in 2000, the year of the ASP, many companies claiming to offer ASP solutions were simply packaging features and benefits of single technologies and trying to market and sell them as application packages. In order to truly emphasize the real benefits of the ASP, Melanie Gordon, cofounder of ChatOverIP (a strategy consultant company for building businesses by creating customized Internet communication solutions) states, "There is a major shift in today's market. Outsourcing is no longer a four-letter word, and partnering is the name of the game. In order to be effective within this new model, the goal of the partnership is not just to broaden your service offering, but to build value as a VA ASP or Value-Added ASP." Building value includes adding new broadband technologies, various technical platforms, and innovative solutions into the partnership. This allows for the services and solutions to be distributed in a seamless fashion; therefore the shift that is actually occurring requires a new perception. Vendors are no longer viewed as *external*. Rather, they are considered part of the team, with an expectation that they will add better functions and support.

More than just renting applications, the VA ASP offers integrated technologies coupled with customer service and strategic consulting, both of which are essential to ensuring that your externally hosted solutions will behave and be managed as if they are an internal part of IT operations.

Unified Messaging

Unified messaging, which is offered by companies like OneBox, iBasis, and 3Com (CommWorks) revolutionizes the efficiency of the way in which we manage our business communications, especially for the road warrior. Unified messaging is not just about cutting costs anymore—it is about the advent of collaborative and interactive services that bring communications together in real time, in a virtual world. Services abound that will unify fax, email, voicemail, and more for a cost-effective approach to local, national, and even international communication. Let's take a look at a few.

Onebox.com (http://www.onebox.com) brings together multiple services for a seamless communications management solution. Onebox offers consumers free, Internet-based integrated messaging services that deliver voicemail, email, and fax, for the Web and phone. After signing up at the site, you are assigned a Onebox account. People call your Onebox phone number to leave traditional voicemail messages or to send faxes. You can send and receive email to your Onebox account, and you can even send or receive voice email, so that you can pick up or send your email over the phone. How do they make money, you ask? Onebox.com rents its telecommunications solutions to companies such as ISPs and large corporations that need this type of service, but do not want to build it in-house. Their consumer service is a constant *proof of concept* and testing bed for new products and services that they will eventually roll out to their corporate customers.

J2, (http://www.j2.com [formerly known as JFax]) is another leading player in the unified messaging space (see Figure 1.4). Tired of missing important messages while on the road, founder Jaye Muller (the J in J2) invented a system that would deliver faxes and voicemail via a universally accessible channel—the Internet. As a result, J2 Free Fax Plus services give you a free personal phone number that you can use to receive voice messages and faxes in your email inbox. The messages are converted to attachments (.tif or .jfx formats), which you click and open to view, print, file, or forward. Voice messages are sent as audio files that you listen to over your computer's speakers. Those who do business internationally will be interested to know that you can sign up for either a U.S. or a U.K. number (90 area codes around the world are available)—meaning that your international clients will pay far less to fax to you via

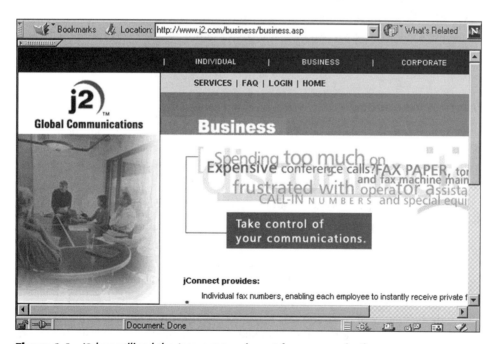

Figure 1.4   J2 has utilized the Internet to reinvent fax communications.

your U.K. account. What about sending faxes? The company offers the ability to send individual faxes, or to broadcast faxes, for a $2.95 per month subscription fee, plus usage costs, in addition to several nifty for-fee services.

An alternate is FaxTel's Internet Fax Box (http://www.faxtel.com). After making a one-time investment of approximately $400 for hardware, FaxTel claims that you'll never have to pay for faxing inside the U.S. again. The Internet Fax Box differs from the crowd of Internet services that offer faxes as email attachments, and web-based services that allow you to send text messages to fax machines. Instead, you plug your existing fax machine into the small Internet Fax Box device. After you plug the Internet Fax Box into your phone line, you can send and receive faxes for free. The device, which is modem-enabled, turns an analog fax signal into packets of data that can travel over the Internet to the FaxTel network. FaxTel routes the fax over the Internet to whichever of its many servers is located the closest to your fax's destination. It then turns the packets back into a normal fax, sending it to your recipient. The service works with your existing Internet service provider. If you and your recipient both have an Internet Fax Box device you can bypass the FaxTel network and send faxes directly over the Internet to each other. In addition, unlike many other free, Net-based services, FaxTel faxes do not contain branding or advertising messages. The company also offers a number of other messaging solutions, including ScanFax!, a software application that transforms any scanner into a virtual fax free of long-distance phone charges.

TIP   The Internet will continue to apply downward pressure on the cost of communication, both on- and offline. Because of this intense competition, a good number of these services will not survive. Therefore, make sure that whomever you go with, online or off, has a good track record and is apt to stay around. The last thing you need is to wake up one day only to find that your fax provider or "communications center" no longer exists. For this reason, it's wise not just to shop on price alone but on constancy, credibility, and continuity as well.

Internet Telephony

What about Internet telephony? Has it improved since the first publication of this book? In many ways it has. It's in your best interest to see if continuing improvements in Internet telephony can work for your company. There are three ways that you can use the Internet to transmit and receive voice messaging:

Computer to computer. Where your computer is the telephone.

Computer to telephone. Where you call someone from your computer and he or she answers on the phone.

Phone to phone. Where you use the Internet as the network between two telephones, rather than traditional long-distance companies such as AT&T or MCI.

Internet telephony is fun; how productive it can really be is something else, although the quality of these services has improved greatly. I remember buying early software that allowed me to talk to my colleague in California. Our phone bills were out of control. Our conversation was pretty comical. We were both shouting at our computer microphones, with a substantial time delay. The conversation went like this:

"... ear you!"

"... 'm fine. _ow about _ou?"

"_ot bad."

"_ear the delay?"

"_es!"

We went back to using the telephone.

Like the faxing capabilities that have morphed into Internet-based communications centers, a number of services are available that supply a full range of telephony options. Some of these services stand alone, such as DialPad.com (http://www .dialpad.com), which offers free long-distance phone calls from your computer to anywhere in the United States, provided you listen to an advertising message before placing your call. Others bring together a complete suite of telephony options. By offering PC-to-Phone, Phone-to-Phone, PC-to-PC, voicemail, e-commerce, and other features, Net2Phone (http://www.net2phone.com) has enabled more than 1 million customers to place calls over the Internet at rates up to 95 percent less than current phone rates.

TIP Before you make an investment in the hardware, try it on a short contract with an outside provider. You might want to test the medium before plunging in. Simply farm out those functions that you're considering and test them during short-term contracts that you negotiate with a provider of such services. If it works, replicate the scheme in-house. If it doesn't, you've just bypassed beaucoup headaches and investments.

In any of these scenarios, it seems likely that you'll maintain a primary long-distance telephone provider and siphon off some of the traffic to a secondary voice network where you can save some money. Look to the major ISPs and phone carriers to aggressively market communications and telephony services. The more bundled services they can offer you, the more apt you are to stay or join up with them in the first place. For the ISP, your loyalty reduces churn and means they can spend less time retaining customers and more time acquiring new customers.

"In 1999 and early 2000, Voice over IP (VoIP) was booming within the IP telephony market, and for voice, it was all about cheap minutes," states Melanie Gordon, who writes the "IP Traffic Report" column for *TelephonyWorld.com* (see Figure 1.5) and who has launched her Internet communications solution company called ChatOverIP (http://www.chatoverip.com). "Voice over IP has completely been refurbished, but IP telephony has been around a long time." According to Gordon, "as with telecommunications, the rates have gone down. The phone you use at home has gotten cheaper, and the same is true with the Internet. The margins for providers are getting narrower and narrower, so unified messaging is growing." Why? Vendors need to have a better impact on the bottom line by providing more services and true value to customers. "Now the customer can shop around," she continues. "Things that were 'luxuries' before, such as VAS fax and email to voicemail are now more likely to be turnkey services, and for tomorrow that is what it is all about—offering true value, turnkey services."

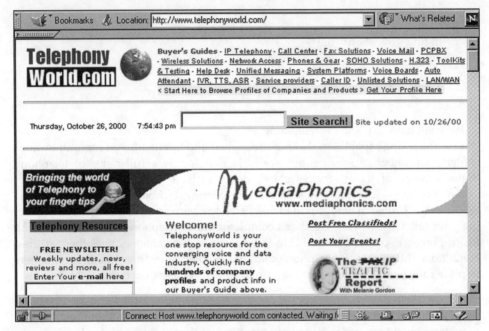

Figure 1.5   TelephonyWorld is a portal for information on telephony products and trends.

After covering the industry for years, Gordon decided to launch her own company out of frustration. "I was traveling too much, and spending too much money to go and see speakers at conferences, but I couldn't interact with them," Gordon explains. Chat-OverIP was initially an Internet chat forum designed to bring telephony professionals together. The team used their influence within the industry to pull in experts and bring business contacts together for online chats and events. "Then we looked at the great response, and decided to bring all these different IP worlds together—fax, voice, unified messaging," she continues.

More and more, the services provided by IP vendors are a commodity. Now, Gordon helps clients make sense of this business. "We at 'Chat' decided to offer full-fledged web conferencing, with personalization and flexibility, while working with different vendors to deliver the best solution," she continues. Essentially, ChatOverIP has readapted a new medium to achieve a higher degree of Internet Communication solutions by combining technology with service, strategy, and collaboration, all developed, coordinated, and managed by their internal team. ChatOverIP partners include Evoke, CMP Media/CommWeb, and eShare Technologies.

"There is a shortage of true Internet Communication Solution strategy consultants available that truly understand where the industry has come from and who are therefore able to effectively guide a solution for the future," Gordon states. ChatOverIP was developed to reduce costs and hassles in travel by building on existing technologies with revolutionary strategies (marketing, corporate, public relations) that enable the user to address true business needs, such as sales training, corporate announcements, and product launches. "Removing the need to physically bring a group together by gathering them online—from wherever they are in the world—without losing the effect of the message was key," comments Gordon. "I use a philosophy I learned in school that was coined by Marshall McLuhan: *The Medium is the Message*. What we do differently is that we understand how to use the medium (Internet communication services), and we teach you how to incorporate your message for effective and efficient dissemination."

Gordon firmly believes in value-added service. "We will work with you personally," she states. "We figure out what works best for you, and what digital multimedia platform is for you. We teach your staff, we teach you how to publicize your events, we tell you what web marketing works, what time of day is best for a chat, web conference, or roundtable. This isn't a fashion show, this is about content, community, and collaborative enhanced services."

Gordon still uses the knowledge she acquired from building a marketing division for a major company producing IP Fax and Enterprise Fax solutions. According to her, like Fax over IP, "eFax for today's simple office use is fine, but for a business it is not OK. Businesses need scalability, carrier grade 24/7 reliability, and accounting management through a carrier network." "Fax over IP is about open infrastructure, peer-to-peer networking availability, and least-cost routing through all the networks, not just the network you are using. It's about truly giving a global reach. You need to look at your future business needs and how you will integrate Fax over IP into your workflow. You need to understand where you need to be and want to be tomorrow. When buying a computer, you buy for the future, you buy more RAM, because you know you will need it eventually. It's a safe investment, because with technology you know you need it. The same is true with your IP solutions."

Whether you are deciding on an IP fax solution, VoIP solution, combining a unified messaging platform, or looking for Internet communication solutions, be sure your due diligence extends beyond your office. Use the same philosophy you would as if you were shopping for a car—*try before you buy*.

The Wireless Evolution

Who needs phones, faxes, or voicemail when your entire communications system can fit into your pocket? Mobile, Internet-enabled cell phones and PDAs have exploded onto the market, both in the United States and in Europe and Asia. According to industry resource allNetDevices (http://www.allnetdevices.com), at the time of writing the United States has the highest penetration for the Internet, but one of the lowest for mobile data. On the other hand, in Western Europe (where Internet penetration is not so high) there is a booming market for mobile services, and Asia Pacific is soon expected to overtake Western Europe as the biggest mobile market. By 2005, mobile data penetration will be approaching mobile user penetration levels in the United States, Western Europe, and Japan. It is expected that by that time, all mobile terminals will be data-enabled and that subscribers will be able to seamlessly access both mobile data and Internet services. In all regions, mobile data penetration is expected to exceed Internet penetration. The ubiquitous use of wireless devices for data access will alter the way service payments are structured, as per-minute or per-second billing will no longer be appropriate. This, in turn, will alter entire business models.

There is much to say about wireless and mobile devices, and how they will impact our business lives. In fact, we could write an entire book about it. There are many lessons to learn from our counterparts in Europe and Asia, who have the benefit of a two-to three-year advantage in terms of wireless technology and protocol. In general, the availability of relevant, personalized content and applications will be crucial to the takeoff and success of the wireless Internet. What kind of information do I need on a timely basis, wherever I am? Certainly not commercials! As we've learned from our online ventures, the user has to see a benefit over and above the technology itself. On the business level, customer retention will rely upon personalization and breadth of services, and a battle for customer loyalty—and the resulting ability to market to that customer—will develop.

Service Evaluations

In addition to using the Net as an alternative network for buying long-distance services and the like, you can also use it to purchase and compare rates and services of everything from traditional carriers like AT&T and MCI to an actual evaluation of the sound quality of various service providers. TeleBright.com (http://www.telebright.com) provides one-stop shopping for telecommunications services. Targeting small- to medium-sized businesses, the company offers a neutral site for comparing and purchasing telecom—all at no cost to the customer. The TeleBright proprietary IntelliRate technology instantly produces customized results, allowing real-time, side-by-side comparisons of telecom services, including long distance, wireless, local, Internet dial-up, DSL, T1, and web hosting. TeleBright also offers free expert analysis and comparison assistance, and provides total service before, during, and after the sale, including email status updates once an order has been placed and a 90-day checkup to ensure that customers have received the most affordable option available. "Our mission is to be the trusted source for consumers when purchasing telecommunications services," states Kristie Hughes, Vice President of Marketing for TeleBright.com. "Our customers have seen savings as high as 68 percent in some cases. For those who have not comparison shopped for telecommunications services, there is money waiting to be discovered. On average, customers see a savings of 50 percent, which can be contributed directly to the bottom line."

Even though your current long-distance company may be providing you with an overall good deal, your calling patterns may warrant a service more finely tuned to your needs.

Using the Internet to Work Together

Document sharing, or collaborative work environments, is another service area that has exploded over the past few years. Whether you are conducting virtual meetings and presentations, or collaborating on documents in cyberspace, you have many options to choose from. Most of these options combine document sharing, virtual meeting space, some sort of telephony services, and even video conferencing—for the ultimate in virtual office environments.

At Astound.com (http://www.astound.com), users can publish a PowerPoint presentation to an online conference room and invite up to two audience members to join them for visuals and chat for free. For larger groups or enterprise-wide conference use, Astound.com offers rentals and fee-based *corporate portals*. Ideally, online conferences reduce travel costs for business and client meetings or training.

It's a collaborative world. Likewise, kudos go to WebEx (http://www.webex.com) for the creation of a free, real-time conferencing service that allows users to set up private, interactive, collaborative meetings on the Web. A complete suite of tools is available to navigate, mark-up, and interact live, in real time, whether on documents in progress or on the Web (with interactive whiteboard capabilities from Mimeo included). WebEx is now the designated meeting place for hundreds of companies and associations.

eShare Expressions Interaction Suite (http://www.eshare.com) from eShare Technologies, Inc., is another provider of collaborative work solutions. It can be used for virtual meetings, live training and conferencing, distance learning, moderated events, and social chat. The user-friendly interface of the eShare Expressions Interaction Suite works with any browser—even behind firewalls. Plus, it does not require users to have special plug-ins or client-side software, which is an advantage when working with a diverse group of people.

InterCall (http://www.intercall.com) offers a suite of audio and web-based conferencing solutions (see Figure 1.6). "We work with several Fortune 500 companies,"

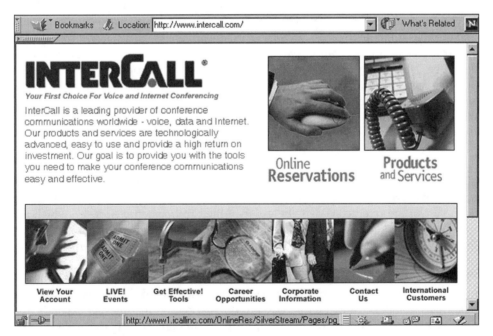

Figure 1.6 InterCall provides voice, data, and Internet conferencing options for both individuals and Fortune 500 companies.

©2000 InterCall, Inc.

states Sharla Sponhauer, a meeting consultant for the company. "InterCall has several different solutions to meet different needs." With InterCall, a web presentation is accompanied by a conference call. The conference leader can control everyone's browser so that everyone is on the same path. "The Gap uses InterCall as a tool to present their stores with visual merchandising guidelines," she continues. "While store managers review visuals of upcoming window and interior displays, they can ask questions and interact. Other clients use the service to launch products or to conduct regular sales meetings."

The cost savings of using such a technology are enormous. With another product called *eInterCall* (http://www.eintercall.com), unscheduled conference calls can be initiated at any time, simply by surfing on over to the site. Calls are conducted through the site for 45 cents per minute per person. "When compared to the costs of time, coordination, and travel, the savings quickly add up," notes Sponhauer. Who is leading the web-conferencing trend? "Dot coms are leading," she explains. "Old school companies want face-to-face meetings with their staff. New economy companies view that as a 'time suck.' They are comfortable with the technology and embrace it with the attitude of 'let's do better things with our time.'"

Using the Net to Trim Travel Costs

The Internet has turned travel services into a commodity-based business. Airline seats and hotel rooms are known as "vanishing commodities." It is considered sinful to let an airline seat fly empty; it would be better to have someone in that seat at 30 percent on the dollar rather than empty at nothing on the dollar. An airline never recoups the cost of transporting an empty seat, and there is always a potential customer who would be delighted to have an airplane seat for a discount. From that premise, Priceline.com (http://www.priceline.com) and the name your own price concept was born. Since its successful launch into the airline travel space, Priceline.com has added hotels, vacation packages, car rentals, and more. Clearly, the Internet is an effective tool for pricing and managing your travel needs.

Travelocity (http://www.travelocity.com) continues to be one of the Web's most popular sites. This site allows a traveler to map out where and when he or she is going. The service will then show the traveler what is currently available, as well as email updates of alternatives. I've known executives at Fortune 100 companies who note that online prices are often considerably less than their in-house travel desks, which are supposed to have good prices due to their purchasing volume. Microsoft's Expedia (http://www.expedia.com) offers similar services. Both sites offer in-depth information on destinations, as well as helpful travel hints, which is to be expected these days. With more and more of these sites arising, each one must differentiate itself in a visitor's mind by providing a unique service or an outstanding deal. This is the result of that highly competitive marketplace referred to earlier. As the Internet expands, the unexpected can, and often does, happen. Keep this in mind from both a selling and a consumer point of view. Exploit this to your own benefit.

One site that has exploited this fact is Biztravel.com (http://www.biztravel.com), which focuses exclusively on the needs of the business traveler (see Figure 1.7). Set up

Figure 1.7 Biztravel.com provides time- and money-saving tools for the business traveler.

an account, and your travel preferences are stored and noted for all future engagements. The site provides travel-planning assistance (via a virtual travel agent), will manage your frequent-flyer mileage accounts, offers a price-protection program, whereby if your flight does not leave on time, Biztravel will compensate you, and even offers wireless paging and notification of any flight delays, departure gate, and other crucial details that you might need on the way to the airport.

In addition to paying close attention to Travelocity, Expedia, TravelWeb, and other travel center sites that will undoubtedly come online by the time you read this, keep tabs on the airlines that fly in and out of your airport as well. Many of them offer their own discount programs, such as American Airlines' NetSAAver (http://www.aa.com), which emails you every week with the latest bargains. US Air, Continental, and other carriers offer similar update services. At this point, it almost goes without saying that these sites also offer ETA (estimated time of arrival) and departure times online, for tracking flights.

While we're on the subject of airlines, let's make sure you get the best frequent-flyer deal possible at WebFlyer (http://www.insideflyer.com). This site will keep you posted on which airlines are offering the best deals on fly miles. There's a calendar that charts who's doing what and when. Be sure to sign up for the email updater when you visit (see Figure 1.8). WebMiles (http://www.webmiles.com) is another interesting program, where you can accrue frequent-flyer miles with purchases from any participating vendor, from Dell Computer to Starbucks. Unlike other mileage award programs, this program lets you earn free and discounted travel on any airline at any time with no blackout dates or seat restrictions.

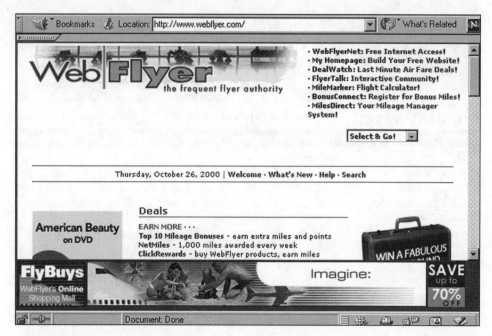

Figure 1.8 Keep tabs on which airline is running what frequent-flyer programs and when with WebFlyer.
© webflyer.com.

As you might expect, there is also a flurry of constant, ever-changing hotel deals. Many of these deals will be found on the Travelocity-type sites mentioned earlier, while others will run stand-alone promotions on their own sites. Obviously, hotels and car rental companies will do package deals with airlines. Just like the rest of the Internet, there is no one source that has a comprehensive listing of all deals that are happening at all times. You may get a great deal on an airline seat with one carrier and not realize that there's a package deal offering you more savings through another airline, hotel, or car rental company. If you're a frequent traveler, it is especially important to sign up for email update services offered by each site. Let's face it, unless your core business is only travel, you're not going to spend most of your time constantly surfing all these sites. If you did, you wouldn't have much time to travel!

Since you're buying airline reservations and hotel rooms online, you might as well consider buying your next company car on the Internet. Whether you're buying a single company car or leasing an entire fleet, the chances are good that you'll only pay a little bit above wholesale on a vehicle. Lots of people are already doing their research online for their next vehicle, so why not you? It makes perfect sense, since a car is a considered-purchase item. In other words, once you're spending a great deal of money, you will want to do your homework in order to make an educated buying decision. As you know, the Internet is excellent at providing this in-depth information. You can bid on rental cars or shop for a new car on Priceline.com, or you can browse for a new car by manufacturer, vehicle type, or price range at Greenlight.com (http://wwwgreenlight.com). Backed in part by Amazon.com, this site lets you choose your make and model, pick a color scheme, and options, and compare models side-by-side in a virtual showroom. If you like what you see, ask for a quote (which includes taxes and fees). If you like the price, put down a $200 deposit and your price will be frozen for seven days. Pick up your new car from the closest affiliated dealer, but not before you read its road-test review, which is posted at the site courtesy of NewCarRoad-Test.com.

Buying the Tools of Your Trade

Chances are there's something significant already happening on the Internet in your niche in the purchasing area. Most industries now have a slew of first-, second-, and third-tier players to choose from. The vast majority of the online Web exchanges already established are awaiting their first transactions, but business is booming among the leaders, who are well on their way to fulfilling analyst predictions that they'll handle sales of nearly $2 trillion by 2003. Who will succeed? It's a tough call. Zona Research sells a directory that includes 1,029 global B2B markets and 262 B2B market-enablers, a reflection of the continuing build out of the B2B market phenomenon. In the directory, B2B markets are segmented by 59 industry categories while B2B market-enablers are categorized by their key technologies, infrastructure, and support services, which B2B marketplaces use to build out their businesses.

While most analysts describe Internet exchanges as being focused on vertical or horizontal markets, or as auctions, information hubs, or trading exchanges, it is becoming increasingly difficult to force them into a single category. For example, news has become just one commodity to be had at the local exchange. Is that fact redefining how we think of a trade publication? Well, weren't there always classified ads in the back of trade publications where people sought buyers and sellers for their brand of arcana? Of course. The Net has simply made this traditional practice more interactive, and has fostered the growth of vertical industry portals, or *vortals* (as discussed in Chapter 3, "Mining the Internet for All It's Worth"). These vortals can generate significant loyalty from participants of that industry as they are more relevant.

TIP According to eMarketer's "eCommerce: B2B" report, to take full advantage of these exchanges, businesses must strategically prepare for the advent of eXtensible Markup Language (XML). XML permits the tagging of data in such a way that it can be transferred between software applications, both internally within companies and externally with their trading partners.

Check out the food-service site that serves as a crossroads for such restaurateur supplies at http://www.supplysite.com. It's quite conceivable that indigenous products for a given industry might have an outside market. We don't think that people will be putting 4-ton steel fittings on their front lawn, but one could see where they may want their own milkshake machine, or an industrial-rated stove or refrigerator.

B2B Networks Explode

Both on a mass scale, such as b2bworld and mysap, which aggregate specific communities, and within industry-specific niches such as eSteel or OrderZone, the B2B market is poised for enormous growth. Horizontal procurement networks, where competitors align on the back end for purchasing, are the marketing tools of the future, as the savings are passed on to the customer.

Nowhere else is the open market principle more apparent than in the scores of auction sites that now populate the Web. Previously the popular domains of consumers selling attic leftovers, the auction space has expanded to include a number of opportunities for business owners. Even consumer-beloved eBay has gotten into the act with a business exchange (see Figure 1.9). At the site, business owners can bid on everything from tractors and trailers to cash registers.

If you're looking for the state-of-the-art computer that just came out yesterday, you may not find it on these auction sites. More often than not, the merchandise auctioned off is close-out products. Very often, there are odd lots bought up that aren't worth putting in the manufacturer's catalog again because there aren't enough left. The computers may be last year's model, without the various bells and whistles, but you may not want or need these extra features anyway. I recommend that you check brand names very carefully, along with the warranties and return policies. In many cases, sales are final.

TIP Put your bids in early. When there's a tie, which often happens, the person who put his or her bid in first gets the merchandise.

Be careful. These auction sites can be addictive to the point of distraction. People get caught up in the bidding excitement and sometimes pay more for things than they

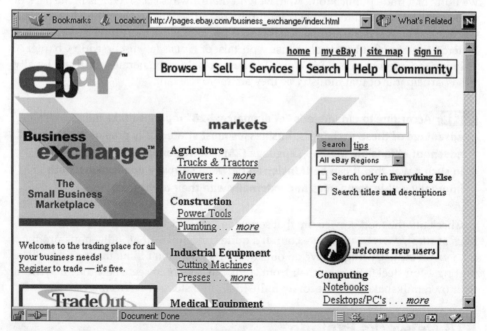

Figure 1.9 Bid on everything from tractors to computers at eBay's Business Exchange.

might have elsewhere. I also know people who buy things for which they have no need, just because the costs are low.

Office Supplies, Support, and Community

The Internet is, as we know, an amazing tool to tap into the special needs of specific target audiences. One of the most lucrative target audiences is the small to mid-sized business. It should come as no surprise that a number of online business communities have sprung up over the past few years. In addition to pens, pencils, and paper, these sites offer services that range from domain name registration and site hosting to complete business support. Most collaborate with other players in the business space to present as complete a suite of products and services as possible. For example, Staples.com has a Business Solutions Center that offers everything from printing services courtesy of NowDocs.com to payroll management courtesy of InterPay (see Figure 1.10).

Why not manage everything all in one place? Most of these services work on an ASP model, where you pay as you go, depending upon your needs. Some of the most popular include:

vJungle (http://www.vjungle.com). vJungle.com claims to be the first Integrated Application Service Provider (iASP) for the small business market. Integrated services simplify daily operations for small businesses with web-delivered software and interactive databases. That means no more upgrading software pack-

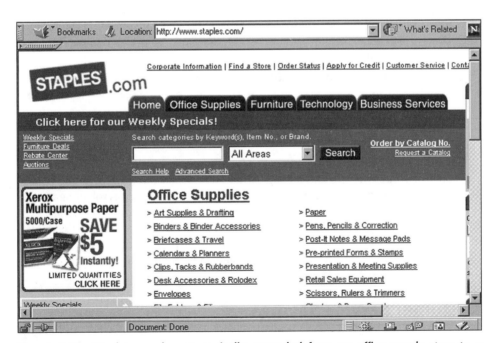

Figure 1.10 Staples.com has strategically expanded from an office supply store to a Business Solutions Center.

ages every few months for a more current solution. Complete database and software integration allows small businesses to simplify tasks such as file sharing, website building, or even payroll by accessing information and resources at one central location.

bCentral (http://www.bcentral.com). This Microsoft-backed site for small business is packed with information. Services offered to start, promote, and manage your online business are monthly fee-based, such as Internet access, search engine registration, email, and advertising programs. The small business directory is quite thorough, with extensive lists of categories and resources. There is also a small business headline news area and a success story feature. Nicely done, and certainly a smart way to bring the Microsoft name and products to the small business market while providing valuable marketing services and information.

AllBusiness (http://www.allbusiness.com). AllBusiness is all business. It offers a comprehensive online resource for essential services, tools, and information for business management. Founded by a group of entrepreneurs who learned firsthand the problems of running and growing small businesses, the site aims to take the guesswork out of running a business so that entrepreneurs can focus on growing their business. AllBusiness supports administrative and professional functions in areas ranging from HR and finance to technology and marketing.

SmartOnline (http://www.smartonline.com). SmartOnline bills itself as the "leading application service provider (ASP) for small business." It combines webhosted applications (priced on a per-use basis or a flat fee of $14.95 per month) with business guidance, business-to-business collaboration, e-commerce, and communications services. Web-hosted applications include Smart Business Plan, Smart Entrepreneur, Smart Financial Statements, Smart Incorporator, Smart Job Description, Smart Legal Forms, Smart Marketplace, Smart Marketing Plan, and Smart Web Storefront.

Office.com (http://www.office.com). Office.com combines best of breed content, commerce, community, and communications to create the place we work when we work online. Original and aggregated content informs Office.com customers of industry trends, news, and gossip in 16 industries, 120 sub-industries, and 10 business management focused areas.

Business Tools from ADP http://www.adp.com/emergingbiz/tool/index.html). Small business owners and managers have a new place to turn for sound advice on day-to-day management issues such as finding funding, payroll obligations, and human resource management. The Business Tools section of Automatic Data Processing, Inc.'s (ADP) site has plenty of advice and articles about small business management. Can't find the form to apply for a federal identification number? ADP has it, and several others, available for free downloading.

Customer Service Savings

Customer service, or Customer Relationship Management (CRM), has become big business on the Web. Why? Because it is where marketing and sales meet—where the dollar hits the road, and the customer has a good experience and comes back, creating a profitable company, or has a bad experience and doesn't come back, leading to business failure.

Traditional call centers and direct marketers have long understood the value of customer service. However, many of the early web companies jumped online with a strong technology focus—they had great technology that could do really cool things. Obviously, the technology is vitally important. However, it's also important to recognize and nurture customers and customer relationships. The growth of the eCRM industry reflects the maturation of the industry, as we move past the gee whiz! stage and into the growth and management of profitable business models. Customer service strategies are covered in detail in Chapter 5, "Your Brand Image and the Internet."

As we know, answering customer service questions on a site instead of by an actual person saves significant amounts of money. But simply slapping up a bunch of help files and product offerings will not induce the customer to use your site rather than the telephone. The challenge here is to make your site not only as effective as the alternative phone call, but more effective. One solution that we respect a great deal in this category is the step-search feature offered by Saqqara (http://www.saqqara.com). Step-search asks you only a few questions at a time. Based on your answers, step-search will come back and present you with an appropriate array of options. This solution goes a long way toward avoiding the user frustration found at many customer service sites on the Internet. Here's why: Very often, customers are asked to fill out lengthy forms on a site and then submit them. Imagine if you take 20 minutes to fill out one of these long forms only to find at the very end that "You cannot get the red Chevrolet Lumina with manual transmission and air conditioning. Please start over!" Step-search avoids both wasted time and frustration.

Another way to keep customers hitting your website instead of your 800 customer support phone lines is to have a discussion group in the customer service area of your site. This discussion group can have many *threads,* or discussion topics. It looks something like a Usenet group or a bulletin board. Each thread may represent a particular product of yours. Thereunder, you might find subthreads, where customers can discuss various aspects of that product. You'll most definitely want to moderate these discussions and interact with them often. There are many free and reasonably cheap software programs that you can put up on your site that run very easily managed discussion lists/bulletin boards. Take a look around. Make sure you use a program that either you or an assigned employee can learn quickly and easily, since you'll want to update it regularly to provide fast customer support.

This solution has an upside and a downside. The upside, as previously mentioned, is that it can save you money. You'll also be delighted when customers answer questions to problems other customers pose. Some of these answers are ones that you might not have even thought of. You can simultaneously collect more solutions about your own products from your customers, while not having to answer those questions yourself: additional input with less output—a powerful combination. The downside is that you might find irate customers trashing your product on your own website. To your horror, you may indeed be sponsoring a revolt aimed at yourself! If the complaints are legitimate, then you're going to have to face the music sooner or later. Isn't it better for you to see this happen on your own site rather than out there on the Net? Most definitely. At your home, you can handle the spin control much faster and more effectively.

If your public relations people start squawking, tell them this is a policy of containment. If you deal with the problems in a forthright manner, it will be seen as such, more often than not. If you try to squelch the complaints in a heavy-handed manner by editing them or replying in an arrogant manner, you're opening up an online can of worms that is best avoided. If the complaints are not warranted, and they're posed by a few persistent cranks out there, the rest of the discussion group will typically see this and appreciate it for what it is. There is something to be said about dealing with your vulnerabilities in an open and upright manner. It can add luster to your credibility and that of your products.

Getting It Together with Intranets and Extranets

Intranets and Extranets used to be privately-built operations whose price tags kept them out of the range of small- and mid-sized business owners. That is no longer true, as the advantages of intranets and Extranets are now available to all through free or low-priced web-based solutions. It is worth your time to explore your options. Here are two of our favorites:

Intranets.about.com (http://www.intranets.about.com). At this site, you can create a private space on the Web where your group can easily access and share documents, calendars, and event information (see Figure 1.11). The company's mis-

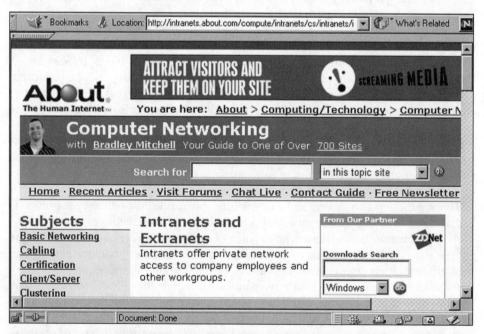

Figure 1.11 At Intranets.about.com, you will find information, strategies, resources, and case studies on intranet *and* Extranet development.

sion is to "get everyone on the same page." Intranets.com began providing free intranets to businesses and organizations via the Web in August 1999. The company's roots, however, go back to 1996, when it was founded as a provider of top-tier intranet software. After winning several industry awards for the product, they developed a powerful Internet application for their intranet technology, and added advertising space and business services to the interface. Voila! A private, secure intranet site for free.

ReviewManager (http://www.reviewmanager.com). ReviewManager is an outsourced client-review tool that is perfect for creative professionals and business owners who want to show their work over the Web. Instead of dealing with the hassle of email attachments, messengers, or having to ask your computer department to help you, set up your Extranet in seconds here. Already have a website? ReviewManager lets you add a "clients only" area to your existing website within one business day, which is far more economical than building or maintaining one yourself. The first 15 users and the first 15 megabytes of space are free.

Strengthening Sales Support via the Internet

The potential for the Net to create friction between manufacturers and sales and distribution channels is very real. But when done correctly, utilization of the Internet can actually enhance those all-important relationships with your channels of sales and distribution. 3Com wisely spent money on developing and marketing its partner support services. Turning well-qualified leads, and sophisticated online tools to support them, over to its resellers can only enhance those existing sales-channel relationships and quite probably attract more due to the extra sales support offered (http://infodeli .3com.com/partner.htm). Helping your vendors locate what products are where is another tactic that can be employed.

The Lee Product Locator allows partners, or anyone else for that matter, to search for a distributor that has a specific product line in the colors, quantities, and sizes needed (http://www.rsvpcomm.com/scripts/foxweb.exe/findlee). Once the specific item is located, users can then find out how many miles that distributor is from them.

BuildNet (http://www.buildnet.com) sells construction management software, including tools for CPM Scheduling, Historical and Take-Off Estimating, Purchase Orders/Work Orders, Job Costing, and Accounting. The site also acts as a clearinghouse for building and construction information on the Web.

One of the most effective sales-support case histories I've come across has more to do with the powers of observation than with technology. Jim Roth works for Document Services Sales Support. The site he administers is behind a firewall, so we can't look at it from the open Internet. The site is devoted to supporting the salespeople out in the field. He checks the logs on the search engine to see what people are keen on. If he sees that a particular product is searched for often, he's apt to put up more information on that product. Remember, though, that what people don't find can be just as important as what they do find. When he sees salespeople searching for things they aren't finding, he moves to put that information on the site.

In a very real way, Roth is using the extensive tracking information as a type of barometer. What's hot? What's not? Since these sites support the people in the field, they get a real pulse for what the marketplace is asking for through the queries submitted by their sales and field analysts. This website now handles 75 percent of the traffic, while the phones handle 25 percent. The site is actually faster because it finds the information in real time, whereas the telephone support team would first have to assign the search and then have someone physically go and get the information and send it to the person who asked for it. Depending on the depth of the request, a physical search can take hours or even days.

"We're a cost center," Roth explains. "This means we're supported and funded by our product divisions. They always ask, 'What have you done for us lately?' The unit of measure we use to answer that question is the amount of returned hours to the field." He points out: "Since the site gets them the information faster, they can return to sell more in the field, or simply get back faster to the prospective or existing client with answers. On average, we return about two days to the field using this method. The old way would have that person out of action because she was either doing the research herself, or waiting for someone internally to complete the task. That's all time out of the field not selling." On the telephone, that person's case would be put in a queue, where it would stay until that queue was looked at twice a day, then assigned to a researcher. The phone system isn't a simple help desk. The questions are more profound than that. Much of the information requested is dynamic. A salesperson might want to locate a particular machine in order to train someone on it, but it's been moved out of his locale. Where is that machine now? is such a question that might be asked. While many people do ask the appropriate question—How much money has the Net saved you?—this case study points out how much time the Internet can save your firm. Many people will rightfully argue that time and money are in fact one and the same.

Distributed Printing

By pushing the production of printed information out to the end user, small and large companies can save enormous amounts of money, time, real estate, and labor. This can apply to running high-resolution, four-color brochures closer to their distribution points, or to printing a single coupon by a grocery shopper. Let's start small and expand out to larger applications from there.

Supermarkets.com was created by a division of Catalina Marketing Network, the folks who currently deliver purchase-based electronic coupons in more than 10,800 U.S. supermarkets. A shopper goes to this site and selects his or her Zip code to find participating grocers. Once the shopper has chosen a grocer, he or she is presented with a list of current specials. He or she chooses the specials, prints the coupons, and takes them to the store. In turn, the store scans those coupons and generates Web Bucks for the corresponding amount of savings. Those Web Bucks can be used as cash on the next shopping trip. The customer saves time and money, as does the manufacturer, and the participating supermarket gets a guaranteed return visit as well. Every coupon distributed online is one less that they had to print, handle, and distribute themselves. This is distributed printing in its most diffuse form, right down to the customer level. Keep in mind that not every coupon the manufacturer prints and distributes gets used.

For the sake of argument, there may be 50 coupons distributed for every one redeemed. In reality, that manufacturer is saving not only on the printing and distribution of a single coupon, but that of 50 coupons.

Pushing the printing of documents down to the end user for everything from cookies to computers is only one form of the distributed printing model. On a different note, on-demand publishing removes the printing, marketing, retailing, and distribution hassles that small software companies, self-publishing authors, and government agencies routinely face. For approximately $1,000 and a manuscript, Trafford (http://www.trafford.com) will partner in your creation by providing an online bookstore, marketing services (including an individual home page and search engine registration), and on-demand printing and shipping. Trafford hopes to appeal to micromarkets that are vitally interested in their offerings to generate slow but steady sales around the world. The author sets the retail price and earns 75 percent of the retail markup. All in all, it's an interesting alternative to the competitive world of traditional publishing.

For those of us thinking there has to be a better way to handle documentation publishing, along comes Fatbrain with a just-in-time answer. Fatbrain (http://www .fatbrain.com) is an online publisher and reseller that delivers documentation on demand for selected vendors through custom stores. From these online documentation storefronts, users and business partners of participating companies will have a quick and easy way to order the most updated versions of hard copy reference manuals (see Figure 1.12).

Going to the local copy shop to make some copies? Think again. Go to the Kinko's site at http://www.kinkos.com and download the free File Prep Tool. Use it to organize

Figure 1.12 Distributed printing comes of age at Fatbrain.com.
© 2000 Fatbrain.com, Inc. Fatbrain.com is a trademark of Fatbrain.com, Inc.

and format your document, which you can then upload to the Kinko's site—where they will print and copy to your specifications. Your order can be delivered in as little as four hours in 60 U.S. cities.

MightyWords.com (http://www.mightywords.com), is the brainchild of Fatbrain .com and its successful eMatter digital publishing initiative. MightyWords.com was created to be the definitive digital marketplace to read, write, buy, and sell written content. Authors, academics, or wannabes can instantly publish and sell work online. The Mighty Network consists of content providers, online content distributors (sites which offer titles for sale), and consumers who wish to purchase titles. The content providers send titles to the Mighty Network which are then pushed out through the content distributors (a form of affiliate program discussed in detail in Chapter 6, "Retail: Setting Up Shop on the Net"). In addition, visitors can always go to MightyWords.com to see all titles housed on the Mighty Network.

In the last edition of this book, I predicted that distributed printing would eventually extend to the point of publishing individual chapters of a book, wherein the consumer could purchase only those chapters of interest. Has it happened? You bet. With eBooks (http://www.ebooks.com), which are published books in digital form, and ePacks, which are specific books, chapters, and pages bundled into a single eBook, the entire world of publishing is undergoing a massive shift. This very book will be pushing the frontiers of digital publishing and distributed printing. Stay tuned.

What we'll look at next is a large-scale printing model that includes higher-volume runs and higher resolutions. While a collateral piece for a trade show in California might be created in New York, it might as well be produced in Los Angeles, rather than paying for it to be shipped across the country. Many print networks, iPrint among them (http://www.iprint.com), offer this capability. By using its Custom Quote Center, you can receive a printing estimate from its network of commercial printers around the world. The Internet puts you in touch with the capability and the company that offers it.

There is a convergence of the fields of distributed printing, publishing on demand, or what some call just-in-time publishing. Xerox plays a major role in these arenas. I helped roll out a product for Xerox a few years ago called DocuTech; in fact, I was part of the crew that helped name it. DocuTech lets someone produce a limited print run of manuals, or even compilations of bits and pieces of editorial, from different sources. It takes electronic files on disk, or transmitted through the Internet or an Intranet, and prints them as if they were coming from an offset press, but using Xerox's print technology instead. A binder unit can turn the product into neatly bound books. For short print runs, it is an excellent solution. A number of efforts have been underway to put a web interface up that would feed DocuTech materials to be printed widely. So anyone, from anywhere, could conceivably print to a remote location where a DocuTech machine resides, perhaps within your own company or at a local print shop.

These sorts of applications help companies work smarter. There's a difference between working smarter and working faster. It's fine to work faster as long as you're not simply running in place at twice the speed. Working smarter makes better use of all your resources, money, materials, and the most valuable of commodities, your time.

The larger projects described toward the end of this chapter are geared for larger operations; however, the Internet is typically utilized for smarter operations by small companies. Large firms would be wise to think small and act accordingly. See how small businesses apply the Internet to make them work smarter, faster, cheaper, and then apply those lessons on a larger scale.

Resource Center

Calendar Systems

Day-Timer Digital   http://www.digital.daytimer.com

Users of the classic Day-Timer time management system will welcome the digital version. Nifty features include the ability to get automatic reminders on your daily calendar and via email messages, and to embed links to top websites for shopping and planning right into your calendar.

ScheduleEarth   http://www.scheduleearth.com

ScheduleEarth is dedicated to being the world's leading information provider for personal and professional development. It also provides a great way to merge your personal and professional calendars, book travel, check weather, purchase products, set up a home page, and more.

ScheduleOnline   http://www.scheduleonline.com

Schedule your meetings, chats, events, tasks, and resources through the click of a button. No more voicemail or email tag! A good free scheduling, calendar, and group office tool.

Virtual Assistants

Freeworks.com   http://www.freeworks.com

Who doesn't want a personal assistant that works 24/7 and never asks for a raise? To get yours, simply log on and set up a free account.

AssistU   http://www.assistu.com

If you find you're so caught up in the day-to-day stuff that you can't find the time or energy to focus on the things that *really* need your attention, you may need a virtual assistant. Connect with a real-world virtual assistant screened to meet your needs here.

iPing   http://www.iping.com

With iPing, you can arrange to send customized audio messages directly from the Internet to any phone. Use it for wake-up calls, reminders to self or colleagues and family, financial alerts, news, motivation, and more.

Communications

MessageBlaster.com   http://www.messageblaster.com

MessageBlaster.com is the first Internet-based outbound messaging service that allows you to send and track messages, polls, virus alerts, and other communications to an unlimited number of contacts by email, phone, pager, fax, snail mail, or overnight delivery. Any database that supports export to a text file (ACT, Microsoft Excel, Microsoft Outlook) can be uploaded directly to MessageBlaster.com.

ELetter   http://www.eletter.com

ELetter comes the closest yet to a truly integrated direct mail solution managed via the Web. Build a targeted mailing list through partner infoUSA.com, upload your database, create a mailing piece with partner iPrint.com, round up some of partner E-Stamp's Internet Postage, and a custom postal mailing is yours in one seamless online transaction.

LetterPost   http://www.letterpost.com

Now you can use the Internet to send messages to friends and family who don't have email access, or people who rarely use email. LetterPost.com is the fast and effective way to send documents straight from your PC to anywhere in the world as real letters. It's speedy, handy, private, and cheap. Send a letter or greeting card anywhere for just 99 cents, including the stamp, letter, and envelope.

Virtual Teamwork

Evoke   http://www.evoke.com

Evoke provides a suite of web-based voice, video, and visual collaboration services. Current services include web conferencing (web plus phone), mobile web conferencing (wireless), collaboration (meeting and seminar tools), webcasting (broadcasting of your events), web talk (voice and text exchange over the Internet), and talking email.

My.PlaceWare   http://my.placeware.com

My.PlaceWare is a free service offered by PlaceWare, Inc. which enables web conferencing. With web conferencing you can conduct live graphical and interactive meetings with anyone, in any place over the Internet with only a web browser and a phone. My.PlaceWare can enhance any conference call or make a meeting possible when meeting face-to-face is impossible.

Lotus Instant!TEAMROOM   http://www.lotus.com/home.nsf/tabs/teamroom

Instant!TEAMROOM is a web application that allows anyone with a browser and an Internet connection to establish a private workspace for managing projects or initiatives with teams of colleagues, partners, and even customers. Users can share files and information, capture discussions, create and store related documents, and track team progress from start to finish—or any length of time. Service is "rented" by the month. ITR is based on world-leading Lotus Domino web server technology and is provided through major service providers worldwide.

PowWow   http://www.tribal.com/powwow

PowWow is a fully integrated instant messaging, interactive communications and online community solution that features instant voice messaging and integrated voice chat capabilities, as well as group chat, instant messaging, buddy lists, and real-time peer-to-peer communication. PowWow users can utilize a collaborative whiteboard and bulletin board system, conduct web tours, and share files, URLs, and sounds. The base level software is free, and requires a download.

GroupBoard   http://www.groupboard.com

Draw on the board using the mouse, and click on Save to store your picture in the gallery for other people to see. You can also chat to other people who are using the board, and leave messages on the message board.

Gooey   http://www.rocketdownload.com/details/inte/gooey.htm

Doing some online research? Surf the Web with your virtual staff using this free software, which includes a pop-up chat room. You can all view the sites, make comments, and chat online simultaneously.

Desktop Tools

MagicalDesk   http://www.magicaldesk.com

A virtual desktop that gives you free email access, a decent calendar, task lists, address book, the ability to store Internet bookmarks and 5 megabytes of storage space is quite magical, indeed. You can even convert your email into a task list or a calendar entry, thereby creating a seamless desktop experience.

Finances

RedGorilla   http://www.redgorilla.com

Do you bill time? Gorilla Time is a free, web-based time tracking and invoicing system that lets you easily capture your time and expenses using a simple web interface, and create and deliver professional-looking invoices online.

PayPal   http://www.paypal.com

Need to send someone money and have it be fast and easy? How about via email or beamed through your Palm Pilot? Try PayPal. Establish an account by billing the amount you wish to your credit card, and "Beam it up, Scotty." With a built-in, fail-safe viral marketing component (if you don't open an account, you don't get your cash), the Internet's largest instant payment network (500,000 users and counting) is coming on strong.

eMoneyMail   http://www.emoneymail.com

A service of Bank One, eMoneyMail enables users to send money electronically to any-one in the U.S. via email message. Here's how it works: (1) the sender goes to the site and chooses one of three possible methods of sending money: Visa credit card, Visa debit card, or checking account; (2) the sender specifies an email address for the receiver and the amount that will be sent (up to $500); and (3) the receiver opens an email mes-sage indicating that money has been sent, clicks on an attachment with a link to the site, and indicates a preferred method of receipt: Visa credit card, Visa debit card, checking account, or a paper check sent by surface mail. Senders pay a $1 transaction fee.

WingspanBank   http://www.wingspanbank.com

The first Internet-based bank saves you time and money by doing things virtually. Ser-vices for both consumer and business customers include online bill payment, interest-bearing checking accounts, free ATM transactions, and more.

Computer Assistance

MyHelpdesk.com   http://www.myhelpdesk.com

Voted one of *PC* magazine's top 100 websites, MyHelpdesk.com is a free service that covers 1,500 tech products, gives vendors resources and phone numbers, has chat rooms for venting about that lousy software or malfunctioning hardware, and pub-lishes tips, updates, and related news. When you sign up, you initially customize your Helpdesk by selecting the software applications that you use and may need help with. Later, you add the hardware that you use. The site covers everything from Internet software to M3P players. It's a great resource for anyone with a computer.

Travel

Expedia   http://www.expedia.com

Whether you travel virtually via mousepad or hold out for the real thing, this Microsoft site is the cherry on top of the traveler's ice cream sundae. Part online mag-azine and part ticketing service, the site features a travel agent, a hotel directory (with more than 25,000 choices), a flight fare tracker (get quotes via email), a slew of forums with places to trade stories with fellow travelers, image galleries, weather reports, and multimedia tours of international destinations. It gives Microsoft's motto "Where do you want to go today?" a whole new meaning.

American Airlines   http://www.americanair.com

This site is a prime example of how classic direct marketing practices can be migrated and employed on the Net. AA lures you in (call this an acquisition program) with its Net Saver discount program, which emails you every week with last-minute cheap seats. The incentive for you to buy tickets online is the offer of an additional 1,000 frequent-flyer miles. You can also find out how many fly-miles you've accrued by giv-ing a PIN that lets you see your account information. Cross-merchandising tie-ins with Avis are featured, just like they are in the monthly hard-copy statements received by snail mail. The more you drill into this site, the more you learn about how to market smartly on the Net.

United Airlines   http://www.ual.com

The skies are amazingly friendly at the United Airlines site. So friendly, in fact, that they are willing to sell you a ticket on a competing carrier. That's right! You can compare fares on identical routes, and if you like the price on American, US Air, or Delta better, no problem. There's lots more information to be had at the site. Picking someone up at the airport? Check the flight status. Traveling overseas? Check out the currency converters. Looking for a good in-flight flick? Peruse the list of scheduled films by flight. If you only had three days in Madrid or Manhattan, what would you do? UAL.com offers ideas with addresses and phone numbers.

Automotive

Auto-By-Tel   http://www.autobytel.com

Auto-By-Tel is a free service that lets you buy or lease vehicles wholesale. Are you tired of those slick car sales sleuths giving you "the deal of your lifetime"? Auto-By-Tel provides you with a convenient, easy, and more affordable way to buy your next car or truck. Be sure you know all the details of the vehicle you plan to lease or buy, such as make, model, series, extras, and so forth. Submit the online request form and a subscribing dealer in your geographical area will contact you. The good part is that you have the option of choosing whether you want to buy immediately, in a couple of months, or later. You can still get the information you seek without worrying about being bugged by a salesperson. Great use of the World Wide Web for customer sales and support.

Volkswagen   http://www.vw.com

This nicely animated site, reminiscent of a tiddlywinks game, encourages online shoppers to scoop up 4,000 new limited edition VW Beetles. Find the nearest participating dealer and design your dream car (interior, exterior, features). If your dream machine is available nearby, it's time to tell them about your finances, credit rating, etc. (which the site forwards to the dealer). Then you access MyVWpage and negotiate with the dealer one-to-one on your own private message board. Hopefully the car is still available. Delivery can take up to six weeks.

Project Management Tools

ThinkFree Office   http://www.thinkfreeoffice.com

No more excuses! With ThinkFree Office, you can do your computing anytime and anywhere from any browser. ThinkFree's suite of office productivity applications harness the power of the Web and revolutionize the way users compute. Designed to complement and not replace standard office suites (think Microsoft Office), ThinkFree simplifies the file sharing and carrying of work between office and home. Advertiser supported, it's free to the user. An 8Mb download is required.

onProject.com   http://www.onproject.com

This site allows you to manage your business as an online portfolio of projects. Services are more professional in nature than some of the free project planning sites; the ability to generate management reports and status reports is a nice feature, and projects can be annotated and planned at a much deeper level. Services include a group calendar, file storage, resource tracking, and most of the usual niceties. One to three projects are $29.95 per month to manage; prices go up from there. You can sign up for a 30-day free trial.

JointPlanning   http://www.jointplanning.com

At this site, you have the ability to maintain to-do lists at the personal and group levels. Manage to-do items by assigning them a category and a priority level. Groups benefit from the ability to assign to-do entries to fellow members. You have multiple viewing options that will assist you in managing your to-do lists. For example, you can view to-do items by group, category, and completion status. You can also store documents, email, and write memos to your entire group, or to specific members. The robust to-do functionality makes it an ideal, free group project management tool.

Onvia.com   http://www.news.onvia.com/tools_marketing.xml

Onvia is a site where entrepreneurs can buy and sell products and services. It does contain productivity tools and a nifty Request For Quote feature, but is most noteworthy for its free business forms and worksheets—so if you are "working from home" to develop a promotional plan, you can do so right here.

ClickTime   http://www.clicktime.com

ClickTime is a web-based time tracking solution for business professionals and their employees. The makers of ClickTime are also the makers of ReviewManager (http://www.reviewmanager.com), which is an online client review Extranet that lets you show work over the Web to your clients.

MyEvents   http://www.myevents.com

By choosing MyEvents, Internet/Intranet/Extranet sites offer their visitors tools for personal organization and group collaboration with little development time or up-front investment. In addition to providing web-based groupware, MyEvents customers have the power to link a user's offline and online activities through synchronization software and a wireless interface. By tethering a user to its website, companies create universal access to files, contacts, calendars, and more for their customers, coworkers, and suppliers.

Using the Net as a Resource for Human Resources

You know that one of your company's most valued assets is your employees. The manner in which you utilize this critical asset will make or break your firm, whether it's large or small. In short, you're managing brain power, or what some call *wetware*. The Net is causing tectonic shifts in the way that all companies find and manage their brain power.

Never mind the lack of technical talent needed by today's Internet companies—which may or may not affect your business. Does your business-development whiz close sales? Today's newly funded dot com needs her desperately. Does your accounting guru make it all add up? There's a venture capital firm with its eye on him. Does your executive VP run a tight ship? The Internet division of a Fortune 500 company has her name on its recruiting list. Is your business partner a networking genius? Beware the next professional event, as business cards are changing hands. The point is, no matter what your business, your employees are highly coveted intellectual assets. The growth of Internet business, and the speed with which employers and employees can find one another on the Internet, means that your ability to leverage the Net for human resources purposes is a critical competitive advantage. In this chapter you will find out about:

- Finding candidates online
- Vertical, college, and diversity recruiting
- Recruitment as a sales function
- How to create a *buzz* about your company
- Telecommuting tips and techniques

- Freelancers and outsourcing
- Distance learning
- Online training

How Jobs and Candidates Find Each Other on the Net

Online employment sites, which consolidate employment opportunities from thousands of companies and offer ways to match them with the appropriate job seekers, have exploded in growth since the first edition of this book. In this competitive market, human resources professionals are pressured to find the right candidates to fill positions—yesterday. What company can afford to spend four months looking for the right marketing director? At today's speed of business, if you are missing key employees, your competition can easily pass you by. Making up that lost time is not always possible, meaning that having the right talent—and keeping it—can make or break your business. Often times, the Internet now connects the employer and the employee, via booming career solutions sites such as HotJobs.com (see Figure 2.1).

Many employment-related websites have capitalized upon this need. One of the early movers into the career matchmaker space is Monster.com. Monster.com first boasted the most extensive array of companies with jobs, and job seekers with résumés, on the Web. Next, Monster.com built tools to bring the two together. From the job seeker perspective, the My Monster profile feature provides a way to store your

Figure 2.1   HotJobs.com is a leading Internet-based recruiting solutions company.

résumé online (up to five versions), to search for jobs of interest, and to apply for those jobs at the click of a button. But it gets better. As part of the My Monster feature, job seekers can create Agents, or personalized searches that will look for jobs that match the seeker's criteria in terms of salary, location, industry, and special keywords. When jobs show up that match (and job seekers can create up to five different Agents), the job seeker is notified by Monster.com. Companies can also search by keyword to find new candidates who have recently added their profiles to the site, and they are likewise notified by Monster.com when candidates of interest have been added into the pool. Connections are made by email; the job seeker can choose to respond (or not) to the interested company's inquiry. Monster.com was also the first to add a Talent Matcher feature for the independent (or freelance) workforce, which we will explore later in this chapter. Monster.com boasts close to 500,000 subscribers to its career newsletter, and also offers a comprehensive resource center for both the job seeker and employers.

BrassRing, Inc., is backed by Kaplan, Inc. (a subsidiary of the Washington Post Company), Tribune Company, Central Newspapers, Inc., and Accel Partners (see Figure 2.2). BrassRing employs a *bricks and clicks* method to find the best candidates both online and off. Using a suite of live and web-based solutions, the company helps organizations reach the best technology and college talent, and provides tools to improve and accelerate every aspect of the hiring process.

What does this mean for the human resources professional? "Matching candidates to jobs was once like finding a needle in a haystack," says Cheryl Brinker, Vice President of Human Resources for Knowledge Strategies Group, an e-commerce strategy and development firm. "Now, I can post jobs and find candidates within minutes—but

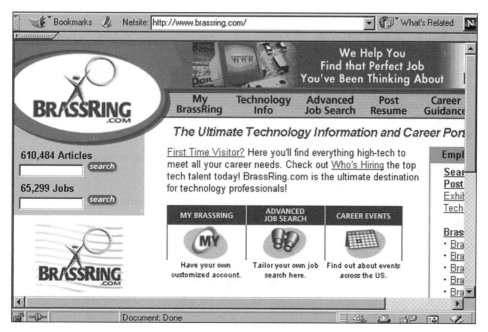

Figure 2.2 BrassRing.com is the largest high-tech career resource online.

so can my competitors. I need to be on top of all the employment sites, and I also need to nurture my relationships with recruiters and with my personal network."

Ironically, the explosion of employment sites has made each individual's personal network much more valuable. Parties, conferences, and other professional events have become common places for personnel talent to be found—or lost. Hiring managers and decision makers on the lookout for talent will often offer jobs over a cocktail, and recruiters use industry events as a data mine for experienced professionals to add to their Rolodex. For example, at a midsummer industry bash in New York City, a talented public relations executive staffing a sponsor booth was offered five jobs over the course of two hours. Was it the cocktails, or the talent crunch? To the company that might lose that PR executive to another company, it really doesn't matter. What does matter is that companies constantly find ways to one-up the competition and woo new talent.

Vertical Recruiting

Vertical recruiting means industry-specific recruiting. In this many-to-many environment, birds of a feather really do flock together and create highly specific beehives of activity both online and off. To anyone outside of that specific industry, much of the information exchange would be more than you would ever want to know about that given industry. But for those within that highly targeted niche, such sites or organizations are a gold mine.

In the Internet marketing world, one must-know association is AIM, the Association for Interactive Media (see Figure 2.3). Since 1993, AIM has been serving businesses that use the Internet and interactive media—and positioning itself as a conduit for talented people and companies looking to hire talent.

"Non-profit associations like AIM help their members and the industry by providing a place of common ground and interest," explains Alexis Bonnell, AIM's self-described DIVA of Marketing. "Whether it is through our job service, a member recruiter, or a personal AIM referral, we can help professionals find the job that is just right for them, and help companies find the talent they need to survive and excel. It is important that companies understand how AIM can help them reach their goals, that is why we exist. To not use your industry trade association is to not understand how your industry works." AIM members can take advantage of many of AIM's services including:

- AIM Job Service—Job search, post, recruiting, and referral service.
- Ask an Expert—Expert referral service.
- Speaker's Database—A listing of qualified industry speakers.
- AIM's Interactive Industry Directory—A "Who's Who" reference guide to people and companies in the interactive space.
- AIM Networking—At events around the world.
- Need-a-Lead—AIM's referral service for leads and potential clients.
- AIM Councils—Specialized councils for every segment of the industry and other verticals.
- AIM's seven free mail newsletters:

Figure 2.3 AIM's diverse corporate members represent interests from email marketing, retailing, online marketing, content, e-commerce, research, and broadband access, and across many verticals like healthcare, finance, entertainment, and retail.

- AIM Member Update—An insider's look at what is going on in the industry.
- Who's News—A synopsis of who is going where, and doing what.
- Research—A compilation of the industry's best current research.
- Politics Insider—An exclusive look at how politics are affecting the direct and interactive industries.
- AIM/DMA Scheduler—A calendar of noteworthy industry events and trade shows.
- Speaker's Link—A listing of speaking opportunities in the industry.
- Sponsor Link—A listing of exposure opportunities in the industry.

If you visit *Advertising Age* at http://www.adage.com, you'll find a job center area there. This is a search engine for jobs that will look for the type of marketing position you're seeking, in the region of the United States you want, along with some other predilections as well. However, the search you conduct at the *Advertising Age* site is actually drawing on the marketing section of the Monster Board database. You could go directly to Monster Board, but you're more apt to be surfing *Advertising Age* if you're in the advertising business. So, in this case, the mountain comes to Muhammad, as it often does on the Net. Another example is Ziff-Davis, which has a searchable job resource using the Techies.com service as the provider of the job database. The point is, these search windows pop up anywhere the candidate is likely to be. It makes the possibility of enticement that much more spontaneous.

It's also possible to pinpoint your employee searches to both an industry and a region. The New York New Media Association is one example of how an industry resource formed, using the Web, around an employment sector (see Figure 2.4). Founded in 1994, NYNMA supports and promotes the new media industry in New York. Over 8,300 individuals representing more than 3,000 companies belong to NYNMA. "Connecting the industry is something that we have done since day one," states Ellen Auwarter, NYNMA's Director of Educational Programs. "At this stage of the industry's development, with start-ups becoming established businesses, training and professional development are needs that an industry association should be able to provide for its members."

NYNMA's members typically connect in an ongoing series of events, ranging from networking CyberSuds to an Angel Investor Program, an Executive Roundtable, evening panel discussions, more than 20 SIGs (Special Interest Groups) and a fantastic online Job Board. Auwarter has added three educational programs to the mix, designed to serve both industry start-ups and those transitioning into new media. "Our 'Building A Successful New Media Business' series was created for seed stage entrepreneurs," says Auwarter. "It's a six-part series that teaches everything from how to write a business plan to how to get funding. The courses are team-taught by successful Silicon Alley entrepreneurs and industry professionals, and serve as a rich resource for networking and new clients as well as education."

What's on the drawing board? "As companies become more sophisticated, they meet up with the proverbial three challenges—management, management, and management," states Alice O'Rourke, NYNMA's Executive Director. "NYNMA can support their efforts by expanding its entrepreneurial education into workforce training,

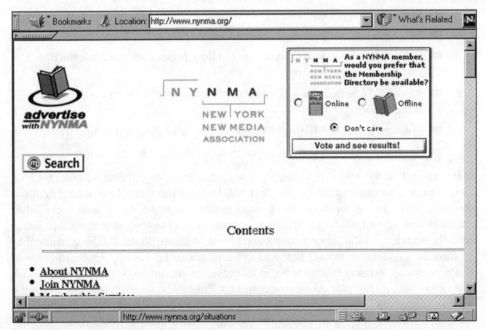

Figure 2.4 Thousands of New York area new media executives call NYNMA.org home.

not only to help management train people to embrace these new challenges, but also to retain people in a competitive market."

College Recruiting

A vast majority of young people today consider using the Internet second nature, the way baby boomers are familiar with television. Therefore, many large firms go to great lengths to woo college students with campus recruitment efforts on the Internet, and many colleges and associations go to great lengths to support students with online career centers and other opportunities. One such effort is an internship program.

"Our internship program started in 1998 with placing 38 students," continues Auwarter NYNMA's Director of Educational Programs, who also runs a successful internship program for high school, college, and graduate students interested in new media. "We placed nearly 200 students in our summer and school-year programs in 2000, and these internships ranged from six to twelve weeks in length."

Why would a new media company hire interns? "Initially, our interns helped fill a demanding job market," she explains. "Now, with a contraction in the job market, our interns can fill interim voids, which appeals to companies that are in need of short-term help but that cannot add to headcount. These companies don't necessarily have a lot of time for training, but they also want qualified people. Students rise to the occasion."

Students who are part of NYNMA's internship program get a firsthand opportunity to view the new media scene in action, and to make valuable connections that will last throughout their careers. The screening process is conducted both by the school and then by NYNMA. The internship program now operates year-round, with events that bring Silicon Alley leaders to the schools and an online system of courses that students can use to increase their skill sets outside the classroom. "We're also starting an alumnae network," notes Auwarter. "Some 300 students have been placed through the program since its inception, and there is an incredible demand for mentoring."

Jobtrak (http://jobtrak.com) is a central feeding source for many schools that accepts student résumés, while also keeping track of companies' available jobs (see Figure 2.5). From a student's perspective, he or she can simply go to the site, submit a password, and access the available jobs from the hundreds of companies that participate in the program. A student can select an industry, a date of availability, part- or full-time employment status, as well as a location. The filtering process is well designed and sophisticated. More than 500,000 employers have utilized Jobtrak.com to target college students and alumni for internships, and full-time and part-time employment opportunities.

A current example of college recruitment on a corporate level can be found at the website of KPMG Peat Marwick (http://kpmgcampus.com/campus/), a top-five accounting and consulting firm. The KPMG campus site targets college graduates who will be participating in on-campus interviews. It's an excellent example of using the Internet to prepare and get acquainted with candidates before meeting them face-to-face. The candidate gets a taste of how KPMG presents itself, while KPMG gets an early-bird insight into whom they will meet when on campus. Basically, on its site, KPMG walks job-seeking students through the entire placement process, from how to submit a résumé to likely questions asked in the interview, to follow-up procedures, all in a question-and-answer format. Other information presented includes KPMG back-

Figure 2.5   Jobtrak.com is partnered with more than 1,000 college and university career centers, alumni associations, and MBA programs nationwide.

ground information and a day-in-the-life piece, detailing what KPMG employees do on a day-to-day basis.

Many schools also have private Intranets that are seen only by the students of that school. More often than not, many are devoted to jobs and career resources. If your company is seeking graduating or part-time students, you may want to figure out how to gain access to these students via their online career centers.

Diversity Recruiting

BrassRing has been an early mover in the "diversity" employment market. In 1999 it acquired Crimson & Brown Associates, a well-established diversity recruiter, and formed a division called BrassRing Diversity (http://www.brassringdiversity.com). Today it is one of the leading diversity recruitment firms, helping companies to identify, attract, and hire top minority and hard-to-find candidates.

"Targeted employment searches for minorities are increasingly essential," explains coauthor Eileen Shulock, who also happens to be the director of Webgrrls NYC (a networking organization for women in new media) on a volunteer basis. "The globalization of business means that talent comes in all shapes and sizes. It's no longer a white male–dominated world, and companies need to find and represent diversity in the workplace."

Companies may need to get proactive to find that talent, which is where organizations like Webgrrls International step in (see Figure 2.6). "I am contacted by recruiters and hiring managers every day," Eileen continues. "Webgrrls is internationally known as a place where Internet-savvy women gather. Whether programmers or marketers,

Figure 2.6   Webgrrls International is an organization for women in new media.

our membership is approached on a daily basis with job opportunities from companies desperate to add women to their workforce." So courted are the members that recruiters, such as the Creative Group (a division of Robert Half International) sponsor the organization on an international basis.

Diversity Expo, created by the producers of JOBEXPO and TECHEXPO (Sales/Management and Information Technology career fairs in the Northeast) is a unique "Equal Opportunity Employment Career Fair." Conducted both in the real world and online (http://www.diversityexpo.com), the event is a platform for professionals and recruiters to meet, network, interview face-to-face, and discuss issues and challenges of today's workplace. Hiring companies can count on Diversity Expo as a resource for IT, engineering, telecom, and business talent (see Figure 2.7).

How to Lure the Best Talent—Recruitment As a Sales Function

It's very easy and efficient to do a broad-based search for employment among a multitude of potential employers, which is why online employment sites are so popular. However, people still do focus their job searches to particular companies of interest, perhaps by profession or region or personal recommendation, so it is to your benefit to shape your website and your brand message to be as job seeker–friendly as you possibly can. In addition, any job seeker who might have found you through an employment network will still check out your website to see what you're all about. It's a sales game.

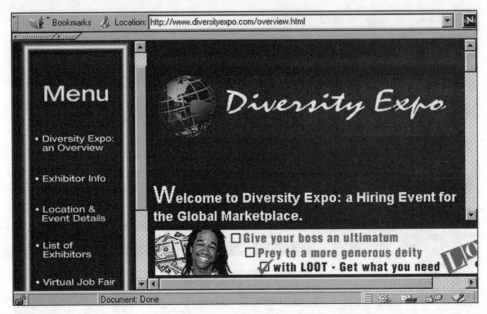

Figure 2.7 Diversity Expo is an "Equal Opportunity Employment Career Fair."

Do I want to work for you? What are you offering? Who are your clients? Does your company look interesting? Have I heard a buzz about how great your company is? Or have I heard that you've recently lost four of your key executives? Talented professionals know that the employment ball is in their court; in many cases it's now the employer that is under scrutiny.

How can you shape your company's web presence and industry image to convey the most positive impression to the job seeker? Let's start with your website. Does it compel the job seeker to want to learn more from the home page? If you are actively recruiting or on the lookout for talent, it must. Let's look at formerly old-line Andersen Consulting, now Accenture (http://www.accenture.com). At the home page level, job seekers are prominently invited to learn more. Enter the career section, and you are invited to "find out how to become part of the creativity, vision, and power of a global leader" as images show happy Accenture consultants at work. You can meet employees by reading profiles, check out a "day in the life" via multimedia presentations, or view webcasts of events and presentations. These innovative uses of technology are designed to appeal to the Internet generation of web-savvy job seekers.

Need we say more? Take a look at your competitors' websites to see how they are pitching themselves to potential job seekers. It's well worth the effort, and often overlooked. From the job seeker's point of view, your website is often the first point of contact with your company. Do you look like a vital and active member of your industry? Or is your site three months out of date? This critical first impression may turn many away before you've even had a chance to begin a conversation.

TIP For examples of firms employing their sites as part of a recruitment campaign, go to http://www.interbiznet.com and look for the Top 100 Recruiting Sites.

Creating Buzz About Your Company

Seventy percent of the people visiting HotJobs.com (profiled earlier in this chapter) are really just passive lookers, who are content with their jobs but curious about what else is out there. One way to keep your company top in the minds of future talent is to position yourself as an industry leader. Of course, we all want to be industry leaders. But if you are serious about raising your industry profile for branding, recruitment, or general buzz purposes, creating a good trade site that really gives a comprehensive snapshot of a given industry is a worthwhile endeavor. It shows clients and candidates that you walk the walk, that you are experienced in your field, and that you are a force to be reckoned with. It also can be used as a tool with which to open up a dialogue with potential candidates.

The Tenagra Group (http://www.tenagra.com), a web marketing, PR, consulting, and design firm, created a hub of activity around http://www.o-a.com, the Online-Ads Discussion List. Tenagra also keeps a high profile with its annual awards program, as well as with industry news digests that are distributed periodically (see Figure 2.8). These efforts by Tenagra afford it the opportunity to get close to many of the practitioners of their trade. Indeed, these venues sometimes act as the equivalent of Budapest for spies of a bygone era. Just like these undercover agents in the Cold War would get to comingle with each other up close and personal, here, too, competitors can eyeball each other pretty closely. Industry intrigue awaits you at your vertical online watering hole!

Survey the information niches already out there that cater to the talent pool you are thinking of addressing. If there is a site that appeals to you, approach it about the cost

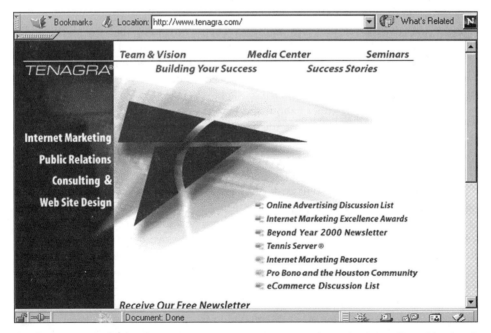

Figure 2.8 Tenagra's activities and site position it as an industry leader in the fields of web marketing, PR, consulting, and design.

© 2000 The Tenagra Corporation (http://www.tenagra.com).

of advertising. You may want to place an overt recruitment ad, or simply announce your own niche publication that is of unique interest to the audience you wish to address. You should have a site that is set up to accept the traffic from such a well-targeted advertising campaign. The readers of your advertisement can then click on over to your site, where they can either retrieve something of immediate value, read and respond to that job placement information, or sign up for a list that will give them periodic updates about industry-specific news.

TIP When guiding subscribers to your ezine, assure them the subscription information will not be used by or sold to any external source. When I put this guarantee in my newsletter, the fulfillment rate increased 10 percent.

You should proceed with caution, however. The information you provide must be of significantly higher value than that which is generally available on the Internet in your niche. Otherwise, your industry perception will be that of a wannabe rather than a real industry player.

To see what's out there, I suggest you check the mailing list databases and zine directories cited in Chapter 8, "Direct Marketing and Sales Support." Remember, nothing on the Internet is complete; there are new sites added every day, as well as sites disappearing. Lists change too quickly to be accurate. After checking these sources, you will want to conduct an extensive search using different search engines in order to see what other sites are serving the niche audience you wish to attract.

The State of Executive Recruiting

I was an executive recruiter for two years and remember finding that any given candidate I met on one job search would probably not be the person to land that particular job; rather, it would be another job down the road that would become the right match. It was a matter of building a relationship with a candidate until the stars were in alignment and everything clicked.

In this book and many others about the Net, the concept of disintermediation is often used to describe cutting out the middleman between two parties, whether they're buying and selling computers or looking for systems analysts. It should also be noted that the Net causes other intermediaries to emerge, as noted in Chapter 5, "Your Brand Image and the Internet."

In many cases, a company will farm out a job search to a Net-savvy recruiter. This concept shouldn't come as a surprise, since the exact same thing happens when trying to filter information. Human filters are becoming a new job classification; while software agents can do some filtering of information, they can never take the place of human judgment. The same holds true in human resources recruitment, where recruiters spend most of their day building relationships with current and future job seekers.

If you happen to be a job recruiter, check out Recruiters OnLine Network (RON) (http://www.recruitersonline.com). Membership is open only to professional recruiters (see Figure 2.9). For an annual membership fee, you can get help in conducting online searches, while also having access to a resource center. Additionally, members have the option of setting up their own sites with RON. Interestingly enough, RON

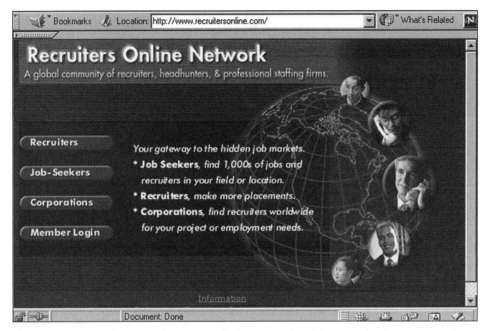

Figure 2.9 Recruiters OnLine Network is a membership organization open only to recruiters.

© Recruiters OnLine Network, Inc.

also offers some affinity marketing services. Recruiters can buy insurance through RON, as well as get attractive rates on things they need in their line of business, such as discounted per-minute rates on toll-free numbers.

Be aware of the image that your recruitment firm conveys to job seekers. Venerable Korn/Ferry International (http://www.kornferry.com), which places senior managers, CEOs, and board members, makes good use of the Net with an Executive Center (http://www.ekornferry.com), an online management recruiting site (http://www.futurestep.com), and a recruitment center for students (http://www.jobsdirect.com). All of these online properties are innovative extensions of the executive recruiter's brand and reach.

Distributed Employment: Telecommuting to Work on the Net

Once your firm has made the leap to recruiting using the Net, you'll find yourself asking the next logical question: If the candidate is already on the Net, is it really necessary to import that person into the office every day, whether that person comes from across the city, the country, or even the world?

If a person's brain power can be harnessed from her home, then both company and employee can have a win-win situation. The candidate saves on commuting time, clothes, gasoline, and so on. The firm saves on office space, electricity, and a host of other built-in HR costs. Employers can also calculate increased worker productivity, since that person won't be hanging around the water cooler or grousing about the coffee in the cafeteria. Assuming that all workers don't have to work together at the exact same time, you'll find that time-shifting is another advantage. Some people work most efficiently in the morning, while others tend to be night owls. For single- or dual-income families with children, this ability to shift workload and place can mean an essential difference in their work lives.

"The best part of the day was at lunch when they said to me, 'Let me tell you about our flexible work program,'" says Martha W. Sears, a veteran telecommuter, about a recent job interview. Sears is the Client Relationship Manager for the Asia Pacific Theatre web operations at PricewaterhouseCoopers, a position that she conducts from her Manhattan apartment and (in season) her sailboat, the *Laura Dee*. Why does she telecommute? "Through the various jobs I've had, I've just realized how much time is wasted working in an office, and how low the time utilization is," explains Sears.

"Discipline and self-initiation are not an issue for me," she continues. "Now, several years into this, and working for a global firm that promotes this, I've realized the whole notion of working virtually or telecommuting is a philosophy and a strategic position that has to start with management and trickle down. It's not suited for everyone, and not everyone is suited for telecommuting. You need to be disciplined, and you need to be able to create your own structure and manage your own time. If you are able to manage your own time, if you have discipline and structure, then your time utilization productivity and time management skyrockets."

After all, it's not how long or how much time someone puts in at the office, it is the results he or she delivers that matters. "In this business, the deliverable is the real thing," emphasizes Sears. "In terms of productivity and time management, telecommuting is a brilliant solution, because not only must you carefully track what you do, but it allows you to clarify what is going on. If there is a call, there will be a follow-up email documenting the conversation and what was discussed, which cuts down the margin for misunderstanding and disconnects." With regard to new media, she states, "In this industry, with its many interdependencies, clear communication is what everyone brings to the table, and telecommuting promotes this. Web operations are less about body language and facial gestures and more about getting things done—this is what we talked about, these are our milestones, this is what we will be working on, and then the subsequent management of both employee and employer expectations."

How do you set expectations as a manager? As a telecommuter, how can your expectations be met? As Sears observes, "That is an arena that is not part of our traditional work history. It's still being defined. It actually taps into a different style of management." At PricewaterhouseCoopers, there is a structure in place to become a telecommuter in that one's staff classification needs to be designated as telecommuter. But, at the time of writing, there is no formal training program. About 80 percent of the 30-person global web team in the United States works as telecommuters.

From a company perspective, the downside to telecommuting is the lack of "facetime." An offsite employee can be diminished in importance if he or she is never seen. "Out of sight, out of mind," as the saying goes. A tendency to marginalize offsite employees is difficult to notice and sometimes even more difficult to correct. But after all, it is a brave new HR world. Maybe a person can come to the office two days a week and use a space that is shared by other telecommuters on other days. Your firm may choose to go halfway and have that employee commute to a telecommuting center located near him. At these centers, there are office support services, such as industrial-strength copiers, videoconferencing capabilities, faster access to the Internet, and other systems.

The employee also needs to address the issue of face-time. "The other component is the relationship building," Sears explains. "How do you build relationships? With the whole notion of building and maintaining collegial relationships and client relationships, there needs to be thought about how you are using the time and how you develop those relationships." Communication outreach includes phone conversations, checking in and saying hello, email, and periodic meetings that have meaning. "When you are taking up your colleague's or client's time, there is now a purpose to it," she emphasizes. "But I am on the phone all day with people. My day is my own. It's not like Sandra Bullock in the movie *The Net* where all I do is stay inside and be a complete recluse."

A potential downside for some businesses is that there are things that happen in a face-to-face encounter that just aren't going to happen in an online encounter, even using teleconferencing or video feed. In many cases, there needs to be a certain spontaneity for inspiration to spawn. That may often only happen when your employees are in the same place at the same time, sharing the same experience.

TIPS FOR TELECOMMUTERS

- Leverage technology. "AOL's Instant Messenger is a brilliant way to build relationships in a telecommuting world," observes Sears.
- Meet face-to-face as a team with defined objectives as needed (PWC meets once a month).
- Establish a format to track and report hours spent by project.
- Establish a day-to-day scheduling database for the team that is used to give everybody's whereabouts.
- Explore new technologies, such as those that allow the group to share applications and conduct a collective work session.

TOOLS FOR TELECOMMUTERS

- Speaker phone or headset
- Fax software
- ThinkPad
- Two telephone lines
- Extremely comfortable chair
- Aquarium (distraction is very important)
- Dartboard
- Palm Pilot
- Cell phone
- Call forwarding
- Direct service line (DSL)

In closing, Sears says, "I recently worked with a 'real world' organization and began to see so clearly where there is low productivity. Just to set up a meeting I had to coordinate with the secretaries of this person and that person. I said, 'Guys, just get Lotus Notes and coordinate your time!' One can identify inefficiencies very quickly, and in a business where time is money, you get the drift." Would she go back to the office? "No," Sears concludes. "I don't think I can go back to an office again."

Telecommuting Forecast

JALA International is an international group of management consultants with a long history of expertise in telework and telecommuting (see Figure 2.10). In the early 1970s, they developed long-range forecasts for NASA (now *there's* a telecommute!) and later helped establish the world's first telework center. According to a study based on a survey of U.S. teleworkers for the Telework America Project of the International Telework Association and Council (http://www.telework.org), JALA forecasts that the expected number of teleworkers in the United States will reach 50 million by the year 2025. On the employer end, telecommuting is on the rise as well. Fifty-one percent of North American companies now permit employees to work at home, and 74 percent expect telecommuting to increase, according to Olsten Center research.

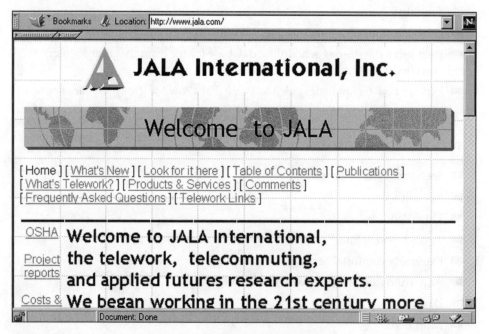

Figure 2.10   Telecommuting experts JALA International "began working in the twenty-first century more than 27 years ago."

© 1998 by JALA International, Inc. Reprinted by permission.

These are numbers that you should pay attention to. To learn more about how tele-commuting will impact your life, check out About.com's resource section at http://telecommuting.about.com/smallbusiness/telecommuting/mbody.htm, and also visit telecommuting expert Gil Gordon's link piles at http://www.gilgordon.com/resources/index.htm.

For a complete guide to telecommuting from both the employee and employer's perspective, check out a pilot project put together by Smart Valley, a Silicon Valley company focused on exploring new models and infrastructures for the work and edu-cational environment. While this particular project has been closed, the online guide covers everything from methods to implement a company-wide telecommuting pro-gram to firsthand reports from both management and employee perspectives. The complete study can be found at http://smart2.svi.org/PROJECTS/TCOMMUTE/webguide/.

TIP Be aware of the differences between offsite contract (or freelance) employees and part-time telecommuters, even if they are using a specific telecommuting center contracted and paid for by your company. There are many legal benefits and compensations that must be clarified and met for each category of employee.

Outsourcing on the Internet

Once your company has embraced the idea of farming work out on the Net, you will most likely find yourself asking the next logical question: "Is it necessary to have this person on staff at all?" In many cases, you will indeed need and want that person on staff, for reasons of consistency, security, workload, and so on. If it's possible to stay open to the idea of simply outsourcing a function (which you may already be doing locally), then why not consider doing so over the Net? Again, the savings can be sub-stantial. You may or may not pay a bit more for the luxury of having just-in-time help, but that is often easily offset by the downtime you have when there is no work for your staff. There you are, the clock is ticking, you have no work for them at the moment, and they're having a good old time buying hotel art in some auction site on the Net. The overall health and welfare of your unit or company is greatly impacted by underuti-lized employee downtime.

In a small business, especially, you will want to work with someone who has skills you don't have. This way, the most skill sets are covered by the fewest people. How-ever, people with different skill sets are often drawn to those pursuits based on their character. The point here is to make sure you can work with someone who may well be your exact opposite in nature, attitudes, and values. I've been in a couple of working relationships that went down in flames solely because of core value differences that weren't fleshed out at the beginning. In addition, make sure that roles, expectations, job descriptions, communications, and so forth are spelled out clearly ahead of time and are continually refreshed as necessary, even more so than in an in-office relation-ship. The same goes for any offsite employees, if you are a manager handling telecom-muters, as noted in the previous section of this chapter.

Another word of caution: If you're looking for someone to work with you on an ongoing project, it is advisable to first meet that person, or at least figure out if you both are temperamentally suited for each other. You can use the Kiersey Temperament Sorter at http://keirsey.com/cgi-bin/keirsey/newkts.cgi for this purpose, although be advised that it is not the be-all and end-all of psychological testing materials. People are indeed more complicated than a few simplified categories of reactions, but this can give you a general idea of how you might interact at a distance. Remember that email/Net interactions can be far different and more difficult than face-to-face ones. Think of how some email flame wars can start so easily over one emphasized word in a posting that in a letter or oral communication would have meant nothing at all. Interaction via the Net has its own pitfalls and advantages, but this medium does add a certain level of complexity to managing virtual relationships.

For example, Eileen and I (the coauthors of this book) have a primarily virtual relationship. Because of my very busy schedule, I am a stickler for schedules, deadlines, and deliverables. I do own my own business, so I am to some degree the master of my time. Eileen would also describe me as a very strategic, *process-driven* marketing professional. Because of her very busy schedule, Eileen is more apt to reshuffle all of her deadlines and deliverables. Eileen works full time in addition to her freelance work, and is more likely to be affected by the changing schedules and meeting times of colleagues and clients. She is also a more out-of-the-box (read, *non-process driven*) brainstormer and business strategist. These totally different work styles do occasionally lead to some prickly moments, but all in all, the relationship works. But we're in the same city, and can meet face-to-face if necessary. Transplant this particular scenario to opposite ends of the country, or the world, and you can quickly see how core work styles or personality types dramatically impact the quality and success of your virtual relationships.

> **TIP** Always check out your potential partner's background via a résumé and references, and keep in mind that the price you end up paying may be closer to the usual contract costs in order to get the best. Using the Internet is not necessarily cheap. You indeed can get what you pay for, from both ends of the spectrum.

Internet teamwork is like dating: Both sides tend to present their best sides at first. Similarly, the medium of email leaves much open for interpretation. Even though I get scoffed at by my Net-cognoscenti friends, I often use emoticons when writing email. This is to ensure the other side will know what I meant to say, since there isn't a common environment and they can't see my facial expressions or hear the tone of my voice.

Knowledge Cottage Labor

In the pre-Industrial Revolution days, work was farmed out to people's homes, where they had looms, spinning wheels, and cobbler benches that were used to turn out the products. It was the Industrial Age that centralized the workplace. Now, in the Information Age, we are shifting back again the other way; only this time, instead of looms, spinning wheels, and cobbler benches, we have computers, modems, faxes, and printers.

One of the dualities of the Net is that it enforces a leveling effect on any given labor market. If the cost of writers in New York City is prohibitive, the Internet provides an opportunity for both the buyer and the vendor of that service to connect outside of their geographical boundaries. If the writer lives in Plano, Texas, where the cost of living is much lower than in New York City or Los Angeles, it becomes feasible for a business owner (or editor, in this case) to farm out the work to the writer in Plano instead of employing a more expensive, local resource.

It doesn't matter if you're farming out programming, spreadsheet analysis, copy-writing, or graphics, it's all information that is more easily transported than actually moving you, your vendors, or your employees. If a vendor is working out of a home or small office, he or she often incurs all the costs of hardware, software, Internet connection, phone, electricity, and so on. While this flat-out Darwinian marketplace can be brutal on small firms and independents, many prefer it because their income is diversified across a number of clients and subsequent revenue streams. I remember I was once let go from an advertising agency because some bean counter in London said the New York office had to cut back 40 people. One of the most stressful aspects of employment is not having control over your circumstances.

How do you find freelancers or contractors to meet your business needs? No matter what your need, there is a website where you can find it. As mentioned earlier in this chapter, Monster.com was one of the first sites to create a freelance Talent Market where freelancers and those in need of their services could connect and actually bid on work-for-hire. Today, sites for freelancers abound. In addition, niche talent sites have sprung up to meet specific freelance, contract, or virtual needs. One example is Guru.com, which boasts 42,000 registered gurus on call to bid for your projects. Need to write a business plan, create a strategy, or evaluate your financial projections? Throw it out to the gurus and see who you find. Another example is the growing number of sites where you can hire a virtual assistant—both live assistants who will work for you for a set number of hours per week, and also a set of virtual assistant tools such as calendars, reminder services, and so on to help organize your life.

Distance Training/Learning

If you have to train a widely distributed group of employees, it can turn into a costly proposition, since you have to bring them to a central location, house, feed, and, of course, teach them. Many companies use Intranets to distribute educational materials across an enterprise. Distance learning/training can be easily implemented over corporate Intranets. A sales force can also be trained by way of Extranets. (An Extranet allows a company to give restricted access to users around the world, often with the use of a password.) Here again, the knowledge itself is more easily distributed than the people to whom you wish to distribute this knowledge.

As predicted in the first edition of this book, distance learning is one of the fastest growing segments of the Internet industry. According to Deborah Lilly, who is the manager on the speaking side of my business, and who is expanding the event training aspect of her speaker's bureau and agency into the corporate training area, "The e-learning tsunami is rapidly approaching the $80 billion training market, and by June 2001, will completely change the landscape of corporate training around the world. It is the solution to the problem of how to reach a global workforce. However, it is a complicated solution requiring a complexity of technology, enablers, delivery systems and that's before you even get to the content or courseware. For each segment of the industry, there are dozens, and seemingly hundreds, of start-up and offshoot companies racing to establish territories in this new market space."

Lilly advises, "Watch how many of these companies merge, partner, change focus, and/or survive as suppliers to the training industry. Once the high-tech infrastructure is designed, installed, and deployed, it will be fascinating to see what high-touch knowledge transference processes emerge."

International Data Corporation (IDC), a global consulting and research firm, reported that $1.75 billion was spent on distance learning and training in 2000. With that much being spent, imagine how much will be saved in gas, time, insurance, and so on. "Competitors, tools, and technology are emerging and rapidly defining the look of training and learning via the Web," said Ellen Julian, a research manager at IDC, in a press release. "The potential of this new delivery system for both IT- and non-IT-related training is enormous; in particular, the ability to provide tools that enable individuals to learn as needed means a giant leap forward for the cause of just-in-time, continuous learning in the workplace. . .Presently, some fine information-technology training sites are up and running, but there is work to be done in the development of full-service sites with varied, desirable features. The key for suppliers who plan to offer training over the Web is to make it possible for customers to tailor the site for their individual learning needs."

Oracle's Learning Network (OLN) is an education portal for customers and portals. Since the last edition of this book, it has evolved to encompass all online offerings from Oracle University. OLN Professional subscription (the first offering from OLN) is a 100 percent web-mediated offering that gives 24/7 access to hundreds of hours of in-depth, self-paced eStudy courses, hands-on labs, quizzes, eSeminars, and instructor eChats, all designed to help Oracle IT professionals stay abreast of the latest products and technologies from Oracle without having to leave their desks.

Southwestern Bell uses its SBC Town, an intranet that employs a bevy of technologies to train its technicians by using Virtual Reality Mark-Up Language (VRML) modeling (3D models) and Java applications, along with the Web. Designed by EDS (Electronic Data Systems), this extraordinary system is called dVISE. The implementation of the project started in early 1997.

Here's how it works: A technician receives a simulated service request that outlines the difficulty level. She then grabs her virtual toolbox and "drives" to the physical location with her mouse. Everything behaves as it does in the real world. A technician opens a terminal box on the screen by clicking on it and is presented with an array of different actions that can ameliorate the problem. Then the technician sends test tones through various terminals to see where the line break is. The system faithfully represents the sounds on the computer the way they sound in the real world. If that technician comes down from the virtual telephone pole without paying attention, she's apt to be run over by a virtual car! Once the technician thinks she's found the fault, she enters the diagnosis into the system to see if she is in fact correct. Throughout this process, the technician is being tracked, so she can later be evaluated on how quickly or how slowly she solved the problem and the accuracy of her results. This is a vivid example of online learning in that it loosely models reality.

Now let's take an example that isn't from a high-tech company. eCollege.com (http://www.ecollege.com) is an application service provider building online courses for colleges and universities worldwide. Comprised of educators and technologists, eCollege.com partners with institutions such as Rutgers University, Johns Hopkins University, University of Colorado, Drexel University, San Francisco State University, and Seton Hall University to deliver course content in a highly interactive and engaging educational manner. North Carolina A&T State University and Northwest Missouri State University, using the eCollege teaching platform, were selected as part of the winning team of institutions participating in the Army University Access Online (AUAO) initiative. Through AUAO, soldiers will have access to accredited associate's, bachelor's, and master's degrees and certificate programs anytime, from anywhere they are stationed. At the secondary level, the company has been selected as the technology and services provider for the Illinois Virtual High School (IVHS) (http://ivhs.org). IVHS will provide Illinois students and teachers increased access to a wider range of course offerings "independent of time and location." On the professional level, the company provides certification in a multitude of disciplines, and has launched eCorporateU (http://www.ecorporateu.com), a division serving the eLearning needs of corporate training providers and corporate universities.

Although most corporate distance training and learning programs tend to be located behind Intranets and therefore not viewable on the open Internet, it is useful to take a look at what some colleges and universities are currently doing in this field. Duke University, among many others, now offers a full-fledged MBA program online

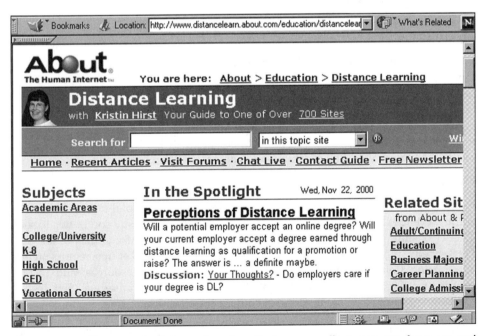

Figure 2.11 About.com's distance learning site is an excellent resource for news and information.

(http://www.fuqua.duke.edu/index_40.html). You must have a minimum of eight years' business experience and already be working for a company that is presumably picking up your tuition. The program takes 19 months to complete and is available in the Americas, Europe, and Asia. A sampling of courses for the North America module includes Decision Models, Managerial Effectiveness for the Global Executive, and International Financial Statement Analysis. In January 2001, Duke University will be the first university to offer a live webcast of a regularly scheduled MBA course to students outside its campus. For an example of a more mass-appeal distance learning model, check out Ziff-Davis's Learn-It Online (http://learnitonline.com). The site specializes in self-paced computer skills training, and is designed for employees who can't make it to the classroom or who need a quick, just-in-time review. LearnItOnline uses interactive, Shockwave-based software simulations to teach computer skills. After purchasing an inexpensive subscription lot, a subscriber can gain access to tutorials for dozens of popular desktop software programs, such as Microsoft Office.

Obviously, distance learning and training will play a role in your future. To learn more, visit the Distance Learning section of About.com, at http://www.distancelearn .about.com/education/distancelearn/ (see Figure 2.11).

Resource Center

Interim Consulting

the hired guns   **http://www.thehiredguns.com**

Wanna go to a Pink Slip Party? It's become a rite of passage for many Internet workers, where glasses are raised to salute fallen companies and the newly unemployed darlings of dot-com disasters swap war stories. This monthly gathering is the brainchild of Allison Hemming, the company's president. If you are currently between assignments, check out the site to determine how to become a hired gun. You'll have access to flexible work schedules, exciting projects, outstanding clients, and a vast pool of free agents to network with—all of whom are as accomplished as yourself.

ConsultingCentral.com   **http://www.consultingcentral.com**

New to the management consulting game? It's estimated that total management consulting revenues hit $100 billion across the globe in 1999 and are still continuing to soar. Check ConsultingCentral.com to see if this expanding market is for you. Sponsored by the Kennedy Information Research Group, the site offers job seeker tips, reports on fees and pricing trends in management consulting, consulting resources, and recommended reading. If your job hunt's got you down, take the humorous "Self Test: Is Consulting For You?" to see if you're cut out for the consulting game.

InstantWork.com   **http://www.instantwork.com**

Dubbed the "first site for buying and selling tasks INSTANTLY!" InstantWork is operating the first online freelance marketplace that uses instant messaging and proprietary "presence-on-browser" technology to give buyers and sellers access to 100 percent virtual projects. InstantWork focuses on outsourced temporary work of the kind that can be delivered immediately via the Web, including creative services, administrative support, foreign language translation, professional services, and technical services. Freelancers can get paid instantly, too, through PayPal.

HR Resources

HR at About.com   http://humanresources.about.com

Site host Susan M. Heathfield, a management consultant, leads you through the maze of human resources issues and resources on this excellent site. You'll find articles and discussions on over 25 different HR-related topics, including strategic HR, labor relations, career development, and much more.

HR.com   http://www.hr.com

Rated one of the favorite sites of HR professionals by *Fast Company* magazine, hr.com offers free membership and easy access to the information, resources, products, and services you need to successfully manage the people side of business. You'll find daily news on HR issues, features from professionals such as Peter Block and Lou Adler, PR/Legal news, and focus points on technology issues that effect the HR community. Take a break from your hectic schedule to enjoy the HR.Comic by Jerry King and look into the future by checking your HR Horoscope.

The Top 100 Electronic Recruiters   http://www.interbiznet.com/eeri

This is the first place to stop when searching for a job or trying to fill a position. A meta-site for electronic recruiting, the Top 100 Electronic Recruiters does a nice job of addressing three different audiences: job seekers, human resources managers, and third-party recruiters. Of particular interest is a comparison price list for popular online recruiting services and reviews of tools and resources for all three audience groups.

Employee Ownership

National Center for Employee Ownership   http://www.nceo.org

Leading the troops and your company toward employee ownership? NCEO provides accurate, unbiased information on employee stock ownership plans (ESOPs), broadly granted employee stock options, and employee participation programs. You'll find articles on how employee ownership works, a conceptual guide to employee ownership for very small businesses and tons of research on employee ownership and participation.

Career Opportunities

monster.com   http://www.monster.com

Job seekers in the U.S., Europe, and Asia are flocking to Monster.com's global network of employment opportunities, and rightfully so. This site has it together. Post your résumé and the recruiters come calling. Search 2,000 pages of career advice, résumés, and salary information. Even senior executives (known as Chief Monsters) can explore employment potential here. Be sure to sign on for the Monster.com email newsletter, which numbers close to half a million subscribers.

CareerBuilder.com   http://www.careerbuilder.com

View and apply for jobs from over 75 of the best career sites on the Web, and read advice on career strategies, getting hired, the working life, and much more at Career-Builder.com. Employers use this site extensively, so it's worth the few minutes to post your experience.

HotJobs.com   http://www.hotjobs.com

Onward and upward with HotJobs.com, in business since 1997. Dubbed a "total employment solutions company," HotJobs.com now has additional offices in Canada, Australia, and in the U.K., expanding across the globe to help opportunity seekers with diverse levels of experience. You'll find 25 different industry channels awaiting your résumé posting, as well as news on hot career events close to home.

CruelWorld.com   http://www.cruelworld.com

The process of entering CruelWorld's site is annoying (splash screen alert) but once inside, you'll find a myriad of job postings and content. You'll find specific sections for job seekers with marketing, sales, finance, development, database, and Java experience. Since a job hunt is, in reality, a marketing job, you'll find loads of good articles on finding your way to career satisfaction.

Headhunter.net   http://www.headhunter.net

With 250,000 jobs and growing, Headhunter.net offers info on permanent placement along with its new site for contractors and freelancers. Search by job type and industry, or delve into specific job communities such as information technology, customer service, healthcare, and more. Read the Success Stories, tour the Resource Center, sign up for the CareerBYTES email newsletter, which is full of inspiration for the job seekers among us.

CareerJournal   http://www.careerjournal.com

Considering all the dot-bomb layoffs, the *Wall Street Journal*'s redesigned career site is just in time. It covers every base for landing another executive, managerial, or professional job. Job seekers can create their own personalized home page, which will show articles and job postings matching their interests. In the job search database I entered "content" and found 200 jobs. There are articles on every topic related to the job search, from résumés and cover letters to negotiation tips and what to expect when changing careers. Check out the salary table to get the skinny on compensation for hundreds of positions.

Jobs.com   http://www.jobs.com

Jobs.com is one of the online employment sites that specifically spotlights job hunting for the military community. Thinking about a military career? Or perhaps you're leaving the military and now you want to use your skills to land a great civilian job. This is the place for you. Students and temporary workers are also invited, along with the permanent placement populace seeking new jobs. You'll also find info on career resources and career fairs in your area. If you're looking to research employers, check this site out.

Distance Learning

ElementK   http://www.elementk.com

With more than 550 information technology and business courses designed exclusively for the Web, ElementK offers instructor-led online courses, self-paced tutorials, a comprehensive reference library, and interaction with experts and fellow students.

DigitalThink   http://www.digitalthink.com

With over 230 courses to choose from, the learning inspired should be satisfied. If not, DigitalThink will customize a course for you. Business-focused courses run the gamut from e-commerce, sales, and IT to more technical training. Simulations, discussion sessions, and quizzes keep things interactive.

Digital University   http://www.digitaledu.com

Distance learning is an explosive web business, and we have only begun to see how it will change the course of education in the years ahead. One challenge has been how to best facilitate the learning process given the obstacles of limited bandwidth, differing operating systems, ranging levels of technical sophistication, and the presentation of often complicated information. DigitalEdu has opted for the killer app of email to present their very informative classes, supplemented by online communities for students, teachers, and chat. Classes are inexpensive, 4 weeks in length, at your convenience, and geared to the technical and professional education of new media types. Get there now for a free class sample and a newsletter that will keep you up to date on DigitalEdu's offerings.

Knowledge Systems

LeadingWay   http://www.leadingway.com

Organizations such as Toyota, Kinko's, and Caterpillar have transformed their training organizations from old linear learning to *knowledge systems* via LeadingWay's software applications, content development, and consulting services. Employees, suppliers, dealers, and clients can gain access to a company's knowledge base with just one click, anywhere, anytime, and on any device—a brand new way to learn, work, and share experience. The result is better productivity and expertise for people and companies.

Ynotlearn.com   http://www.ynotlearn.com

According to the folks at Ynotlearn.com, U.S. corporations lost close to $12 billion last year due to the inability to effectively access their own intellectual property. Ynotlearn.com will help you spend some of that revenue with a browser-based suite of products where all courseware authoring, editing, assessment creation/maintenance, and learning management functions are available via the browser. No need for a direct connect to the organizational LAN/WAN and Windows desktops.

Tcert, Inc.   http://www.tcert.com

Tcert.com of Atlanta, Georgia, has developed a learning application called Edapt that assesses the unique skill level of the student and generates a personalized path of instruction. It acts as an online tutor so students are always challenged at the appropriate level. Result: efficient and effective learning. Visit the online Learning Center for self-directed demonstrations.

Knowledgeware

HorizonLive.com   http://www.horizonlive.com

MetLife, the Employment Channel, Blackboard.com, the Princeton Review, and others are interacting in real time with customers, students, and employees using Horizon-Live 2.0, an application that enables the presenter to show still or video-based text and visual content, project his or her voice, demonstrate live applications, and use a white-board. Very popular with the healthcare, manufacturing, financial, and professional services industries, HorizonLive 2.0 is 100 percent web-ready with no plug-ins or downloads required and can be accessed via any Mac, Unix, or Windows platform. Visit and sign on for a free demo.

ReadyGo.com   http://www.readygo.com

Did you know that 80 percent of corporate training materials are produced internally? ReadyGo of Mountain View, California, has the ReadyGo Web Course Builder solution that sells for less that $500. It's an easy-to-use authoring tool that dramatically reduces online courseware development time. Best of all: All courses created with the software are the property of the author—not ReadyGo. Download a fully functional trial version of the ReadyGo Web Course Builder at the site today and see for yourself.

Scientific Learning Products   http://www.scilearn.com

Talk about brain waves. Scientific Learning combines the latest advances in brain research and proprietary technology to create programs, products, and services that develop learning and communication skills. Participants spend 90 to 100 minutes a day, five days a week, for four to eight weeks with these adaptive exercises, which train the brain to develop language and reading comprehension, phonological awareness, organizational skills, and overall communication skills. In addition, teachers and parents can track data and monitor progress online for each student. Check out the quotes from satisfied parents and educators and check out the company's BrainConnection.com site for every fact you could ever want to know about the human brain.

eLearning

Ninth House Network   http://www.ninthhouse.com

Recently named among the Best of the Web in corporate training by *Forbes* magazine, Ninth House Network provides one of the leading broadband e-learning environments for organizational development. Partnering with respected business thought leaders such as Tom Peters, Ken Blanchard, Larraine Segil, Peter Senge, and others, transformation is the keyword for the services and products Ninth House offers. All are geared to help companies achieve meaningful organizational change through employee development skills, including management, leadership, communication, project management, teamwork, and business essentials.

Caliber Learning Network, Inc.   http://www.caliber.com

Caliber, located in Baltimore, has eLearning solutions that serve up unique learning and interactivity. When live collaboration is needed, check out Caliber inClass. . .perfect for product roll outs, channel training, supply-side communication, and professional development classes. Caliber liveCast provides full, immediate interactivity without live collaboration and Caliber onDemand produces messages that have a longer shelf life, such as softskills IT training, HR/Benefits training, and employee orientations.

EduCommerce

LearningBrands.com   http://www.learningbrands.com

Brands should teach. That's the word from LearningBrands.com, a company that's developed a unique, online brand-building tool to create this reality for all companies that produce, sell, or service. Take the time to visit the site to learn more about adaptive learning, the one-to-one teaching experience that strengthens the relationship between you and your customers, similar to the bond between a great teacher and a student. Sign on for the free newsletter and read the Case Studies to find how other companies are using learning as their most powerful sales and marketing tool.

Powered, Inc.   http://www.powered.com

Formerly known as notHarvard.com, this online education pioneer has developed online branded universities and the concept of eduCommerce—the use of online education as a sales and marketing weapon. Powered's client list includes Barnes & Noble.com, jobs.com, Metrowerks, Web Street Securities, and Talk City, Inc., among others. Powered's aim is to make learning free and accessible to everyone. Visit the Powered site to find out about learning opportunities hosted on their customers' sites and the teaching opportunities that abound due to the company's growth.

Mining the Internet
for All It's Worth

You are very lucky. Why? Because in this crowded, cacophonous dot-com world, many companies desperately want your attention. So desperate are these companies that they are willing to give you valuable information for free (or almost free), as information is now a commodity that will continue to decrease in price. And guess what? You will continue to get even luckier. In an effort to keep up with the increasing competition, these companies will continuously need to offer higher quality information to capture your attention. How lucky you are will be determined by your ability to exploit this happy circumstance. In this chapter, you will discover some of the most delectable offerings out there. In addition, you will learn the tricks of the trade to find what you are looking for quickly, because your most valuable commodity is your time.

If the beloved American monologist Will Rogers were alive today, he might say the following: "You know they're telling the truth when they say there are over 1 billion web pages on the Internet, because when you do a search for something, you get 950 million of them back." In this chapter, you'll discover how to separate the wheat from the chaff, and learn how to whittle down what seems like millions of search results to a meaningful few that deserve your attention and focus. You'll find some new starting points that may make your current search efforts seem archaic. Or maybe you're not looking for a piece of information that's on the Net, but rather an answer to a question. You'll find some places where you can get those questions answered.

Information is like oil. You have to know how and where to drill for it. That knowledge gives you two competitive advantages: First, if your cost of gathering information is low, you can run smarter and leaner than your competition. Second, unearthing information your competition doesn't know about opens up doors of opportunity. Imagine if your main competitor didn't use computers today. He wouldn't be a competitor very long, would he? The same is true for finding and using information on the Internet. If you can't find information quickly and easily, you will not be a competitor in your field, whether that information is statistics, government regulations, market research, or customer feedback. If you can get to those nuggets of knowledge first, you're that much ahead of everyone else. After reading this chapter, you'll be armed with information about:

- Search engines
- Search directories
- Search services portals
- How to focus your searches
- Boolean search strings
- Vertical industry portals
- Filtering agents and search tools
- Sweet spots for information
- Online focus groups and market research

Search Engines and Directories

To novice surfers, the concept of a *search* means going out to any number of seemingly identical sites, typing in a word, and crossing their fingers in hope of a good result. In reality, search engines and search directories are quite different. Understanding the differences between the two and leveraging their unique strengths will turn your information-gathering efforts into a laserlike stealth mission.

Search Engines

Search engines are driven by software. They use *spiders* to explore entire websites. Essentially, the search engine periodically sends its automated emissaries out to the Web and instructs them to "crawl" through a website, electronically picking up keywords, metatags, titles, and other text. The information collected is stored in the search engine's *index*. The index, or catalog, is a giant database of information covering every site the search engine has ever visited. Finally, that information is categorized and ranked by the search engine using proprietary rating methods. Examples of search engines are AltaVista, Excite, FAST Search, and Google.

Google (http://www.google.com), one of the fastest growing search engines on the Web, is a good example of a search engine on the move (see Figure 3.1). According to a newsworthy press release, Google enables Internet users to search more than 1 billion URLs, which includes 560 million full-text indexed web pages and 500 million partially indexed URLs. "Google's new gigantic index means that you can search the equivalent of a stack of paper more than 70 miles high in less than half a second," says Larry Page, Google CEO and cofounder.

Figure 3.1   Google indexes 1,060,000,000 and counting.
© Google, Inc.

In addition, Google uses a variety of innovative technologies, including sophisticated text matching and advanced, patent-pending technology called PageRank, to organize information so that the most important results always come up first. Google's technological innovations have garnered numerous awards for the company, including a 2000 Webby and People's Voice Award for Best Technical Achievement, Best Search Engine on the Internet from *Yahoo! Internet Life*, and more.

Search Directories

Search directories are driven by human editors. They are usually compiled manually by humans, and are based on user submissions, editorial selection, and other categorization processes. Search directories involve a level of human editorial analysis to determine which sites will or will not be included in the directory's categorical offerings. Examples of search directories include Yahoo!, Snap, LookSmart, and Open Directory, which actually powers the popular directory sections of AOL Search, Netscape Search, AltaVista, and others.

But wait! You just read a few paragraphs ago that AltaVista was a search engine. Now you've read that AltaVista is also powered by a search directory. How can this be?

The Search Services Portal

The answer is the hybrid search engine/directory, or the *search services* portal, which has become more and more popular. Why? People like to find information in different ways. Some like to search by keyword through the enormous database of a search engine. Others may prefer to browse through the editor-determined categorical hierarchy of a directory. In an effort to gain market share, and to be all things to all people—including a source for news, commerce, email, games, maps, stock quotes, weather reports, and so on, ad infinitum—the quest for the ultimate search services portal is generating strategic alliances among industry players at a record pace. For example, AltaVista, which we will discuss later in this chapter, is a search engine. AltaVista licenses its search engine capabilities to LookSmart, a directory. AltaVista also provides for its users both a directory option, which is powered by Open Directory, and a natural language question and answer service, which is powered by Ask Jeeves.

Confused yet? It's also possible to search a search engine of search engines—called a *metasearch engine*—which queries multiple search engines simultaneously. Metasearch engine sites may also offer portal-type services in an effort to generate user loyalty.

With so many options, what's a searcher to do?

Search Strategies

Focus: It's what you need to stay on mission. The sophisticated information sleuth knows that the first step in an information quest is to select the best place to start looking for the information. Basically, you have four choices:

Search engines. The bigger the better, right? Sometimes, but not always. For example, Google has a strong consumer focus. If you are searching for vacation tips or sporting events, your search here might be very productive. However, if you are searching for information on conveyor belts, you might spend a lot of time wading through extraneous results.

Search directories. Ah, the human touch. Danny Sullivan, an industry expert on search services and publisher of SearchEngineWatch, a website and email newsletter devoted to the search services industry, predicts that directories are the future of web search. Why? "They make the job of finding sites easier for searchers," Sullivan says. "For instance, a searcher may discover (using a directory) that there is a whole category of information related to a particular business topic. Entering that category would show them a list of sites on the topic. In contrast, without human help, the searcher might have had to try and search a crawler-based search engine to create such a list from scratch." Some directories are general, such as Yahoo! and About.com, and some are focused on specific niche markets.

Search service portals. The best of both worlds? Maybe. But where is your information coming from? Is it coming from the search engine and the directory most relevant to your search?

Metasearch sites. Recognizing that all this searching was bound to be frustrating and time-consuming, metasearch sites were developed that query multiple search engines simultaneously. One example is Mamma.com, which queries more than ten sources, including Yahoo!, GoTo, Excite, Lycos, AltaVista, and Kanoodle. To demonstrate the efficiency of each, let's do a sample search.

Search Tactics—Choose Your Weapons

Before you dash off, randomly looking for what you want, think of how you might filter out the noise that can easily distract you from finding the gold. In this section, you will learn how to frame your inquiry to achieve the best results. Recognize the phrase "garbage in, garbage out"? Searches work the same way.

Let's say we're searching for the optimum temperature for a chicken egg to hatch in an incubator. First, think of a few keywords that might succinctly express this search— we need a *chicken egg* in an *incubator*. Take all the articles, such as "the" and "a," out of your search phrase. Remember to remove all of the conjunctions, such as "and" and "or." Now, look at what remains:

chicken egg incubator

What can we do with this odd little series of words?

Searching a Search Engine

First, let's try putting that phrase in the search engine of your choice and see if it narrows the field a bit. It should. If it narrows it too much, which is doubtful, try inserting other descriptive words that could conceivably be found on the web pages or newsgroup archives you're trying to unearth. At the time of this writing, Google returned 2,300 results (in 0.40 seconds) in answer to this query.

TIP Since no one search engine has a complete database of the entire Web, you should try your query with a few different search engines. Remember the steps required to spider and then to index a search engine's offerings? Web pages and newsgroups change daily. Search engines can't possibly keep up.

The next thing you should do is take that same search phrase and go to HotBot (http://www.hotbot.com). Look for the Advanced Search tab on the home page and click on it. There you will find one of the most useful tools on the Internet. Paste your search phrase in the text field and put quotes around it:

"chicken egg incubator"

By doing this, you ensure that those words within your search phrase will appear within 10 words of each other on the pages HotBot digs up for you. This should help you zero in pretty quickly to what you're looking for. Even if you still get back 100 pages, click on the Revise Options button and you'll then be able to easily toggle on and off various words, dates, and more to narrow down the sites returned. Get rid of those that are off track, and then press search again. Bingo! You've got a much finer grain of a search this time—a link to a document about Incubation Troubleshooting leaps to the top of our list. If it's still too large, you may wish to refine some more, or you may try to Refine Your Search with HotBot's preprogrammed suggested search topics, which are generated based upon your keywords (see Figure 3.2).

> **TIP** The ability to support user-directed searches, like HotBot's Revise Options feature, is increasing in importance as the technology to do so becomes more readily available. By empowering the user to direct his or her search based upon analysis of the results (for example, "Show me more like this"), sites will deliver increasingly relevant results much more quickly.

Essentially, the Revise Options feature is a user-friendly way of letting you write what are known as *Boolean search strings* without even realizing it. To get an idea of the extended Boolean search phrase that HotBot wrote for you based on your refinements, press the Back button and look at the text field in which you entered your original search phrase in quotes. You'll see that it's much longer and more complex than what you wrote. By comparing that much-extended search phrase to the refinements you checked off, you'll begin to get an idea of what an advanced Boolean search phrase looks like and what you would have had to write yourself in order to get the same results.

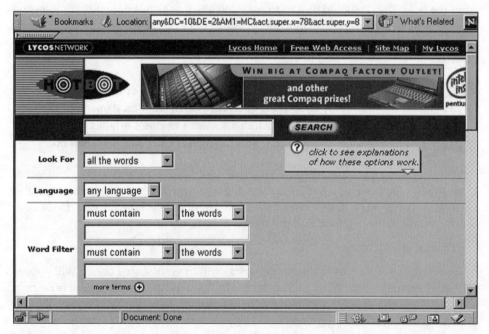

Figure 3.2 HotBot Advanced is one of the more sophisticated tools for power searching the Web.

TIP Longing for some signs of human contact? Visit natural language recognition search site AskJeeves, found at http://www.askjeeves.com. There you simply type your search question in natural language—Where can I find information about the optimum temperature to hatch chicken eggs in an incubator?—and multiple suggested links from multiple sources are delivered to you. Since the technology is not perfected, results can sometimes be off base at best and comical at worst. However, watch for increasing use of natural language recognition technologies as a search option.

Search sites increasingly aim to remove the need to understand Boolean searches and other advanced search tactics, to give the user a seamless experience. However, until technology is perfected, we encourage you to learn a few advanced search techniques that will work for you across the board. Remember, it's your time and your competitive advantage.

TIP If at any point during a search you hit pay dirt, then SAVE the actual results as an HTML document to your hard drive. This way, you don't have to redo the entire search the next time you're looking for the same thing, or if you can't finish your research in one sitting. Remember, saving that web page of the search results is like saving a snapshot of a horse race: The results you get tomorrow may well be different from the results you got today. Search, save, and be merry, for tomorrow you won't find it.

Searching a Directory

For comparison's sake, let's take our string of words to a search directory. At NBCi (formerly known as Snap, http://www.nbci.com), our string led us to the top-ranked choice (as selected by the section editor): Chick Master at http://www.chickmaster .com, an incubator manufacturer that is listed within the category of Bird Incubators. The categorical hierarchy also suggests that we might find sites of interest with the Egg Incubator, Hatching Chickens, and Poultry sections. These categorized lists of sites make it easy to focus right in, as long as the sites that will help us best are categorized in this particular directory.

TIP Some search engines and directories are focused on niche topics. You will find a great list of specialty search spots at industry expert Danny Sullivan's Search Engine Watch site (http://www.searchenginewatch.com/ links/Specialty_Search_Engines).

Doing a Metasearch

You may want to now attempt a metasearch. A metasearch engine searches other search services. For example, you can search AltaVista, Direct Hit, Excite, FindWhat, Lycos, and more than 700 others by simply going to CNET's Search.com (http://

www.search.com). While you'll get a snapshot all at once of what each service has about your search subject, your results can be overwhelming. In addition, the Search.com site can't perform advanced searches on each of the search engines—it can only do one big simple search on one engine at a time. This may be all you need or want. However, if you are looking to get a very specific piece of information in your crosshairs, it's going to be pretty hard if your gun sight is as large as all outdoors.

Sampling a Search Service Portal

Each search service portal offers different slices of the Web and different services. My favorite search spot is AltaVista. Since AltaVista also offers a directory service, powered by Open Directory, it is actually a search portal—but AltaVista began as a search engine and continues to develop sophisticated search engine technology. If you prefer to use the stripped-down version of AltaVista without the extraneous portal services, you can find it at Raging Search (http://www.raging.com).

You might also ask, Why don't you use Yahoo!? It is consistently one of the top-ranked websites according to Media Metrix. Well, at the time of this writing Yahoo!'s search engine is powered by Google. Remember, Yahoo! is a directory, not a search engine, but Yahoo! is strategically aligned with Google to provide a search engine to users as well. Google? I've already been there and done that. However, Yahoo!'s indexed directory is very useful. When you don't know exactly what you are looking for, take a browse through Yahoo! by category to see what turns up.

TIP Your search results may reflect the sites with the largest budgets. Some search services allow sites to buy a top ranking in their results. Also, many services rank sites in order of importance based upon an algorithm that includes link analysis (the number of sites pointing to a site; the more the better) and popularity analysis (the number of visits to the site and the time spent there). You may have to work hard to find exactly what you need, especially if it doesn't rank high on the advertising or popularity meter!

Hit a Bull's Eye with a Boolean Search

Until now, Boolean searches were the purview of gray-haired, granny-glassed librarians; in fact, many of the original Internet publications were aimed at librarians. In this age of limitless digital information, informed search skills are becoming more and more useful to a greater number of people. You can get much more out of many databases if you know some basic Boolean techniques. Although search engines such as AltaVista are set up so you don't really need to know how to construct a Boolean search string yourself, it's a good idea to know how to do so anyway.

Basic Boolean search parameters follow the two-valued logic system, where there are only two answers to any query: True or False. The query can use three parameters, or values, in order to reach an answer: OR, AND, and NOT. OR means that both or either can be included in an answer. AND means that both values must be included in an answer. NOT excludes a certain parameter from the answer, narrowing it even further. The following list shows typical Boolean search parameters using both two and three values. For example, if you are still searching for that optimum chicken egg hatching temperature, you could set up a query string as follows:

"incubator AND chicken egg". AND statement, which would yield anything with both temperature and chicken egg in the text.

"incubator OR chicken egg". OR statement, which would yield either temperature or chicken egg in the text.

"incubator AND chicken egg NOT dead". NOT statement, which excludes anything including the word "dead" in the text, yielding, we hope, a quality website focusing on successful chicken egg hatching for your needs.

While Boolean logic applies to any database-driven search engine (in other words, all search engines), each search engine has slightly different rules for wording personally created Boolean strings, using different symbols or words to represent the three values. Be sure to check the help file of the Advanced section of any search engine before you try to create a Boolean search statement of your own.

TIP Keep your search skills tuned by subscribing to the Search Skill of the Day list, found at http://www.tipworld.com.

Veering into Vortals

Vortals, or Vertical Industry Portals, are one of the fastest growing segments of the Web. These industry-specific websites usually combine a number of features—a search engine, an industry-focused directory, news, discussion groups or other community exchanges, auctions, and/or other e-commerce offerings. What are the advantages of a vortal search? Again, choose your weapons wisely. If you are in an industry that is well served by one of the blossoming vortals, you may find:

■ More relevant search results, news, and information (selected specifically for your industry)

■ Industry-specific terminology and categorization

■ The latest research and statistics for your industry

■ A professional networking community

■ Business-to-business support and commerce opportunities

Searching a Vortal

One last time, let's attempt a search for "chicken egg incubator." This time, we're going to farming industry vortal JoeFarmer.com (http://www.joefarmer.com). In this case, JoeFarmer.com (see Figure 3.3) seems to have been tailor-made for our searching needs. Not only can we search for the phrase "chicken egg incubator" and hit pay dirt within a second (The Chicken Site! Who knew?), but we can also peruse a very targeted series of category options that range from AgriBusiness to Veterinary Medicine.

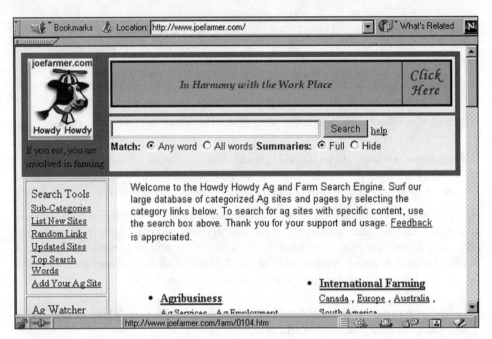

Figure 3.3 Farming industry vortal JoeFarmer.com serves up targeted content and community options for the farming industry.

© Joefarmer.com by Brett Tabke.

Should we want to spend more time at the site, we could check out the Ag Calendar, Classifieds, Ag Weather, or even add our own Ag website.

Finding a Vortal

"Where's my vortal?" you may now cry out. Well, we can't counsel each of you individually, but vortals are reviewed in the weekly email newsletter *Web Digest For Marketers*, which you can subscribe to for free simply by sending an email to join-larrychase@sparklist.com or by going to http://wdfm.com and entering your email address. At the site you can also freely search through hundreds of cream-of-the-crop site reviews by using the handy WDFM archive search tool. You may find your vortal already there, just waiting for you to discover it.

You are also now armed with powerful search tactics that will help you find your vortal. Should your Boolean strings get tangled, you can also try the following:

VerticalNet (http://www.verticalnet.com). VerticalNet is a leader in the vortal space and owner/operator of more than 55 business-to-business communities ranging from Bakery Online to Wireless Networks Online.

EoExchange (http://www.eoexchange.com). A specialist in the building of B2B exchanges, EoExchange powers several VerticalNet sites as well as RedHerring.com (financial and stock information), plus dozens of vortals for the healthcare, financial, insurance, and small-business markets.

Office.com (http://www.office.com). Office.com combines content, commerce, community, and communications to create "the place we work when we work online." Original and aggregated content informs Office.com customers of industry trends, news, and gossip in 16 industries, 120 subindustries, and 10 business management focused areas.

BusinessWeb (http://www.businesswebsource.com). BusinessWeb features news, information, and organized access to web content from 11 different industries. Industry links, upcoming events, and breaking news headlines are also searchable by industry, providing search access within highly targeted business content—from chemicals to professional services to transportation.

ClickZ Network (http://www.clickz.com). ClickZ Network is one of the most comprehensive resources for those in the Internet marketing and advertising industries.

SearchEngineGuide (http://www.searchengineguide.com). SearchEngineGuide is the guide to search engines, portals, and directories, with over 3,000 to choose from. Today's best? Porschezone.com—an Internet portal dedicated to Porsche enthusiasts. Find everything Porsche; new and used automobiles, classifieds, and discussion forums.

Filtering Agents

Instead of going to the search engines and letting your fingers do the tapping, you can have agents scan the Net for you. You tell these agents what you want to see. They, in turn, scan the newswire services or the Web itself for documents that contain those words most important to you. These agents can deliver the documents to you via email or on the Web—or both.

News Index (http://www.newsindex.com). One of the original news-only search engines. Choose your topic, and News Index will track stories from hundreds of sources and create a free personalized news experience. The News Index Delivered service will automatically deliver the results of your personalized searches to your email account every day.

My Yahoo! (http://my.yahoo.com). Essentially, a way for users to create listings of favorite sites, Yahoo! categories, and keyword searches. There are also areas for custom news, quotes, sports, daily tips, and personal information management. For the novice Net user or Yahoo! devotee, it's a way to keep information and news nicely organized in a familiar, friendly interface.

My Excite (http://nt.excite.com). Best described as a digital clipping service. The Excite NewsTracker service monitors material published by hundreds of digital news sources and packages them by topic, which the user can then choose and modify to create an individualized daily news folder on the site.

Individual.com (http://www.individual.com). Gives users the opportunity to build a personalized NewsPage that can either be accessed online or delivered by email every business morning. The site pulls the free, customized content from 40 worldwide news sources and also includes the opportunity to filter press releases by keyword from over 15,000 companies (see Figure 3.4).

CRAYON (the acronym for Create Your Own Newspaper) (http://crayon.net). Another service that assists users in navigating the wealth of web-based information sources. Users build personalized newspaper editions using hundreds of sources linked by CRAYON. So if your ideal personal paper includes NFLNews, Garfield, AP Newswire, and Cool Site of the Day, this is the source for you.

StreamSearch (http://www.streamsearch.com). Looking for news or information in a multimedia (audio or video) format? StreamSearch is a multimedia database that contains millions of streaming and downloadable files, including entertainment, news, sports, music, movies, lifestyle, and web-only special events. Within the first 45 days of availability, StreamSearch signed up 100,000 members to its MY STREAMS personalized online multimedia community, which allows members to select the genres, formats, and styles of playable content they wish to view and hear.

Figure 3.4 Individual.com delivers an individualized news website and a customized daily email briefing.

© office.com, Inc., a service of Winstar.

Search Companions

Finally, a growing assortment of search tools will accompany you on your journeys through the Web, making it possible to launch a search, find related sites, store information and more, on the fly.

Alexa (http://www.alexa.com) is a free web navigation support tool. It appears as a toolbar along the side or bottom of your browser window, and provides additional information about each site you visit. Alexa Internet was created to provide web navigation that learns and improves over time with the collective participation of its users. As you view a site, Alexa will indicate the address, launch date, traffic numbers, and other useful public information about the site, and will make recommendations for similar sites based upon the travels of other Alexa users.

Why search when EntryPoint (http://www.entrypoint.com) delivers? EntryPoint is an Internet toolbar and service that, upon download, delivers personalized news and information to your desktop.

Copernic (http://www.copernic.com) is another software companion for download that simultaneously consults the best search engines, brings back relevant results with summaries, and removes duplicate information and dead links (see Figure 3.5). Basic services are free; a fee for the software garners dozens of specialized search categories and hundreds more information resources.

Bullseye 2 (http://www.intelliseek.com) is another free software download that searches over 800 web sources simultaneously—both search engines and databases. In

Figure 3.5   Copernic is a powerful search companion, available as a software download.

addition to tracking news and information, Bullseye can be used to search for job candidates or sales prospects, or track product pricing or even your competitors. A professional (fee-based) edition of Bullseye offers even more nifty features.

Sweet Spots for Information

While you're quite apt to find the Top 100 Sex Sites on the Net or the Top 100 Sports Sites on the Net, we've yet to find the Top 100 Databases on the Net, although About.com's Web Search section (http://websearch.about.com) comes darn close (see Figure 3.6). In this section, you will not only learn about free databases that will be valuable to you, but also about other sites that frequently post new information. Let's start with databases.

Databases

Aside from search engines, which are essentially searchable databases of web pages and Usenet postings, you can search for more specific information, especially from governmental resources, at targeted treasure troves of information.

American FactFinder (http://factfinder.census.gov) is a wonderful data access and dissemination system that provides useful facts and information gleaned from some of

Figure 3.6 About's Web Search section is one of the best places to learn about both search strategies and the latest and greatest search sites.

the U.S. Census Bureau's largest data sets. The data can be organized in multiple ways according to preferences. Preformatted "quick" items enable users to create tables and maps by industry, geography, or other data in seconds. More detailed reports allow users to create customized data reports out of unique combinations of summarized data. The final way to access data is to build your own query, which is easily formatted so that even if you can't spell "query" you will soon be reviewing the exact data that you need.

The Delphion Intellectual Property Network (http://www.delphion.com) is a premier website for searching, viewing, and analyzing patent documents. This site provides free access to a wide variety of data collections and patent information including United States patents, European patents and patent applications, PCT application data from the World Intellectual Property Office, Patent Abstracts of Japan, and INPADOC family and legal status data. Care has been taken to make the tedious job of research fast and easy. The server supports simple keyword, phrase, and patent number services, as well as field searches by title, abstract, all claims, assignees, inventor, and attorney/agent.

SAEGIS Trademark (http://www.thomson-thomson.com) is a collection of 16 international trademark databases featuring two powerful search engines: custom searching and AutoQuery (see Figure 3.7). Custom searching allows users to quickly conduct sophisticated trademark searches by name, owner, design, or other fields found in a trademark record. AutoQuery defines the best possible trademark search strategy, producing results that only the most experienced trademark researchers would have previously found. The SAEGIS reference library allows you access to a number of Thomson & Thomson publication sites, such as the TRADEMARKSCAN Design Code

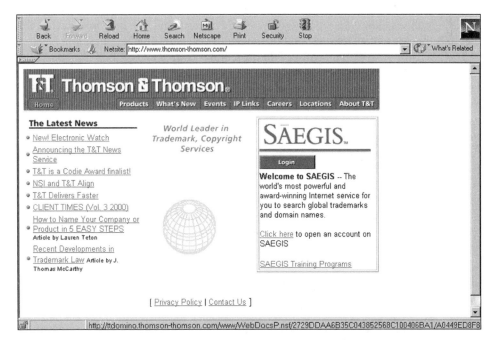

Figure 3.7   SAEGIS is a collection of 16 international trademark databases.

Manual and the International Guide to Trademarks, as well as many links to intellectual property resources on the Web. Some services are free, others are fee-based.

The Stanford University Copyright and Fair Use website (http://fairuse.stanford .edu) is devoted to statutes, cases, issues, and other resources for copyright law.

The U.S. Securities and Exchange Commission (SEC) FreeEDGAR database (http://freeedgar.com) offers free, unlimited access to fundamental financial data as it is released to the SEC. Corporate financial reports created from EDGAR filings, downloadable Excel spreadsheets of all SEC filings, and financial analysis and reference resources are a click away. The FreeEDGAR Watchlist will notify you by email when any company on your list submits an EDGAR filing to the SEC. Services are customizable and free.

Free Advice

The old adage says that free advice is worth what you pay for it. The Internet is changing that theory. There are many high-powered consultancies, law firms, accountants (and a vast array of other professionals) who are willing to entertain a query from you in the hopes of turning you into an ongoing client. You see, the answer to one question usually prompts another one. Don't count on these professionals to endlessly answer all of them. It's a good idea to have one well-thought-out question when approaching sites like these.

This approach reminds me of a technique practiced many years ago by a chiropractor. When he first came to this country, he used to promote his practice by going into shoe stores. While the patrons were waiting for the salesman to bring them their shoes, he would offer to adjust the bones in their feet. When a patron liked what she felt, she would ask him to do the other foot. At this point, he presented his business card. This is exactly what's happening today on the Net. Professionals will help you part of the way, but they do expect to turn you into a client if you want further attention.

The law firm of Arent Fox Kitner Plotkin & Kahn (http://www.arentfox.com) specializes in technology and information law, and its site is a good starting point for Internet-specific legal information gathering. At this site, you can participate in discussion forums moderated by members of the legal team. At the time of writing, the Advertising Law, Consumer Product Safety, Contests and Sweepstakes, and Online Privacy Law forums were active.

Have a question for the Mortgage Professor? Jack M. Guttentag, Professor of Finance Emeritus at the Wharton School of the University of Pennsylvania, nationally syndicated columnist, and recognized expert on mortgages, will answer your questions for free at http://www.mtgprofessor.com.

If you're looking to publish a nonfiction book, visit Cader Books at http://www.caderbooks.com/pubfaq.html, where the FAQ is a work-in-progress dialogue between the publishers and site visitors.

At iDecisionMaker (http://www.i-on.com/know/know.asp) visitors will find a library of articles and tools that guide e-business decision making in the areas of marketing, technology, and management.

Court TV's legal help section (http://www.courttv.com/legalhelp) gives free legal advice on a multitude of subjects, such as the legal dilemmas one faces when getting older, small-business legal information, and family issues, such as divorce and prenuptial agreements. Looking for a new lawyer? Court TV will help you find one according to the preferences you set up. You can even link to Quickform Contracts Online (http://www.quickforms.net), which provides agreements and policies for basic, day-to-day business issues, such as running a company email system or purchasing hardware. Use one of the already-made documents or draft a new one yourself.

TIP Know when to get off the Net. Sometimes it's just faster to pick up the phone and call directory assistance or call a company directly for information.

Outstanding Free Content

Another way for professional services to vie for your attention is to publish white papers on their sites that contain extraordinary amounts of well-considered and well-researched content. It is not easy to know or predict when and where these reports will go up, unless you subscribe to one of the agents mentioned earlier. Hopefully, they'll pick up a news story or press release that contains keywords that match the ones you are looking for. If these high-value white papers are indigenous to your industry, then your trade magazines and journals should carry news of them. However, you want to know before the rest of the industry at large does. If you are always the first one to have vital and pertinent information, you attract others to you, since you are considered a source and, by extension, a gateway of information. This can only help your company, your project, and your career.

Morgan Stanley Dean Witter regularly publishes technology news and research, which can be found at http://www.msdw.com/research/index.html. At the time of this writing, the following reports were available at the site:

The Internet Data Services Report. A primer on the critical tools and infrastructure that enable companies to participate in the *digital economy*.

The Internet and Financial Services Report. The macro trends reshaping the consumer financial services industry over the next two to three years.

The Internet Credit Card Report. A primer on the card industry and how the Internet will impact its profitability over the next five years.

The Internet Company Handbook. A profile of 90 Internet companies, providing descriptions, user information, screen shots, and, when applicable, stock price charts and financial models.

The European Internet Report. A review of leading Internet companies across 12 industry sectors and an in-depth look at trends related to the European Internet.

WHITE PAPERS

Traditionally, *white papers* are government reports on any subject, but in the Internet Age, they have come to mean any definitive documents or reports created by any company or entity, which are then posted as reports on websites.

PDF FILES

PDF (Portable Document Format) files are standard files created by Adobe to produce fully-formatted documents from PostScript files. PDF files are ubiquitous on the Net nowadays. Adobe (http://www.adobe.com) offers a free application called Acrobat that reads these files, which is available for download on its site. As PDF files are both easy to create and read, white papers are often published in PDF format, which cannot be altered by the reader. Gartner Group (http://gartnergroup.com) offers technology and marketing information in the areas of e-business, CRM, enterprise and supply-chain management, and the mobile and wireless industries.

Arthur Andersen's Knowledge Space (http://www.knowledgespace.com) provides free access to company resources across practice areas, including trends and statistics, global best practices, and extensive reports.

Cyber Dialogue's re:Source section (http://www.cyberdialogue.com/resource/index.html) provides data, insight and analysis on interactive markets, including Internet users, e-commerce, entertainment, healthcare, finance, and small business.

Even if you're not a Forrester Research client (http://www.forrester.com), you still can have access to a select group of reports and briefs, including the Forrester Power Rankings of the top e-commerce sites.

Dataquest (http://www.dataquest.com) is a Gartner Group resource that packs facts, figures, and interpretation into this research-oriented site. Search through Dataquest research reports, register for the news alerts service, set up a customized page, or just browse through the highlighted research. It's all free, unless you want a full-length report. Then you'll have to give Dataquest your credit card number.

If you can't get enough of research reports, go to Internet.com's allNetResearch at http://www.allnetresearch.com, where you'll find all Internet research, all the time. Email updates serve as notification when a new research report is available (currently over 1,000 are on the site). While many reports are for sale, abstracts and comprehensive free information are more than available for those willing to do a little research.

Trade Publications

No longer do you have to wait for your trade news to come once a week or once a month. Nearly all the major trade publications are on the Net now, as well as some that don't even exist in print. The majority of trades seem to be moving toward a daily update model, such as *Advertising Age*. Some publishers will give you a daily update for free on their sites, while others may charge you for the convenience of pushing it to you via email. Here are some of the better examples:

Advertising Age (http://www.adage.com). One of the first marketing publications to hit the Net and continues to stand out in its category with its constant innovations. These include a daily update, chat boards, and a search engine that enables you to look for jobs, freelance talent, or agencies, local or national, within the advertising industry.

Bookwire (http://www.bookwire.com). The online home for *Publisher's Weekly* and much more, features a news section, original reviews and features, and a behind-the-scenes column written by industry insiders. The site is simple to navigate, provides all the necessary weekly news for this fast-moving industry, and keeps visitors entertained with whimsical features such as Flap, a voyage into book trivia. Other notable sections include Soapbox and its lively discussion areas; Bestsellers, a weekly list of bestsellers from *Publishers Weekly*; and a calendar showing a comprehensive listing of book industry conferences and meetings.

Meeting News (http://www.meetingnews.com). Published by Miller Freeman Inc., Meeting News provides you with updates on what's new in the travel and meetings industries. You can also search the Meeting Site Selection Service, featuring more than 7,000 meeting and event facilities, post an RFP, or ask Meeting News for an answer to a problem you might have planning your company's annual conference in Spokane.

The Internet Advertising Discussion List. Moderated by Adam Boettiger, this is a good place to expand and share one's knowledge of the world of Internet advertising. Started in January of 1997, it has become a hit among its over 12,000 subscribers in 77 countries. The list often includes newsworthy tidbits of direct interest to online marketers. You can take part by going to http://www.internetadvertising.org.

If you'd like to go straight to the source, at MagPortal.com (http://www.magportal.com) you can search for individual articles from hundreds of online consumer and business magazines by keyword or topic.

Soliciting Customer Input on the Net

Except for the section on where to get free advice, this chapter has focused on secondary research, which is information already compiled and packaged by others. However, the Net is an excellent medium for gathering primary research as well. You can utilize both time-tested focus group and market research techniques as well as new, technology-enabled methods to engage your customers in a dialogue on a range of issues, such as:

- Product and service feedback
- Thoughts on a proposed product
- The effectiveness of your website
- Brand awareness
- Impact of online advertising campaigns
- Expanding product or service offerings
- Overall suggestions for improvement

While the Internet will not replace the insights gained in face-to-face, personal interaction with customers, it can be used to save much time and money for all kinds of primary research.

How can you leverage the Internet to take advantage of the speed, efficiency, and lower costs of online focus groups and other information-gathering methods? Industry veteran Nick Nyhan, founder and chairman of Dynamic Logic, has much insight to share.

Dynamic Logic (see Figure 3.8) is an online marketing information and research company that uses proprietary technology to collect data about consumer attitudes and behavior. The company was founded in 1999 by Nick Nyhan, the former Director of Online Research of ModemMedia/PoppeTyson. Dynamic Logic is often approached by its clients to do online market research because it is seen as being faster and less expensive than traditional methods. In some cases, as Nyhan points out, there is no substitute for old-fashioned focus groups.

Online versus Offline Data Gathering

"There are limits as to what an online focus group, or chat session, can accomplish," states Nick Nyhan. For example, a moderated Internet discussion using chat is not as effective as a traditional focus group because of the nature of the medium. The conversation is staccato—people type in spurts and then have to catch up with what others are saying. The faster typists may tend to dominate the conversation. The slower typists may not be able to get their full points across, so they may end up truncating their thoughts in order to participate. In addition, the moderator doesn't have as much control as he or she would in a real world-session, although he or she may have the ability to delete participants who are not behaving, or actually approve comments from the group before they make it to the entire list. Most importantly, emphasizes Nyhan, "You also lose the give-and-take chemistry that you would get face-to-face, in addition to

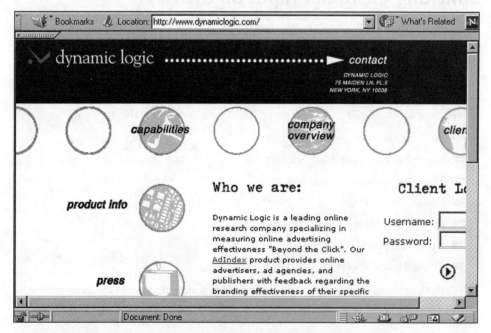

Figure 3.8 Dynamic Logic utilizes proprietary technology to conduct online research into consumer thoughts and behavior.

body language and facial expressions. Finally, it's impossible to gauge silence online, which is often more telling than words."

A focus group is a qualitative practice, and you will indeed sacrifice the quality of communication to some degree when conducting one online. Online chat environments are better used for concept testing and creative feedback, such as, I'm going to give you three benefit slogans. Which do you like the best? "After spending a lot of time behind a one-way mirror," Michael Carlon, a Dynamic Logic director, concludes, "I found that the nonverbal communication respondents exhibited when a web page was brought up or a new concept was introduced was one of the most important learnings of the test. It is a lot easier to see confusion on someone's face than to infer it from chat sessions or transcripts."

Online Methods

Dynamic Logic does utilize very sophisticated technology to take advantage of the online medium. "There are things that can be done online that are impossible to do in the real world," states Carlon. "We use web traffic analysis to determine how customers are moving through and reacting to a website. We also offer extensive data-mining services."

One service, AdIndex, uses online surveys hosted by Dynamic Logic to determine the effectiveness of a banner ad campaign. The AdIndex system can identify whether a respondent has been exposed to a banner ad, and if so, it will dynamically generate a set of appropriate questions that measure brand awareness levels, message association, purchase intent, and design appeal—all of which provide extraordinarily valuable feedback as to how well banner ads are working. "This type of research goes well beyond standard clickthrough measurements," explains Nyhan. "The Internet enables marketers to track the actions and reactions of web surfers in very sophisticated ways so that they can make informed strategic decisions."

"Our research is designed to quantify the effectiveness of online advertising on an attitudinal rather than behavioral level," continues Carlon. "We look to see what role web advertising plays in behavioral patterns. Since 99 percent of all online ads do not get clicked on, we feel it is crucial to provide the industry with this type of data, which offers a more complete picture of the efficacy of the medium."

What about email? It's ubiquitous and the time pressures faced in chat are then removed. Nyhan points out that email becomes a self-administered questionnaire. Using that methodology, you open yourself up to getting a lot of bad data. Why bad data? A respondent can put his or her answers anywhere in the email document. The tabulation process may not be able to read the answers. Even worse, you would have to manually recode the received email, which defeats the whole purpose of saving time and money.

A definite positive to online research as opposed to face-to-face research is that nobody judges the answers of the people being surveyed. The people filling out online surveys don't have to worry about anyone else's opinion; it is an objective, neutral environment. You can get a clearer picture online because those being surveyed are more apt to let their guard down when they're not being confronted by others' opinions.

It is important to find the right audience in order to conduct meaningful research. While the online audience has greatly matured from the "white male tech geek" composition of its early days, it is still a challenge to find the right sample groups for a study. In the real world, telephone-based researchers use random digit dialing (RDD) in order to generate a good random sample.

To address the need for a diverse sampling pool, the company has also built its own community of potential research participants at QuestionMarket.com (see Figure 3.9). This is a survey site operated by Dynamic Logic where visitors can register and be on call for research events. They may be asked to test new ideas, evaluate strategies or websites, or take surveys appropriate for their demographic profile. Rewards are offered to encourage repeat participation.

Sampling Methods

Subjects in a research project are often *order biased*. That is, if you ask for their preference on three different logos, many will choose the first one, simply because it's the first, or the third one, because it is the last one they saw. To compensate for this order bias, we suggest that marketers change the ordering of the examples.

It's abundantly clear that the Internet is quite appropriate for some kinds of research and not for others. Because of its quick turnaround and potentially large savings, there are many more companies coming into this space. Another firm to watch and explore is Decision Analyst (http://www.decisionanalyst.com), which boasts a market research service that taps into the opinions of more than 1,000,000 consumers in the United States, Canada, Europe, Latin America, and Asia who can be reached via the

Figure 3.9   QuestionMarket.com is a consumer survey site operated by Dynamic Logic.

Internet. It is one of the largest consumer panels in the world, with significant membership in over 150 countries.

Called American Consumer Opinion Online, the service surveys panelists over the Internet on such topics as copy effectiveness for online, television, radio, and print advertising campaigns, as well as product market testing. Decision Analyst forms panels from its database, works with clients to develop online surveys, conducts the surveys or market tests via a private website, then tabulates and analyzes the results. Pricing depends on the project. Decision Analyst offers a free product at its site called STATS, an IBM PC Windows program designed to perform several commonly needed statistical functions for marketing researchers. The software generates random numbers, calculates sample sizes needed for surveys, computes the mean, standard deviation, standard error, and range for keyboard-entered data, determines the standard error of a proportion, and more.

Customer Feedback

Undoubtedly you've heard the expression, "If you want to make a friend, ask his or her advice." The Web is no different in this respect. In fact, its instant interactivity serves as a perfect feedback loop to conveniently solicit advice from your customers (and prospective customers). The product users can be queried for any amount of information you may want in order to improve existing products, or even develop new ones—often with only a little incentive for their time.

Pinging the Product User

What's the easiest way to determine if your site visitor or customer is satisfied with his or her online experience? Ask! cPulse (http://www.cpulse.com) created the cPulse Satisfaction Network for that very purpose (see Figure 3.10). cPulse is a site visitor satisfaction monitor—the company is dedicated to the single task of measuring and monitoring online customer satisfaction. cPulse provides free 60-second surveys to hundreds of websites. Approximately 1 percent of visitors to sites in the cPulse network are presented with a survey. "Approximately 30 percent of site visitors choose to answer the surveys," says Jody Dodson, executive vice president of Marketing and Research. "The best ways to encourage visitor participation are (1) keep your survey short (two minutes or less); (2) offer a good (nonbiasing) incentive; and (3) don't interrupt a critical process like placing an order."

Websites utilizing the cPulse surveys receive a continuous, immediately accessible information stream as provided by the survey results. "Businesses use these reports to identify major problems and opportunities," continues Dodson. For example, at the end of summer 2000, Crutchfield.com (a consumer electronic products site) conducted real-time online interviews with 7,267 consumers using cPulse's proprietary web tools. The data indicated, using a scale of one to nine, that "complete product description" received the highest importance rating from these consumers. Crutchfield.com utilized this and other consumer feedback to completely redesign its site in preparation for the holiday season.

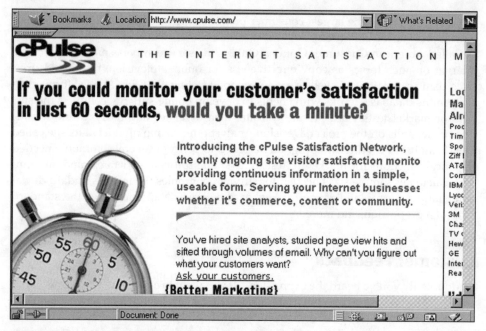

Figure 3.10 The cPulse Satisfaction Network is a collection of hundreds of sites that are using 60-second surveys to continuously evaluate their customers' wants and needs.
© 2000 cPulse LLC.

Dodson suggests that members target user groups by inserting custom profiling questions into the survey itself. An example of customer profiling questions for a commerce site selling running shoes might be:

- Have you ever purchased our brand before? (Y/N)
- Have you ever purchased running shoes online before? (Y/N)
- How frequently do you run? (Once a month, once a week, several times a week)

Then the client can, using the respondent's answers to these custom profiling questions, segment their total respondent base into more relevant subsegments for deeper and more relevant analysis. "For example," explains Dodson, "the client might want to delve into the differences between the wants and needs of someone who's purchased their brand before as compared to someone who hasn't."

Finally, cPulse also aggregates the data gathered through tens of thousands of surveys and provides industry benchmarks so that members can compare the performance of their site against that of their competitors, their industry, and even the Internet as a whole. "Benchmarks are the final and most important step in analyzing customer satisfaction," concludes Dodson. "To see that you received an average satisfaction score of 7.2 for ease of site navigation is interesting. To also know that your competition is averaging a score of 8.3 helps you understand that this issue is a priority."

As cPulse demonstrates, it is no longer necessary to retain a consumer research firm or implement complex technology to communicate with your customers. Informative's SurveyBuilder (http://www.surveybuilder.com) is another easy-to-implement, automated solution for conducting online research that helps businesses quickly, easily, and cost-effectively perform professional custom market research on the Web— from customer profiling and usability testing to customer satisfaction measurement and concept testing. Companies can create online surveys in minutes and instantly view results in real time, with remote access from anywhere in the world, using a web browser. There's no software to install, no programming involved, and no administration required. All operations are automated and performed via the Web—from survey design, respondent invitation, and data collection, to analysis and results reporting.

Discussion Lists as a Straw Poll Medium

Another very quick and simple way to solicit customer feedback is through email discussion lists. These can either be private or public lists. If they're private, you can control who joins and therefore you will have an easier time authenticating potential subscribers. You may create a list explicitly for a given product and urge the users to join. Will this protect you from your competitors eventually catching on? No. You must keep this in mind when soliciting input. For this reason, you may want each of your respondents to reply privately, rather than in front of each other. You can even run this type of list right from your email program, until you get up to a few hundred participants. At that point, you'll want to consider more elaborate systems to manage the load. You can learn more about managing and using these mailing lists in Chapter 8, "Direct Marketing and Sales Support."

Using a public list leaves you wide open to both your competitors and cranky customers. Nevertheless, you might choose this route if you're simply looking for a quick read of a niche market. It's also important to remember that you might tip your hand to your competitors as to your plans. If you're using an already existing public mailing list, controlled by someone else, be sure to ask the moderator's permission before posting your queries. Many lists have protocols for just this purpose. For example, in the subject header (assuming they allow you to do this in the first place), you might have to put the word *SURVEY*, so that readers instantly know that your post to this list is expressly for the solicitation of feedback.

If the moderator doesn't want you to ask the list about a product idea, offer to run an ad soliciting participants on the list. You can offer people an appropriate incentive for their feedback. Don't offer T-shirts unless you're selling T-shirts. I once saw a major New York ad agency offer a T-shirt as the incentive for coming to its site three times over three weeks and filling out three questionnaires. What was on the T-shirt? Why, the name of the advertising agency! If my company ran such a campaign with the moniker "Chase Online Marketing Strategies" on that shirt, I don't think I'd want to be associated with those people, let alone have them serve as human billboards for my firm. The offer must have drawn in large numbers of kids and people with too much time on their hands who thought it was an attractive deal. This is not what you would call a "scientific technique."

Although doing a public solicitation exposes your ideas early in the game, it also has the advantage of quickly testing the waters to see if you should continue to proceed with your idea. It also happens to be very inexpensive.

Selected Sites to See

We've selected a few sites in different categories that we believe you'll find useful, because we use them all the time. These sites are by no means the only sites to see, nor are they quintessential sites that serve the needs of all people. There is no such thing, and don't let anybody convince you otherwise. However, these are good places to start. You can also visit the *Web Digest For Marketers* site at http://wdfm.com for a comprehensive archive of thousands of site reviews, searchable by keyword. But since you're within the pages of this book right now and presumably not online, the following sections offer a few sites to get you started.

Financial Sites

Visit Investorama at http://www.investorama.com as a financial research starting point (see Figure 3.11). It offers a good link pile for investors and investing information, which you can pick apart to your heart's delight.

It's hard to beat StockMaster.com (http://stockmaster.com). You can get up-to-the-minute stock prices and performance graphs on demand for free. This site is part of the RedHerring.com network.

Figure 3.11   Investorama offers a comprehensive collection of links to all things financial.

The *Wall Street Journal* (http://www.wsj.com) requires a fee of $29.00 to access online if you subscribe to the print edition, and $59.00 a year if you don't. This online subscription gives you the current print *WSJ* edition, access to the past two weeks of the Dow Jones archives, and the Barron's Online edition. Additionally, you have access to the Asian and European editions, as well as frequent updates throughout the day, stock quotes, and nearly every imaginable financial index you can think of.

The International Weekly Journal of News, Views and Analysis, otherwise known as the *Economist*, can be found at http://www.economist.com. The entire contents of the *Economist* are available online by 10 P.M. London time on Thursdays. Archived articles from the *Economist* are searchable on the website. Weekly email and mobile editions are available for direct feed to registered users' email accounts and PDAs.

For a global view of finance and investment news and trends, it's hard to pass up the free online companion to the *Financial Times*, found at http://www.ft.com.

The free, professional-level tools at BigCharts (http://www.bigcharts.com) make this investment research site an example of incredibly valuable and incredibly interactive functionality.

Raging Bull (http://www.ragingbull.com) provides individual investors with access to the discussions and information previously reserved for investing professionals. With free real-time stock quotes, news, original editorial and more than 13,000 dynamic discussion boards, and an alliance with ipo.com for access to high-level initial public offering information and discussion, the site is a savvy guide to investing.

Personal Mining

Sometimes you're looking for people, places, or things. The Net is excellent at helping you find all of these. The key is knowing where to go to find what you're looking for.

Switchboard (http://www.switchboard.com) can help you get in touch with people you've lost track of over the years. Of course, it isn't complete, as nothing on the Net is, but it is very deep. I know people who have no listed phone number or address and no magazine subscriptions or property, yet they're in there. You can also search for businesses and email addresses.

↗ InfoSpace (http://www.infospace.com) does all sorts of intriguing tasks, such as reverse number lookup (see Figure 3.12). Give it a phone number, and get a name (sometimes). Give it an email address, and get a physical address. Give it a name, and get an email address (but everyone does that). Give it an email, and get a name or a list of all the email addresses at that domain name. Search for a business, and find houses, restaurants, and more near that business. While information may not always be the most current, if you are trying to learn more from a caller ID phone number or a fragment of an email address, this is an excellent tool.

Ever wonder what happened to your high school honey? At ClassMates.com (http://www.classmates.com) you can become part of the largest U.S. and Canadian high school alumni directory on the Net, with over 6.8 million self-registered alumni. Basic membership is free; additional services are fee-based.

Learn2.com (http://learn2.com) is an incredible how-to site. You can learn how to jump-start a car or how to wrap gifts without getting the tape stuck to your fingers. This is the perfect site if your mantra is, "Each and every day, I'm getting better in every way."

Figure 3.12   What ever happened to. . .? Find them at InfoSpace.

Gomez (http://www.gomez.com) helps you shop smarter and safer online. Free membership includes expert reviews of e-commerce sites, consumer ratings and reviews, great deals and rewards, and weekly email alerts.

For Your Business

Interested in business news and trends from over 40 cities across the United States? Surf on over to BizJournals.com (http://www.amcity.com), where trends and head-lines from Albany to Wichita are literally at your fingertips. Comprehensive coverage of each city (plus an option to receive weekly lists of new businesses and home own-ers) is fee-based, but the site does offer an interesting glimpse of trends across the nation with a free weekly upload of new content, city by city.

The Thomas Register (http://thomasregister.com) is a print and CD-ROM-based catalog of information about 155,000 U.S. manufacturers, featuring products and ser-vices, company profiles, and catalog information (see Figure 3.13). After registering, web users can search the large database for companies, products, and services.

At the Credit411.com site (http://www.credit411.com) you can easily order, either over the telephone or the Internet, your public and private records to be delivered straight to your doorstep. You cannot order anyone else's, unless you have his or her key personal information. Choose from three packages: Basic, Plus, and Premium, and get as little as three credit reports, an FBI disclosure form, and a mailing list removal letter, or as much as your education, employment, medical, motor vehicle, and Social Security records.

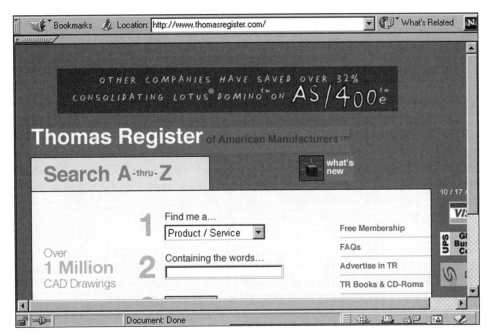

Figure 3.13 Thomas Register Online contains information on over 155,000 companies.

Business Tools from ADP (http://ebs.adp.com/tool) gives small-business owners and managers a place to turn for sound advice on day-to-day management issues, such as finding funding, payroll obligations, and human resources management. This section of Automatic Data Processing's site has plenty of advice and articles about small-business management. Can't find the form to apply for a federal identification number? ADP has it, and many others, available for download.

Citibank's Bizzed (http://www.bizzed.com) gives you news to grow your business, tools to power your business, and networking to help you get ahead.

AllBusiness.com (http://www.allbusiness.com) provides a one-stop online resource that delivers everything the business owner could need, from comprehensive HR to sales and marketing solutions, plus a marketplace that consolidates all business-related purchasing into one convenient location.

For the fast track to personalized news and information, try CEOExpress (http://www.ceoexpress.com) where you will find a compilation of the best business links for senior executives.

At TSCentral (http://tscentral.com) you can gain free access to up-to-the-minute information about trade shows, expos, conferences, seminars, event industry suppliers, virtual tradeshow and online floorplan management solutions, webcasts, and more.

News

Say what you will about Matt Drudge's reporting, his site (http://www.drudge.com) is an incredibly useful compilation of best-of news. From there you can also search Reuters, AP, and UPI, plus regional and international wires.

"Delivering news at the speed of television with the depth of print" is Stratfor.com's (http://www.stratfor.com) claim to fame and it delivers. This Internet news company explores international trends with an eye toward corporate intelligence. Originally focused on supplying information to business clients, and providing metacommentary on world events via the highly touted Global Intelligence Update (GIU), Stratfor.com is transitioning from a private intelligence company to open-source cyber-intelligence.

Getting the facts straight isn't always easy, especially if you're on a deadline. FACS-NET (http://www.facsnet.org) is an excellent research site (designed by journalists for journalists) that provides just the facts, ma'am. Additional reporting tools, tips, and worthy online resources are just a registration page away. This is a must-have bookmark for freelance writers and those who require an unbiased, incisive news source, brought to you by the Foundation for American Communications.

Legal

If you know where to go, you can often get answers to your questions without consulting a lawyer. Even if you do have to consult a lawyer, in order to contain legal fees it's better for you as a client to learn as much as you can on your own.

Free Advice (http://www.freeadvice.com) is designed to provide the basic legal information people need in order to address most legal situations arising in their personal and business lives. It provides easy-to-understand answers to thousands of the most frequently asked questions compiled by attorneys from leading law firms nationwide, and covers dozens of legal topics, from accidents, bankruptcy, and divorce to business, tax, and trademark law.

Venerable legal research source LEXIS-NEXIS (http://www.lexis.com) now allows its subscribers to tap into its databases via the Web. In addition to its subscription service, the site offers a free alert-type service called Hot Law. Sections within Hot Law include Hot Topics, which is an overview of important current cases in specific legal areas such as California criminal law or Florida family law; Hot Cases, a listing of cases most commonly requested by customers; and Hot Bill, a rundown of current legislation. There's just enough free information to keep it interesting and tease serious users into the paid services.

Imagine a free service for legal solutions (if you can). LawOffice.com (http://www.lawoffice.com) provides profiles of lawyers and law firms broken down by city and state. There are also topic-driven resources to assist consumers and small-business owners with frequently asked legal questions. Looking for trademark advice? Questions about incorporating your business? Is a hotel responsible for guests' property? What rights do nursing patients have? Find your answers here. You can also raise your legal IQ by searching the Oran dictionary of more than 5,000 legal terms and related link piles.

Internet

CyberTimes from *The New York Times* (http://www.nytimes.com/yr/mo/day/cyber) is one of the Net's best resources for insightful articles about the Internet itself.

At WhoIs.Net (http://www.whois.net) you can register and protect your domain name, change your current domain name, or search for other domain names by keyword. The site will suggest names for you based on three keywords, and will also present a list of domain names that have been dropped recently that you just might want to snap up.

Iconocast (http://iconocast.com) is the brainchild of Michael Tchong, founder of MacWeek and CyberAtlas. This free weekly ezine (launched in 1997) manages to be provocative, insightful, visionary, and entertaining while serving up consistently excellent industry insight. Don't miss the irascible Jacobyte, a column filled with inside information and gossip about the latest and greatest on the Web, plus news on the international new media networking scene from the scribbler of Silicon Alley herself, Courtney Pulitzer. If you're looking for facts, figures, and trend analysis, plus irreverent commentary on the Internet marketing industry, sign on now.

Since 1993, *Red Herring* magazine (http://www.redherring.com) has evaluated technology as a strategic asset for industry leaders around the world. Sign on for their series of ezines if you're fishing for facts on the business of technology. Catch of the Day reels in a fresh take on the trends, people, and companies shaping the New Economy. The Red Eye is a close look at the architects of business today. Fishwrap bundles up and delivers a summary of the week's news, and Fish or Cut Bait is a detailed look at a stock per week. There are more, so sign on. You'll be hooked.

Significant research and insight on the industry are yours through Industry Standard's site and group of ezines (http://www.thestandard.net). From Wireless News and Media Grok to newsletters focusing on European Internet trends, specific industry segments, key industry players, and financial movers and shakers, the Standard covers it all. Do sign on for the *Net Persuasion* ezine, a report on the meeting of marketing and the Internet.

Marketing

The original marketing ezine, *Web Digest For Marketers* (http://www.wdfm.com) delivers short reviews of websites that should be on the radar of every Internet marketer. Born in 1995, this ezine was created at a time when the launch of a website that delivered horoscopes was as exciting as the launch of a website that delivered sales leads. Publisher Larry Chase and his faithful team of editors continue to scour the Web for the latest and greatest in trends, business strategies, and online tactics for marketers in the categories of e-commerce, DM, branding, PR, advertising, research, reference, marketing, and plain ol' smart use of the Net. WDFM is now delivered weekly, and at the site you will find a free searchable database of six years' worth of website reviews. What other publication would have the gall to review itself, and favorably at that?

With over 100,000 subscribers and no signs of stopping, the free *Web Marketing Today* from Wilson Web (http://www.wilsonweb.com) delivers a solid supply of ideas, tutorials, and links to help the web marketer succeed. Published since 1995 by Dr. Ralph F. Wilson, owner of California-based Wilson Internet Services, it's an amazing resource for both marketers new to the Web and industry veterans. Dr. Wilson also publishes *Web Commerce Today,* a monthly newsletter about direct sales on the Web, which will cost you $49.95 a year, and it's worth every penny. Most recently, the prolific Dr. Wilson launched *Doctor Ebiz,* a free ezine designed in a Q&A format to help small businesses succeed online.

If you want tell-it-like-it-is numbers and commentary, eMarketer (http://www.emarketer.com) has e-telligence for you. A leading provider of Internet statistical information in the form of printed eReports, eMarketer also provides a peek at what's happening through their *DailyeNews, DailyeStat,* and *WeeklyeNews* opt-in newsletters. Beloved by over 50,000 subscribers, eMarketer watches all the other research houses and then gives its take on what the research is saying.

ClickZ (http://www.clickz.com) offers daily thoughts and research about the Internet marketing and advertising industry. *ClickZ* serves up a number of new columns every day, written by industry luminaries such as publisher Andy Borland, editor Ann Handley, and industry analyst Dana Blankenhorn. Each gives their hands-on take on the currents and eddies of this quickly evolving and mutating medium. Articles and primers cover everything from affiliate marketing to rich media. You'll find comprehensive directories of Internet marketing business resources, at the site and in the free daily email newsletter.

Offering "useful ideas for creative business people," the *A-Marketing-Idea-A-Day-by-e-mail* (http://www.ideasiteforbusiness.com) ezine has been providing free marketing ideas daily to subscribers worldwide since 1996. Sponsored by Idea Site for Business, recently chosen as one of the 103 great e-biz websites by *Newsweek eLife* magazine, *AMIAD* offers unusual and inexpensive marketing ideas for small-business folks just getting started. Experienced marketers can also receive a daily dose of creative thinking through this service.

iMarketing News Daily (http://www.dmnews.com) brings the top Internet marketing news stories to you each day, under the sharp-eyed, skeptical watch of editor Ken Magill. A division of venerable DM News, iMarketing News Daily focuses specifically on the news of interest to interactive marketers. It's a must-read before starting your interactive marketing day.

Digitrends (http://www.digitrends.com), known as the "information network for interactive marketers," hosts a collection of opt-in email newsletters (an extension of the quarterly print publication) for every marketing mind. Senior-level marketers can benefit from *Digitrends Daily,* which is chock full of up-to-date reports on the latest interactive marketing and advertising campaigns and industry developments. *Ebiz Daily* relates the latest business and consumer e-commerce industry news, and *Entertainment Beat Daily* keeps entertainment professionals informed through its daily email news service. Digitrends' editors also keep busy by developing Internet marketing and advertising campaign case studies (found at the site), that merge news with real-world examples of marketing in action.

Fast Company (http://www.fastcompany.com) was launched in print in November 1995 by Alan Webber and Bill Taylor, two former *Harvard Business Review* editors, to chronicle how companies are reinventing business. *Fast Take* is *Fast Company*'s free email newsletter, which alerts readers to what Fast Company is up to, in print and otherwise. Sent out each Tuesday, the newsletter offers occasional features not found in the magazine or on the site, and previews of upcoming print articles. If you're interested in change agents, evangelists, or visions of how the Internet has affected the world of work and marketing in the twenty-first century, Fast Take will take you there.

It's worth checking out *Business 2.0* (http://www.business2.com) online, as the content is excellent. Several ezines will even bring the content to you. Daily Insight offers New Economy thoughts from *Business 2.0's* editors. The biweekly *Business 2.0 Lineup* supplies summaries, headlines, and links to the content found in the current issue of the magazine. Best of all, *Marketing Focus,* also mailed biweekly, focuses on the ever-changing world of digital marketing, with a critical look at what's working and what's not in the areas of online ad issues, customer acquisition strategies, and one-to-one marketing.

Statistics

The U.S. Department of Commerce Bureau of Economic Analysis (http://www.bea .doc.gov) provides a wealth of current economic reports and statistics on U.S. states, regions, and international trade.

CyberAtlas (http://www.cyberatlas.com) has tremendous depth and breadth and should be on every Net marketer's hot list (see Figure 3.14). It is one of the best spots around to find statistics about Internet usage patterns, demographics, and similar information. The site points users to recent Internet-specific reports from analysts and more.

NUA (http://www.nua.ie) is a repository of Internet surveys from around the world. The site is a must-visit for up-to-the-minute Internet statistics on usage patterns, demographics, and more.

The Bureau of Labor Statistics' site (http://www.bls.gov) provides an overview of the organization; access to regional and national labor statistics, such as employment and unemployment, hours, earnings, and productivity; the Consumer Price Index and Producer Price Index; and details on BLS surveys, publications, and research reports.

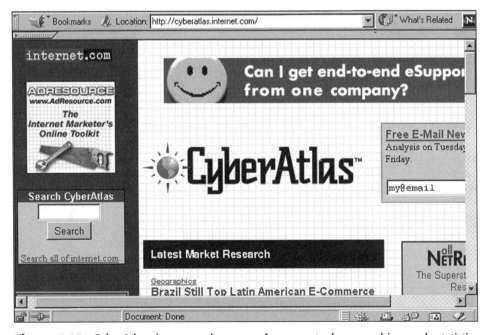

Figure 3.14 CyberAtlas is a good source for recent demographics and statistics concerning the Internet's growth.

There was a time when marketers paid dearly to find what Nielsen/NetRatings Report (http://www.nielson-netratings.com) delivers for free every week. This ezine (with information gathered by Nielsen Media Research, ACNielsen eRatings.com and NetRatings, Inc.) reports on headline news and how that news affects web behavior and traffic. But wait, there's more! You'll receive weekly listings of the top websites, with traffic reports, number of unique visitors, and time spent at each site. Plus the top ten Internet advertisers, the top ad banners viewed (with reach percent and creative message), and average Internet usage stats—divided by those surfing from home versus those surfing from work. Need we say more?

TIP **Always have the text field that lets you see the web address (URL) showing when you surf. On most browsers, it is at the top of your screen. It comes in handy when you hit an error page and get the dreaded "File Not Found 404." What do you do if this happens? Well, if you are going to http://chaseonline.com/marketing/articles.html and you don't see anything there, go up to the URL box, highlight /articles.html and delete it. Then press Enter. You'll be sent to http://chaseonline.com/marketing, where you can navigate to all the subpages of the site. It's quite possible the subpage still exists, but the specific address may have changed.**

By the time you read this, there will be many more resources of all kinds. That is the nature of the Net, which is like a living, breathing organism with tens of millions of people and their collective knowledge adding to it every day. The Net is sometimes described as a giant CD-ROM. This isn't true, as a CD-ROM is considered finite once it's manufactured.

For a continuing stream of new sites that are rich with resources, subscribe to *Web Digest For Marketers*, at http://www.wdfm.com.

Finally, know when to stop. The Net is an infinite place. Your life is not. We strongly suggest that you train yourself to set coordinates for what you are looking for, and then get out once you've found it. We say this with one caveat, and that is, be aware of what you don't know. You will find times where you are looking for something and inadvertently bump into something else that is entirely unanticipated and outside the scope of your search project. Don't be so slavish as to ignore the happy happenstance, but rather go with the flow until you reach a point of diminishing return down that path.

http://007: Spying on Your Competitors and Yourself

The exponential growth of the Internet has created a frenzy among privacy advocates, who believe that the implications of worldwide information collection and sharing have yet to hit us. They may be right. As business owners, access to massive amounts of information (most often free) represents a significant competitive advantage. There are fountains of hard-won knowledge that are directly relevant to you and your business on the Net. Knowing how to undertake competitive intelligence sleuthing is a skill that will save you enormous amounts of time and money.

Find out what your rivals know and what they don't know. If you do it right, you'll uncover far more than how web savvy they are. You can peer into their plans and thinking. Your aggressive investigations should uncover holes in that thinking, and those holes have your name on them. Your mission, should you choose to accept it, is to identify and exploit these holes to your advantage. Despite themselves, your competitors will teach you the best practices to adopt and what boneheaded directions to avoid. In short order, you will reap sizable dividends from a modest investment of time.

This chapter shows you how to get under your competitor's skin and how to prevent them from getting under yours. You will explore:

- Benchmarking strategy
- The invisible Web
- Anonymous sleuthing techniques
- Metatag magic
- How to win the Web popularity contest

- Secrets of InterNIC
- Usenet, lists, and more
- Essential databases
- Ego surfing
- Competitive intelligence strategy

Benchmarking Strategy

You can get so close to your competitors on the Net that you're practically able read their minds.

I once queried a search engine to show me all the available pages on a competitor's site. The search revealed an entire new business presentation, replete with cue cards and selling points. I then called the company that was going to receive that presentation and had a discussion about where the strategic thinking of my competitor was flawed. The prospective client was impressed by my reconnaissance, and very concerned by the lack of discretion on the part of the competitor. The whole exercise took 15 minutes and instantly established my firm as a player in the prospect's mind.

Benchmarking can be defined as comparing your company to both industry standards and to the products, services, or sites of your competitors. Knowing where you stand in the playing field as compared to your competitors is essential information. From there, you can determine where you need to improve, how you can differentiate yourself from the competition, and where the sweetest opportunities can be found.

Coauthor Eileen Shulock is, by day, Vice President of Retail Strategy for Knowledge Strategies Group, found at http://www.kstrat.com, an e-commerce strategy and development firm. KStrat constantly conducts benchmarking studies on behalf of its clients. "We call it competitive analysis," explains Eileen in an interview with herself. "It's important for our clients to know exactly where they stand with regard to both their competitors and to established industry standards. Our clients need to deliver an e-commerce experience that meets or exceeds customer expectations of what they can find elsewhere. We also strategize for our clients to determine which areas of possible improvement will yield the most significant results."

KStrat developed a benchmarking methodology specifically for e-commerce sites that rates tangible, industry-recognized criteria for a successful e-commerce business. Each benchmarking criterion can be backed up with data, surveys, or other statistics about best practices. The analysis is a weighted system that compares the client site with that of its competitors (or with recognized e-commerce leaders such as Amazon.com) in the areas of functionality, customer service, merchandising, and value-added services. The weighted architecture insures that core elements such as database categorization and product imaging are much more important than nice-to-haves such as product reviews or same-day delivery. By constantly surveying the marketplace, the company is able to point out trends and best practices as they gain in importance, and weight them accordingly. The client receives the complete analysis with scores for every criterion, scores by category, and a final total score. That information can be dissected to determine where the best opportunities for improvement can be found.

Since the consumer's attention span is steadily decreasing, Knowledge Strategies also created a microanalysis specifically for e-commerce home pages. "Industry standards say that you have seven seconds or less to make an impression upon your visitor and entice them to explore further," says Eileen. "State-of-the-art shipping methods aren't going to be too useful if the customer can't get past the home page." The home page examination includes an analysis of page structure, ease of navigation, branding, and merchandising—for example, is it obvious that an e-commerce site sells products? Can core products be purchased from the home page? "It's amazing how many e-commerce sites don't feature a single product or a clear product categorization on their home page," Eileen laments. "The customer is frequently required to investigate to figure out exactly what the site sells. That does not make for a happy customer experience or many sales."

The Radar Screen

My company, Chase Online, also conducts benchmarking surveys for corporate and association speeches as well as for clients. Called the Benchmarking Radar Screen, I start out by finding best and worst practices in a client's respective category or industry (see Figure 4.1). Then I move one order of magnitude out to a contiguous category,

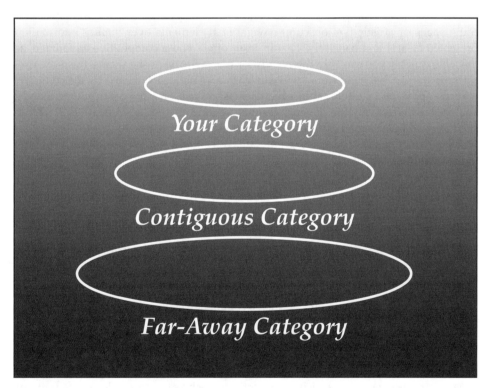

Figure 4.1   The Chase Online Benchmarking Radar Screen places the client in the context of their industry and contiguous categories.

and finally zoom all the way out to far-away categories from which the client can still learn something.

I show a client three examples of best practices in their category, which gives them an idea of how sophisticated they are relative to their peer group. If the peer companies are way ahead of them, they know they've got to get moving and have much to learn. I also point out bad practices to avoid. In the contiguous category, I show practices that are being employed that can easily be migrated into their immediate category. Finally, in the far-away category, I look for best practices that the client can adopt and quite possibly be the first to use in their own respective category. Being the first to employ such tactics in their respective category can yield a significant competitive advantage.

In these benchmark studies, a client usually likes to zoom in on a couple of arch rivals and learn all there is to know about them—not just how they're using the Net, but hints at what they might do next and where there are chinks in their armor that might be exploited online or off.

Site Analysis Standards

While every industry will differ in terms of what is standard and expected by the online customer, there are basic benchmarks that can be applied to any type of business website. Too often, companies choose bells and whistles such as slick animated welcome pages or artistic (yet obscure) navigational elements over quality information presented clearly and concisely. That in itself offers you a competitive advantage, as the more quickly you can help the site visitor find what he or she wants, the more useful your site will be. In addition, you can learn a lot about a business by the company it keeps—pay special attention to advertisers, sponsors, and site contributors. Finally, analyze how effectively the site engages the user and encourages repeat visits. Tactics such as permission email programs, promotions, or interactive tools show a level of web savvy that you should strive to emulate. You should analyze and note the following at a competitor's site:

- Time required for the home page to load
- Plug-in requirements
- Ability to see what the site offers without needing to scroll
- Consistent branding experience conveyed through design, content, and look and feel
- Obvious, understandable, and consistent navigational structure
- Permission marketing efforts, such as email newsletters or membership programs
- Partnerships, strategic alliances, advertisers, and sponsors
- Promotional efforts, such as coupons or other incentives
- Methods to encourage visitor interactivity, such as quizzes, calculators, polls, or discussion boards
- Ability to create a personalized site experience

- Customer service efforts

- The level of sophistication of the hidden text, found in the source code

- The overall transaction process (for retail sites)

- The quality of the content or product offerings, or the lack thereof

You should also ask the following questions:

- Is there a site-wide search engine available from every page?

- Are there any fancy databases? If so, what is the level of complexity?

- Does the text load before the graphics, so you have something to look at while the rest is loading?

- How easy is it to find company contact information on the home page and throughout the site?

- Does your competitor live up to its brand image and deliver brand value, as discussed in Chapter 5, "Your Brand Image and the Internet"?

Benchmarking is to some degree a subjective analysis, and as such, is most often done by physically comparing one site to another. You know your industry, and you can best assess how useful a site might be to the customer, or how important a competitor's strategic alliances are as compared to your own.

However, there are a growing number of software solutions that support competitive analysis efforts. One such solution is from WebCriteria (http://www.webcriteria .com), which uses a browsing software agent to spider through, or *browse*, both your site and selected competitor's sites much as a user would. The software measures accessibility (how quickly and easily users can navigate pages), load times (how long it takes for pages to download), and content (how quickly a page can be scanned and understood, the types of plug-ins needed, and how recently the content has updated). The resulting report provides a high-level comparison of sites, link-to-link page analysis, and page-view-by-page-view analysis (see Figure 4.2). This level of detail can be especially useful when comparing large sites in depth.

WebCriteria also provides free industry benchmarks, which are rankings of the quality of user experience for hundreds of leading e-commerce, corporate, and entertainment sites to which you can compare your site. A free demonstration of the software and the industry benchmark database are available at the WebCriteria site.

Diving into the Deep Web

It's important to note that when benchmarking, you are not only comparing website to website, but also business to business. The information you have gathered will help you look at where your company stands in relation to the competition. From there you can build your competitive intelligence—the informed decisions that you will make about your company growth and long-term strategy.

Before turning a microscope to the sites and tactics of the competition, you may want to take a deeper look at your industry itself. The Web is an excellent place to do that—and the Web is bigger than you think it is.

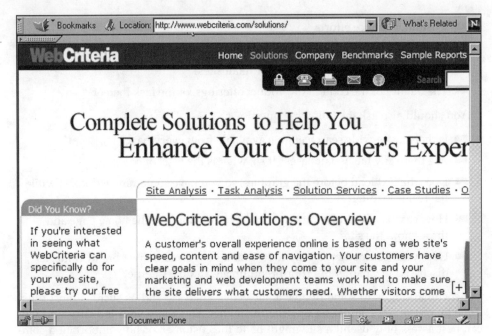

Figure 4.2   WebCriteria's software solution automates parts of the benchmarking process.

One of the most fascinating trends for those who use the Web for competitive reconnaissance purposes is the concept of the *deep Web* or the *invisible Web*, as the industry has termed it. What is this? The Web is full of information that is stored in databases. Unless you know how to access a particular database, the information stored therein will be invisible to you, because it cannot be accessed by search engines. Why? A searchable database serves up results dynamically to answer a direct query. Though search engines may point to these databases, they cannot reference or search the contents housed inside of them. In addition, in a traditional search, a result that leads to a database will be listed along with all the HTML web pages that match your query—burying the database itself even further in a sea of information.

According to a survey by search company Bright Planet, the invisible, inaccessible part of the Web housed in these databases is about 500 times larger than what search engines can show you. Think about it. Quite conceivably there are hundreds of billions of pages of information out there. Knowing how to access the invisible Web as a competitive intelligence tool, right now, as the technology to do so is being developed, means that a treasure trove of information is at your fingertips. Dig in.

TIP   To keep up with database news and trends, bookmark searchDatabase.com (http://www.searchdatabase.com). This site offers both a search engine for databases and up-to-the-minute database news and related tutorials and information.

The easiest way to start is to access a database of databases. Much like a web page search engine, these database search engines will yield a list of database results that match your query.

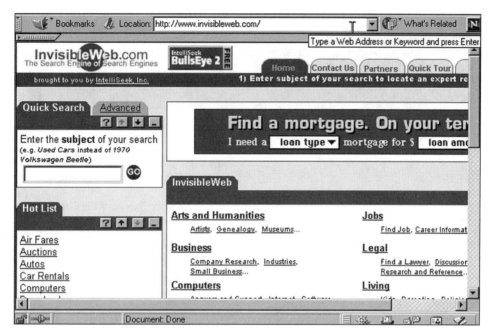

Figure 4.3   Search the invisible Web at InvisibleWeb.com.
© 2000 Intelliseek, Inc.

For example, at Intelliseek's InvisibleWeb site (http://www.invisibleweb.com), you can search for "venture capital," and then be shown databases that house information relating to venture capital. While you will have to search each resulting database one at a time, the ability to dive directly into databases in search of information (instead of reviewing a list of 1,347,982 links to static web pages that might have text content about venture capital) allows you to access specific information about venture capital firms and funding activities that would otherwise take hours, if not days, to find (see Figure 4.3).

Direct Search (http://gwis2.circ.gwu.edu/~gprice/direct.htm#SearchCenter), is another database search vehicle. A quick browse through the database categories available led to the discovery of several competitive intelligence database gems:

Bitpipe (http://www.bitpipe.com). A search engine for IT information, this site houses thousands of analyst reports, case studies, standards, test results, and white papers from vendors for the IT community, and provides a place for IT professionals to share knowledge on everything from DSL market overviews to enterprise computing.

eComp (http://www.ecomponline.com). At this invaluable site, you can access current executive compensation data on more than 32,000 executives at more than 9,000 U.S. public companies. The database can be searched by company name, ticker, symbol, state, and sector or industry classifications to view salary, bonus, option grants, and option exercises (see Figure 4.4).

Salary.com (http://www.salary.com). An interactive Salary Wizard will pinpoint salary range by job title based upon your zip code. It will then suggest additional salary surveys, resources, government studies, and trade associations for supplemental data.

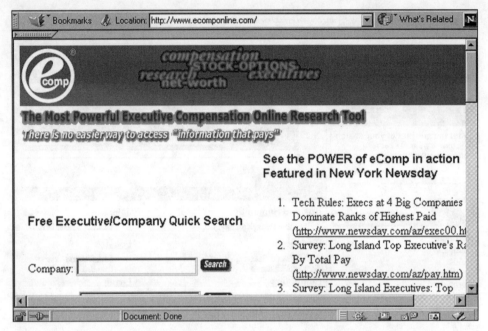

Figure 4.4 Find the compensation packages of thousands of executives at eComp.

As you can see, the discovery of a few of these database gems can potentially be very advantageous to your company. What's next? The crème de la crème of competitive reconnaissance tools: the multidatabase search tool.

According to BrightPlanet's tutorial, *The Deep Web: Surfacing Hidden Value*, found at http://www.completeplanet.com/Tutorials/DeepWeb/index.asp, the deep Web is the fastest growing category of new information on the Internet—and a full 95 percent of the deep Web is free, publicly accessible information.

BrightPlanet also has a database search site, which can be found at http://www.completeplanet.com. At CompletePlanet, you can search for databases offering hidden information. BrightPlanet is raising the *deep Web* bar by offering its LexiBot search tool, which will search multiple databases at once for you (see Figure 4.5). At the moment, this tool looks at your search request, then selects the most relevant of 600 different deep Web resources and forwards your query to them. After that, as with traditional metasearch tools, your information will be returned. The plan is for this tool to query against all 100,000 significant invisible websites that BrightPlanet estimates are in existence today. At the time of this writing, a 30-day free trial of the LexiBot tool is available at the site, and the cost of the software itself is a mere $89.95—an investment that could pay off a thousandfold in terms of information potentially at your fingertips.

Cloak and Dagger Tactics

When you're crawling over your rival's site, you should be aware that he or she can identify you as well. There are a few tactics that will help you research anonymously, should you so desire.

Figure 4.5 Search multiple databases at once with BrightPlanet's LexiBot software.
© 2000 BrightPlanet.com.

The Nom de Plume

Remember what the Godfather said: "Keep your friends close, and your enemies closer." If your rival offers an email newsletter, subscribe to it. Of course, if you subscribe to your rival's newsletter, he or she will know who you are. . .or maybe not? Using an anonymous email address is one way to get around this potential problem. Acquiring an anonymous email address costs nothing and is very easy. Simply sign up

---

WEBSITES CAN SEE YOU

Without any fancy technology, a site can identify a visitor just by using free or very inexpensive software. You can identify a user's domain name, browser type, machine, and where he or she last came from on the Web. For example, a server can see me as chaseonline.com using Internet Explorer 5.0 on a PC. Even though it doesn't know that larry@chaseonline.com is the one on the site, it knows my company has been there. I may not want to leave that impression behind. Set up a dummy account from another domain name, such as bobt@panix.com, or from a free email service, such as bob@hotmail.com. This way, the site will not know that someone from your company using Internet Explorer 5.0 on a PC has visited. In other words, leave no trail of bread crumbs when you're on a recon mission in the enemy camp. With more sophisticated software that accesses *cookies*, which are files parked on your machine, sites can learn much more about you, including your name, snail-mail address, demographic information, and a history of where you've been surfing for the past 30 days.

for free email service from any number of search engine services, such as Excite or Yahoo!, or from free email providers like Hotmail or Mail.com.

Your nom de plume will be especially useful when you request email newsletters, sales brochures, or make sales calls to check the level of sophistication of your rival's sales force. At most locations, you can take out several different accounts under pseudonyms. Do be careful when you fill out the sign-up information, as many spiders around the Web are very good at tracking down the true owners of accounts. Simply using one of your other screen names on AOL will probably not do the trick. I know a number of people who are quite upset that their email addresses can be found by entering their names in any number of people/address search engines. In many cases, you can even get a map to their houses along with exact addresses and fax numbers.

The Anonymizer

If you are only an occasional snoop, you may just need to cloak yourself at the Anonymizer (http://www.anonymizer.com), shown in Figure 4.6. Passing through a site like this makes it much more difficult for a rival to identify you. It prevents him or her from knowing certain things he or she would otherwise automatically have, such as:

■ Your domain name (i.e., chaseonline.com) and possibly your actual name (for example, larry@chaseonline.com)

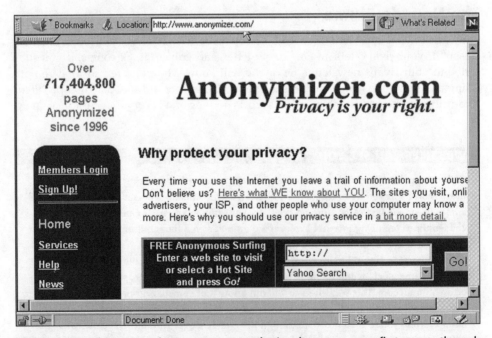

Figure 4.6 When snooping on a competitor's site, you can first pass through Anonymizer.com, so your competition can't tell where you're really from.

- ■ Your current IP number (which tells your rivals exactly which ISP you use and where you are located)
- ■ The kind of browser and computer you are using
- ■ What country you come from
- ■ What site you just came from (which web page you last looked at)—in this case, your rival's referrer logs will tell him or her that you came from Anonymizer.com, rather than some identifiable site, like your home page

You go in one side of this site and come out the other anonymously, so your rivals can't see your domain name when you hit their pages. What they see instead is "anonymizer.com." The downside here is that security-sensitive sites can and do filter out specific domain names, and you can be blocked access to the site you wish to snoop. I know a number of sites that not only filter out the Anonymizer, but also specific domain names that belong to their competitors. Some sites have a filter that can break through the Anonymizer's *network proxy* as well, revealing your true information. Of course they can and do get access through other accounts; it just serves as an inconvenience and makes it harder for them to stay right on top of you, unless you have a cloaked account.

Looking under the Hood

Now it's time to turn your attention back to the competition. Go to http://www .altavista.com and enter your competitor's URL in the advanced search engine offered there. If AltaVista doesn't have the site listed, no problem. Just add your competitor's URL in AltaVista yourself, and come back a few days later after AltaVista has had a chance to examine that site and load its contents into its own database. You can then slice and dice it into bite-sized pieces for analysis. This is exactly how I found that new business presentation I mentioned at the beginning of this chapter.

You, or one of your techies, should also examine the hidden text on each page of your competitor's site to assess the sophistication of the programming. A good programmer can quickly assess the level of sophistication of a web page by looking at the source code, as shown in Figure 4.7. If you wish to examine all 432 pages on a given site, that might take a while.

Looking at the way the site has been coded will tell you how sophisticated your competitors are. It will also tell you if they are using metatags to help better their

---

URL

URL is geek-speak for *Uniform Resource Locator*. It's the address for a website. Many URLs have Ws before their name, as in www.chaseonline.com, while others don't. Make sure your web address is represented both ways, with and without the Ws. Some people just type in your company name, sometimes with the Ws, sometimes not. When you have represented it both ways, it increases the odds that someone can find you the first time out.

```
<BASE HREF="http://wdfm.com/">
<html>
<head>
<title>Larry Chase's Web Digest for Marketers - Internet Marketing Reviews a
<META Name="description" content="Larry Chase's Web Digest for Marketers...f

<META Name="keywords" content="Internet marketing reviews online marketing ne

        <script language="JavaScript">


        <!-- hide from JavaScript-challenged browsers
function openWindow() {

  popupWin = window.open("http://www.wdfm.com/thanks.html","remote","scrollbe

}


closetime = 0;
function Start(URL, WIDTH, HEIGHT) {
windowprops = "left=150,top=50,scrollbars=yes,width=" + WIDTH + ",height=" +
preview = window.open(URL, "preview", windowprops);
if (closetime) setTimeout("preview.close();", closetime*1000);
}
```

Figure 4.7   The hidden HTML text behind WDFM.

search engine standings. If you notice they are not using metatags, they haven't done their homework in figuring out how to help the search engines rate their sites. Chapter 7, "Online Events, Promotions, and Attractions," discusses in detail how to promote your site to search engines with the sophisticated use of metatags, and how to track your search engine ranking success.

By simply taking a peek at your competitor's metatags, you may find they're doing some naughty things, such as embedding keywords hundreds of times to fool the search engines into rating the site higher than it should. I once heard of a major airline embedding the word "sex" into its metatags thousands of times. This tactic is not only crude, but ineffective. Not only does it draw people who are looking for sex to the site, where they will be severely disappointed (unless they happen to be looking for a flight bargain as well), but search engines are increasingly aware of and reactive to such techniques. Many search engine executives admit that they will gleefully delete a site, an

MAKING THE MOST OF HIDDEN TEXT

Underneath every web page you will find the "code," or programming language, that helps your browser figure out where to place things and how to make them look. You can see what this looks like in many browsers under the option View Source. It's like looking under the hood of a car. You can see much about how the page was constructed and (in some cases) even copy it verbatim.

METATAGS

Metatags are keywords relating to the subject of your site which are inserted into the code of your site. Search engines look for metatags in order to catalog a web page. All web pages should have them in order to get cataloged in the engines properly. Unfortunately, every search engine likes to see metatags organized in slightly different ways. Unless a special page is built and optimized for each search engine (called a *gateway* page, the merits of which can be debated), you will have to compromise and strategize so that your metatag solution works well enough for most. A good primer on the use of metatags and how search engines work is located at Northern Webs (http://www.northernwebs.com/set).

---

entire series of sites, or all the sites of a particular offender from their search engine, and basically put them on a black list and ban them for life. There is no legal recourse at this time. So it's to your benefit to either understand metatag and search engine positioning techniques yourself, or to make sure that you hire an ethical professional to handle them for you.

By looking under the hood of your competitors' sites, you might also find that they're entirely clueless and not taking advantage of all the legitimate ways to mark up a site so as to actually help search engines and users themselves (by using alt tags, for example).

Finally, you can benchmark by looking at the credits for design and development of your rival's site. Take these names down and contact the vendors later to get a handle on what your rival is paying for his or her site. Very often, these vendors, in their exuberance to get your business, will reveal what is currently on the drawing board for the next phase. Getting the skinny on a rival from one of his or her indiscreet web vendors is a phone call or email away. Ask them for quotes on the sorts of things they did for that particular site and you will get an idea of what your rival paid. You might even get it for less, as it gives the vendor the chance to resell something that has already been created.

ALT TAGS

Alt tags are what a programmer inserts whenever there is an *embedded* graphic, sound, or video file on a web page—these are simply lines of descriptive text that show up on a web browser where the embedded object is, or will be. For example, if there will be a graphic with a picture of your logo, the alt tag should say "company logo." This not only gives site visitors with slow modems something to read (and look forward to) while a page is loading, but provides content information to the search engines. In addition, if the visitor has images turned off, or if they are unable to view images at all, the alt tags will indicate what appears in the graphic image. With the increasing availability of voice readers (technology that actually reads websites, using HTML text and alt tags), site owners should ensure that everything on their site can be read at the code level.

Link Popularity

Remember those good old high school days when your popularity quotient determined everything from your prom date to whether you were voted Most Likely to IPO? Alas, the same is increasingly true in the web world, former home of the nerd and the geek, as link popularity is beginning to factor into more and more search engine algorithms and resulting rankings.

Once you've surveyed every inch of your rivals' sites, you can then see who has links pointing to them. Granted, the Web is huge and changes very quickly, so no one engine can accurately catalog it in its entirety. But it is worth the time to get down to the business of seeing who's pointing to your rival. Then go to these links and see why they're pointing to your rival's site. Are they pointing to your site as well? If not, why not? Do you need to contact them and ask them to point to you as well? If yes, where do you stand in relation to your competitor in these other companies' eyes?

TIP At LinkPopularity (http://www.linkpopularity.com) you can see exactly how many sites are pointing to you, or to your competitor, according to AltaVista, Infoseek, and HotBot. Simply type in the URL and you will be served with the number of referring sites according to each search engine. Click on the number and you will get a list of each and every pointing site (see Figure 4.8).

Your popularity in cyberspace is often referred to as your *site visibility*. With the Word of Net Visibility Index, found at http://www.wordofnet.com, web marketers

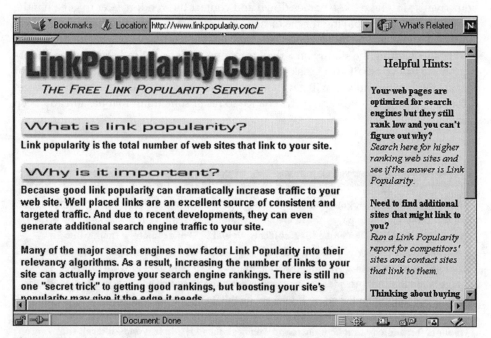

Figure 4.8 LinkPopularity will tell you how popular your site is in cyberspace.
© 2000 The PC Edge, Inc.

can obtain the popularity quotient of their site and assess how visible it is on the Web. The Visibility Index factors in how many sites link to your site and how popular the sites are that link to you. A 1,000 point index measures and tracks the online visibility of your site, as compared to competitors of your choice. The index considers search engines, directory listings, and third-party pages that reference you and/or your competitors, and weights them according to the quality referring sites to obtain the Visibility Index.

Perhaps some of the links you'll discover are advertisements your rival is running, in which case you're now starting to unearth marketing budgets and strategies. You might find other links heavily concentrated in certain geographical or industry areas, which will reflect the direction in which your rival is focusing.

If your rival is a big company, you may turn up some antimarketing sites, such as http://www.flamingfords.com, where disgruntled customers publicly vent their misfortunes from having dealt with your rival. These people may well be low-hanging fruit for you to entice into your camp. Based on this, you could fashion a marketing plan that's solely aimed at the disgruntled users of your opposition.

If, on the other hand, you are one of those unfortunate firms that is the object of the ire of these antimarketing sites, you will most definitely want to contain the problem by addressing it head-on, if possible.

Often these reverse-link lookups will uncover ad banners that your rival paid for out of his or her advertising budget. Go to the site where that link is, find the banner, and note the message on it before clicking. You will be taken to your rival's site and shown a corresponding page. Is that banner advertising a special promotion, a branding campaign, or a new product or service that you should know about? If that banner was a recruitment ad, that corresponding web page will give you rich information about who your competitor is looking for, the job description, and sometimes salary ranges. You may even want to have someone outside your company go through the motions of applying for that job to see how the follow-through process works. Keep in mind that the ad running may or may not be drawing qualified leads. If the ad stays up forever, it may be a sign that it isn't reflecting reality when it comes to compensation, qualifications, or geographical expectations. Still, it's an indicator of your rival's movements.

TIP If you would really like to get the inside scoop on your competitor's plans, go to a job posting site such as Monster (http://www.monster.com) and create a personal profile set up to scan job leads every day by industry or even by company. Every time your competitor advertises a new job on one of the major recruitment sites, you will be notified by email the very same day!

Search and Ye Shall Find Yourself

Concerned about your competitor's online popularity as compared to yours? Keep in mind there's a right way to increase your overall visibility, and there's a wrong way. Spending your time trying to dupe the search engines is a lose-lose proposition, as I mentioned previously. Some engines take punitive action by deleting your URL should you continue to attempt to abuse the parameters they lay down for fair and reasonable placement. Furthermore, your time is much better spent being more proactive and aggressive, grabbing mind share by devising campaigns that rewrite the rules so that your competition gets caught up in a game of follow the leader—namely, you. Packing your site's code with thousands of keywords to trick the search engines is not a productive use of time.

Having said that, there's no reason why you shouldn't know your standings in the search engines by using handy tools such as The Detective (http://www.did-it.com) and PositionAgent (http://www.positionagent.com). Both of these sites systematically check the popular search engines to see if your site (or your competitor's) is indexed, and where it stands in the various search engine rankings.

TIP If you want an idea of what words are most commonly used in searches, you can get a listing of the week's hot search topics with the Lycos Top 50, found at http://www.lycos.com. Excite's WebCrawler (http://www.webcrawler.com) will let you look behind the scenes at live keyword searches. I'll tell you right now, people aren't searching for zinc alloy or gallium arsenide. Nevertheless, it will give you an idea of how people go about looking for things on the Net using search engines and keywords.

It's a good thing to stay on top of your standings in search engines, but I wouldn't put too much effort into it; there most certainly is a point of diminishing return. In my case, the engines account for maybe 30 percent of my traffic, with the rest coming from advertising, press coverage, trade-outs, and referred links from sites with resource sections for marketing.

Curiously enough, there's another way you can increase your online visibility: Put keywords in the signature file that appears at the end of your email. When you submit postings to newsgroups and mail to some discussion lists, it tends to get archived on the Web. Your post is archived with many other documents with similar words. That means something to the search engines that come around with their virtual clipboards. Furthermore, you easily and automatically create a higher incidence of coincidence. If you're an online marketing consultant, and that fact is in your sig file, which has been sorted on some discussion list of authors and agents, it might very well come up when someone submits a search for "online marketing" as well as "online advertising." I've had people contact me who read a newsgroup post I made years ago.

WHAT'S IN A SIG FILE?

Sig is short for *signature*. At the bottom of every email you send out you should have a sig file that gives your contact information and what you do, or even a promotion or an offer. Most email programs let you write this standard signature once and then automatically append it to every email you send. This sig file should not be more than six lines long, after which it is considered overkill. I suggest you use the horizontal space across the page as much as possible. Here's my example:

Cordially, Larry Chase Consultant/Speaker/Author of "Essential
Business Tactics f/t Net"
Sample chapter - http://LarryChase.com
Publisher: Web Digest For Marketers
Subscribe @ http://wdfm.com

What's in a Name?

Visit the InterNIC, the place that keeps track of all domain names, at http:// www.internic.net, and you'll learn even more about your rivals. In addition to finding out when they registered for their domain names and who is responsible from an administrative and technical point of view, you can also enter the companies' names into the search field (called "WhoIs") at http://www.internic.net/whois.html. This is a little known fact. If you enter Procter, for example, you'll turn up all the domain names that Procter & Gamble has registered, when it registered them, and if they're currently assigned to a website—whether or not the site is currently being used. You will not be able to determine if the site is active; you will have to go to each individual URL and see if it is active. If not active, the domain names are on reserve for future efforts or to protect them so that competitors cannot use them. The very names themselves will give you clues as to what companies are planning for future sites and how long they've been in preparation.

For example, if we check on Procter & Gamble's registered domain names, we see that it has pampers.com and vidalsassoon.com—and both of these URLs yield sites dedicated to those two trademarked products. However, Procter & Gamble also has names such as sinus.com, badbreath.com, flu.com, dish.com, and dozens more generic names that have to do with diapers, cold and flu medicines, and household cleaning. The company, however, has reserved all these domain names for future development; no one else can use these domain names unless Procter & Gamble is willing to sell them.

While you are searching for information about your rival companies, identify the names of specific key people employed by your rival. Then use your newfound sleuthing techniques to do searches on these people. See what trade shows they're speaking at, what articles they've written, and what they said in those articles. These articles may include newsletters or press releases that are now, in part, posted at your rival's site.

How much does all of this searching cost? Not much at all, except for your time or that of some college whiz kid who is interning for you and understands your search criteria. Unfortunately, whiz kids are not always available, as they have their studies and their own IPO ventures, and are not always as keenly tuned to the nuances of com-

---

Sig files can and should be used to promote your company, products, and services in a noninvasive, compelling way. Here's an example of the sig file that coauthor Eileen Shulock used during the writing of this book:

Eileen Shulock, Managing Editor, Web Digest For Marketers
Free subscription at http://wdfm.com
Coauthor, "Essential Business Tactics for the Net 2.0"
Get Ready. Spring 2001. Wiley. Are you in it?
Email me at es@wdfm.com for book queries, interviews, product reviews, and site suggestions.

> **INSIDE THE INTERNIC**
>
> You can think of the InterNIC and other domain name registrars as the central post office of the Internet. They know who holds which domain names and will give you the names and physical addresses of the owners of each name, in addition to the technical administrator. The NIC can tell you how long someone has had a name and when it was last updated, as well as what other names that person or company has registered.

petitive intelligence as a seasoned business professional. So be prepared to spend between $30 and $100 an hour for a business and Net-savvy pro who can get it right the first time (that hourly rate is an approximate range—your mileage may vary). Ask for his or her search strategy, and be prepared to compare it to your own criteria and expectations in order to determine the right professional sniffer for your needs.

TIP Go to WhoIs.net and use the Suggest A Name feature, which lets you list several keywords that pertain to your company. For example, if you are Chase Internet Marketing, you can enter those three keywords and find out which combinations of those words are available—and which are taken, with links to the information as to who might own ChaseInternet.com, for example. Even if you don't plan to register every single combination of your business name, it doesn't hurt to know what is available, and what others with similar business names and keyword matches are up to.

Using the Usenet and Listservs for Undercover Work

As you probably know, the Web is only the most visible part of the Net. In addition to the discussions happening all over the Web on online bulletin boards, there are tens of thousands of Usenet newsgroups, which are essentially public discussion groups on the Internet that you can read and/or post to yourself. Using the same search engines as mentioned before, you'll want to search the Usenet for any references to your competitor's name, products, services, or people. You may even want to contribute a comment or two when appropriate. There are literally thousands of newsgroups available; be prepared to take some time to find the ones your search engine adventure turned up for you to check. You can access and search many newsgroups through the site Deja (http://www.deja.com/=km/usenet).

In addition to Usenet and online bulletin boards, there are tens of thousands of email discussion lists that you can explore as well. Instead of going to the Usenet in this case, you'll want to subscribe to the email discussion lists that are relative to your industry and rivals. In fact, your rival may already be running a discussion list. If he or she isn't, you may want to start one yourself. Both Usenet and mailing lists are good tools to have in your arsenal when collecting information. When you first join, just *lurk* for a while and do not post anything. *Lurking* is simply reading and not saying anything. Most groups and lists are composed of lurkers, with a comparatively small percentage of people who actively post. It's like talk radio in this respect: many listeners, few talkers. See who's active, what topics are being discussed, and how they're handled. You may want to build goodwill by introducing yourself and offering up a valuable piece of information, in a few short words, or give the URL of your site. This is done to build good relations with the landed gentry who came before you.

TIP Find email lists that relate to your topics of interest at Liszt.com (http://www.liszt.com), which is one of the original listserv compilation sites (see Figure 4.9). Search by keyword through over 90,000 email lists, or browse through a topical directory to find lists of interest.

There has been a great deal written about the use of proper netiquette when posting to newsgroups or mailing lists. The culture that has grown up over the years is quite distinct, and it's quite easy to ruffle feathers with typical *newbie* mistakes. Sometimes even asking basic questions about the topic at hand, rather than taking the time to read the group's FAQ (Frequently Asked Questions), can ruin your chances to get "in" with the mailing list group. Take your time and let them get to know you by posting a few polite and short follow-up statements to an ongoing discussion; in other words, test the waters. After a while, you might float a few questions that solicit the input of the members on a given topic. Don't say, "Hey, what do you think of my rival?" Rather, ask for discussion on points of disagreement between you and your rival. This is an effective and inexpensive way to ping your trade or marketplace.

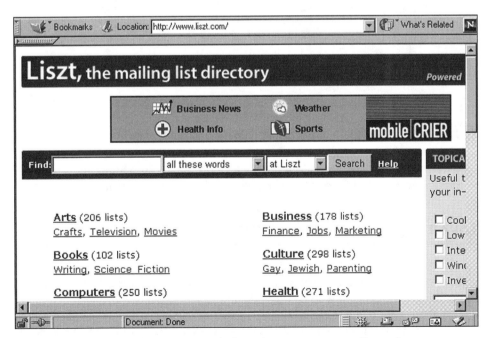

Figure 4.9   At Liszt.com, you can search through over 90,000 email newsletters.

MINDING YOUR OWN MAILING LIST

Many firms find it very handy to stay in touch with their constituencies via broadcasting news updates and the like to those who have requested it. This is what my *Web Digest For Marketers* (WDFM) does (see Figure 4.10). WDFM is a one-way mailing list. Others are two-way and accept messages from the recipients so that discussions between all can take place. If you start a mailing list, make sure the quality of content is high enough so people have a good incentive for subscribing and staying with you.

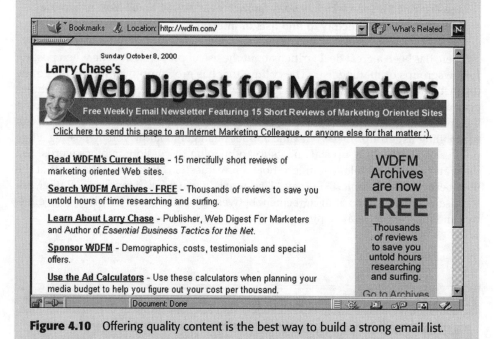

Figure 4.10   Offering quality content is the best way to build a strong email list.

TIP   An online guide to Internet etiquette, or *netiquette*, can be found at http://www.albion.com/netiquette/. This overview is excerpted from the book *Netiquette* by Virginia Shea (Albion Books, 1994). Shea's Core Rules are the classic introduction to the subject and are widely cited in cyberspace.

Touching Base with Databases

As discussed earlier in this chapter, databases can offer up a gold mine of information to the cyber sleuth. There are certain databases that we turn to time and time again for competitive intelligence research. These databases will potentially yield much information about your target companies.

If you go to Trade Show Central (http://www.tscentral.com), you can look up who's exhibiting at tens of thousands of conferences, trade shows, and seminars worldwide. Are your competitors there? Should you be if they are? Are your competitors advertising an aggressive promotion to bring traffic to their booths?

You can go to American Business Information's infoUSA (http://www.infousa.com) to get a top-line business credit report rating on over 10,000 companies. Dig a little deeper and you'll find out who gets paid first: the phone company or the landlord.

LEXIX-NEXIS, the Public Records database (http://www.lexis-nexis.com/business/public_records/), contains information from a national consumer reporting agency, limited to a person's name, address, birthday, and sometimes alternate names, previous addresses, and phone numbers. It is marketed to law enforcement, legal offices, businesses, and government agencies. The service is priced on a flat rate, hourly, or transaction basis, depending upon your needs.

In the United States, government requires public companies to disclose a huge amount of information. This information is available online in the U. S. Securities and Exchange Commission's Edgar Online database (http://www.edgar-online.com) which is a searchable archive that can provide invaluable insights into the competitive and financial activities and plans of a company.

DeBarcode (http://www.debarcode.com) is an Internet directory service specializing in bar codes and universal resource identification. Given the bar code or Universal Product Code of a product, deBarcode will locate its maker's website.

The Library of Congress Online Catalog (http://catalog.loc.gov) contains over 12 million records representing books, serials, computer files, manuscripts, cartographic materials, music, sound recordings, and visual materials.

Don't Forget the Press!

Of course we haven't yet touched on basic tracking by way of press releases and statements to the press. There are dozens of options for employing the electronic version of Beryl's Clipping Service, many of which are discussed in Chapter 9, "Public Relations, the Internet Way." Or you can do it yourself. It really depends on how much this information means to you versus the time you spend doing it yourself. I myself tend to spot-check every now and again. I feel it's good for sharpening my research skills, as well as adding knowledge to my business relationships.

The PR Web Press Release Database (http://www.prweb.com) contains thousands of business press releases that have been released online within the past 90 days that can be searched by keyword.

There are also services that will monitor specific newsgroups and web pages for you, alerting you to any changes in the page's content or to the mention of your rival in a newsgroup, for instance. One such service is eWatch (http://www.ewatch.com), which provides extensive monitoring capabilities for less than it would cost to employ a staff member to do so.

I've also used electronic news-clipping services to good effect. Individual.com's NewsPage (http://www.individual.com) offers a free news-clipping service, as well as more sophisticated, fee-based levels of information gathering. With Individual.com and others like it, you can dial up the selectivity of the words, so that you only see stories in which those words appear most prominently in the document (see Figure 4.11).

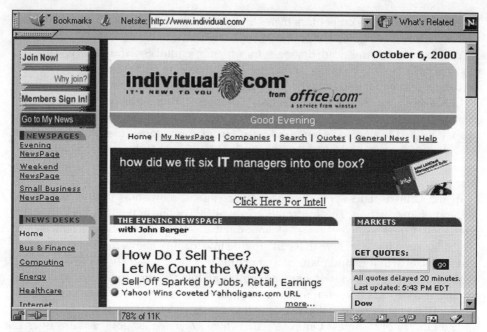

Figure 4.11   Individual.com will filter through a myriad of news and wire services looking for articles of interest based on your preferences and will then email them to you.

© office.com, Inc., a service of Winstar.

Spying for New Business

If you're on the prowl for new business (and who isn't?), you'll want to employ all of the tools in this section to strengthen your chances to score that win. You probably have companies in mind for new business leads. Start by targeting them. Even more than a brochure, a company's site speaks volumes about how it perceives itself. The closer you can get to them before making first contact, the better. Subscribe to any online mailing lists they offer. See if they have members of the department you're targeting listed on the site. If so, grab their names and do a Net-wide search for information. It can come in very handy when you bump into someone in the hall when you're first visiting.

Say, for example, you visit the site of a client that you are planning on pitching. You can use some of the information gleaned from your visit to this site as a reason to make contact. An opener for you might be an email gently pointing out that a few links on the site are no longer working. He or she might email you back and thank you for that helpful information, and you pick it up from there. You may also find that this company has interests in an area in which you excel. You might call or email the company saying that you vend a solution that is integral to what it talked about on its site. I've also found that if I email such a company about having found some very interesting sites pointing to it, it always elicits an eager response: Who is it? How did you find them? What are they saying about us?

Remember the example I gave at the beginning of this chapter in which I pointed out to a prospective client my competitor's presentation that was publicly available for anyone to bump into? When I mentioned it to the prospective client on the phone, he had to stop and listen, then go to the site online, where he and I critiqued the positioning the rival had in mind. This prospective client got a number of messages from me in one burst:

- My rival was not being discreet.
- I was sophisticated enough to detect it.
- I was aggressive enough to mention it.

Knowing a prospective client's business that well has to be respected. He or she will think about the value you can bring on a sustained basis and quite possibly, by inference, the lack thereof by your rival. It's a very potent selling message.

Spying on Yourself

One of the very first things I searched for on the Web was my own name. Everybody does, to the extent that the term "ego surfing" was created to fully capture the nuances of a complete self-search. You can easily conduct your own soul-searching at EgoSurf .com. During my search, I found eight other Larry Chases out there. I'm sure there are more by now. What that told me to do was register larrychase.com as a domain name. I suggest you do the same for both your name and all or some intuitive part of your company's name.

Just as with your competitive reconnaissance discussed earlier, you can use many of the Web's search engines to sniff yourself, as it were. Pretty much the same applies when trolling the Usenet groups and mailing lists for your company or self as you did for your rivals. Using the very same techniques, you can see whose web page links point to you, and why.

When people consider advertising in my *Web Digest For Marketers* newsletter, their comfort level goes way up when they see big, blue-chip names pointing at it and saying nice things about it. Think of it as a hyperlink seal of approval. . .unless, of course, they are saying negative things about you. Many of the same search engines that search the Net can also be used to troll Usenet groups. If you are a large company, this can give you an early heads-up about potential problems before they get out of control. This voyeuristic technique is especially effective when you want to find out what your constituents really think about you. They are more apt to speak freely if they are not prompted by you directly. Some people ask other members of a Usenet group or a mailing discussion list to mention their product or service so that they can get totally honest input. Unfortunately, at the time of writing, there seems to be no one resource that scans all publicly accessible mailing lists—the search engines on the Web only catalog web pages and Usenet groups. Therefore, it is best that you simply join those mailing lists that are relevant to you.

TIP You can also find out what the public is saying about your company's products or services by visiting one of the many public opinion sites, where customers share their comments and rate their experiences. One example of this type of consumer-power site is BizRate.com. Of course, you can always post favorable things about yourself there as well.

Client Focus

Thus far, we've talked about casting nets out to pick up snatches of information about competitors, potential new business, and ourselves. But what about knowing the users of your products or services better? Just as you should troll the Web, Usenet, and mailing lists for individual competitors and yourself, you should see what you can turn up on your clients. Once a company I was working with was coming out with a new product. The company was extremely sensitized to the prospect of other companies coming out with something similar. When one of these competitors showed up on my radar screen with a product directly pitted against this company, I immediately gave my client the heads-up. This told him to put more manpower behind his product to market it sooner rather than later. The pricing of this newly released competitive product told him what he could charge for his. He could also adjust his marketing copy to accentuate the stronger aspects of his product, while he quickly moved to improve upon those areas in which he was weaker.

We've found other bonding points for our clients on the Web. Many don't even realize they're mentioned on the Web until we tell them; it makes for great conversation. I remember one was amazed to find out he was listed by the New York Road Runners Association, while another had a yen for fly fishing. As a consequence, whenever I see something in my cybertravels on fly fishing or road running, I pass it along to them via email so they can surf over. It only takes a few seconds, but it consistently builds a stronger bond over time that will be less apt to be broken by a lower bid or what have you from a competitor.

You might also want to capture intelligence on behalf of your clients, whether you are providing web-related services or not, especially if they are less web savvy than you. All of the tools and resources outlined in this chapter can be used on behalf of your clients as well as your own business. By doing so, you add value to your relationships and keep tuned in to your clients' businesses.

Protecting Yourself

How can you protect yourself from your competitors' sniffing you? The bold truth is, you can't do much about it. Just as the Web provides an opportunity for you to grope your competitors, they can do the same to you. Nevertheless, there are some precautions you can take. Be sure that all of your site staging areas are password protected; neither the search engines nor your rivals will penetrate this easily. You can stop competitors from sniffing you out when you put up new information on your site by using some HTML code (<URL-MINDER-IGNORE>). This prevents the sniffers from seeing that new info (more information on this tactic can be found at http://www .netmind.com). The downside is, if you have customers who use this software to alert them as to when you update your pages, they will also be excluded, and thus unable to receive notification when your pages have been updated.

When you send out your newsletter, do not put all of the recipients' email addresses in the "To:" or "Cc:" fields if you are using a basic email program. If you do, everyone on your list (assume your competitors are in there) will see who the other subscribers are. If using a simple email program, put all the recipients' names in the "Bcc:" field.

That way, the names appear as "list suppressed." This is a paranoid-sounding phrase, but at least it protects the anonymity of each and every recipient. Or you can create a *group name* and put all the addresses under the group; only the group name will show in the "To:" field (such as "All Customers"). A majordomo program or a web-based list service such as eGroups (http://www.egroups.com) can also be employed that will send everyone your newsletter, but the "To:" field will have the name of the list, rather than the recipient. If you will be sending occasional group emails, this may be the most cost-effective way to go, next to using your own email program and a group name.

You can't prevent your competition from scanning you closely, but you can at least know they are doing so. Hopefully, they are not as sophisticated as you are, so you'll be able to identify them (for example, they may not be cloaked or anonymized, as explained earlier). In this way, you at least know what they know about you or know what they don't know about you. You can also block entry from specific domain names. So, for example, the search engine Google may prevent its competitor Lycos from checking out its new interface or technology by simply disallowing entry from anyone from Lycos.com to its site. Of course, the Lycos person can simply bypass this block by going into Google via his or her own AOL account. You can just make it more troublesome for your competition to get information about you.

Putting It All Together

You've sleuthed and surfed and sleuthed some more—now what? It's time to analyze what your newly collected data is telling you so that you can create winning marketing strategies and make strategic company decisions. How do you extract the relevant data to make the right decisions?

It will be helpful to put the information you've gathered about yourself and your competition in the context of a larger industry profile. Industry benchmarks can be particularly helpful at this point, whether for actual site evaluation as outlined in the *Benchmarking Strategy* section of this chapter, or for general business conditions.

If you are introducing competitive intelligence techniques to your company for the first time, you will want to establish some guidelines and procedures. There's no point in gathering all this information only to have it languish on your hard drive. First, you will want to document what you have discovered, and pinpoint those sources or tools that are needed to provide an ongoing stream of information. These may include news-clipping services, competitor alerts, email discussion lists, and market studies and reports.

Next, determine where and how this information will be stored. Who in your company will be responsible for gathering information, and with whom will the information be shared? Don't forget to include your sales staff and marketing staff, customer service personnel, and other company members who are in a position to both share and analyze competitive intelligence information.

Finally, you will need to establish a regular sleuthing schedule to check online visibility and to benchmark competitors' websites. The Web doesn't stand still—neither should you. In order to be effective, competitive intelligence needs to become an integral, daily part of your business strategy.

What do you do with all this information? You'll want to divide your focus into three areas:

External market. What are the industry trends? What are the current economic conditions? How do you foresee your industry changing and growing over the coming months and years? What are the greatest challenges for the industry at large?

The competition. Who is your competition right now? Who might be your competition in the near future? What does it look like your competition is doing to establish its competitive advantage? What does the competition offer that you do not?

Your company. What are your company's strengths and weaknesses? How does your company compare to the competition? How is your company positioned to take advantage of industry trends and competitor weaknesses?

With this information, you will be able to outline a number of industry and competitor predictions, and recommendations for your own strategic direction. You will be in position to take advantage of early warning signals in the market—downturns or upturns in business, new products or services, the changing needs or wants of your clients or customers. You will also be able to assess the moves of your competition, and analyze how potential new products or strategic alliances will affect your company—and you'll be able to get there first. You will be able to build a vision for the industry and for your company, and act aggressively upon that vision.

Fuld & Company (http://www.fuld.com), an international leader and pioneer in the field of competitive intelligence, provides many helpful tutorials and resources at its site. The company goes so far as to provide an Intelligence Organizer, which is essentially a game board that outlines possible situations—for example, your competitor launches a new product—and then offers suggestions on the intelligence needed and how to address that particular challenge.

Are you ready? Take Fuld & Company's Corporate Evaluation Questionnaire to find out. A series of 40 questions explores the issues that any company embarking upon a competitive intelligence mission needs to consider. The questionnaire covers everything from strategic issues to the motivation of those charged with the reconnaissance—after all, it's "your mission, should you choose to accept it."

Caution: Don't Get Carried Away While Carrying Out Your Spy Mission

The naked truth is, snooping around can be loads of fun; in fact, you can have almost too much fun under the guise of a work-related project. This is particularly true of obsessive types, of which there are teeming hordes on the Net. Just like surfing the Web itself, you can more easily than not get sidetracked or go far deeper than is necessary. In other words, if you take it too far, it can actually prove injurious to the health of your project or firm. Know when to stop.

You can get pretty far down in the trenches while gathering information on yourself, your rivals, your clients, and prospective clients. As more and more information becomes available and the tools to perform such tasks become more sophisticated and cheaper, you'll be able to go even further. The question is: How far do you want to go? Do you really want to gauge the traffic flow hitting your competitor's site? Some of you will find this extremely relevant, while others will consider it overkill. The true answer is: How valuable will the information be to you once you've mined it? If the upside is great, then go for it. If it's questionable, then forget it, or have someone else do it, or perhaps assign a piece of software to the task that regularly checks patterns and notifies you when things are noticeably different.

The Web has made information practically infinite, but there is one commodity that is very finite: your time. I suggest you set up an information-to-time or information-to-money matrix so you can identify that point of diminishing return and not exceed it. If your corporation is large, then it may well pay to have someone on staff trained to snoop around regularly. If you're a smaller firm, you might consider disciplining yourself to do only as much as you can reasonably manage on a periodic basis. You might also consider farming out to an outside source some of your specific recon missions on rivals or new business prospects. How can you find these companies on the Web? Well, just do a little digging with some of the practices learned in this chapter. You'll turn something up.

Resource Center

Competitive Intelligence Indices

Competitive Intelligence Resource Index   http://www.ciseek.com

Could it be possible to find a search engine and directory of competitive intelligence resources? 'Tis true, although almost too simple to believe. A recent search for patents, for example, turned up over a dozen sources for patent-pending information ranging from drug applications to science and technology inventions. The site is stunningly simple to use, and offers everything from online categorical resources to news, tutorials, educational programs, and a directory of CI-related companies. Bookmark this one.

Fuld & Company Internet Intelligence Index   http://www.fuld.com/i3/index.html

Think of the I3 (Internet Intelligence Index) as the research center for intelligence research. Created by Fuld & Co., an international leader in the field of competitive intelligence, this resource is designed to help you gather competitive intelligence information by providing over 600 intelligence-related Internet sites covering everything from macroeconomic data to individual patent and stock quote information. While at the site, be sure to check out other useful sections such as the intelligence dictionary, the War Room CD and general intelligence-gathering primers. As they say, competitive intelligence is "research diligence, not magic."

Financial Intelligence

Edgar Online WatchList   http://www.edgar-online.com

It's *the* source for SEC information. This personalized system allows you to customize your own portfolio of companies, industries, and SEC information, with instant notification based on the criteria you select. If it's a newly minted company you're interested in, sign up for the IPO Express to receive automatic email notification about new public offerings as they are filed, priced, postponed, or withdrawn. If it's people that you need to track, with Edgar Online People you can type in a name and instantly get back details on any executive included in an SEC filing—including salary, stock ownership, options, and sales, overall compensation packages, employment contracts, and corporate board memberships. For under $100 per month for the top-tier services, this is one source of information you can't afford to live without. Don't pass it up because of the cost, however—basic site services are free.

Company Sleuth   http://www.companysleuth.com

Company Sleuth is an online covert information specialist providing free, legal, inside information on publicly traded companies. At the site, users have the ability to stakeout and track company business activities, financial moves, Internet dealings, and legal actions. Daily customized updates are delivered via email or wireless application. After selecting the companies you would like to track, Company Sleuth will deliver information on new patents, SEC filings, earnings estimates, discussion group postings, stock quotes, analyst ratings, trademarks, job postings, press releases, business news, stock rumors, and more.

News Feeds

Individual.com   http://www.individual.com

Individual.com, now backed by office.com, is one of the Web's original resources for personalized news delivery. Simply choose your sources of interest, and you will receive a custom-built rundown of filtered news headlines (either on the Web or via email) daily. It's amazing how powerful a customized news feed can be—rather than surfing from source to source, you are sure to catch what you need to know, saving time and gaining intelligence in the bargain. Unlike many other news-clipping services, Individual.com will also include corporate news and press releases (as predetermined by your preferences) in your daily news bulletin.

Business Wire   http://www.businesswire.com

Business Wire delivers breaking news and multimedia content to traditional and online newsrooms, targeted journalists, and your desktop or wireless device. One of the original web-based industry news sources, the site has grown to offer quite an experience in state-of-the-art news delivery. Here you will find multimedia news, industry-specific reports and trends, or simply a guide to the latest business events via partner TradeShowNews.com. While at the site, be sure to check out TradeTicker, which offers quite a competitive advantage. TradeTicker features editorial exclusives generated by the more than 1,000 leading industry trade publications that are affiliated with American Business Press. These items, limited to 100 words in length, are advance previews of breaking news stories being reported by the nation's influential trade media.

PR Newswire   http://www.prnewswire.com

Much industry and competitor insight can be gained by reviewing the press releases of industry competitors. To gain a perspective on a competitor's growth strategy, visit Company News On-Call—a searchable three-year, archived database of all stories appearing on PR Newswire from participating companies. Information can be accessed as daily news, by market, or by specific areas of interest such as international, financial, or in multimedia format.

Business Intelligence

Hoover's Online   http://www.hoovers.com

Hoover's is well known as an excellent resource for company and industry information, and its Company Capsules provide information on more than 12,600 public and private companies around the world, often with extensive links to financials, operating information, and lists of key competitors. What isn't as well known is the fact that the company has extended its expertise to provide a business-oriented perspective on other topics important to users: money management, career development, news, and business. Be sure to sign up for one or more of several informative newsletters: Hoover's Today (editorial insights); Capsule of the Day (companies in the news); IPO Update (weekly IPO happenings); and Hoover's Week at a Glance.

Brint.com   http://www.brint.com

While there are many news-clipping-type services that will deliver filtered headlines to your desktop, Brint deserves special focus as a premier business and technology portal and global community network. If you can't find what you need to know about business and technology here, then you don't need to know it. The site delivers the news and more, with a special focus on business research and knowledge management. The site's claim as a "knowledge metaportal" is well deserved. Bookmark it.

Strategy

Sookoo   http://www.sookoo.com

What if you are searching for information about a concept, rather than a specific company or person? Try Sookoo, the business strategy search specialist. At this site, you can drill through categories such as big thinkers, leadership, trends, or change management—or search on just about any term you can think of. According to Sookoo, "the Strategy Search Specialist is a pioneer in a new breed of search engine—it doesn't try to be everything to everyone. It focuses on a specific content area, Business Strategy, and instead of trying to link to every related site in the world, only links quality, active sites." The right-brained thinkers among us may have just found our new best friend.

StrategyWeek.com   http://www.strategyweek.com

Sometimes competitive intelligence is not about facts and figures or cold corporate data, but more about insight and learning from the successes (and mistakes) of market leaders. StrategyWeek.com is an excellent publication that delivers compelling interviews with industry CEOs. If you are overwhelmed by the sheer volume of information you can collect during your competitive sleuthing, learn how to manage it all in an interview with Martin Brouchard, CEO of Copernic. Each interview is skillfully conducted by StrategyWeek.com founder Karen Lake. Be sure to sign up for the free update newsletter, and for a bit of inspiration, also try the CEO Daily Quote.

Internet

Axie   http://www.axie.com

Do you know how many sites are launched each week? Do you know how many of them apply to your interests? Are you going to wait for a search engine to index them to find out about a new competitor or alliance? We think not. Axie automatically extracts new listings from the Open Directory project (the definitive search engine directory resource), and delivers the ones that match your interests to you. So if you are in the business of ball bearings, you can sign up to learn about the new ball bearing-related sites published by the Open Directory well before your competition does. It's competitive intelligence at its best.

Spyonit   http://www.spyonit.com

There are many things that we need to know online, and Spyonit delivers the goods. The site's spies include the Ultimate Stock Spy, which notifies you of splits, analyst rating changes, new SEC filings, and an end-of-day price movement summary for multiple ticker symbols; the Auction Aficionado, which searches all major auctions for items of interest; the Fare Finder, whereby you can enter a departure and destination airport and get notified when the fare is below what you want to pay; stock headlines, team wildcard standings, bad weather finders, baby product recalls—and for the creativity-challenged, a create-your-own spy, which will notify you when anything on an URL of interest changes. In addition to Spyonit's proprietary technologies, fanatic fans have added their own spies to the growing offerings.

Anonymizer   http://www.anonymizer.com

Anonymizer.com is a pioneer of Internet privacy technologies, and has offered users the ability to surf the Web in a private and anonymous fashion since 1996. It's still best of breed. By going through this site to surf the Web, you effectively put a Klingon cloaking device around a body of information that would have otherwise been discernable to the web server that you are visiting. Why hide? Because you are spying, remember? Hide the make and version of your browser, the type of operating system that you use, the last site you just visited, as well as your email address. If you are spying on your competition, why let them know? A must for all cyber Sherlocks.

Reference

InfoSpace   http://www.infospace.com

InfoSpace does all sorts of intriguing things, such as reverse number lookup. Give it a phone number, and get a name (sometimes). Give it an email address, and get a physical address. Give it a name, and get an email address (but everyone does that). Give it an email, and get a name—or a list of all the email addresses at that domain name. Search for a business, and find houses, restaurants, and more near that business. While information may not always be the most current, if you are trying to learn more from a caller ID phone number or a fragment of an email address, this is an excellent tool to find out who's sleuthing who.

Society of Competitive Intelligence Professionals   http://www.scip.org

SCIP (as it's known to industry insiders) is surprisingly easy to find. Dedicated to helping professionals develop expertise in creating, collecting, and analyzing information and disseminating competitive intelligence, this professional organization is an excellent resource for industry information, articles, research, and compelling events. If you are new to the field, don't miss Competitive Intelligence for Beginners, which can be found in the *Competitive Intelligence Magazine* section.

Media

Competia   http://www.competia.com

If you can't get enough of this competitive intelligence stuff, then *Competia* magazine may be your next purchase. For a price of $89 per year, a subscription will deliver unlimited content access, monthly bookmark updates, strategic analysis templates, coupons that can be applied to events and products, and a question and answer network to personally answer your CI needs. A free one-week trial subscription is available at the site. The free Bookmarks and Links section may also prove useful; for example, if you are a CEO, a browse through the links brought three new sites to our attention—CEO Exchange, CEO Refresher, and CEO Wall Street Executive Library.

Integrating the Internet into Your Marketing

Your Brand Image and the Internet

Just because you're not Amazon.com or Nike doesn't mean you shouldn't be concerned about your branding—quite the contrary. No matter who you are or the size of your company, you should think of yourself, your firm, and your products or services as brands in this age of one-to-one marketing. You may have the best intuition about where the marketplace will move to, or the best technology, or the most cogent advice, but if you don't package yourself and your firm correctly, it'll be your own little secret.

In this chapter, we're going to start with presenting you as a package on the Net. Whether you own your own business or are part of a small or large company, the reality is that you actually work for yourself. How do you create a brand? What should you obsess over? What should you ignore? Where and how should you spend your money to promote your brand? We're going to look at new types of brands emerging on the Net, such as intermediary brands. Perhaps you should be one. But right now, let's address just one thing: You. In this chapter, you'll learn all about:

- ■ Personal branding
- ■ How the branding is in the doing
- ■ Tribal marketing
- ■ Time branding
- ■ Creating brand value
- ■ What's in a name?

- Brand migration
- Community-building
- Web design as brand extension
- Ad buys and ad networks
- Syndication models

Personal Branding

Since you have your own unique destiny, skill set, and character, it's in your best interest to present yourself as a package or a brand. It's your responsibility to identify what 1950s advertising legend and author of *Realities in Advertising* (Knopf, 1961) Rosser Reeves called the *Unique Selling Proposition* (USP) for that brand called you. The Net will help you, if it doesn't force you, to concentrate on what benefits you offer to which constituencies. Whether you're in manufacturing or modeling, the key to establishing your personal brand on the Net is *reputation*.

Why is your personal USP so important? Branding guru Tom Peters, author of *The Brand You 50: Fifty Ways to Transform Yourself from an "Employee" into a Brand that Shouts Distinction and Passion!* (Knopf, 1999) predicts that over the next ten years, 90 percent of all white collar jobs will be eliminated (see Figure 5.1). It's akin to what happened to hand laborers during the Industrial Revolution. They were replaced by machinery, and

Figure 5.1   According to Tom Peters, "you either stand out or you are road kill on the information highway."

Used by permission of tompeterscompany!

those who did not adapt or learn new skills were left behind. The Internet has done the same for the white collar worker, as technological advances have made much of middle management obsolete. Workers can no longer expect to retire with a pension and a gold watch after 45 years of service to corporate life. You are as good as your last project, your unique skill set, and the creativity with which you market and brand yourself.

If you do work for a corporation, you will want to carefully measure what is appropriate for you to do as you brand yourself, so as not to conflict with your company's products or services. However, as Tom Peters rightly points out, branding yourself as an expert in a particular area is a USP both internally and to your company's clients. If you are known as the person to count on to produce high quality work in a particular area of expertise, that is your brand—and one that reflects positively upon yourself, your manager, and your company.

Branding Defined

Before we begin our branding journey, let's first define exactly what *branding* is. According to Phil Carpenter, author of *eBrands: Building an Internet Business at Breakneck Speed* (Harvard Business School Press, 2000) branding is more than just a name, a logo, or a tagline. "Crafting a powerful online brand requires paying just as much attention to developing other facts of the brand as well, such as customer loyalty and influential distribution processes," Carpenter states.

In reality, the branding is in the doing. The branding of you, your company, and your product or service takes place every time you touch your customer. Whether you are building awareness through a branding/marketing/advertising campaign, moving traffic through your site, engaging in actual transactions, providing customer care or follow-up support, or building an ongoing relationship with your customers, every single encounter creates a positive or negative brand impression. You must craft and manage your brand to create a positive impression at every stage of your business process.

The financial incentive to create a successful brand is enormous. Consider the numbers: global consumer commerce is projected to generate $1.3 trillion a year by 2003; business-to-business commerce is predicted to reach $1.5 trillion that same year. The Internet advertising sector should hit close to $22 billion in annual revenues by 2004. Who do you buy from or advertise with? The brand that you know and trust—the brand that consistently delivers a positive experience. The days of flash-in-the-pan branding, where $20 million advertising budgets blasted a dot com name out into the universe—with little return or value to the customer—are long gone. The competition for customer loyalty and actual revenues online is fierce. Good branding will get you there faster.

Big Place, Small Place

"The Internet is a very big place. The Internet is a very small place," observes long-time Net columnist Daniel P. Dern. What does he mean? In the aggregate, the Internet is a huge environment, now too large for any one person to fully comprehend; in fact, it's kind of intimidating in that way. However, you shouldn't be concerned with branding yourself to every being on the Net; that's too unfocused. Your mission is to laser-target one, two, or three niches within that huge biosphere and concentrate your power, your expertise, and your brand within those spaces. In this way, the Net is a small place, kind of like a village. Unix wizard Chris Graham calls this "Tribal Marketing." In this tribe or village, reputation is everything. You don't want to risk ruining your reputation for short-term gains at the expense of losing your long-term face. Contribute to your tribe. Figure out what your target tribe needs, and then fill that need if you can—whether with a website, an email newsletter, or a moderated discussion list.

Courtney Pulitzer, founder of Courtney Pulitzer Creations, describes this phenomenon well. "I started in a small pond with a good core group of people, and focused on delivering value to the people in the room—not to the millions and millions of 'eyeballs' out there," Pulitzer explains. "I think of my business as not so much of a hard sell, but as a conversation, a human connection. I don't worry about 'closing the deal' at every meeting. People get to know me, and they are then impressed enough to do business with me. If you make the connection, the sales will come."

TIP Go to where your constituents *aren't*! It's very well and good to talk to your peers, but, if they're like you, you'll learn from each other but you may not close many deals. That's why new media lawyers, such as Jonathan Ezor, belong to online ad discussion lists, as well as law lists. They have affinities with marketers because they're intellectual property lawyers. They establish a presence with potential clients, which is very smart on their behalf.

Personal Branding Strategies

Begin your personal branding by asking yourself the following:

- What makes you unique and valuable? What are your "brand assets"?
- Can you describe your USP in ten words or less?
- Will your target market find this USP valuable? More valuable than your competitor's USP? Why?
- Who is like you and what are they doing out there to promote themselves? What can you learn from them? What mistakes of theirs should you avoid?
- What do you want from your target audience? Referrals? Sales? Leads for jobs or potential clients? Or simply to expand your network and learn from what Tom Peters calls "cool dudes and dudettes"?

These needs are all very valid reasons to employ the Net to propagate your brand and your USP.

Getting Your Name Out There

To further illustrate this, let me give you a page out of my own book (so to speak). I started my newsletter, *Web Digest For Marketers,* in 1994. It was a $50 subscription service at the time. When the *Wall Street Journal* put its entire paper online, and then some, for $49.95 per year, I realized that the boom had been lowered on the cost of content for the consumer. So I made the newsletter free. However, before doing so, the legendary Dick Rich (cofounder of Wells Rich Green Advertising) advised me to change it to *Larry Chase's Web Digest For Marketers.* Now my name is seen, at a conservative estimate, by over 150,000 marketers every month. Over 2,000 sites point to my publication. This is about a hundred times more than the number of sites that point to my actual company web page. What's the branding lesson here? Give something away of value and put your name prominently on it. WDFM accounted for a large percentage of my consulting and seminar work last year. Obviously, carefully strategized personal branding can and will pay off.

WDFM gives me a *sphere of influence,* which is all-important to establishing your personal brand. People ask me to review their sites, and over 30,000 people receive WDFM by email every week. I must admit I am delighted when people come up to me at trade shows and seminars and tell me how much they appreciate the service. It opens a dialogue through which potential business can and does flow.

I try to have a wide range of services or products—a Larry Menu, if you will—that my readers can purchase; in fact, you're reading one of these products. It may be a website review, advertising space in my newsletter, a seminar, or a retainer relationship. I try to let the customer buy whatever type package of me that he or she can

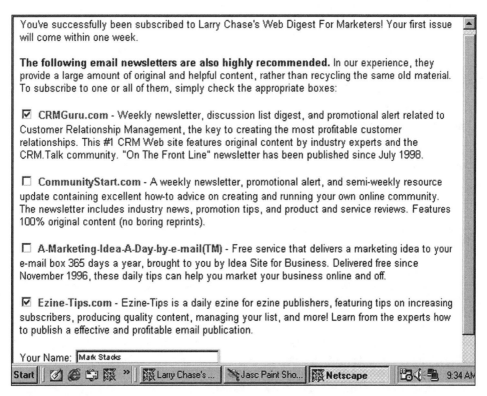

Figure 5.2 WDFM's thank you page suggests other email newsletters that the subscriber might find useful.

afford. If they can't afford, or don't want to afford, anything right then, fine. They get a free subscription to the email edition of WDFM. Some will never buy anything. But you know what? That's OK, because I even make money from their free subscriptions by selling advertising in WDFM.

Whenever people do subscribe to WDFM, they first see a thank you page that also suggests other high quality newsletters that they might be interested in subscribing to (see Figure 5.2). Not only does this build great relations between myself and other newsletter publishers, but it also exposes the new subscriber to very useful information that they may not have otherwise known about—therefore, delivering value within seconds of their new WDFM subscription.

New subscribers also get an email back from me, confirming their subscription and telling them a little bit about the other products and services that I offer. Notice how the welcome message informs the reader about things he or she will predictably want to know about WDFM while at the same time embedding information about me and my services.

```
Dear New Subscriber,

I'm Larry Chase. Thank you for subscribing to my Web Digest For Mar-
keters (WDFM). Every week, you'll get WDFM via email. Each issue usu-
ally contains 15 short reviews of the latest business-oriented sites.
Each review (usually not longer than 120 words) offers a constructive
critique of a site that might be useful to you. Some of the categories
covered are: E-Commerce, Finance, Media, Advertising, Research, Auto-
motive, Hi-Tech/Telecom, Recruitment, Outstanding Content, Smart Use
of the Net, Trends and more.

I've been publishing WDFM since April 1995. It was the first publica-
tion of its kind and has been syndicated throughout the industry to
publications such as Ad Age and Business Marketing Magazine and DM
News. Over 100,000 people read WDFM reviews monthly. Many hundreds of
websites point to wdfm.com. The New York Times, USA Today, CBS, CNN,
CNBC, Business Week, Bottom Line Business and scores of other well-
known magazines, journals, and newsletters have quoted, reviewed or
recommended WDFM.

WDFM's parent company is Chase Online Marketing Strategies, which
offers Internet seminars and consulting. I speak in the U.S. and
Europe mostly, but will go anywhere. Just ask me. :) My most popular
seminars are those where I customize the presentation for the audience
I'm addressing. Fidelity Investments, KPMG Peat Marwick, Internet
World, American Society of Travel Agents, Nationwide Insurance and
PG&E are all events and organizations that have had me present.

My consulting clients include Electrolux, Con Edison, EDS, New York
Life and 3com. They often ask me to help them determine what a company
like theirs should be doing in a medium like the Net right now, and
down the road. I call this "Market Mapping."

My book, "Essential Business Tactics for the Net," is published by
John Wiley and is on bestseller lists at both Amazon.com and
```

```
Barnesandnoble.com. It's been quoted or reviewed on CBS, ABC,
Bloomberg (TV and radio), Publisher's Weekly, Crain's New York Busi-
ness, Worth Magazine, and a slew of other media outlets. It's also
been excerpted in DM News, Target Marketing Magazine, Promo Magazine,
and a few others. For an excerpt and Table of Contents, visit
http://LarryChase.com.

I could go on, but I won't. :) If you do want more information on my
consulting and seminar services, please visit http://chaseonline.com
or email me at larry@wdfm.com. In the meantime, enjoy my Web Digest
For Marketers.

Cordially,
Larry Chase
CEO, Chase Online Marketing Strategies
Voice: (212) 876-1096 Fax: (212) 876-1098
Free subscription - Web Digest For Marketers - http://wdfm.com
"Essential Business Tactics for the Net" sample chapter at
http://LarryChase.com.

PS—If you'd like to see a rate card for advertising in WDFM,
mailto:steveng@wdfm.com and put "rate card" in the subject header.
```

Respecting Your Tribe

One of the most crucial components to consider in the presentation of your personal branding message is to respect people's time. Time is our most valuable commodity. *Time Branding,* or how well you handle people's time, is an important concept. Since many of us don't have the reputation of Procter & Gamble or IBM, we're obliged to tell a visitor to our site what we do, why we do it, and how we do it. Often, personal and small company sites are rather vague when it comes to telling the visiting surfer what exactly it is that they do. Some may feel that they are creating buzz by presenting a mysterious front. I also frequently run into flowery mission statements that sound too self-absorbed: "This company was founded on a deep-seated philosophy that every-thing is everything. . ." Believe me, your site visitors will get bored and end up going somewhere else rather than play the mysterious "what does this company do?" guess-ing game. This is why it is imperative to predict what visitors to your site want and to present it in a clear and concise manner. In short, be your customer, or potential cus-tomer, then create a site that you would want to visit.

You are probably more at ease when a telemarketer says, "Ms. So and So, I know you're busy, so I'm not going to take much of your time." The exact same thing is true on the Net, both on the Web and in email. The A&E cable TV network has a great tagline: "Time Well Spent." Adopt this principle in all your online and offline endeav-ors. Is my time on your site well spent? If I have to grope around to find your point, it isn't. If I have to wait for your graphics to load on my slow or average modem connec-tion, it isn't. But if you give me a *time experience* that pays off by adding value, it is. Fig-ure out what *it* is and serve it up sooner rather than later.

This goes for email, too. Get to the point fast. People respect focus and speed. When I see an email from someone who is always asking for something, I tend not to open it right away. . .if ever. The old cultural protocol of the Net still holds: Give in order to receive. This doesn't mean you have to give the family farm away, far from it, but do give something if you expect people to give to you—either their time spent in looking at your site, or later, perhaps, a favor you may need from them that falls in their purview, even if all it is is a reciprocal link to your site, or, heaven forbid, a sale. The concept of using your email communications to extend your brand message is what I call Inbox Branding, and with over 70 million emails being sent per day, you should never, ever underestimate the power of your email communications.

Whether in a discussion list of your peers, a one-to-one email, or on your site, people in this medium respect you for having done your homework. This is rarely explicitly stated, but definitely is a truism. If you ask questions of a discussion list that could've been found elsewhere with ease, you're either a newbie or lazy. If you're a newbie, that list will hopefully treat you with respect and point you to the information, usually in the form of the list's Frequently Asked Questions (FAQ). If you're lazy and repeatedly take without giving, you start to tarnish your personal brand in that community, which consists of the very people you wish to influence. It is to your advantage to be prepared. Be patient with newbies once you're no longer one—as with everything on the Net, it can and probably will pay off down the road. You never know where a potential contact lies.

Be Memorable

Put your name, contact information, and USP or some offer of value in your signature at the end of all your email messages as well as any newsgroup postings. I have booked seminar engagements simply because someone read my signature file.

When naming your firm or site, give it an obvious name from a branding perspective. "Larry Chase's Web Digest For Marketers" tells you exactly what you get. It's also helpful for optimum search engine positioning, as explained in Chapter 7, "Online Events, Promotions, and Attractions." Clever names are too cryptic for this day and age. KN2KB Inc. may look cool today, but you don't want a trendy name that will look like a has-been tomorrow. People like names that spell out exactly what a company does, such as Eric Ward's URLwire Service, or John Kremer's Book Marketing Tip of the Week.

Branding and marketing gurus Tom and Laura Ries have devoted an entire book to branding online, entitled *The 11 Immutable Laws of Internet Branding* (Harper Business, 2000). The chapter on site naming is a thought-provoking rehash of the early days of dot com domain snatching. In reality, what is so memorable about business.com (sold for $7 million) or sports.com? The authors advise website owners to "own a word" in their market, and to build their brand around that word. The word should be memorable and unique. It might even be your own name.

Dr. Tony Alessandra, an internationally renowned sales and motivational speaker, has expertly leveraged the Web to present his brand image (http://www .alessandra.com). Alessandra's site sets a branding standard by truly expressing his personality in design and function. Raised in New York City's Hell's Kitchen, Alessandra went on to initially develop a professorial attitude, which came across in his personal brand. He then made a strategic decision to "go back to his roots" and express his more mischievous, streetwise self. His more playful approach to personal branding resulted in the site's most popular features—the personality profile tests and charisma quotient.

Alessandra's site serves as a business center to showcase his speaking, products, and books—all components of his brand. He has successfully utilized multimedia to highlight these elements, which is far more effective than plain text descriptions. For example, at the site visitors will find audio and video clips of Alessandra's previous engagements (the videos get accessed more frequently), audio testimonials, and a digital press kit complete with audio clips. Companies considering him for a speaking engagement can easily see him in action right at the site. Many times, a committee will evaluate potential speakers, which previously meant that at least one, and possibly several, videocassettes had to be sent out upon request. The digital press kit has eliminated the time and expense of creating and mailing hundreds of tapes, as each individual can review and evaluate Alessandra's "brand" at their own convenience.

Address for Success:
What's in a Domain Name?

Branding for individuals and companies begins right here, with your domain name. If you're an individual and your name is still available as a domain name, grab it. If it isn't, and if you want to use your personal name as your brand identity, then get something close to it, such as your first initial and last name before the .com, or use a hyphen between first and last names. You may not use the domain name right away, but it's good to have it reserved for you. At the time of writing, this costs $35 per year to own the name. When I found eight other Larry Chases on the Net, I went directly to the InterNIC (http://www.internic.com) to see if any other Larry Chases had registered larrychase.com. They hadn't. So I did. You can also check for domain registration at Whois.net. There you can search by keyword to find those who have a domain name similar to yours.

Try not to obsess over your domain name. Yes, it is important and pivotal to everything you do with regard to branding, but if someone has already registered your last name (more than likely), or your first and last name, or your company name, relax. It isn't the end of the world. Netscape was called Mosaic Communications in the beginning. Its domain name was mcomm.com. The company was pressured not to use the name of the original web browser developer. It agreed and became Netscape Corporation at http://www.netscape.com—although do keep in mind that a name change down the road can be a tedious undertaking.

TIP If you are domain name-obsessed, there are many others like you out there, and many services are available to help you find a domain name that meets your needs. DomainGames (http://www.domaingames.com) is a domain name search engine and manager. You can search for specific or partial names, monitor daily new domains and dropped domains, and sign on for the value-added service of domain name management and tracking.

Be as Accessible as Possible

Keep in mind, when choosing your domain name, that people are going to get to your site from a number of different directions, just as they travel to your company or house using different routes. Some people will come in by the search engine route, while others may have already bookmarked you in their browsers. Many will try to go directly to you by typing what they think your web address is in their browser's address field. For example, if you wanted to go to Fidelity Investments, you might assume you know what its domain name is and simply type www.fidelity.com—and you get there. However, this easy route wasn't always the case for Fidelity. Its original address was www.fid-inv.com. I once wanted to write an article that included the wide array of calculators Fidelity offers on its site. It was after business hours and I was on a deadline. For the life of me, I couldn't find Fidelity's address even using my extensive expertise with search engines. Therefore, Fidelity missed out on a great free reference due to an arcane domain name. It did eventually add the "fidelity" domain name, which stands in its favor—although these days such a straightforward domain name may no longer be available.

> **TIP** Be aware of all current top-level domains. At the time of this writing, .com, .net, and .org are the three top-level (non-country-related) domain suffixes available, although the Internet Corporation for Assigned Names and Numbers (ICANN) has approved .aero, .coop, .museum, .name, .pro, .info, and .biz. If possible, we suggest that you register your domain name with as many extensions as possible to prevent others from purchasing any version of your hard-won name. Do try for .com, however, as that extension is top of mind with people and will be for some time, in the same way that it is preferable to have an 800 number over an 888 or 877 toll-free alternative. Ultimately, the old and new extensions will become interchangeable, once they've all propagated thoroughly. Having said all that, it is better to have underwear.biz than TheLongestAndMostForgettableURLinHistory.com. It's still more important to get a sound business model together than some (supposedly) easy-to-remember domain name. Can you spell gazoontite.com? I remember it, I can't spell it, and even if I could, it would have gone out of business anyway.

When you are registering your domain name, think of every conceivable way that a person might enter your site's name into the browser. Not only do I have www.chaseonline.com, but I also have www.chase-online.com. Have your address set up with and without the www. prefix. Those Ws are not necessary to make a web URL connection, even though many think they are.

Keep in mind that many people are still fuzzy about the difference between a website address and an email address. You must communicate your email and web address in the lowest common denominator when talking to your constituents. Simply saying, "Go to chaseonline-dot-com" can confuse your audience, although it is becoming more acceptable in advertising, marketing, and the media. When possible, clearly specify that larry@chaseonline.com is the email address and that http://chaseonline.com is the web address. And *s-p-e-l-l i-t o-u-t*! Many times, a domain name may sound like it could be spelled or hyphenated in several different ways. For example, Shop4Shoes .com contains a numeral rather than the spelling of the word "for," as one might expect. Also be aware of the different ways that people may read your domain name. "RightsExchange" may seem like a good domain name until it is read as "RightSex-Change," for instance. It is vitally important that your domain name is very clearly conveyed both verbally and in print so that your audience can find you.

If the name you want is already taken as a domain, think of a "solution name" that people can remember, such as www.NoBugsNow.com if you're an exterminator. In retrospect, you may even find it was a better way to go. Once you settle on your domain name, keep it. I can tell you from personal experience that it's a nightmare to change it after you've let it propagate online and offline. For example, *Web Digest For Marketers* used to reside at http://advert.com/wdfm. When I moved it to its own domain name at http://wdfm.com, I had to tell hundreds of sites to change their links. There are still wayward souls who bookmarked the old URL and found out about the change over a very long period of time. I have had to set up pages that redirect them to the new site. My logs show that every day, people still go to the old address, even though I changed the domain name years ago. Remember, you will also need to change all your stationery, business cards, collateral, and advertising materials. The lesson here: Think very hard before you change your domain name. It's like changing your street address or phone number, but worse.

Putting Your Domain Name to Good Use

Once you have your domain name registered, use it across everything: your web address, email, mailing lists, stationery, business cards, printed collateral, and so on. Remember that conformity is the key. If your site has one domain name, such as Red-SledCompany.com, and your email address is BigBobMan@aol.com, you have a few options to marry the two to prevent branding confusion for your clients.

You could get an Internet Service Provider to host your website on its server. This server may hold hundreds of other sites, each with its own domain name, which is called a *virtual domain*. At the time of writing, this option costs between $20 and $40 per month for a relatively small site. Make sure you can access and edit your site from your own desktop so you don't get tied in to using the provider's services for each and every change you wish to make to your web pages, unless you want to buy their services and let them do that work for you. Then, ask your provider how much it will cost to forward email addressed to your domain name to your existing mail account (such as in the previous example, in which the person has a domain registered and hosted on a server under the domain name, but has email going to AOL). It shouldn't be much—most providers will actually give you up to five or so email aliases, as they are called, for free. So you can set up info@redsledcompany.com, sales@redsledcompany.com, and so on, and have them point to your existing email account. Your site visitors will not know that you are actually receiving that email at an AOL account.

Keep in mind, however, that when you reply to those who have sent email to your virtual domain name, they will see that you're emailing from AOL. You can set up another system in reverse with your provider to prevent this from happening. This means that your mail sent back will first have to be routed to your provider, and then sent out from there to the recipient. The extra routing shouldn't take much longer than going directly.

> **TIP** A virtual domain is one that resides on someone else's web server, but the address is the domain you registered and own. In other words, a client will type in http://www.yourdomain.com into his or her browser, and arrive at your site. However, if you are housed as a virtual domain on, say, panix.com's server, it's really going to panix.com, even though the URL shows your domain name.

Or, instead of setting up this labyrinth, you may want to simply have an Internet account with a provider that hosts your site with your domain name, as well as provides you with Internet access with an email account that uses your own domain name. (For instance, you could be both http://www.RedSledCompany.com and big-bob@redsledcompany.com, using that method.)

Many Internet access providers offer you 5 or 10 megabytes of space on a web server when you get an Internet access account. The downside is that although I may have an email address of larchase@blueclambox.com, my website will be http://www .blueclambox.com/user/chase/index.html, unless I pay to have a virtual domain created for me on my ISP's server. This is a cheap way to go (between $20 and $35 a month usually), but try giving someone a web address like that verbally! It's like renting a post office box. If you can possibly afford it, be your own person with your own domain name.

If you have a mailing list, use a service that can *spoof* your email address. Spoofing or faking your email address is done to make it seem as though your email is coming from you when in fact it's coming from a third party. This is helpful if you outsource your mailing list and want it to seem as if it is coming directly from you when, in fact, it's coming from the provider of the list service. In other words, pretend your company is called Red Carpet, and your mailing list address is admin@RedCarpet.com, but SparkLIST is housing and sending out your mailings for you. You want to make sure that the return address, as well as the originating address, shows as RedCarpet, not SparkLIST! Remember to use branding to prevent, not cause, confusion.

> **TIP** You can easily start a mailing list for free. Companies such as eGroups (http://www.egroups.com) will let you send your mailings to your subscribers for free in exchange for putting one of its ads at the bottom of each message. Cheap? Yes. Confusing for the reader? Very. Easy to work around? Yes. At the time of this writing, a $4.95 monthly payment removes all advertising from your eGroups email list. Alternate inexpensive email list options are reviewed in Chapter 8, "Direct Marketing and Sales Support."

Protecting Your Domain

If you choose a name that you believe someone else will challenge, you should protect yourself. Right now, if another firm challenges your right to a domain name, the Inter-NIC informs you that you have 30 days to vacate the domain while the dispute is settled. At that point, it will be in a type of stasis until the dispute is resolved. In order to prevent this, you may want to quickly protect yourself by trademarking or service-marking the letters or words that make up your domain name. Do note: If you register it through the U.S. Patent and Trademark Office, your potential adversary may pick this up on a standard trademark search if he is looking for such things, and many do. However, it is in your best interests to protect your brand name(s) as much as you can, especially as trademark rules and regulations as they pertain to the Internet will be battled for a long time to come.

Okay, enough about your domain logistics; let's talk about your company's image on the Net.

Your Company's Image and the Internet: Brand Migration

Obviously, most offline brands must consider the migration to the online world, if they have not done so already. In addition, many online brands are migrating to offline channels such as retail stores or catalogs in order to reach a wider audience via multiple channels.

Brands that have migrated from the offline to the online world are known as *crossover* brands. According to Phil Carpenter, author of *eBrands: Building an Internet Business at Breakneck Speed*, crossover brands that expand their businesses to take advantage of the Web share three best practices:

Respect for core brand elements. The unique attributes of the brand are equally recognizable both online and off. One example is BarnesandNoble.com, whose site echoes the colors, look, and presence of the store branding and packaging, and whose popular in-store author readings have been duplicated in online chats at the website. The shopping experience presented to customers is reinforced from one medium to the next.

One-up the offline brand. The Web provides enormous potential for interactivity with your customers—interactivity that may not be feasible in an offline environment. Can you really talk one-on-one with Martha Stewart through the pages of her magazine, during her TV show, or via her products on the shelves of Kmart? No, but you can interact with an entire Martha community and with Martha and her special guests at her site—and you can also purchase her products right there.

Leverage key offline assets. Offline businesses enjoy assets that pure online players do not have—for example, a physical presence in the real world that can be branded with your URL, such as you will find in all of the Gap stores around the world. Many businesses are embracing what Knowledge Strategies Group (http://www.kstrat.com) calls an *omnitailing* approach to business by creating an integrated brand message across multiple channels. This is what coauthor Eileen Shulock calls the *portable brand*, meaning that the brand, products, and services are available no matter where you are—at home on your computer, on your cell phone or your PDA, in the real-world location, or browsing a catalog.

One of the first things you have to ask yourself is whether you should keep your brand name as the domain name or *Net-ize* it. Columbia House (music company) uses its name as a domain name. Its mission online is quite clear: sell music and entertainment products. But what about a company that makes detergent? Do you really expect Tide to sell its detergent on its website? If not, then what is its raison d'être? Procter & Gamble answers this challenge well. They have created a portal (http://www.pg.com) to house more than 300 P&G brands (see Figure 5.3). There you will find all kinds of helpful tips and tools "sponsored by" the various P&G brands. Need to know how to launder safely? You'll find out from Tide.com. In addition, the site serves as a test bed for new products and services before they reach the real-world stores, which allows Procter & Gamble to work with their online customer base to test market new ideas and products. This brand smartly made the migration from offline to online. That's not a bad impression to leave with a consumer. Who says you can't do good branding for "low-involvement packaged goods," such as laundry detergent, on the Net?

Finally, many pure online players have seen the advantages that a real-world presence can offer. Whether by expanding into a print magazine or catalog that can be held in the hands of offline consumers, such as done by The Knot and RedEnvelope, or by expanding into real-world stores or offices such as eTrade.com, online businesses are quickly beginning to realize that it's a big world out there, and not all of it is online. Branding—and business in general—needs to take place at every possible point where the target audience can be reached.

If you do expand your online offerings, make sure they all support each other in some way. I use management and sales consultant Barney Zick's "Three-Legged Stool"

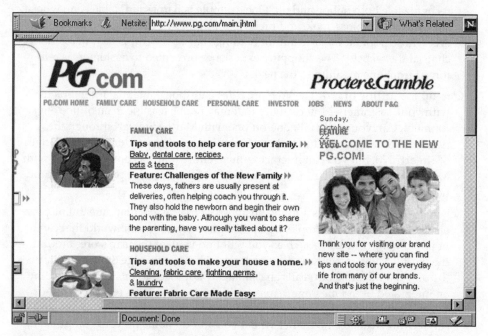

Figure 5.3   Procter & Gamble's portal is a good example of how offline consumer goods find a niche online.

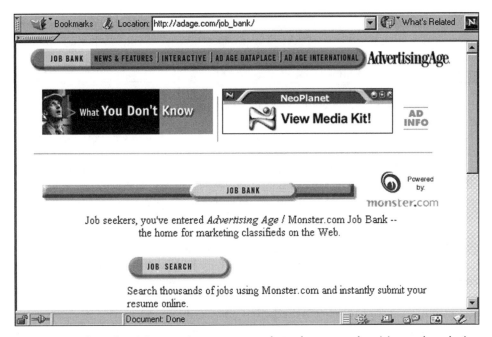

Figure 5.4 The *Advertising Age*/Monster.com Job Bank targets advertising and marketing professionals in search of new jobs.
Reproduced with permission. © 2000 Crain Communications, Inc.

analogy. Each line or leg of business helps the next one. My publishing activities help my consulting and speaking lines of business, and vice versa. Be sure to create a top-level brand, or *umbrella* brand, with a consistent name and image. Your secondary services or products should comfortably reside under your umbrella brand, so that you are not suddenly in the business of promoting multiple brand names.

Another way to extend your brand is to ally with a complementary line of business. For example, the *Advertising Age* magazine site (http://www.adage.com) has a jobs section. *Ad Age* didn't want to actually get into the jobs database business, so it set up a cooperative arrangement with the Monster Board jobs database, found at http://www.monsterboard.com and also at http://www.monster.com—another example of registering two site domain names that refer to only one URL. The *Ad Age* site delivers added value to its readers, while giving some exposure to the Monster Board database (see Figure 5.4).

One way you can raise the barrier of entry for your competitors is to excel so far ahead of them that the cost of entry to leapfrog over you becomes prohibitive. In fact, the worth of your brand may well be assessed by how much it would cost to duplicate or exceed it.

Marketing Professional Services on the Net

Let's face it, a lawyer or highly paid consultant is going to have image problems if he or she starts sending out coupons in those Carolyn Wright card decks you get in your regular mailbox. On the Internet, however, professionals and their services are right at home when expanding their reach to new prospects. Why? Because whether you're a lawyer, accountant, or highly paid consultant, you're in the information business. The Internet handles information very well, as you know.

The consulting firm of Ernst & Young not only represents all its divisions online, but also fashioned an entirely new product called "Ernie." Ernie gives you unlimited email access to specialists at Ernst & Young for $6,000 a year. From there, you have the option of upgrading to telephone access for more money. I must admit, I was very skeptical of this in the beginning, as it was my thinking that Ernie diluted the prestige of Ernst & Young's offline brand. I was wrong. In fact, quite the contrary is true; Ernie has turned into a success. Ernie has been instrumental in bringing in new business, not only at the email level, but also by upgrading services to higher forms of contact, including phone access, where the dollar volume is more substantial. This is brilliant!

Creative Good (http://www.creativegood.com) is an Internet consulting firm focused on customer experience. The company consults with websites from American Express to Macys.com to help improve site usability and overall experience. Resulting improvements have raised conversion rates (and other metrics, like revenues) between 40 and 150 percent. Creative Good has established itself in the industry as the expert on the customer experience, and its marketing efforts support that strategy. At the Creative Good site, industry professionals eagerly await free white papers on everything from the "Wireless Customer Experience" to the "Dot Com Survival Guide." The site's many free resources, as well as the informative white papers, make Creative Good's site a destination for the Internet industry—and effectively market the firm's consulting services (see Figure 5.5).

Figure 5.5 Creative Good's mission to improve the online customer's experience is supported with savvy marketing of its professional services.
© 2000 Creative Good, Inc.

Starting a Brand Online

Yahoo!, Excite, CNET, Amazon, Netscape—these names weren't in our vernacular just a few years ago. In fact, if you went back in time five years and listened to yourself today, you probably wouldn't understand much of what you're saying: "HTTP this . . . "; "email that. . ."; " . . .what about WWW?" Will your online brand become a household word in five years? Anything's possible. Yahoo! (Yet Another Hierarchical Officious Oracle) was started by two college students at Stanford University as simply a browsable search directory compiled by humans. Originally, the two founders set a goal to add 1,000 sites per day to their directory. Seems quaint in retrospect, as today it gets 40 million page views a day. I think it's more likely that your brand will resonate within a specific category; so while your brand may not turn into a household name, it should be a well-respected one on key desktops.

If you're going to start up a brand, you must practice due diligence. In other words, use the cybersleuthing skills taught in Chapter 4, "http://007: Spying on Your Competitors and Yourself," and find out everything you can about those who are already in that niche. Be hard on them and even harder on yourself. What do you offer that they don't? Is it enough to make a difference? Also, beware if there are no competitors. It may be that you've stumbled onto a niche first. Then again, maybe someone else found it and decided not to proceed. Why? What did they find out? Or was it just not right for them and might be for you? This is what I mean by being tough on yourself. Management and marketing consultant Mac Ross once told me, "Beware of having no competition: there may be a reason."

> **TIP** What we recommend here is blasphemy to site developers: If you have limited funds, spend less on the bells and whistles of your site and considerably more on marketing. By marketing, we don't mean one blast of marketing at launch, but rather an ongoing promotional program that keeps you in front of your target group on an ongoing basis. If you don't have the amount of gunpowder needed to do this, you may want to rethink your business plan. The world will not click a path to your site unless it knows about it.

If you do launch a brand that starts out online, you should seriously consider whether it "has legs." That is, can you extend the brand online as well as offline? Excite Corporation started out as a search engine. Now it has expanded into offering chat and email. This is something I would never have thought of: "Hey, let's go hang out by the search engine and chat." Wouldn't you assume that someone who gets to a search engine has email already? I would, yet the growth of free email accounts and services as provided by every search service portal is explosive. Perhaps people are using the Excite accounts as stealth accounts for competitive reconnaissance, heeding our own advice from the last chapter!

Look at how Yahoo! has extended its brand, both on and offline. My Yahoo! offers a filtering service for news and press release wires. A journalist recently said to me in passing that he likes to get his sports news from My Yahoo! Could this take away at least a little piece of *attention-share* from *Sports Illustrated*, or the sports section of a newspaper? You bet it could, and it does. Attention-share is otherwise known as time, which is a finite commodity. Therefore, this fight is a zero-sum game; if I get 10 minutes of your time, some other site, channel, station, or newspaper loses that 10 minutes. Chances are I will get 10 minutes of your time every day when you return to see updated scores and statistics for your teams of interest. That's 3,650 minutes per year. Successful online brands can and do take away customers and attention-share from offline brands, if utilized properly.

Additionally, the people working at Yahoo! have extended their brand awareness smartly offline. I heard a radio commercial here in New York City telling me to go to the web page of "Yahoo! New York" for more details on its local retail outlet. While visiting Maidstone Arms, a country inn in East Hampton, Long Island, I saw free postcards with the name of the inn on it and the printed question: "Have You Yahoo!'d today?" *Yahooligans!* and *Yahoo! Internet Life* are online sites and print magazines. Yahoo! is so ubiquitous a brand now that it is oozing out of the walls. It's using branding the way it's meant to be used, as a preconditioner. When Net newbies come online, they'll check out Yahoo! because it's familiar from offline campaigns. They'll let their kids read *Yahooligans!* because, after all, Yahoo! has a reputation to protect. Therefore, it is a trusted product. That trust traces directly back to branding.

Online Intermediary Brands

It's commonly thought that the Net "disintermediates" middlemen. It's true, it does. Most people with the words *agent, reseller,* or *broker* in their names should take note. Indeed, the Internet is creating a certain amount of friction between manufacturers and their respective sales channels because those manufacturers see the potential for selling directly to the end user, without the help or commissions of the middlemen. Fortunately, the Net is also opening up new opportunities for middlemen. These middlemen don't usually need much inventory. Their job is to bring buyer to seller, just like in traditional terms.

One example of an intermediary brand is Kozmo (http://www.kozmo.com), which is essentially a local storefront stocked with brand name products such as videos, magazines, drugstore items, and food (see Figure 5.6). What Kozmo does is deliver the products that I order to my door within an hour. Kozmo is essentially a messenger intermediary that acts as a middleman between location-bound retailers and too-lazy-or-too-busy-to-leave-the-office consumers. Coauthor Eileen Shulock rarely sees the outdoors during her business day—everything from lunch to errand services to Xeroxing and printing are ordered over the Web and delivered right to her desk.

Quotesmith (http://www.quotesmith.com) is a different kind of middleman brand, this time for insurance. Here again, it offers value to both buyer and seller. The seller—in this case, the insurance companies with whom Quotesmith has a commissionable broker relationship—gets prospects it otherwise wouldn't have. The browsing customer, who is probably doing research on what sort of insurance to buy, gets loads of good information to help him make up his mind. Now, insurance is a grudge purchase if ever there was one, but when you get down to doing your homework, you're going to appreciate someplace like Quotesmith assisting in that task.

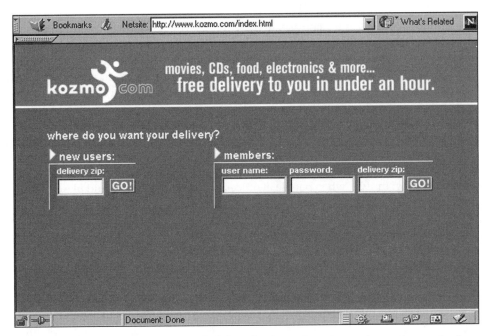

Figure 5.6 Intermediary Kozmo will deliver food, movies, electronics, and more for free, in under an hour.

© 2000 Kozmo.com, Inc.

Some new middlemen are direct challenges to old middlemen. Trade Show Central (http://www.tscentral.com) is one such example. Before it existed, you had to buy a costly print directory of all trade shows in the United States that had to be frequently updated. Now that information is not only free at Trade Show Central but it's also more timely, as updates are made daily to the database of trade shows and events worldwide. This is an interesting example of what I call *contiguous cannibalism,* referred to in Chapter 7, "Online Events, Promotions, and Attractions." Succinctly put, contiguous cannibalism causes one man's core business to be another's loss leader. Trade Show Central gives away what the bound volume charges for so that Trade Show Central can get your attention for its advertisers. In the near future, look for online brands to expand into other lines of business that feed them income. It isn't too hard to imagine an overnight shipping company offering free catalog software and even website housing for your catalog if you give it your shipping business. We've already seen long-distance telephone companies offer Internet access as a loss leader in exchange for your long-distance business. We now predict that cellular phone providers will soon give away cellular phones and service in exchange for the ability to advertise directly to the user.

Marketing to Yourself: When Should You?

Years ago, I got into an argument with an ex-vice president of NBC. He said the Net would never become the norm. I said he had missed the point. The Net wouldn't be a single norm, but thousands of norms. In these niches, you are quite apt to be marketing to people who are just like you. When you're setting up marketing strategies and sites from now on, you should ask yourself if you would click on that banner or investigate that site. Do you like waiting 40 seconds for a screen to load on your computer? No? Then it's a good bet your target group won't either. But it goes much deeper than that.

As mentioned earlier, be tough on yourself. If you aren't, your prospects and clients will be. Be predictive in what your audience wants. After all, they share many traits with you. Don't just give them what they want at the time they are expected to ask for it. Delight them by giving them something they didn't expect. Don't leave it entirely to market research to tell you exactly what they're going to want next, because they usually don't know! In 1939, when people in offices were asked if they would like dry copy documents, many replied, "What for? We have carbon paper." Remember, people by nature do not like change. However, if you can spark their enlightened self-interest, you may not only have changed their habits (the hardest thing for any marketer to do), but you may have also gained a devoted and passionate prospect or client. When Xerox finally did come out with its copier, people bonded with the brand, once they understood the impact of its value. This is something those people in 1939 couldn't possibly have projected from what was then an abstract concept.

So how do you find those nuggets that delight your constituency? Look to yourself. My *Web Digest For Marketers* originally had a market of one: me. Then I found other people wanting the same information. If you ever catch yourself saying, "Why can't I simply ...," write the thought down and see if you can *product-ize* it and deliver it on the Net. Maybe there's a newsletter for your industry that hasn't been done yet. Perhaps there are already six, but they're too long, or not in-depth enough, or have some other weakness that you can identify as the niche to fill.

Another idea is to visit other industry categories for ideas you can migrate into your category. This ingenious approach was given to me by marketing guru Jay Abraham when I visited the financial categories on the Net for my client Con Edison. There were no other utilities offering online customer account information at the time. One year later, Con Edison broke new ground by offering customer account information and online payment options. This was considered a breakthrough in the otherwise risk-adverse industry of utilities.

When Shouldn't You Market to Yourself?

There are times when we truly are only talking to ourselves and no one else. What I find fascinating is that some of these expressions turn into websites. Companies are like biospheres, each with its own culture. It's quite conceivable that an interface makes perfect sense to a group of people who live and breathe that culture day in and day out. This is like viewing your company from within the goldfish bowl. Remember, a website can be accessed by anybody. You need to look at your company from *outside* the bowl and create the interface accordingly.

I suggest you live in the shoes of your customer or prospective client. I remember visiting the site of a large brand of soda. As I hit the home page of the site I was presented with a dialogue box while the page was coming in. The dialog box told me that in order to fully appreciate this site, I would have to download some application that would let me play the audio that went along with the visuals on the screen. What kind of branding impression is the visitor left with after going to all that trouble? "Diet Cola: You're Inadequate"? To avoid this dilemma, ask yourself some questions: What sort of things will make visitors delighted they came in the first place? Is it appropriate for them to smile or laugh out loud, or be intrigued by a juicy news abstract or idea? What will make them bookmark you so they can return again and again? How can you keep them in your sphere of influence? Ask these questions for every page you create in your site, not just the first page. The average surfer is on your home page for seven seconds. If they are intrigued by your site, they might stay through two to three clicks (or pages), if you're lucky.

Bringing Value to Your Audience

Your brand needs to be perceived as providing value to your audience in order to be successful. In the online world, that means your brand should be interactive—a two-way flow of information from you to your audience, and vice versa. Such is the nature of the Web. Ignore this dynamic at your own peril, as it is one of the greatest advantages that the Web has to offer. Your audience is no longer passively absorbing your brand message through a print advertisement or a TV commercial. They are experiencing your brand, assessing your willingness to listen to their needs, evaluating your ability to meet their needs, and pondering their willingness to come back to you for more. How do you create customer loyalty for your brand?

Walk the Walk

How can you demonstrate to your target audience that your branding is found in your doing, or that you not only talk the talk, but you walk the walk as well? I suggest you start a newsletter that caters directly to the needs of your audience. The next question is, what should your newsletter specifically be about? Should it be your pontifications? Probably not, as few people have time for the pontifications of others when they're trying to get the in box down to a manageable size.

The answer is to deliver value to your audience. Answer questions that need to be answered. Share information that needs to be shared. Marty Edelston, the wizardlike founder and publisher of BottomLine Business and BottomLine Personal, observes, "I have to find the things that are troublesome to you. I then have to press the buttons that open the doors that have the important questions to which you want answers. So, if you then like what I do, it's because I'm in step with you."

The information you deliver to your audience needs to be quickly understood as valuable and having good utility. "Most news is a narcotic," Edelston notes. "The less time you spend with it, the better off you are." The trick is to help the reader understand an issue, reach a conclusion, or in some way inform, educate, or entertain. "The Internet is very much like life itself. Both are confusing. Both are chaotic and people try to seek some order to it, though little or none is to be had. Anyone who brings clarity is honored and listened to, though few actually deliver on this," Edelston concludes. I submit to you, reader, that you be that one who delivers clarity and order to your readers' reality and in box. When they see your name in the "From" field, they will associate it with good tidings, which will set you apart from your competition. It is highly likely that your competition is only adding to the chaos and confusion that Mr. Edelston, and everyone else, finds so pervasive.

Online Communities

Since the debut of the World Wide Web in 1994, there's been a great deal written about online communities. At first, the Web was one big happy community filled with surfers jumping from site to site, saying, "Gee, isn't this great? And it's all free!" Then the Web quickly became a very valuable communication, information, and sales channel. Businesses both large and small dot commed themselves to take advantage of this new medium. And freedom became "just another word for nothing left to lose," to quote Janis Joplin.

However, interactive exchange between people online is one of the core components of the Internet and the Web. A community where people who share common interests can exchange their views in many ways is an essential expression of the medium. That being said, online communities may not be your road to a profitable business, and online communities are very demanding to nurture and maintain. The question is: Does a community serve your needs, or can you serve a community with a product or service that adds value both to the business and the community?

People gravitate to that which ultimately serves them best. Adam Smith's invisible hand of capitalism is at work here. If another community sprouts up that serves your visitors better, some of your members will go to the new place—believe me. Brand loyalty off and on the Net is a fleeting thing that must be constantly nourished. Since the cost and barrier of entry are low, anyone can and does try to poach your community.

To determine whether an online community will benefit your company and/or your customers, ask yourself the following questions:

Who is my target audience? How likely are they to appreciate an online community? The demographics of the online audience have changed dramatically over the past few years, as have the ways that information is shared, the technology to do so, and consumer expectations. For example, if your target audience is primarily women or teens, online communities, or community-type features, may be essential for your business success, as those audiences (and the businesses that serve them) have frequently embraced collaborative features.

Do my competitors have online communities? If so, conduct a careful evaluation of your competitor's communities. Are they active? If there is a bulletin board, are there many posts by a number of different people? Is there a moderator that steps in to make comments from time to time? Are any posts allowed, or do the posts of visitors need to be approved before they make their way onto the board? If your competitor has an email list, by all means get on it and evaluate the quality of interaction. Are there other forms of community available? For example, product reviews or other forms of content input by site visitors create a feeling of ownership among site visitors.

Do the members of my target audience need to communicate with one another? If so, then you need to create a community environment. The transfer of information between customers, such as in a business-to-business exchange, fosters a community to which you will want your site visitors to remain loyal. As such, you should be thinking of sophisticated ways to foster this information exchange. Perhaps bulletin boards don't work for your audience—your challenge is then to think outside the box and to research constantly evolving community-building tools and techniques. Many customer relationship management providers include what are essentially community-building tools as part of their service offerings. Even auctions or other e-commerce exchanges are forms of community, as members interact with and rate one another's products, services, and professionalism.

When Not to Create Communities

There are points where it is actually in your best interest *not* to create certain communities. An example is the story of a major bank that was preparing to set up communities for its clients. It obviously was not in the best interests of that bank to have its high-level clients talking to one another about their respective relationships with that bank. We've heard of another firm that made a similar effort and found that clients were sharing negotiating tactics with each other on how to get the best deal from the sponsor of said community!

Ask yourself before you get into the community-building business: Do I *need* a community? If I had one, what would I do with it?

Customer Relationship Management

It is possible to engage in an ongoing dialogue with your site visitors or customers in other ways. Customer service, or *Customer Relationship Management* (CRM), is this century's buzzword; one that has in many ways replaced community-building as the perceived essential ingredient for online success.

What is CRM, exactly, besides a potentially expensive undertaking that many sites feel compelled to include on their corporate checklists? "The most important part of CRM is the strategy," emphasizes Bob Thompson, founder and president of Front Line Solutions and Chief Guru Officer of CRMGuru.com (see Figure 5.7). "Companies think they can automate their way to a better customer relationship. I compare this attitude to spending thousands of dollars on the latest and greatest tools to build a house, and then taking them home and starting to build without a blueprint or any plans. It's a 'let's see what happens' mentality." CRM technology is just that—technology. "It's just another application," he continues. "When it's up and running, are you deriving benefit from it?"

A good place to start your online branding strategy as related to CRM is with a careful evaluation of what your customer wants, not what the latest hype says you should have. "You don't need to install a CRM solution to offer a great customer experience," Thompson says. "Companies are looking for a magic pill to make a good business. Yes, conceptually, all your channels should talk to one another. But does your customer really want that? The real power of CRM lies in lots of thinking and hard work to create a good experience."

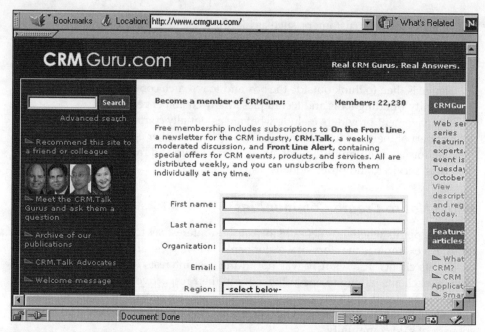

Figure 5.7 CRMGuru is an industry-renowned source for CRM insight and information.
CRMGuru.com is a service of Front Line Solutions. All content is copyright Front Line Solutions.

At the base level, customer relationship management means being available to your customer, whether through email, live chat, phone, mail, or in person. One of the most effective things a business can do to establish and protect its brand is to establish communications standards. "Set a standard and stick to it," advises Thompson. "Customers do have increasing expectations with regard to email response times, in particular. Email is not instant response, although many expect it to be." Manage your customers' expectations and provide alternate means for urgent contact. "Tell your customer if it's urgent, do not send an email," Thompson concludes. "If your house is on fire, don't email the fire department. Call 911."

There are many, many technologies available at all price ranges that will assist in your customer relationship management efforts. Some are even free, such as cPulse (http://www.cpulse.com), which provides a survey to random site visitors as they view your site, as discussed in Chapter 3, "Mining the Internet for All It's Worth." Your visitors can evaluate their experience and share their thoughts with you about how you could improve your offerings to better meet their needs.

Most advanced CRM solutions begin to integrate both customer service and marketing solutions to build relationships and extend the lifetime value of your customers. Some are available for monthly lease as an ASP (Application Service Provider) model, where you actually lease the right to use and maintain your CRM using their solution. If you would like to own the software solution, there are also multiple vendors to choose from.

TIP To learn more about the rapidly evolving CRM industry, you can also visit searchCRM.com (http://www.searchcrm.com), a CRM search engine and information portal. It's particularly useful as a resource for vendor information, as all 2,000 of them are classified both alphabetically and by categories in Vendor Central. Each vendor has a virtual booth space within the site, so that you can easily compare services and even request quotes.

Web Page and Site Design and Your Image

As you know, first impressions mean a great deal in business. That first impression frames how we're going to feel about a given company. More and more, people will get those first impressions of your firm online, where they can see your site and hopefully interact with it. Your thoughtfulness of the visitor's encounter speaks volumes in terms of how that person will feel about your firm. The look and feel of your site has everything to do with what people think of you and, therefore, of your brand.

The Web has done to interface design what desktop publishing did to page layout. Being *able* to use 10 different fonts and numerous unmatched graphics on one page doesn't mean you should! The same is true for a web interface. Technology has made it easier than ever for self-proclaimed designers to produce bad layouts for both the printed page and the home page.

Don't Fool Yourself with Fancy Graphics

There's often a big disconnect between designers and the sites they're designing. I've seen clients look at dazzling web pages and watch them swell with pride at how beautiful the site looks. When the designer demos a new page for them, they'll notice how quickly the page loads. . .or does it? Many people don't realize that the desktop PC doesn't stay in constant contact with the web server. It brings in the page and stops talking to the web server until another page, which hasn't been previously asked for, is requested. The point is that many of those graphics that seem to be flying up onto the screen with alacrity are not coming from the server at all. They're already stored locally on the PC you're looking at—if that page has been viewed before. Even if you press Reload, you may not see or experience what a first-time visitor to your site experiences. If you want to be absolutely sure your computer is void of any images on the server, flush your cache, quit your browser, and yes, actually reboot the machine. This is the only way to guarantee that you're looking at something that is loading fresh right off the Web, in real time.

Visiting a site is not just a graphic experience; it's also an experience of time. Many site designers look at each page as a single experience, rather than one of many site views that are loaded onto the screen of an impatient surfer. I know of some art directors who are very proud of their design work and have hard copies of the screens laminated and put in their portfolios. However, a laminated page in an art director's portfolio isn't the primary reason a site should be designed.

I'm not suggesting that you strip out all your graphics. Far from it. When I hear people complain about how they hate to wait for the graphics, I tell them I can solve their problem in one second. Simply surf with graphics turned off. They sheepishly smile and say, "Oh, but I like the graphics; it adds to the experience." They will wait a small amount of time for a pleasant interface. For an ongoing collection of the best in site design, check out Project Cool's Sightings section at http://www.projectcool.com/sightings. This resource is a gold mine from a conceptual, artistic, and user point of view. Started in part by Glenn Davis, who originated the Cool Site of the Day genre, a new site is added every day. We often look there for new sites to review for *Web Digest For Marketers*

I advise clients that no home page should be more than 30K in size, with secondary pages no larger than 20K. "This doesn't allow for much creative room," complain many designers. Tough. Those are the real-world limits, and even that is pushing it. There are survey statistics showing that an astonishing number of people don't know the speed of their modems. It's a reasonable thing not to know, when you think about it. They probably bought the computer with an internal modem, and the speed was just one more specification in a blur of megahertz, RAM, gigabytes, and so on. Many people are surfing at below optimal speeds without even knowing it.

If your site has many people visiting from AOL, think about this reality check: When an AOL user logs on to that service, he or she often gets downloads of graphics before he or she can navigate. It's sort of like an inoculation. What happens is that your computer receives graphic files at the beginning of a session, so they don't have to be loaded each and every time you go to that part of AOL. Therefore, most of the graphics AOLers see are already local on their machine; to them, AOL pages load quickly. When they go out onto the Net, though, the graphics are often flying in for the first time to their machines. When designing your pages, you must keep in mind that if you have many people visiting from AOL, they may think that your pages load slowly.

Other problems occurring on the open Internet can and do happen with regularity. The Net could simply experience a bad hair day in the entire Northeast for some known or unknown reason. Accessing U.S. sites from Europe after noon can take forever, too, as the transatlantic circuits are nearly always jammed. If you want an idea of how slow your site comes in from overseas, try accessing a site over there at the worst time of day for your region on the Net. That will give you some idea.

This medium clearly employs the design principles of the Bauhaus, where less is more. Brevity is appreciated, if not demanded. Study how Helmut Krone, the incomparable advertising art director, brought these principles to advertising by looking at the original Avis and Volkswagen ads. I had the distinct pleasure of knowing this icon of advertising. He once said that an advertising page should be identifiable to you from 40 feet away. The impact and impression made on readers was that much greater when they were even closer. When someone approached Helmut, they would sometimes start babbling about themselves, out of nervousness. In that Bauhaus way of his, he would raise his hand and say, in that unmistakable low dulcet tone, "I don't want to know that much about you." Part of your job is to figure out when visitors to your site want to know that much about you, and when they do not. Less is more. The following is a list of design don'ts:

No clueless banners please. I want more than just a name; I want "Here's a darn good reason to stop what you're doing and click here" banners.

Making me wait is bad branding. It leaves a bad taste in my mouth. If that long download that I didn't expect doesn't pay off with a major paradigm shift, I'm out of here.

Don't force me through too many screens to get to the point. It's far too manipulative in this medium, where the customer is in the driver's seat. If I have to keep clicking and reading and searching to find what I want, I'll go elsewhere.

Don't talk to me like I'm reading a brochure or watching TV. Those are other media. This is the Internet. Talk to me in your online voice. Don't have one? Get one.

I'm more interested in me than I am in you. Remember that when I visit your site. What's in it for me? is what you must answer with every click.

Screen Real Estate

The browser window that you use to design your web pages should look just like the majority of browser windows out there. The lion's share of surfers still have 17-inch monitors; yours may be larger or smaller. Average screen resolution is also set at 800 x 600 pixels (picture elements)—yours may be set to a higher resolution. Make sure all the toolbars of the browser are showing when you design a page set to that size and resolution—you don't want your visitor to have to scroll vertically and horizontally because your web page is just so big. Users may scroll down past that first screen if you've sufficiently captured their attention right in front of their eyes, or simply click on a link in that first screen. Yes, many people see more than that with bigger monitors and better screen resolution. If you're sure your entire audience has that increased viewing window, then design to that. But I advise clients that you can't go wrong with designing to have the primary elements fit the least common denominator of viewing. Someone with a bigger monitor may then actually see your home page without a vertical scroll bar. Have you ever seen the delight on someone's face when that happens? It says you are well organized and know how to design for a web audience. Many firms simply won't be able to do this. Some will try to cram everything into that first screen, and that in itself is overwhelming, scrollbar or no. Use your best judgment when designing, then change your mind a few times.

You should also make available to a user a search tool that specifically searches only your site. That search feature should appear on every page of your site so the visitor can get from anywhere to anywhere quickly. A site map is also a good idea to give a bird's eye view to those who want it. When you have a search engine, clearly indicate it is for searching your site only.

TIP **Atomz.com Search (http://www.atomz.com) allows you to quickly add a powerful free search engine to your site in about 5 minutes by copying a few lines of HTML. There is no programming and no hardware or software to install.**

Buying Media on the Net

Since branding budgets tend to be larger than other marketing budgets, I decided to park this aspect of marketing right here. Why? Because the dollar volume does start to get significant in this realm of media buying. You have several basic options when looking for media to purchase for your website, and, therefore, add value to your brand: search engines, content sites, e-commerce sites, discussion, and mailing lists (which are covered in Chapter 8, "Direct Marketing and Sales Support"), and making your own channel of communication. You also have advertising networks, which we will address as well.

Search Engines

In Chapter 8, "Direct Marketing and Sales Support," we explain how to buy actual words on search engines that will increase your ad banner clickthrough rate, due to a more tightly targeted audience. That audience will see your ad come up each time they search for the words you purchased. Here, we'll cover *general rotation* buys, which means you don't buy anything but a general placement on the search engine page for any search word that hasn't been purchased and reserved by someone else. A search engine sales representative will like you much better if you come with a budget that will sustain over months.

Like any other media, the search engine companies have rate cards. These rate cards are a starting point for negotiations. Every scenario is different. Here are some basic negotiating tactics you can employ with the search engine companies.

Getting a Good Price

First off, you should know that they typically run loads of unpaid slots every day. They will sell out in certain categories, and they'll be sure to tell you that. For the most part, though, they have extra inventory. The key is to get that inventory for the best price. If a sales representative from one of the search engines tries to come on strong (and some have) about how powerful his brand is and how he is selling out, listen patiently, as I do. Thank him for sharing the information and ask if he would like you to share your information with him. Of course, he will say yes. You can then tell him that you have a budget—but quote him *20 percent less* than what you really plan on spending— that you're approaching three other search engines with that same budget, and you encourage him to offer a plan that will make the best of that budget. At this point, ask him if he would like to participate. So far, no one has ever said no to me. In this way, you've turned the tables. You make your needs the common denominator that the reps must cater to, rather than trying to untangle all their sales programs to figure out which one has the best value.

Getting the Right Number of Impressions

Once you've narrowed the field, listen to how your needs are being met. The important word here is *impressions*. Make sure they are offering you real impressions. I've had sales representatives use an interesting closing tactic by telling me that extra impressions are had by people clicking on the Back button after they've finished looking at the web page from a search result, and therefore, hitting the search results page again that has my client's banner ad still on it. I tell them that my client is paying for initial impressions. If a user happens to click "back" and see the ad again, that's great. But you cannot prove it, and I do not count that as an initial impression. If anyone is still trying to sell on hits, just leave. What you want are impressions. Hits are very misleading. Here's why: When you go to a website, you may see five graphics plus the text for that first page. Technically, that constitutes six hits. You are interested only in your banner being viewed by your target audience and nothing else. Some sites will put your banner at the top and bottom of the page and may claim you are getting two hits or two impressions. Don't buy it.

> **NOTE** An *impression* is considered to be one banner ad hitting one targeted user. Only proven impressions should be counted in a media buy. You should require proof of how many users from the target audience actually clicked through the banner ad to your site.

Remember I mentioned to quote the previously mentioned sales representative 20 percent below what you actually planned on spending? That extra cash can come in handy when you get down to the wire. Offer to up the ante by that extra 20 percent and see what the reps do in return. Make sure to ask if they offer an agency discount, which is typically 15 percent. Some do and some don't. If you're not an agency, become one quickly in order to take advantage of this extra margin. Some media outlets will want to see stationery or a bank account specifically dedicated to your agency or media-buying service function. If you're going to be buying media repeatedly, it's worthwhile. If not, try to get them to give you some kind of break on that end of the deal anyway.

Make sure that you have the opportunity to change your banners a few times a week, as you weed out the weak ones and replace with fresh attempts. See what the reports look like and choose the most successful ads to run again, and create new ones based on the successful ones. How often do those reports from the search engine company come out? The more often, the better, as it gives you a closer read on how your clickthroughs are coming. Remember to ask that of the representative when you're thinking about buying ad space. You do want clickthrough even though this is *just* branding, right? Getting your name up in front of potential customers isn't enough. Don't you want to show them something slick back at your site, designed for this media flight especially? Of course you do.

> **TIP** Start your negotiations much earlier than you actually need your banner ads to run. Have the approval to purchase in hand, but keep that to yourself. At the opportune time, ask the rep if there is a signing bonus if the deal can be closed that very day. The signing bonus may come in the form of extra impressions or an additional discount on the purchase itself.

Get the Type of Contract You Want

Finally, it may be in your best interest to have short-term contracts, unless they really give you an incentive for going longer. I've noticed that clickthroughs will go up when changing search engine companies. I suspect it's because different users are seeing the ads for the first time, since users have brand loyalty to search engines, too. Having said all this about negotiating with representatives from search engines, I will say they are very good people to have on your side. If you ever want to buy keywords (as explained in Chapter 8, "Direct Marketing and Sales Support"), they can tell you which ones are most popular in your category. You may find some surprises. If you happen to be one of their favorite clients, you might just get a few more impressions than you bargained for as well.

Content and E-Commerce Sites

There are many media buyers who prefer buying banners on content and/or e-commerce sites. This is usually due to the nature of the content or the shopping environment, which is likely to attract a targeted audience. High-tech and travel sites are often in high demand on the Net as these categories are now hot and heavy for consumers. Sometimes these sites are related to print trade publications. If you're currently running ads in print, try getting the publishers to throw in some online impressions as well, to keep you happy as a print advertiser. If they avoid doing this for you, at least expect a very favorable discount on your online ad purchase. I know that some publishers divorce these two operations. I think that's nuts. They should be heavily cross-merchandising each other. Visit the sites you wish to advertise on and see who is currently advertising there. Do this before contacting the sales representative for those sites. If your ad is going to rotate around the site, ask to see exactly where it rotates; you may or may not like parts of that rotation. By all means, get a guarantee on how many impressions will be delivered each month. After all, you are guaranteeing them a certain number of dollars. You deserve a definable value in return.

Once you've purchased ads on someone else's site, it's only natural to want ongoing information. This can be handled in a number of ways. I/PRO (http://www.ipro.com) is a third-party firm that audits sites to verify that the statistics the sites are claiming are, in fact, correct. In this medium of instant information, people want to know in real time what's going on. CNET gives its advertisers a password that allows them site access to see charts that depict what's going on with their avails in close to real time. Other sites will simply give you access to their off-the-shelf referral log software, such as MS's Usage Analyst, which shows you in a more basic way what is happening: what pages got which hits from where, how many, and when. The rule of thumb here is, the higher the dollar volume, the more demanding you can be about feedback and the speed at which that feedback comes to you.

NOTE *Avail* refers to an advertising availability. It is simply a space that is available for an ad. Think of it as an empty airline seat looking for a passenger. The term comes from the traditional print, audio, and video advertising markets.

Growth of Advertising on the Web

The general outlook on advertising on the Web remains a skeptical one. After a deluge of dot com ad blitzing both online and off, many of the dot coms are now "dot gone" and cooler heads have prevailed. Internet advertising revenues for the third quarter of 2000 increased 63 percent over the comparative quarter for 1999, and showed a slight decline of six and a half percent when compared to the second quarter of 2000, according to the Internet Advertising Bureau's (IAB) Internet Ad Revenue Report, which is conducted independently by the New Media Group of PricewaterhouseCoopers. Third-quarter 2000 revenues grew to $1,986 million (63.2 percent) over the same period in 1999, and showed a decline of $138 million (6.5 percent) when compared to the second quarter of 2000.

"This slight decline in online ad revenue should come as no surprise to the industry. The slowdown we are seeing this quarter has its roots in a number of factors that affect the medium. The pullback of advertising by many companies in the dot com sector, combined with the traditionally weak third quarter, and the transition of the advertisers' focus on how to best take advantage of the Internet, all have contributed to the third-quarter slowdown," said Rich LeFurgy, Chairman of the IAB and General Partner of WaldenVC. "There is no doubt that traditional advertisers are increasing their online spending, as the $6 billion year-to-date attests. With publishers offering a variety of new and innovative ad formats, these advertisers are now transitioning their objectives. Increasingly aware of the power of the medium for branding and direct marketing, these savvy advertisers are no longer looking for the most traffic, rather, they are seeking different ways and new creative formats that publishers are offering, to build their brands. This is an industry of innovation, and the serious players are in it for the long haul." At the time of writing, there are precious few sites that are solely supported by ad revenues. In addition, there are many thousands of new ad avails coming online every day. In the magazine world, you have about two new titles a day, so I figure there are maybe 120 new ad avails in the magazine world daily. Match that with the thousands of new avails available on the Web daily. What does this mean? It means ad rates will drop precipitously due to an open market. In fact, web advertising may drag down advertising prices across all media. I can hear it now: "Why should I pay $30 per thousand readers in print when I can get it for $17 dollars per thousand on the Web?"

One reason might be the ability the Web offers to reach a targeted audience and to track return on investment. Jupiter reports that 73 percent of advertisers plan to increase online advertising spending over the year 2001. Currently, extra services—such as targeting of the audience that will see your ad—increase the cost of your advertising buy. As clickthrough rates plummet, however, online marketers will need to demonstrate better results for their marketing expenses. Extra services, such as targeting, may well become part of the standard advertising buy. An alternative is to price the buy based on the delivery of definable actions, such as clickthrough, lead, and sale. Yes, more people will come online to see more ads, but the growth of sites wanting to show you those ads is increasing at an unprecedented rate as well. Keep all this in mind when negotiating the media you wish to purchase.

TIP Keep up to date with online advertising trends at ICONOCAST's Dotcom
Marketing site (http://www.iconocast.com/dotcom/). This resource synopsizes
demographics, trends, and metrics, in easy-to-understand textbook chapters.

Beyond the Banner

Now that the Net is becoming omnipresent, big brand advertisers are asking themselves how to use this interactive medium as a branding tool. Are banners enough? We
hear much talk about *going beyond the banner*. In many cases, it's a lot of hooey. Banners
are just fine, just like envelopes are fine. Both beckon you to click or open an envelope
to see what's inside. You can't leave a huge impression on someone with a banner.
You've got to pull him or her through to your site. New banner shapes, such as the
long, vertical "skyscraper," allow more room for content and interaction. If used well,
both the consumer and advertiser can benefit. Some mass merchants feel they don't
have anything to say on a one-to-one level. I presented Tide detergent as an example
earlier. Procter & Gamble found its online voice—so can the others. *Interstitial ads* have
been touted as the second coming for quite some time now. This is a bunch of
malarkey. These advertisements are splash ads that come up between pages. You click
on an icon on a website, and while the next page is loading, you get the interstitial. To
me, it looks like subliminal advertising in slow motion. I liken them to seeing commercials in a movie theater where I just paid $9.50 and all I want to see is the movie.
The only site I've seen where interstitials work is something like the online game show
You Don't Know Jack (http://www.jacknetshow.com) where, between live game sets,
you get what they are calling *interstitials.* I'd call them commercial breaks, just like on
TV, complete with animation and sound. But the growth of *static* interstitials that interrupt a website for no reason at all—those are interfering and only make the site visitor
uncomfortable.

Advertising Networks

The challenge for big brand marketers is interesting. As more attention-share goes
toward the Net, it must come from somewhere else. Time is a zero-sum game, as mentioned earlier. The source of that attention is other media. If big brand marketers still
want to reach the people who have turned partially away from other media, it is
becoming more apparent that they have to make impressions on the users in this interactive medium.

These big brands often are looking for demographics rather than interests. If you
have a child, you will buy Pampers whether you're a techie or a teacher. Advertising
networks have sprung up to deliver those demographics to brand marketers. DoubleClick (http://www.doubleclick.com) was the first and most well known of these ad
networks. The DoubleClick Network is a collection of the most highly trafficked and
branded sites on the Web. This network of sites is coupled with proprietary DART targeting technology. DoubleClick will sell you advertising impressions only on the sites
that it represents. In other words, it makes money two ways:

■ DoubleClick represents high-traffic sites, such as Edgar Online, Dilbert,
Zagat.com, and over 1,449 more.

■ The company makes money selling you a more specific demographic on and across those sites that it represents. For example, if you want to target women with graduate degrees from Canada across a number of sites, that will cost you a bit more than simply buying banners on individual content sites.

Leveraging Your Brand Name through Online Syndication

Once you have created a brand, it is necessary to establish that brand in the minds of your customers through as many means as possible. Remember when branding consisted of mounting multimillion dollar advertising campaigns to blast a company's name out to the world? Those days are long gone. Advertising still plays a very important role in the branding game, but there are many other ways to bring your brand to the attention of a wide audience. Are there tangible payoffs to devoting so much time and effort to your branding? You bet.

One of the most lucrative ways to make money from your brand name is to repackage, or in some cases develop, branded content and database-driven tools that can be syndicated across the Web. Just as hundreds of newspapers around the world purchase the rights to print "Dear Abby," a syndicated advice column, on a daily basis, so will websites around the world pay for the rights to include content or information from others in their sites.

Why? Your content or expertise allows sites to supplement their own offerings, and, through a mix of syndicated content, create a unique, relevant, and useful site for their target audience. "Our clients need to present constantly changing content in order to retain their audience," explains Nandita Jhaveri, Director of Content Business Development for iSyndicate (http://www.isyndicate.com). "Syndicating branded content is far less expensive and far more powerful than paying a staff to develop it."

iSyndicate is a leading online syndication company that acts as the middleman between content providers and those seeking content for their sites. It is important to note that content can be defined in many ways. An editorial column, news headlines, stock quotes, weather, or a database of website reviews are all content. iSyndicate refers to the information syndicated through its service as "digital assets." As a matter of fact, the traditional editorial column or news article is probably one of the least creative forms of content in the interactive world of the Web.

"We're in the business of helping content partners develop saleable content for syndication," says Jhaveri. What's saleable? Branded content that is published on a reliable schedule. iSyndicate works with its content partners to develop packages, or modules, which can be sold separately. "We have more than 4,500 content products from over 1,200 partners. Those products include sports scores, personal calendaring, calculators, games, and databases of information," she explains.

For example, WDFM syndicates each weekly edition of *Web Digest For Marketers*. That is static content that is delivered on a weekly basis. In addition, WDFM plans to syndicate a database wherein users can search the WDFM archives for individual site reviews by keyword. That is an example of an application, or tool, which is incredibly valuable to marketing-oriented sites.

The rapid growth of iSyndicate, and other syndication services such as Screaming Media, is a bellwether of the changes in Internet business models and business realities. Instead of paying for an editorial staff to create content, many sites have decided to save money and bring in better, more valuable, and potentially more recognizable content than they could create on their own. Syndication fees range from $500 to $2,000 a month per content package, with well-known, branded content generally earning the higher prices.

What's in demand? "We're focusing on wireless content, such as personalized call-to-action, or time- and location-sensitive information," states Jhaveri. "Anyone who is sitting on content that can be repackaged for mobile devices—such as traffic information, travel schedules, restaurant reviews, local city guides, event guides, and games— is in the driver's seat. Rich media, especially in the business and technology section, is appealing, as is anything that can be syndicated to an international audience."

On the content provider end, "Syndication provides a wonderful opportunity to extend brand while increasing site traffic and building revenues," Jhaveri explains. "Our content providers range from freelance journalists to web brands to content aggregators. There is an enormous amount of content produced on the Web, and it doesn't have to only live in one place." As surfers see your branded content again and again on their journeys online, your brand is enforced. Content syndication allows you to live beyond your own website while establishing yourself as an authority across the Web on your particular topic.

Karen Lake, CEO of StrategyWeek.com, offers a weekly interview with an industry CEO. In addition to publishing the interview on her site, she syndicates both the text and audio versions of the interviews, which are downloaded and listened to by executives during commuting time.

Syndication also extends the shelf life of your work. Why generate and archive content week after week on your own site, when you can easily share it elsewhere? Savvy content providers are also thinking of ways to repackage content for syndication purposes. And with good reason. According to Forrester, quality of content is the number one reason visitors return to a site. Updated, brand name content turns a site from so-so to a desirable destination. Because of the demand for content, many sites have found themselves in the business of content publishing, but most are what Forrester terms "accidental publishers"—lacking the necessary resources and experience in this area.

TIP According to Forrester, the median number of distribution deals is set to jump from 14 per site today to approximately 69 in 2003. Get your brand out there!

What's the bottom line? Comfort. That's what branding is all about, whether it is for you personally, your firm or organization, or a can of pineapple chunks. Whether people are going to buy your brand online or offline, they are going to want to feel comfortable in the knowledge that they are getting a product or service that has a reputation to live up to. You can think of it as a preconditioner. Very often, the most effective branding will hit the target audience using a number of different media at the same time. This causes a resonance in the target audience that often causes them to act. No single message may be responsible for that action, but rather a team-selling approach may be the order of the day. This team approach sets the target up with a brand image, then attempts to convert that target to buying the brand with some sort of incentive.

In this way, the target feels that he or she got high value (perceived as such by the branding efforts) for a good price (the financial incentive that lures customers into the buying cycle). The coupon without perceived value is valueless. Like it or not, you must have a branding strategy. Failure to do so will result in perception as either a pure commodity brand, whereby your price is forever headed downward in competition with others, or ignored altogether. To bring it down to a personal level, branding is the kind of suit you wear, the tie you select, and your watch that does more than tell time. Keep this is mind when you design your site and the outbound communications to bring people back to your site. Remember, *everything* you say and do is branding.

Resource Center

Branding

Tom Peters   http://www.tompeters.com

Get ready to WOW! Tom Peters describes himself as a prince of disorder, champion of bold failures, maestro of zest, professional loudmouth, corporate cheerleader, lover of markets, capitalist pig. . .and card-carrying member of the ACLU. If it's time to create the Brand of You, then it's time to visit this site, where you will find all the support (and community) that you need.

Rob Frankel   http://www.robfrankel.com

According to branding expert Rob Frankel, "Branding is not about getting your prospects to choose you over your competition; it's about getting your prospects to see you as the only solution to their problem." At his site you will discover a treasure trove of articles and information on branding, as well as a discussion list and many gems of wisdom from the man himself.

Branding Tools

NameProtect's NameGuard Monitor   http://www.nameprotect.com/freemon.html

Is your business safe on the Internet? Are competitors or unscrupulous individuals misdirecting your traffic, tarnishing your name, or stealing your brand? NameGuard, a service of NameProtect, is an amazing (and free!) service that will let you know if your domain name, or a variation thereof, has been registered by others. In addition to a monthly report that details anyone who has registered a domain name that contains part of your domain (such as ILoveCoke.com), the report also includes a trademark section designed to keep you informed of new U.S. trademark activity that may impact your ability to use your domain name or other brand name. Another section details conflicting domain names that are similar to yours, which will help you identify potential competitors and assess the potential for your site traffic to be diverted.

Thomson & Thomson Connotation Services   http://www.thomson-thomson.com

Trademark and copyright research firm Thomson & Thomson offers two unique brand research services. Connotation Check and Connotation Evaluation will help businesses researching trademarks, corporate and product names for international launches to identify possible negative connotations and associations with their name in foreign markets—before these could affect sales or create potential image problems for the company and its products in international markets. Some services are free, others are fee-based.

Advertising

Bannerstake   http://www.namestake.com

Bannerstake is a free online advertising monitoring tool that marketers can use to find out if their competitors have purchased a specific keyword on leading search engines. Bannerstake works like this: You enter a keyword. Bannerstake queries the search engines, then delivers to you a page that shows the banners resulting from that search. If the banners are unrelated to the products and services offered by the brand indicated in your search, then the keyword is probably not purchased. If the banner is for a competitor's product, that competitor may have purchased said brand name as a keyword. Bannerstake is offered as a service of Thomson & Thomson, a company that has positioned itself as the guardian of trademarks and brand names in the wild and wooly land of Internet domain name-ville.

Customer Relationship Management

searchCRM.com   http://www.searchcrm.com

searchCRM.com is a technology-specific search engine and information portal covering CRM. It's particularly useful as a resource for vendor information, as all 2,000 of them are classified both alphabetically and by categories in Vendor Central. Did you know you needed Analytical Applications, Knowledge Management, and Sales and Marketing Automation? You do. Each vendor has a virtual booth space within the site, so that you can easily compare services and even request quotes. Another cool touch— the ability to store your search results for future reference.

CRMGuru   http://www.crmguru.com

Hats off to Chief Guru Officer Bob Thompson, who continues to deliver one of the Web's best CRM research and reference sites. Whether you're at the What Is CRM? stage (Tip: According to this site, "CRM isn't about technology any more than hospitality is about throwing a welcome mat on your front porch") or are a seasoned marketer looking to implement smart strategic CRM practices, you'll find the information you need here. If you don't, you can always ask the CRM Gurus a question directly (what customer service!). Free membership to the site includes several newsletters.

CRM Community   http://www.crmcommunity.com

Baffled by eCRM? Confused by the multitude of choices and players that seem to merge and emerge daily? For more than you ever wanted to know about Customer Relationship Management, join the CRM Community. We have found it to be an invaluable guide to the peripatetic world of customer service, especially as related to marketing efforts.

DestinationCRM   http://www.destinationcrm.com

What are the most important trends that will impact the direction of e-business and the way businesses manage customers? According to Peggy Menconi, DestinationCRM .com's expert on call, "Self-service will hit the power curve in a big way in 2001, thanks to several examples of companies saving money by offering their customers the option to self-service. These examples range from B2C companies like Eddie Bauer, which is experiencing an 80 percent inquiry resolution rate through its Ask Eddie feature, to B2B companies like Cisco, which is enjoying more than 60 percent resolution through self-service." To learn more or access news, information, and community, visit the site.

Customer Experience

goodexperience.com   http://www.goodexperience.com

Customer experience consulting firm Creative Good practices what it preaches—this informational arm of the company is designed solely as an online resource dedicated to monitoring the online customer experience. Free white papers and reports are devoted to establishing CRM strategy that will help you on the Web and beyond—including a guide to creating a good experience for the mobile or wireless customer on the move.

Measurement

Engage I/PRO   http://www.engage.com/ipro/

How would you like to measure over 9 billion web pages and 1.4 billion user sessions from over 350 customer websites each month? The folks at Engage I/PRO do, interpreting the numbers generated from sites and reporting what websites really reveal about online businesses. Most interesting is the company's online Unique Visitor (UV) audit that provides sites with independent, census-based reach, frequency, and duration calculations in order to verify a site's unique visitors to advertisers and investors. Another offering is the I/PRO Velocity service, which measures and monitors user experience so you can ensure your site delivers.

BPA International   bpai.com

BPA International, an independent, not-for-profit, self-regulating organization specializing in audited data for the marketing, media, and information industries, has been around since 1931. And now they're taking on the Web. Their Interactive web audits are based on census data from a site's log file(s). They employ a series of real-time and historical tests to clearly portray site traffic. Since their audits are not dependent on installed software at the server location, the BPA process doesn't interfere with site operations. Slick.

Domain Names

Alldomains.com   http://www.alldomains.com

Here you can do a free search for your domain name or your company name in every currently recognized domain extension (which currently numbers over 675) for matches, ownership, and/or availability. This includes the usual suspects plus all country-code domains and subdomains. Alldomains.com provides basic domain registration, hosting, and web forwarding services, as well as corporate services created to handle, track, and protect brand names online at an international level. Quite nifty.

NameBoy   http://www.nameboy.com

What's in a name? NameBoy generates hundreds of domain names that are available, taken, and for sale/auction from a few keywords. It even performs cool tricks such as finding names that rhyme, and tracks names that are registered or newly available with a report that is emailed to your desktop. NameBoy speeds up the process of finding a relevant, memorable, and available domain name, for free. Bookmark it.

DomainGames   http://www.domaingames.com

DomainGames is a domain name search engine and manager. You can search for specific or partial names, monitor daily new domains, and dropped domains, and sign on for the value-added service of domain name management and tracking. If you do not feel the need to snatch up every good domain name that becomes available, you will still benefit from the extensive information available on domain name issues, governance, and disputes, which is consolidated at the site.

Retail: Setting Up Shop on the Net

The electronic commerce arena has changed dramatically since the first edition of this book was published; perhaps more dramatically than any other concept updated in this edition. The explosive adoption rate—by both business and consumer—led online consumers to more than double their holiday spending in 2000, according to figures from Goldman Sachs and PC Data Online.

From the beginning of November through December 17, holiday shoppers spent $8.7 billion online, up 108 percent from 1999's figure of $4.2 billion. Whether or not you are in the business of manufacturing and selling products, e-commerce should be part of your overall Internet strategy. But at what cost? In this chapter you will learn about:

- What consumers expect from e-commerce
- What will make consumers buy
- Master merchandisers
- Free and low-cost e-commerce options
- Micropayments and credit card alternatives
- Personalization
- Customer relationship management (CRM)
- Affiliate program strategy
- The lure of cyberbait

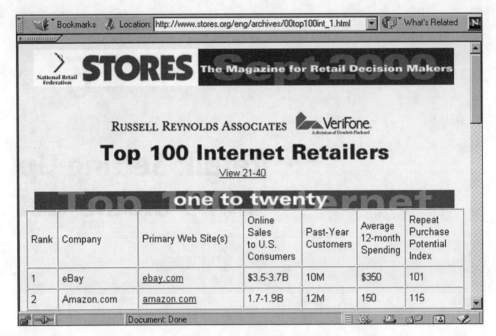

Figure 6.1 T-shirts are catching up to technology as best-selling online categories shift.

The Shift in Consumer Buying Habits

The first edition of this book advised that "you shouldn't ignore the Internet as a viable sales medium simply because the category in which you sell currently isn't the most popular on the Internet." In retrospect, that turned out to be pretty good advice. At the time, computer software sales accounted for close to 50 percent of all online purchases, and computer hardware accounted for another 18 percent. Remember those days—when geeks bought tech toys online and the thought of purchasing pantyhose, engagement rings, or custom-made cars from an e-commerce site sounded like something out of the Jetsons? The times, they have a-changed.

Today, if a major retailer is not online and e-commerce-enabled, customers and industry press are more likely to ask Why not? A ranking of the top 100 business-to-consumer e-commerce sites by *STORES*, the magazine of the National Retail Federation, is quite telling—of the top 100, 80 are non-technology-related businesses (see Figure 6.1).

The Shift in Consumer Expectations

Not only are consumers more and more likely to buy the most unlikely of products online, but they also are learning to raise the bar as to their expectations of a sales experience. According to a study by Jupiter Communications, less than 20 percent of online retailers deploy well-accepted and widely supported web technologies such as Java, Flash, or chat functions to enhance the online shopping experience and help close sales. Jupiter actually advises that online retailers abandon conservative website development practices and optimize their interactive presence in order to match the technical capabilities of most online consumers, which can now adequately support a rich interface. "Many retailers have designed their sites for the lowest common denominator, which is shortsighted, particularly for vendors of high-consideration goods," explains Lydia Loizides, an analyst with Jupiter, in a press release. Jupiter's survey of online merchants found that 60 percent cited customer feedback as a primary factor in their decisions to add advanced technologies to their sites. A Jupiter Consumer Survey of online shoppers found that more than 50 percent of respondents indicated they would use the technology if it were available. Specifically, 56 percent said they would use items such as virtual dressing rooms, and 51 percent said they would use zoom-and-spin technology if available.

It's important to note that the sales experience does not only take place online. "We are seeing a fundamental shift of power from industry to consumer," states Cynthia Hollen, CEO of Knowledge Strategies Group (http://www.kstrat.com). "It used to be that business took place at a retailer's convenience, from 9 A.M. to 5 P.M., or perhaps via a toll-free number. Now the consumer is in charge, and expects to interact at his or her convenience, whether in a bricks and mortar store, online, through an interactive kiosk, or via a wireless device. This concept of retailing 'anytime, anywhere, anyhow' is what we call omnitailing" (see Figure 6.2).

As a matter of fact, according to a report by Ernst & Young LLP entitled "Global Online Retailing," despite the fact that 2000 was a year of devastating defeat for many pure-play e-tailers, and caution for the investment community, consumers around the world continue to be very satisfied with the online retailing channel. Ernst & Young

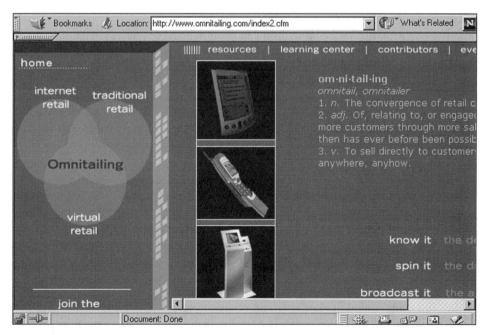

Figure 6.2 Omnitailing.com provides a forum to discuss the convergence of traditional, web, and virtual retail.

found that while shoppers are concerned with shipping costs and generally are price sensitive, the overall number of online buyers continues to increase, spending more on a greater range of merchandising categories. Ernst & Young's fourth annual special report shows four patterns clearly emerging in 2001 from the ever-shifting picture of online retailing:

- A multichannel strategy is the key to success today and a critical driver for the future. For anyone who offers consumer products, whether they are retailers or manufacturers, the online channel isn't just an option—it is an absolute necessity.
- The same consumer who buys in stores is now buying online.
- What consumers want to buy online is the same as what they demand in stores, and they expect the same merchandise selection, product quality and brands, and shopping experience across channels.
- Consumers will continue to push companies to make their online technology work the way users want it to work; and it's more than just modem speed.

The STORES e-commerce retailer ranking cited earlier in this chapter contains some interesting data about multichannel retailing. According to the accompanying report, "A look at the companies ranked #11 to #20 on the STORES list attests to the strides traditional retail companies have made in developing e-commerce as part of the reinvented business model. It also suggests that multi-channel retailing, complete with integrated IT systems, remains the future of retailing. Retailers like Lands' End, Spiegel Group, Fingerhut, JCPenney, and Gap, which built their strength in traditional store-based and catalog retailing, are successfully transferring their brand recognition to the Web."

This *new* way of thinking is quite ironic to many who have witnessed media predictions ranging from the death of bricks and mortar to the demise of the dot com to the current frenzy surrounding the wireless Web. The fact is, business is business. Making the most of every possible touch point with your customer, as appropriate for your business and your customer, is simply good business sense. Rather than scurrying after the latest media hype, the savvy business owner is asking himself or herself, What will make them buy?

What Will Make Them Buy?

There are three variables that converge in order for the consumer to feel comfortable and positive about purchasing online: financial incentive, convenience, and added value. These features are similar to the ones that moved people to change their habits and use ATMs and mail order catalogs. When my coauthor Eileen Shulock isn't writing a book, or editing *Web Digest For Marketers,* she is Vice President of Retail Strategy for a New York City consultancy called Knowledge Strategies Group (daytime job). The company creates omnitailing strategies for their clients, blending all channels and media for a complementary customer and brand experience.

It's not just about selling on the Web, or in email, or by fax, phone, or carrier pigeon. It has much to do with how you use all points of touch with your customers and prospects in tandem. In Chapter 8, "Direct Marketing and Sales Support," we feature a top-notch example of an email that sold a cigar. That cigar came from JRCigar.com. But the story doesn't stop there, for I found out about JR from stumbling upon one of their eleven stores. As a result of being in the store, I received a catalog, which featured the 800 number. When calling the 800 number, they ask you for your email, which is how I received the email featured in Chapter 8, "Direct Marketing and Sales Support." The email pulls you through the site. You sample cigars from the store, then order from the catalog and 800 number, then get email, and finally reach the site. This is merchandising. I interviewed the author of those emails, who happens to also be the CEO of this public firm. Lew Rothman is quite a guy, with a very wry sense of humor.

"We're in a great business," he says offhandedly. "People buy our products, take them home and set a match to them. If they bought suits and set them on fire, that might be a good business to get into as well." The brass tacks character I came to know in the email copy is coming through loud and clear. The man doesn't use ghostwriters. He has a reputation for speaking his mind.

Q. How much time do we have for this interview?

A. As little as possible.

Q. When you trash a cigar in your weekly email specials, I realize you're building credibility up with your readers so they'll believe you when you praise a cigar. But doesn't trashing a product destroy the sale?

A. No. Because we're asking a trash price. You have to understand who our customers are.

Q. OK, who are they?

A. They're usually people who came from modest backgrounds. Whether they are well-to-do now or not, they all understand the value of a buck. So whether they are looking for a trash cigar or an expensive cigar, they want value.

Q. Do you do much research on your audience?

A. Not so much. They want value. What does it matter if they are 26 years old from the Southwest or an MBA over 50 from the Northeast? It doesn't matter.

Q. You seem versatile online and offline. What works and what doesn't?

A. Display ads don't work. Every so often I indulge myself with a full page ad and get a few dozen phone calls, no big deal. Email and the site work for us; it's the future. Billboards work in those areas where we have stores. They do increase traffic.

Q. Online is the future for you?

A. Oh yes. We'll be able to sell internationally, now that overnight couriers make it easier to ship product anywhere.

Rothman is a master merchandiser. He innately knows what sells and how to sell it. He's been buying up huge amounts of cigars that were made for the cigar boom (which has gone up in smoke). One of his recent emails was labeled: "The cigar that never should have been made." He talks about suppliers needing to get rid of inventory for which much of the demand has evaporated, thus making it quite believable that a great cigar can be sold very inexpensively.

On my way back into New York City from his headquarters in Whippany, New Jersey, the car service driver told me Rothman's merchandising was uncanny. A few years ago, there was this soccer craze and too many golf balls were made to look like soccer balls. So Rothman buys them out and sells them for $7.00 a dozen. "How can you refuse?" the driver asks. He shows me a very sturdy collapsible umbrella. . ."Five bucks! I'm telling you, the guy's a genius." All this from a corner store that was started in Brooklyn by Rothman's dad in 1946. "I flunked English," Rothman notes, and now JR is a public company with eleven stores around the country.

The point is, selling on the Web is just that—selling. It's not all this pie in the sky extrapolation of inner psyche and modem speed. A well-grounded understanding of people and what makes them act will lead to success. Our tip? Find the Lew Rothmans of the world—the naturals in the business—and watch what they do. It's knowing how to sell, not how to guess the future.

Financial Incentive

Let's take the first variable: financial incentive. Online goods frequently sport attractive pricing as compared to competing sales channels. The cost of sales online can be less than the cost in the real world for a number of reasons: You don't have to own or rent a store; there are additional savings in reduced inventory; and you are able to sell directly to consumers while disintermediating many middlemen. The savings are passed on to the consumer in this open marketplace, not because of any altruistic notion, but rather to stay ahead of the competitor's pricing.

The self-service style of selling also offers the consumer the option of completing the transaction online and making the purchase for less, by way of auctions and last-minute deals on vanishing commodities, such as airline seats. In addition, many online retailers are in a battle for market share, and steep price discounts are one way to bring customers to their sites. Not always the most successful way, as giving away one's products does not a business strategy make—a slew of bankruptcies in the e-commerce space will attest to that.

Convenience

The second variable is convenience. Instead of trundling down to the library to access a *Consumer Reports* review of lawn mowers, the customer looking for a lawn mower can simply pull the review up on screen at his or her desktop. Multiply that by a few hundred buying occasions in one's life and you're looking at saving an enormous amount of time. Even though users don't think of it on such a grand scale, the day they do in fact look up the information about a lawn mower on the Net means they have indeed initiated a new habit for one part of the buying cycle. Users may or may not finish that cycle online, but may make the actual purchase offline instead. If consumers don't complete the transaction online, they are still one step closer to doing so for a purchase in the future.

Many web technologies, such as online registration and storage of personal information, have made purchasing online far more convenient for consumers. How much easier is it to do your holiday shopping at the Gap online, where the addresses of friends and family are stored, and products can be selected, purchased, wrapped, and sent with a few clicks? You can probably complete your holiday shopping from your desktop in less time than it would take you to find a parking space at the local shopping mall on a busy holiday weekend.

Convenience can also be measured in the amount of time it takes to actually get the product you need into your hands. Over the past few years we've seen that convenience can no longer be measured in days; it is measured in hours. Services like Kozmo.com—which will deliver books, videos, food, CDs, and more to your door in an hour or less—stand toe-to-toe with a growing number of same-day delivery solutions for online retailers. Ironically, the ability to tap into actual bricks and mortar retail or warehouse outlets now gives *bricks and clicks* retailers a distinct advantage over pure online players.

Added Value

The last variable is added value. To paraphrase an old saying, "Value is in the eye of the beholder." For example, there are specialty food sellers out there who sell directly over the Net, such as http://www.pastrami.com, which originates from the Mill Basin Kosher Deli in Brooklyn. It is a robust and worldwide business selling New York deli food to homesick New Yorkers. Another microniche player in the food category (especially if you're a salsa fan) is HotHotHot! (http://hothothot.com). Note the tight focus on the site's raison d'être, as well as the presentation of product categories, which gives the user several different ways to shop. The site is clever and efficient, and consumers do notice. The ability to purchase products or services that were previously not easily available is a great value-add to consumers (see Figure 6.3).

Figure 6.3 HotHotHot! knows how to sellsellsell! on the Net.

Figure 6.4 Pick your own ink color, font, and words and see your Fine Stationery come to life online.

We have tried to avoid using the overused Amazon.com site as an example, but here we feel compelled to do so to demonstrate added value. Amazon.com is the leading e-commerce site on the Web for one reason—the company has continually focused on using technology to its best advantage to provide value for its customers. From suggested reading to the ability to request and receive the latest installment of the Harry Potter book series the day it is published—by express mail—Amazon.com is a great example of how to meet a customer's needs, often before the customer even knows what those needs are.

Added value also includes the concept of improving upon a customer's real-world experience with the creative use of technology. For example, at FineStationery.com (http://www.finestationery.com) you can create your own customized stationery in an interactive Design Studio that combines the actual stationery product of interest with your own words in your choice of fonts. That way, you can easily see what your choice will look like before committing to the purchase—a feat that is impossible when purchasing customized stationery, invitations, or other printed materials in any other way (see Figure 6.4).

The Real Costs of World Class E-Commerce

Right about now you may be saying to yourself, But I don't even sell products! Indeed, product manufacturing and/or sales may not be part of your business today. But the sale of products (and services) from your site should be part of your Internet strategy starting right this minute. Why? Because you have real people—a targeted audience—visiting your site for any number of reasons. In today's increasingly virtual world, your audience gives you power.

Retailers recognize that fact, and are increasingly providing ways in which you can sell to your audience without ever touching a product. Your recommendation, through an *affiliate* program (covered later in this chapter) can translate into commission on every sale. You can even add a store to your site and choose from a catalog of products, offering only those that you think will be of interest to your site visitors. This is a win-win situation, as you can establish new revenue streams while providing products or services that may be quite valuable to your site visitors. You are also creating a competitive advantage, as your visitors learn to rely on your site not only for your business information, but also as a convenient place to purchase related products and services of interest to them.

Since your coauthor is an e-commerce strategist involved in the strategy and development of many high-end retail sites, we wanted to take this opportunity to address the not-so-level playing field that is e-commerce today. As noted earlier in this chapter, today's consumer is growing increasingly sophisticated. Computers come equipped with more power and memory, as well as the latest browsers and plug-ins, so that sites with Flash animations, audio, sophisticated product imaging, or other fancy techniques are well within the realm of experience of the average web surfer. Certainly, sites with online registration, membership or loyalty programs, address books, wish lists, and other shopping conveniences are growing increasingly common. Therefore, the customer's expectation level is increasing exponentially—and is definitely increasingly more quickly than the technology budgets of most small to midsized businesses.

In general, shopping is as much about the quality of the experience as it is about the product itself. After all, you can purchase a pair of jeans from innumerable retailers. Why do you choose Banana Republic over Old Navy? It may have to do with the look of the store, eye-catching advertisements, the quality of the product assortment, or the ease of purchase. Online, the website is the environment in which a sales transaction takes place. The look of the site, its ease of navigation, its value-added functionalities, and the comfort level with the brand and with the security of the transaction process play a huge role in your purchasing decision. If you are the owner of Joe's Books, your site visitors may already know what it is like to purchase a book from Amazon.com. Do you offer a comparable experience? If not, why would the customer choose to purchase from you?

That question has difficult but not insurmountable answers, as you will learn throughout the rest of this chapter. However, we do want to make one thing very clear—it takes a lot of money, meaning significant six figures well into the millions of dollars, to create a world class e-commerce experience. By world class, we mean the type of seamless experience that covers everything from innovative design and ease of use to personalization, retention programs, integrated customer service, real-time inventory updates, and well-branded, on-time delivery.

The good news is that technology is constantly evolving, so today's million dollar innovation may well be within the affordable range from a number of providers, at least in a scaled-down version, in the very near future. Leading online retailers are creating the future of e-commerce with the help of well-staffed technology teams and constant research and development. Leading e-commerce solutions for the small to mid-sized business owner are incorporating those learnings into a variety of packages that bring e-commerce into the affordable range.

We'll show you what to focus on and how to find the most affordable way to integrate e-commerce into your business today.

High Impact Solutions with Low Impact Price Tags

Can you add an e-commerce component to your business for free? Yes, actually, you can. One of the most innovative e-commerce opportunities on the market today is the free e-commerce store offered by Freetailer.com (http://freetailer.excite.com). Backed by Excite.com, Free*tailer* is the first major Internet portal to give away a fully functional store in one free package. With Free*tailer*, you get:

- A site-building wizard with step-by-step instructions
- Free hosting with 25 MB of web space
- Listing in Excite Shopping to help drive traffic
- Unlimited products, 100 free transactions
- Functional shopping cart and cash register from day one
- Orders accepted securely through SSL (Secure Socket Layer) encryption
- Automatic shipping and sales tax calculation
- Accepted cash and check payments
- Ability to upload custom graphics and insert customized text
- Merchant "backroom" with store traffic statistics
- Ability to change site and retrieve orders online, anytime
- Upgrade options that help drive traffic and make processing orders easier

Excite's Free*tailer* gives anyone the ability to create a professional looking store with sophisticated e-commerce functionality. For those who are leery of leaping into e-commerce, and all the associated price tags, this solution provides the tools you need at a good price—free.

How can Free*tailer* work for you? Let's say you are a travel agent specializing in adventure vacations. In addition to your core site offerings, which probably include both information and the ability to purchase an adventure vacation package, you can create an online store using the Free*tailer* service. Your store might include everything from hiking boots and tents to scuba gear. Your audience—adventure vacation travelers—might welcome the opportunity to pick up a few adventure-oriented products for their vacation at the very moment that they book their trip with you. Why should they leave your site, full of excitement and inspiration, only to purchase the items they need somewhere else? You can satisfy their travel needs and get them ready for their vacation at the same time.

What's the catch? First of all, the service is free until it reaches a certain sales level. If your store is wildly successful, you will move on up the Free*tailer* food chain and begin to incur costs for the maintenance of your store. That's not such a bad position to be in—you're so successful that you need to pay a bit for what was previously free. But you have added a revenue stream that didn't exist before, for zero start-up cost. Another drawback is that your store must reside under the Free*tailer* domain, so that if your site is called WildTravel.com, your store would actually be at WildTravel .Freetailer.com, and your customers would leave your site to go to shop in your Free-*tailer* store. Again, not such a bad trade-off, although it does indicate that your store is not a privately-owned endeavor. Finally, while you do have a choice of templates and designs and products to choose from, you are limited to the store designs, product assortment, and display methods established by Free*tailer*.

This limited ability to customize your store in look and feel, product display, or ancillary support services such as customer service or inventory management is one of the key drawbacks to free or relatively low cost e-commerce solutions. For some, this may not matter at all. For others, the lack of control, or a cookie cutter solution could be a disadvantage to their business. Once again, the good news is that these e-commerce platforms are growing and changing daily in response to competitive pressure and customer demands.

TIP It's best to fully explore and test any e-commerce solution up front, with a good idea of how you would like your commerce efforts to expand in the future, in order to find the best solution for your needs.

What if you have your own products that you want to feature in your online store? There are hundreds of e-commerce solutions out there, and an analysis of their pros and cons could be the subject of another book. Take a look around. It's likely that your own Internet Service Provider offers a combination of e-commerce services to create, host, and sell products, including secure transaction capabilities. At the time of this writing, basic e-commerce solutions from ISPs were available for as little as $40 per month. IBM (http://www.ibm.com) offers a WebStarter Kit with an e-commerce solution that includes online ordering, multiple pages, and limited credit card capability. Setup costs $799 at the time of this writing, and hosting is $40 a month. Others such as Secure Pay (http://www.securepay.com) offer credit card processing and shopping cart functionality that can be integrated into your own site. Finally, e-commerce solutions such as iCat (http://www.icat.com) provide more sophisticated (yet reasonably priced) ways to either build or integrate an e-commerce store. These starter e-commerce solutions are a boon for the small to midsized business, and also an easy way for large businesses to get their feet wet in the e-commerce waters.

Key E-Commerce Issues

In addition to your e-commerce store itself, there are a few services you must secure to complete transactions, such as the ability to process credit card transactions (if this is not offered by your e-commerce solution provider). There are other services you can offer to customers that will create value, bringing them to your site again and again. Let's look at several of them now.

Getting an Online Merchant's Account

If you had a physical store, you would go to the bank with which your company has an account and ask to have a merchant's account set up in order to accept credit cards. If your firm's credit history is good, this shouldn't take too long or be a problem. However, even if your company's credit history is flawless, companies quite often have problems getting a merchant's account specifically for the purpose of online credit card transactions. For this reason, there are brokers who will match you up with an institution who will accept the risk. Ad Merchant Accounts (http://www.admerchantaccounts.com) is one such service. These brokers are remunerated one time, often by the application fee you are charged by the sponsoring institution. Once these brokers are paid, they leave the process permanently. For a list of additional brokers, go to any search portal, such as Yahoo!, and type in "merchant account." You will be served up with hundreds of suggested links.

Once your merchant account is secured, there are basically three players: the buyer (with his or her credit card), your site, and the clearinghouse that tells you whether or not the buyer's credit card is legitimate. Two examples of these clearinghouses are FirstData Corporation and FirstUSA. If you have a big company, you're going to need a vast quantity of sales to support the huge infrastructure consisting of your server, industrial-strength connectivity to the Internet, and a full staff. More often than not, a company is apt to farm out this process to a web service provider. There's usually a setup fee that can range from a few hundred to a few thousand dollars, depending on the scope of the store. Then there's a monthly fee that usually ranges in the hundreds of dollars as well. Depending on the pricing structure, that provider may also take a percentage of each sale or have a minimum charge per transaction.

When you're shopping around for a provider to house your store and take credit cards, try to figure out about how many sales you'll have per month, as the provider will often quote you a price based on predicted transactions. For the sake of argument, let's say you have 50 products to sell online. Let's concentrate on the options you have to accept payment. It's easiest to accept orders through a toll-free number or by fax, but in order to be competitive you will need to offer the ability online. The following is what often happens.

A buyer selects an item to purchase. He or she proceeds to the checkout part of your site. Behind the scenes, this often means the buyer goes from your shopping cart or catalog into a more secure place where credit card numbers can be exchanged. All pages are not automatically secure, as secure pages run much more slowly. The buyer is actually transported from your site to what is known as a Secure Socket Layer (SSL) site at your provider's site. The buyer sees a dialog box that notifies him or her of this and sees either a solid key or padlock in the lower-left screen. When that key or padlock is made whole, you know you're communicating with the server at the other end in a much more secure fashion. Try this yourself on some sites and keep an eye on the URL to see if the domain changes to "https," which indicates a secure transaction location.

The actual appearance of the screen may look exactly the same as the rest of the catalog or shopping cart, while the URL is in fact different.

All information is heavily encrypted and is passed in a file. One of the key components of that file is a certificate that must be renewed annually. This certificate tells the surfer's PC that you are, in fact, the site that you claim to be. Breaking this file apart would entail decoding the encrypted information. This would take a hacker a very long time, even with the help of a supercomputer—all for only one measly credit card number. It just doesn't pay to steal credit card numbers this way.

Once the card number has been given in this secure area, one of two things will happen:

The card number is sent to a clearinghouse to establish whether it is a valid number and if there are enough funds available on the account to cover the purchase. This real-time checking of card numbers is a more expensive option, but it might be worth the extra expense, as you immediately are alerted to insufficient funds or invalid card numbers. Unless you are handling hundreds of transactions a day, it will probably be more practical to implement the next option.

The card numbers are simply stored and forwarded to you so you can check them all at once at the end of the day, or every few days. This is called batch processing. If you're taking in only a few orders a day or week, and you're not selling instant deliverables, it's probably more cost efficient to batch process the orders, rather than doing so in real time. However, if you batch process at the end of the day, having already delivered online software or content, you run the risk of parting with the goods prior to knowing whether you've sold them to a legitimate cardholder or not. On the other hand, if you're selling physical goods that must be delivered, you can simply withhold the sending of such items until you are sure you're dealing with a legitimate customer. If someone is brazen enough to use a fraudulent credit card and have you mail him the merchandise, he's likely to mask his physical address, thus making it harder for you to track him down.

TIP If you accept monetary or credit card transactions from outside the United States, always insist on the transaction being denominated in U.S. funds. This puts the burden and cost of conversion on the consumer, not you. Multicards (http://www.multicards.com) accepts in U.S. dollars or British pounds.

The higher the cost of a product, the more occurrences of fraud you're apt to encounter. It is especially important to keep in mind that even with real-time transactions, there is a risk on the merchant's part. You see, someone could be using a credit card number that is indeed valid and not stolen, but merely "borrowed," perhaps by a waiter who took the card the night before in a restaurant. When the real-time checking is done, it comes back saying that this card is fine and to let the purchase proceed.

However, some weeks later, the true cardholder sees this charge from you on his monthly statement and denies having made the transaction. Your merchant account is then notified that the money you thought was now yours must be returned. In fact, you're likely to be charged a fee, usually about $25, to reverse the transaction. As a result, you're not only short of the money you thought you had from the purchase, but you're also $25 in the hole! A credit card holder has up to 90 days to contest purchases. If you do sell instantly deliverable items online, you won't know for sure that money is truly yours until three months from when the purchase is actually made.

On a more positive note, fraud screening is getting better all the time. In the United States especially, it is getting faster and more accurate. Since Europe and points beyond don't have a unified standard for checking and reconciling such claims, it will be harder to limit fraudulent use from overseas at this time. You may elect to not accept credit cards from overseas for this reason, though it seems a shame to shut down markets that were heretofore not necessarily available to you.

Alternate Payment Methods

The kinds of online transactions we've discussed thus far have primarily been credit card oriented. There are other approaches, either for smaller transactions or in order to purchase without a credit card. Either of these payment methods might be effective and useful to your audience.

Micropayments are designed to fill a niche that covers small transactions that aren't worth putting through the credit card system. They work by having a virtual purse on your computer, out of which you can spend small amounts of money. However, as mentioned in previous chapters, the noise level out on the Web is deafening. Therefore, people are giving away things of higher and higher value all the time in order to get your attention.

Ask yourself, Why should I pay next to nothing for something that I can get for nothing somewhere else? You might answer: convenience. It might be worth 15 cents or $1.52 to pull up that article from a database while you are right there at a site, on a deadline, rather than trying to go find it for free on the open Net, where it may exist somewhere else. Will you spend small amounts of money for useful information while on a research mission rather than spend your time finding the right information for free? Just as some people will drive out of their way to avoid paying a toll on a bridge or highway, there are people who prefer the free route. However, many who need to find accurate information fast, such as journalists, librarians, research analysts, students, and so forth find that paying for small amounts of information via micropayments is a convenient path to a speedy solution.

As a matter of fact, the policy has been implemented by the Great Grey Lady herself, *The New York Times* (http://www.nytimes.com). While daily content remains free (for up to one week), retrieving articles via a Premium Archive search (which dates back to 1996) costs $2.50 per article. *The New York Times* partnered with Qpass, a micropayment system, to handle these small transactions. Users set up an account with Qpass (which is free), give their credit card number, and are then assigned a user ID and password. Any time the user wants to pay for a service offered by a Qpass partner (partners also include the *Wall Street Journal*, *USA Today*, and AT&T Prepaid Wireless), they simply give their Qpass information. Qpass aggregates the microcharges and then deducts the total of all Qpass purchases from the user's credit card each month (see Figure 6.5).

Should you employ a micropayment scheme for your online retailing? The litmus test to use here is to ask yourself if your target audience is apt to use it themselves.

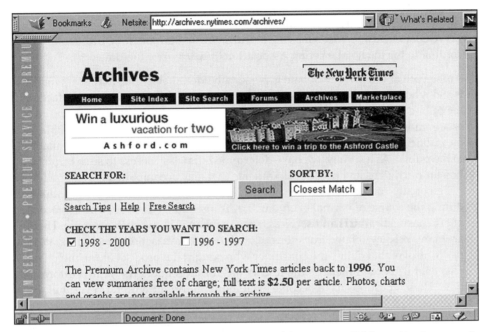

Figure 6.5 Articles from *The New York Times* archives are available at $2.50 a pop via micropayment processor Qpass.

© 2000 The New York Times Company. Reprinted by permission.

Another alternative is to offer a form of cashless payment that utilizes a prepaid gift certificate or currency alternative. Flooz (http://www.flooz.com) is the creator of an online gift currency. The company pioneered a unique new method of gift-giving for the Internet by combining email and electronic greeting cards with a *stored value platform*. As a result, Flooz users can send online gift currency to anyone with an email address. Recipients can spend their Flooz at any online store that accepts Flooz. Flooz selected and aggregated stores in every consumer category to create an online shopping destination for Flooz recipients. Retail partners include BarnesandNoble.com, Toysrus.com, TowerRecords.com, marthastewart.com, Babystyle, Fogdog Sports, and MotherNature.com. Recipients of Flooz get a Flooz account, which allows them to keep track of their purchases and their remaining Flooz balance. It even gives reminders for special occasions. While Flooz works well for gift occasions, other solutions, such as PayPal, allow buyer and seller to transfer money to one another from preestablished and prepaid PayPal accounts. PayPal is the number one method of payment used at auction site eBay, which eliminates the need for checks and money orders and the time lag involved in waiting for payments to clear for relatively small purchase amounts.

Privacy

In addition to the security issues inherent to online payment, consumers are also concerned about privacy online. While organizations such as TRUSTe (http://www .truste.org) push for an international privacy standard, e-commerce sites must balance the need for consumer trust with the need to gather and analyze customer data to better serve customers and—let's face it—to learn how to become more profitable. According to the Direct Marketing Association (http://www.the-dma.org):

> At the core of the privacy debate is personally identifiable information—what it is and who has access to it. In the United States, many forms of data are, in fact, in the public domain. Name, address, telephone number, birth certificates, and real estate transactions are just a few of the types of information that are available to the public. The telephone book is another example of information that is available to the public. As a society, we have determined that easy access to such information far outweighs any possible detriments that may accompany it.
>
> Personally identifiable information is generated every day by individuals during the course of normal everyday life. Transactional data, such as the record of purchasing products and services from merchants, is one such example. There are many privacy-related questions related to such transactions, including; Who has control of that data—the consumer who bought the product or the merchant who sold it? Should there be the restrictions on subsequent use of that information? These questions have become even more important with the advent of the Internet.

As marketers, we must balance the ability to ascertain more and more information about online visitors and customers with an open recognition of what data is being collected and what is being done with it. Consumers do understand that by explicitly sharing certain kinds of data, they can in turn receive targeted offers or even a complete online experience that is personalized to their preferences. With technology, it is also possible to deliver targeted messages by using data implicitly gathered from the site visitor. Is it appropriate to gather and react to that information without the visitor's consent or knowledge? These issues will be debated for years to come. Our advice? Do what works for your business while being very upfront with site visitors and customers as to how you use their data. Honesty is always a good policy.

TIP Create a privacy policy online in minutes using the Direct Marketing Association's interactive Privacy Policy Generator tool (http://www.the-dma.org/library/privacy/creating.shtml#form). This tool was developed to help marketers create policies that are consistent with the DMA's Privacy Principles for Online Marketing. Answer a series of questions about your site and your use of customer data, and your new policy will be emailed to you for upload to your site.

Leading E-Commerce Trends

There are trends in e-commerce development that can be tracked and analyzed to understand where the industry is going, and ultimately what your customers will expect from you. This section peers into the future to assess how cutting-edge technologies will impact e-commerce over the months and years ahead.

Adding Value with Personalization

We mentioned before that it will be necessary to add value to the online purchasing process by featuring items the user finds helpful and can't find in any other medium. Personalization is one such added value. LikeMinds, Net Perceptions, and Broadvision are three of the better known personalization providers on the Net. What is personalization? Personalization is actually quite misunderstood. It is used as an all-encompassing word, when in fact personalization comes in many forms (see Figure 6.6).

Customization allows visitors on a site to indicate their preferences according to their needs, such as specifying what sports scores and weather reports are of interest to them.

Rules-based personalization allows a marketer to specify fixed rules to change or adapt a site based on visitor behavior. For example, a marketer might establish a rule that if a visitor puts a Palm Pilot in his or her shopping cart, the visitor is always presented with an upsell of the latest Palm accessories. Or a user may go to a music site and fill out a form that asks questions about musical tastes. The user is helping the merchant to rule in or out possibilities that may be of interest to him or her. If I tell it I like Bob Dylan, it may come back and inform me that there is a tribute album to Jimmy Rogers he produced that I might not otherwise have known about. It could also tell me that Dylan figures prominently in the book *American Folk Lore Anthology*. Rules-based systems do not learn from customer reactions. Do the upsells work? The marketer would have to study traffic and sales reports to determine that.

Figure 6.6 Personalization.com is an excellent source of information on personalization thinking and technology.

Adaptive personalization takes rules-based personalization one step further by reacting—in real time—to what the customer is doing on the site, learning from that behavior, and applying it to future scenarios, without intervention. One example of adaptive personalization technology is *collaborative filtering*, which is employed by many e-commerce sites. For instance, with a collaborative filtering system in place, a music site may discover that customers who purchase Bob Dylan music also tend to purchase new stereo systems. In a rules-based scenario, it would be difficult to predict or determine that kind of behavior. Who knew? Collaborative filtering efforts continuously learn about visitor behavior, and compare visitor predilections with those of others who have similar tastes. As time goes on, they can make more sophisticated recommendations to you because they better understand the behavior of the group. Collaborative filtering can greatly increase revenues, as customers are presented with products, content, and even entire websites that are targeted to their preferences, thereby making them more likely to buy. A better site experience also means that they will return more frequently and purchase more often. Incorporating personalization technology such as collaborative filtering into a site is an expensive endeavor today, although more options will become available at more affordable price ranges. As the cost of new technologies typically comes down precipitously, these added-value goodies will become more accessible to smaller players sooner rather than later.

It is possible to offer a scaled-down version of rules-based personalization with a bit of savvy web strategy. For example, if you are in the business of selling sports memorabilia, you might want to first categorize the products and content of your site into major sports divisions, such as football, basketball, baseball, and hockey. The visitor who is interested in hockey would be taken directly to the hockey-focused section of your site, leaving the sports that are not of interest behind. You then might want to further categorize the hockey section into decades, or teams, so that the hockey fan can dive right in to the specific era or team of interest to him or her. In this way, you have allowed the user to quickly navigate through a morass of information and products to the exact area of interest. You can cross-reference products as appropriate between teams and eras. You might also offer registration for targeted newsletters within each of the subsections, so that the fan can be updated when new merchandise or content arrives. While you are not providing a dynamic personalized solution, where products and promotions of interest are predicted on the fly and served to the visitor based upon preferences, you are personalizing your site to the extent that it provides a very valuable, targeted experience for the user.

This may seem like a lot of work, but industry studies indicate that a user who registers or opts in for targeted information at an e-commerce site accounts for the majority of purchases where that opportunity is available. Using this example, you will want to evaluate your potential e-commerce solution to make sure that it allows you to categorize and subcategorize products exactly as you need to, and that you are able to mix informative content with your product selections. A year ago, such a solution would have to be custom-built. Today, it may well be within the range of competitive online or off-the-shelf technologies.

Eric Norlin, Managing Editor of Personalization.com, elaborates further: "Jupiter Research estimates that fewer than 20 percent of all websites use personalization technology. And Forrester estimates that only 16 percent of those sites using the technology actually measure the results. The bottom line is that personalization has just emerged from its adolescence. As personalization matures, it will come to mean not just a software package that runs on a website, but a shift in attitude as well. The personalization of the future will demand that business move past the discrete moment of the transaction to the ongoing process of individualized interactions."

Dana Blakenhorn, who publishes the *Get A Clue. . .to Internet Commerce* newsletter, suggests you watch which personalization scheme Netscape and Microsoft choose. Those endorsements and possible financial backing will be good indicators as to who will be around for the long haul. This is true for any plug-in, package, or technology standard on the Web today: The two big browser companies, as they continue to duke it out to be number one, will decide for the rest of us which programs will become the standard.

Adding Value with Cookies

Another way to bring value to your customer is with the use of cookies. A cookie is a file that sits on the surfer's computer. It can tell your server a number of things, including the domain name of the surfer's provider, such as netcom.com. You'll know the type of browser being used by the visiting surfer, such as Netscape 5.0. The cookie also carries with it a virtual trail of breadcrumbs that divulges which site the surfer visited prior to coming to yours. It won't tell you the actual name of that surfer, unless of course you ask him or her, then marry that information with the cookie to identify the surfer the next time he or she visits. Just using simple cookies can help you personalize your site.

E*TRADE (http://www.etrade.com) uses a combination of registration and cookies as a tool for making its site a more efficient and personalized experience for the user. If you're using the same computer each time you surf and return to the E*TRADE site, it might say "Welcome back, Eileen Shulock. Click here for the latest information about the stocks that interest you." Here again, people will, for the most part, accept this knowledge of who you are in favor of the savings, convenience, and intuition it offers as a tradeoff. If surfers don't like the use of cookies and feel they are an intrusion on their privacy, they can turn off the cookie function in their browser's preferences.

TIP Using cookies as a form of personalization familiarizes your server with the surfer's PC, not the surfer himself. If multiple users use the same computer, your server will not have an exact fix on one person's profile, since numerous people are using that machine.

Adding Value with Customer Service

Good online customer service may be one of the most valuable areas on which to focus. According to industry studies, 66 percent of online shopping carts are abandoned, most often due to unanswered questions or other point of sale difficulties. A good customer-focused strategy on both the front end and the back end, combined with some low-cost customer service tools, can go a long way to helping you close your sales.

According to Mark Hurst, founder and president of customer experience consulting firm Creative Good, "In consumer tests of top e-commerce sites conducted recently by my firm, basic problems on these sites caused customers to fail in over 40 percent of their buying attempts. These customers *wanted* to buy, but the sites were so confusing that the customers literally could not figure out how to get to the end of the transaction. For example, customers got confused when sites asked them to 'create a new account' before they could buy their selected items. A buying failure rate of 40 percent translates to billions of dollars in lost sales per year for e-businesses worldwide." His advice? "To succeed, sites must be easy for customers to use. But 'easy to use' is not easy to attain. Don't rely on your internal resources to get the 'objective eye' you need to fix your site. By definition, resources inside the company are already biased with insider knowledge. Instead, get an experienced, professional third party to help."

In a real-world store, customers can usually find a salesperson to help them with their purchasing decision. However, that salesperson may be busy, may not be particularly knowledgeable or friendly, or may have a bias toward certain products (such as those that pay higher commissions) that in the end do not best serve the customers' needs. A website offers the opportunity for pure customer support, with the explicit goal of helping the customer close the sale.

CRM, or Customer Relationship Management, is discussed in detail in Chapter 5, "Your Brand Image and the Internet," as we contend that your branding depends on executing flawlessly at all customer touch points. A site can be strategically structured to provide the best possible customer experience. Make sure that your site includes:

Contact information **(phone, email, or both) on every page, along with a clear definition of service hours or turnaround time for a response.** For example, if customer service is available 24 hours a day, by all means make that perfectly clear. Also let the customer know when their email queries will be answered. Today? Tomorrow? With many companies, it's never. Don't let that happen to you.

Complete, easy-to-read *product descriptions* **with every possible bit of information included.** Don't make the customer have to ask how much it costs, whether or not necessary parts are included, and so on. When structuring your product pages, you may want to make the top level of information very clear and easy to scan, and then provide links to the details or questions that a customer is likely to have for each product. That way, the customer can access information as needed, right at the point it is needed.

In addition to a FAQ (Frequently Asked Questions) section on your site, *provide brief questions and answers throughout your site* **where problems are likely to occur, or where questions are likely to arise.** For example, as the customer enters the purchase process, you may want to highlight your secure transaction capabilities. Why should the customer have to search out the answer to a frequently asked question in the FAQ section, leaving the purchase process? Intuitive placement of questions and answers eases the customer through the transaction.

Product reviews **from an unbiased source, if appropriate.** These reviews are often more credible than the manufacturer's slick promotional spin. Amazon.com's book reader reviews are a good example of how unbiased content and opinions can be solicited from your purchasing audience. You might also want to pull in information from another unbiased content source, such as *Consumer Reports*, to help customers assess your product choices.

Related information **about how to use your products or services, success stories, news items, or other content that relays just how important it is for the customer to own what you are selling.** For example, you may want to incorporate articles or testimonials from happy customers. You might also even consider pulling in content from another source, such as a newsfeed, if it relates to and sincerely supports your product assortment. The latest news on product recalls in your segment, for example, could be perceived as a very useful tool if applicable.

TIP **To learn more about how to create a good customer experience on your site, sign up for the goodexperience.com free weekly newsletter by sending an email to update@goodexperience.com, or by visiting http://www.goodexperience.com.**

In addition, carefully plan and execute your customer service strategy. This includes scripted, professional handling of all email inquiries, and potentially an integrated CRM solution. While many customer service solutions can cost quite a bundle to integrate into your site, there are no-cost and low-cost ways to add effective support. HumanClick (http://www.humanclick.com) provides free live online chat capabilities for the low traffic site (see Figure 6.7). Using this service, you could easily establish "customer question" hours where you will be available to advise on purchase decisions. If you are not available, customers can leave a message for you for future follow-up. LivePerson (http://www.liveperson.com) is the provider of the HumanClick service as well as more robust, yet low-cost, live customer support alternatives.

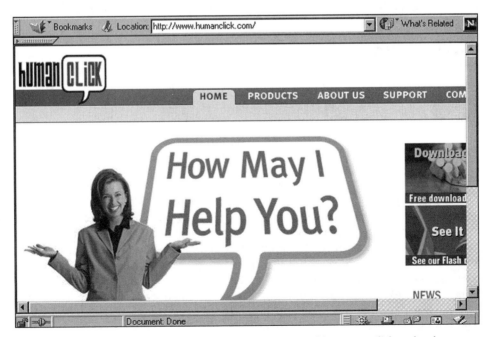

Figure 6.7 Free, live customer service is minutes away with HumanClick technology.

LivePerson's sophisticated technology allows you to automate responses, push product pages and promotions to the customer, and archive all conversations for datamining purposes.

Adding Value with Cross-Merchandising

No matter how your online store is constructed and maintained, you've got some very interesting possibilities to amortize the investment you've made in the solution itself and the advertising it took to get shoppers to your site. Cross-sells and upsells are two ways to help your customer spend more money at your site. Not only can products be suggested from content pages, but you can also predict what your customer might be interested in based upon the product they are looking at.

Of course, sophisticated merchandising technology will do so automatically, but a more homegrown solution can also be effective. You can look at each of your product pages and imagine what else the customer would be interested in, and then suggest that product with a link to it. For example, every page of your store that features a hiking boot could cross-sell a sports sock. You can also incorporate upsell suggestions, which encourage the customer to buy more of whatever he or she is considering—instead of buying one pair of sports socks for $10, a promotion could offer three pairs for $25. A recent trip to the Speedo store here in New York City serves as a good parallel to real-world cross-selling. I went in to buy a bathing suit. The second one was half price, so I bought two. That allowed me to save additionally on swim goggles, so I bought a pair of them. At this point, the dollar amount of my purchase entitled me to buy anything else in the store for 40 percent off, so I bought a day pack. By the time I got out of there, I had spent over $150! I went in looking to spend around $30. They got me.

Affiliate Programs

One of the easiest ways to add e-commerce to your site is to participate in an affiliate program or an affiliate program network. Basically, an affiliate program, or associate program, is a sales and marketing tool that a retailer can use in order to extend their products and brand awareness into the sites of others, thereby tapping into much more traffic and a much wider audience than they could reach at their site alone.

The most popular affiliate program on the Web is the one offered by Amazon.com. Just about anybody with a website can recommend books that might be of interest to their site visitors. Amazon.com pioneered the affiliate network concept by empowering site owners to link to specific books within the Amazon.com site. Whenever a visitor clicks on the link and purchases a book, the site owner receives a commission for the sale. Amazon.com has created proprietary technology that tracks and analyzes affiliate sales to the purchase level, rewarding those sites that perform well with higher commissions. The site owner benefits from the revenue stream, the site visitor benefits from the ability to directly purchase books of interest to them quickly, and Amazon.com benefits by having hundreds of thousands of sites promoting Amazon.com through the affiliate network.

What if you want to sell more than books? An affiliate network is the answer. Affiliate networks are companies that bring together dozens of retailers that wish to offer affiliate sales opportunities. The affiliate network then goes out and finds hundreds of thousands of websites to participate in driving traffic to the retailer's site by placing generic banner ads or specific products from the retailer on the affiliate's site. Affiliates are rewarded (usually with a commission) when their site visitors click through to purchase on the retailer's site as a result of the affiliate promotion.

Each site owner can apply to sell products from any number of retailers in the network. If you have a website about alternative medicine, you might apply to sell aromatherapy candles from retailer 1, vitamins from retailer 2, and exercise equipment from retailer 3. Your site would be reviewed by those three retailers, and if approved, you would simply link to store banners or specific products of interest wherever appropriate within your site. Again, you receive a commission whenever one of your links results in a sale, as visitors will click through your link to purchase on the retailer's site. Affiliate networks have built very sophisticated technology to link and track the retailers and site owners, site performance, product sales and commissions, and are responsible for making the entire relationship run smoothly.

One of the disadvantages of affiliate programs is that the retailer will want to establish a relationship with the customer that you have just sent to them. Therefore, you must constantly update your content and affiliate links in order to encourage your site visitors to buy specific products. Otherwise, the next time they need an aromatherapy candle, they will go straight to the retailer's site—there's no reason to link once again through you to make future purchases. Therefore, to keep your commissions coming in, you must work hard to continually merchandise products and links throughout your site.

LinkShare (http://www.linkshare.com) is one example of an online affiliate network. You can either initiate the offer to other websites via LinkShare, or, as an affiliate you can see what other deals and percentages other sites are offering you for referring business. In either event, LinkShare offers a good index as to who's offering what team-selling programs on the Net.

Affiliate programs have exploded over the past few years, as they do offer an efficient means to connect merchants with affiliates that would like to sell products online. "We'll see more and more emphasis on training for both merchants and affiliates," predicts Dr. Ralph Wilson, industry veteran and publisher of WilsonWeb (http://www .wilsonweb.com) (see Figure 6.8). "That's the weak link. Ninety-five percent of all affiliates have one main business plan—set up a site, put up affiliate links, and get rich quick. But they have no traffic."

Lack of traffic leads to lack of sales, which leads to unhappy experiences with affiliate programs for both retailers and affiliates. According to Dr. Wilson, education is in order for both parties to help affiliate programs succeed. "Merchants need to identify which affiliates are valuable to them," emphasizes Wilson. "Merchants must then contact the affiliates personally and encourage them to join their affiliate network. They must then create a personal relationship." This personal, ongoing relationship between retailer and affiliate is like the relationship between a manufacturer and its sales force. Is the sales force left on its own to do whatever it wants? Never! The sales force is the backbone of the company, responsible for knowing as much as possible about current

Figure 6.8 Dr. Ralph F. Wilson's WilsonWeb site is one of the best sources on the Web for e-commerce and web marketing information.

and future products, the company, and the market. Manufacturers spend millions of dollars to educate their sales forces on an ongoing basis. In contrast, says Wilson, "Typically the merchant's attitude is 'Let's spend as little money as possible on this.' But if merchants would work to build relationships with their key affiliates month after month, then everybody wins."

Wilson has advice for affiliates as well. "Affiliates, like all e-commerce sites, need to develop realistic expectations and work on creating a good customer experience." This can be a challenge, as affiliates are essentially driving traffic and sales to the merchant's sites. Affiliates are also not necessarily skilled retailers who are able to lead their site visitors to a sales opportunity. How can affiliates create more successful and profitable customer experiences?

■ *Present e-commerce opportunities in support of good content or information.* A sea of links or banners to products with no contextual relationship to the site or to customer's needs is simply a bad retail strategy.

■ *Focus on core offerings.* Rather than being a department store or portal for every product under the planet (there are already enough of those), develop a special niche and concentrate on developing the best content, information, customer experience, and product selection in your market. Loyalty will follow.

■ *Don't forget about marketing!* Once you have established a niche offering, you must let the world know about it, or you will be the best site that no one has ever heard of. Learn how to market your site in Chapter 7, "Online Events, Promotions, and Attractions."

■ *Promote your niche, not your store.* Aim to be the very best micromerchant on the Web. And do it.

Greg Helmstetter and Pamela Metivier, authors of *Affiliate Selling: Building Revenues on the Web* (Wiley, 2000), suggest that the site owner answer the following questions before entering any type of affiliate program:

■ What are your goals?

■ Is affiliation the backbone of your business model, or is it a supplement to other revenue?

■ Will your site be big or small?

■ How many products will you place on the site?

■ How frequently will the products change?

■ What impact will merchandising have on your management and production teams?

■ Will you integrate product links with content tightly, loosely, or not at all?

■ Will your editorial plan, design, or navigational scheme require major alteration?

■ Will the boat float? (How much will it cost, and how much will you make?)

By defining your expectations and the potential impact on your business, you will be in a better position to evaluate programs and initial results. The authors stress, "As soon as possible, stop planning and start experimenting! Any test data you collect will help you move forward and plan with confidence. Where possible, base your assumptions on data that is generated from your site. Data from other sites can give hints, but unless these sites are very similar to yours, and are visited by a similar audience, then the data may be misleading."

Declan Dunn, CEO of ADNet International (http://www.activemarketplace.com), is author of numerous books about affiliate programs and online sales. He has the following advice for those participating in an affiliate network:

MERCHANTS

■ Consider affiliate programs as a media buy. You want to get the best price to lower your marketing costs, but getting free ad space is not the game. A good affiliate program pays its affiliates, just like a good media buy.

■ Your job is to convert, not to send people to a home page. Most affiliate programs try to steal traffic, but the good ones convert and pay their affiliates. Conversion is your job.

AFFILIATES

■ Build your opt-in email list or become a search engine expert. By far the best affiliates use email or search engines to generate huge revenue. Websites are nice, but to get potent traffic that converts you need email and search engine positioning.

■ Create your own network of *super affiliates,* which are sites that can generate incredible sales and revenue, like we do at ActiveMarketplace.com. When a merchant comes to you, share the wealth with your network. It's a game of volume, and if you generate the most sales, you win.

Finally, get creative! Find ways to lift your product and site above the crowds in cyberspace. When self-published author Ken Evoy wrote his book, *Make Your Site Sell,* several years ago, he recognized that he had a very useful product, but did not necessarily have the clout or the money to launch a huge marketing campaign. Instead, he used every single sales technique found in his book to create a website that would sell his book. He was rewarded with 10 percent visitor-to-buyer conversion rates. But that was not enough. Evoy spent $10,000 on a visitor survey to find out why 90 percent of his site visitors did not purchase. The answer? Visitors wanted a cut-to-the-chase sales option, such as the "5 minute sales tour" tool that Evoy added to his site. Evoy decided to share these tools with others, and created an affiliate program for his book, rewarding affiliates with 25 to 30 percent commissions on every sale. The result? A proprietary affiliate sales system, which can be found at http://buildit.sitesell.com, a growing affiliate network, $750,000 in sales, and a new business publishing books for other selected online authors.

Planning for Sales

There are many ways in which your online store is just like your physical store (assuming you have one), but this analogy can be taken too far. Just like a real store, you need to build foot traffic in order to generate sales. However, many sites make the mistake of designing their sites to merely simulate a mail order catalog or the physical space of an actual store. Like so many misconstrued notions about how online commerce and culture will unfold, these attempts will seem quaint to us in the coming months and years. While I urge you to see the similarities, be sensitive to where the analogy stops and the new way begins.

Cyberbait

You want to have some sort of ongoing lure or *cyberbait.* Why should someone shop with you? Do you offer the most informed way to purchase scuba gear for the adventure vacation? Do you offer free hiking boots with every purchase of a trip to Mount Kilimanjaro? Or do you offer a 20 percent discount to first-time purchasers? Whatever it is, it needs to flow naturally out of your product or service. I recommend you have this type of loss leader year round.

I recently consulted for a company that sells liability insurance to health care professionals. I advised them to create an archive of helpful hints to reduce their target audience's liability exposure. The archive is located at the company's site, while short tips on avoiding risk are mailed out on a weekly basis to subscribers. An online and offline campaign was devised to push the target audience traffic to the site to sign up for additional services. In the outbound tips, there are lures put in to get the audience to visit the site again. The archive works as one of these lures.

The key here is to promote one's added value on one's site, both online and offline, and then try to engage the visitor to your site for an ongoing relationship. This can be done through a Tip of the Week service or via an updating service, like that of one of my first clients, 1-800-Flowers. An email reminder program was put in place, so a previous purchaser would be reminded two weeks ahead of an anniversary or birthday that the event was coming up and what was sent the year before.

These email tip and reminder services, along with large databases of relational information, can cost a substantial amount of money to establish and maintain; however, it is the cost of business to build that all-important foot traffic. Bloomingdale's may heavily advertise a huge sale on canvas bags and may sell you the canvas bag at, or even below, cost. When you go to Bloomie's to get that bag, you see a blue sweater that's on sale for $185. You simply must have that sweater now. You wouldn't have known that you needed that sweater had the canvas bag special not gotten you into a position to see and want that sweater. Now, with bag and sweater in tow, don't you think those navy pants would. . .

Bloomie's takes a gamble on buying a bunch of canvas bags to sell at or below cost, and then spends even more money to advertise that fact. The canvas bags and the advertising to promote the come-on are the equivalent of your ongoing loss leader at your website. Amazon.com's investment in continually improving upon its core database of books, reviews, and personalized suggestions is equivalent to Bloomie's canvas bag campaign. You would be right if you argued that Bloomie's campaign constitutes a sale or promotion. What I'm suggesting here is that your online store needs an ongoing lure, where Bloomie's doesn't. It has people getting catalogs in the mail and walk-in traffic every day it's open. However, no one walks by your site or the umpteen others that pile into your category. Your competitive edge will be your ongoing loss leader campaign.

Another reason you want an ongoing loss leader at your site is that your timed promotion may or may not coincide with the buying cycle of your target group. More often than not, they'll go looking for some sort of information or utility, whether they know it exists on your site or not. Your mission is to make sure they know that it does exist.

Contiguous Cannibalization

One of the scary things about playing in the online arena is that the marketplace is so wide open. In this brutal environment, one man's core business can become another man's loss leader. For example, in order to capture your long-distance business, a large telecommunications company could offer you Internet access for free or at highly discounted rates. This practice puts enormous pressure on smaller ISPs. It wouldn't surprise me at this point to see an overnight shipping company give you a catalog or shopping cart software that lets you display your wares on the Net for free, just so it can capture your shipping business. In other words, your competition could now come from anywhere. You may find yourself loss leader-ing something that a vendor or supplier next to you on the food chain offers for money. They could do the same to you. Make it your business to stay one step ahead of your obvious—and less obvious— competitors.

Search Engines Sending You Business

Having told you all this, it is important to remember that many of your prospects aren't even going to see your carefully crafted online and offline campaigns. They're going to first go to a search engine and enter in. . .what? What they enter into the search engine is all-important because it determines how they'll find you, or not find you. Much of this information is covered in Chapter 7, "Online Events, Promotions, and Attractions"; however, I do want to address a few issues here about search engines as they relate to retail.

If you have a catalog, it is probably in some sort of database. Search engines typically visit your site and scan for words on the pages of your site, but not in your database. Once the search engine has cataloged the words on your web pages, it makes determinations as to where your site should rank in its search results. If you've got 42,000 varieties of gardening tools in your database, the search engine may pick up only the specials you've listed on the few pages that are readily apparent to the visiting agent with its virtual clipboard.

Have available on your site a substantial amount of content that is readily accessible by the agents of the search engines so they get a better idea of what your site is about. You'll come up higher in the search results this way. One strategy is to include large amounts of content on your web pages for these agents to peruse and catalog when they come visiting.

Designing for Retail

Many of the rules of good site design remain the same for retailers. For a design checklist, you can look at Chapter 5, "Your Brand Image and the Internet." Keep in mind that the prime real estate of an average 17-inch computer screen is 800 x 600 pixels, with the toolbar turned on in the browser. You want to make sure that people see your special offers prominently displayed in this space. Make sure that your visitors see what they came for *above the scrollbar* at the bottom. We suggest you design a slot for the upper left-hand part of your screen, where you can slide specials or updates in and out. Since the upper left of the screen is where the eye tends to go first (which is the opposite of print, where right-side placement is preferred), many feel that this space has the most *screen real estate value*. As a result, people often try to cram everything into that confining space. *Little Tokyo* is what my former associate Nina Rich used to call this graphic phenomenon.

Use well-orchestrated outbound messages that entice the user into your site. Being well-orchestrated means a few things:

Timing. Not only should your online advertising efforts to build foot traffic be coordinated with your site, but your print advertising needs to do the same as well. Lead time on print is often longer than online lead time, especially if you are running color ads in magazines.

Fulfillment. Brace yourself for increased traffic and notify your provider. Remember the commercials about the successful marketing executive who suddenly realizes that he "forgot to tell the web guys" about his huge promotion? Don't do that.

Ask for the sale. It seems extraordinary how often websites neglect to close a sale. Don't be bashful.

Consider working with a promotional partner. In addition to co-op dollars with advertising, you should consider working with a promotional partner. Notice how the search engines are all making deals with top retailers. You should think the same way on your scale. This may be as simple as setting up trade links or trying to bundle someone else's product with yours. In other words, try to sell the customer opportunity to someone else in order to bring more sales in for your own site. If that customer is in a buying mode, he or she may well be persuaded to buy related products.

When you are designing your retail site, you will also need to consider the presentation of your goods, using both (or either) catalogs and shopping carts. If you are working with a promotional partner, you may, in fact, need a more sophisticated sales area that supports the cross-linking of products from other sites.

Stretching Your Online Ad Dollars

If you want to stay in it for the long haul, you're going to have to promote your site on an ongoing basis. We just went over several ways for you to improve your site so that it adds value for the customer. I often advise my clients to spend less money on their site and more on the marketing of their site, as mentioned in Chapter 9, "Public Relations, the Internet Way." You may have the best gold lamé Elvis jumpsuits in the world, but who will know if they can't find you or have never heard of you? You also don't want to have an overpromised site that's a letdown when surfers come visiting. It's a tricky balancing act you must manage in order to succeed and make a profit.

One way to strike a balance is to look for cooperative ad dollars. In the physical world, it works like this: Let's say you're a Chevrolet dealer. Chevrolet Corp. makes co-op advertising dollars available to you, the dealer. Chevy may pay between 50 percent and 80 percent of the retail advertising. The result is a full-page ad in the newspaper that touts a Washington's Birthday sale, with eight Chevy dealers listed at the bottom, yours being one of them. Chevy gets some extra branding impressions, while the retailers get a full-page ad in the newspaper, each attracting local customers. It's a win-win situation.

Most of the top 20 visited sites have either transaction components to them or key relationships with retailers. Expect many of these cross-merchandised and cobranding relationships to come together and fly apart when it becomes apparent that the configuration isn't working as planned. In short, the Internet marketplace is a real-time focus group.

Unintended Consequences

One of the things I have noticed about setting up shop on the Internet is that often what you expect to happen doesn't, while other things you never dreamed of happening, do. One of my first clients was Hotel Discount. Client Dave Ray and I guesstimated that 20 percent of the traffic to this site would come from Europe. It did, but what we didn't expect was that Europeans would account for about 50 percent of the room-nights booked. Using retro-logic, we deduced that someone coming from Amsterdam to Chicago will book more room-nights than someone from New York, since the European is coming from a greater distance.

This is the exciting part of the Internet, where unexpected things happen with regularity. It's the sign of a medium rife with possibility, success, and yes, even failure; in fact, there will be many more failures than there will be successes. Predicting what will fail and what will work is very difficult because there are so many variables and forces at work simultaneously. That's the nature of any medium. Intellivision Dumont TVs went out of business, while TV dinners became a hallmark piece of Americana. We suggest that you attempt a few different angles that are all somehow related to each other, so that if one or two fail, you've got the remaining components that survive. Remember not to spread yourself too thin, as then no one retail endeavor will enjoy enough of your resources, attention, and focus in order to succeed. Although the Elvis site that sells gold lamé jumpsuits may not survive, the Elvis Sighting of the Day list, used to remind subscribers about the site, might turn into a minimedia property of its own.

Resource Center

E-Commerce References

Shop.org's "Complying With the FTC's Mail Order Rule"   **http://www.shop.org/ forums/Hhftc.ppt**

Do you know the steps to comply with the Mail and Telephone Order Rule, which applies to online retailers? Ship when you say you will, and if you don't say, a 30-day shipping policy is implied. Seven online retailers paid $1.5 million to settle charges they were in violation of as part of Project TooLate.com. To help Shop.org members with compliance, Heather Hippsley of the Federal Trade Commission participated in Shop.org's Holiday 2000 Countdown audio forum. As a public service, Shop.org made the presentation available to everyone.

Gomez   **http://www.gomez.com**

Gomez, "the e-commerce authority," provides innovative services for both businesses and consumers. E-commerce merchants can take advantage of GomezPro (e-commerce customer experience measurement tools and analysis) and GomezNetworks (a real-time, globally distributed service that measures site and transaction performance from over 50 geographic locations and 20 backbones). Gomez.com, the consumer site, provides consumers with rankings and merchant certification for more than 6,000 firms in over 75 industries, based on over 120 criteria points. How do you measure up?

Syndicated Commerce

EPod   http://www.epod.com

What takes an affiliate relationship one step farther? The ePod! What's an ePod? It's a transactional advertising and merchandising unit that bundles interactive content with branded merchandise. It's like a website within a website, wherein visitors can browse information and purchase products within the unit itself (called a *showcase*) without leaving the original web page. These ministores are great for retailers, and good for affiliate sites, as traffic and loyalty are maintained while generating sales revenue. It's just one more step until affiliates can truly create an "e-commerce without borders" experience that marries the best of multibrand retailing with the freedom of the Web.

WebCollage   http://www.webcollage.com

WebCollage is another of the new breed of syndicators of e-commerce and more. Actually, WebCollage virtually clips an application from a site and places it seamlessly in another site, thereby creating the opportunity to syndicate something—for example, e-commerce—all around the Web exactly as the merchant wants it to appear. The Syndicator is a patent-pending technology, and according to the company, with its use, "in essence, two distinct sites are fused into one by individuals' browsers without messy and expensive integration hassles, and with no back-end integration required." Sounds like a plan.

Red Cart   http://www.redcart.com

It's an e-commerce maven's dream come true—a hosted ASP e-commerce solution. With RedCart, you can tap into a burgeoning merchant network and offer digital marketplaces on your site. What makes it stand out? A universal shopping cart and a digital wallet, which gives users access to the storefronts of multiple merchants without leaving your site. A turnkey mobile commerce offering. Plus a transaction engine that places orders with over 100 merchant sites, extensive customer reporting, sophisticated cross-merchant merchandising technology, and automated partner reporting to simplify merchant reconciliation.

Merchandising Avenue   http://www.merchandisingavenue.com

If you have online real estate and a content-rich or e-commerce site, Merchandising Avenue will plop a related palette of merchandise onto your page for free so your customers can spend. You receive commissions once a month. Sounds like upscale affiliate marketing. Merchandising Avenue provides e-merchant partners an alternative method of channel distribution without expensive advertising, and merchants only pay commissions for products sold.

E-Commerce Research

ZDNet's E-Commerce Channel   http://www.zdnet.com/enterprise/e-business/

Where do e-commerce pros go to keep up with e-commerce? Try ZDNet's E-Commerce channel for more than you will ever want or need to know. Who are the top ten bricks and mortar retailers? What's going on at Internet World today? Where can you find web technology and e-strategy trends, all in one convenient place? This is a great source for reports, articles, and product reviews, more so than news, as the in-depth information deserves a more thorough read-through than daily headlines usually allow.

E-Commerce Times   http://www.ecommercetimes.com

This site provides a global overview of the e-commerce industry, and is a great resource for those in the industry to find out what's going on. The overly caffeinated and e-commerced among us (who are desperately trying to meet site deadlines) will greatly appreciate the daily cartoon. Little known fact: There is a dearth of e-commerce humor on the Web. Headlines, a stock index, research, resources for the multimillion dollar enterprise as well as small business, and great newsletters make this site a must-visit. While there check out sister publication CRMDaily.com for the latest in customer relationship management insight.

Internet.com's E-Commerce News   http://www.internetnews.com/ec-news/

For those who have been dying to know, this is coauthor Eileen Shulock's start page. A half a dozen or so key e-commerce headlines are served up daily, and before coffee, that's about all she can handle. This site is a great resource for those who need to key in on what they absolutely need to know about e-commerce in 60 seconds or less. The articles are timely, well-edited, and definitely hand-picked by Internet.com.

Personalization

Marketing 1to1   http://www.1to1.com

Most marketers will have read, or browsed, or at least heard about *The One to One Future*. Published in 1993 by Don Peppers and Martha Rogers, Ph.D. This best-selling tome on how technology is changing the way companies build relationships with customers has not only proved prescient, but has generated a *one-to-one* universe at the company's site. See why Peppers and Rogers Group was named to the Inc. 500 list of the fastest growing companies—and learn a great deal about CRM, e-strategy, personalization, and direct marketing while you're at it. Be sure to check out *One to One Online*, the latest report on how the world's leading sites create customer loyalty, and sign up for *INSIDE 1to1*, a free weekly email newsletter.

Personalization.com   http://www.personalization.com

Underwritten by NetPerceptions, a leading personalization technology company, this site provides an objective and informative forum for the discussion and sharing of information on personalization and how it will affect Internet commerce with increasingly targeted marketing opportunities.

Affiliate Programs

B2B LinkShare   http://www.b2blinkshare.com

Here's a B2B affiliate program from the creators of the industry's first B2C affiliate program, LinkShare. By creating partnerships with B2BLinkShare's merchants (Verio Web Hosting, eLETTER, OfficeMax.com, etc.) you enhance the value of your site and generate revenue for all involved. As a B2BLinkShare merchant, you expand distribution sale channels and build brand awareness. Free sign up.

Commission Junction   http://www.commissionjunction.com

If commissions are your mission, Commission Junction is striving to drive an e-commerce option called EnContext that enables online information and entertainment sites to sell products and services that relate to their content in return for e-commerce revenues. EnContext lets affiliate content sites place revenue-generating products, ads, and links from leading Internet merchants in and around the content of their websites in exchange for the almighty commission dollar. EnContext creates a powerful impulse to buy by matching products with content relevant to the reader—enabling consumers to buy anything, anywhere, anytime, directly within information or entertainment that matches their interests. Put commerce in context.

Refer-It   http://www.refer-it.com

Launched in December 1997, Refer-it.com's comprehensive listing of 2,481 affiliate programs is still fresh, with programs rated on revenue share, ease of implementation for the website owner, responsiveness if problems arise, reporting capabilities, and clarity of each affiliate program's terms and conditions. Each listing also includes program description, direct links for joining, fee information, program launch date, and, most importantly, a list of websites that currently belong to each affiliate program. Bookmark it.

AssociatePrograms.com   http://www.AssociatePrograms.com

AssociatePrograms.com is maintained by Allan Gardyne, a former journalist who lives in a pole home among gum trees, palms, and jacarandas in sub-tropical Queensland, Australia. Allan makes his living through web affiliate programs and e-book sales, and has compiled this directory of 2,806 affiliate programs with no "adult, multi-tier, or MLM affiliate programs or companies included." Visit to read his 32 useful hints about associate/affiliate/referral programs and submit information about your own affiliate program so others may send business your way. It pays to associate—even in a gum tree.

Online Events, Promotions, and Attractions: How to Make a "Scene" and Draw Them In

If you have a website, any kind of website, it automatically puts you into two businesses you may not have been in before: publishing and promotion. Running a site feels like running a catalog, newspaper, or magazine, as it needs regular updates. In this environment of many-to-many, you also need to promote your site in order to draw in your target audience. This way, they can see exactly what you've updated, be it content or merchandise. The attraction that you create should relate to your core business, product, or service.

The delicious irony I wish to share with you here is that this notion of promotion reaches back much further than most of us realize. In the introduction of this book, you probably noticed a picture of a letter from Thomas Alva Edison to my great-grandfather, Edmond Gerson. My great-grandfather was a showman and promoter in the 1870s and Edison, the "Wizard of Menlo Park," wanted him to take his version of the telephone out "on the circuit." Just as Barnum & Bailey put the Ringling Brothers' Circus on tour, there were those like my great-grandfather who would bring around the wonders of the world, like Gertrude the Headless Woman.

The point is that *the more things change, the more they remain the same,* with or without the technology. If you want to get people's attention, sometimes it's a good idea to put on a show, especially in a crowded environment like the World Wide Web, where so many sites are howling for your attention. Web marketers spent approximately $13.1 billion on website promotion in 2000 (or 10 percent of revenues), according to Activ-Media Research. Whether on free T-shirts to new customers, or $50,000 grand prize sweepstakes, there's a whole lot of showmanship going on.

In this chapter, we'll explore different kinds of promotions you can hold and discuss some of their respective tradeoffs. Should you have one big annual blowout, or should you parsimoniously dole your budget out on a monthly (or even weekly) timetable? Well, this is your lucky day, because in this chapter, you'll find the answer to these questions and many more. . .step right this way! Take a look inside and find:

- The promotion checklist
- Database-building techniques
- Contests, sweepstakes, coupons, and more
- High-impact email promotion
- Loyalty and rewards programs
- The value of live events
- The lure of broadband
- Viral marketing
- How to promote professional services
- Site optimization techniques

Promotional Goals and Objectives

Before you begin crafting specific promotions, you should first determine what you would like your promotions to achieve for your business. The choice of appropriate promotional vehicle or partner may vary depending upon your goals and objectives. You may want to:

Drive traffic to your site—the more the better. In this case, you would most likely choose big, splashy promotions and aim them at a wide audience in order to get those numbers up.

Create prelaunch hype so that the public is breathlessly anticipating your site launch. Your promotions will need to be carefully designed so that your audience is not disappointed to find a site that has not yet launched. . .and you will need to give your visitors a compelling reason to return when you do launch.

Create brand awareness. You may specifically want your promotions to establish your brand online, in response to a competitor's move or to establish your business as a first in the market. Promotions that focus on branding will be different, and potentially more difficult to measure, than promotions that focus on tangible elements such as traffic numbers or new subscribers.

Sign up members. If your site offers membership privileges, you may want to drive qualified traffic to the site and then give visitors incentives to share some of their valuable personal information by becoming a member of your community. As your mother probably told you, share and share alike. This concept holds true for information-sharing on the Web. You must give a little to get a little.

Build an email list. Hopefully, your site has an established email list as a marketing tool. (If there is one thing you learn from this book, it is to establish an email list on your site. Today.) Your promotions may be designed to add subscribers to your list. These types of promotions are not as complex as promotions designed to generate members, as the email sign-up process should be less complex and time-consuming than a membership form.

Generate qualified leads. In other words, create a database that can be mined for future business opportunities. Your promotions will need to be finely honed to generate conversion within your niche market.

Generate sales. You may want promotions to drive qualified traffic to your site, and then compel those visitors to make a purchase right then and there. Promotional tools and techniques that assist in generating online sales are becoming increasingly important, and we will explore them in this chapter.

The Effect of Promotion on Online Behavior

As the online landscape becomes more and more competitive, the tactics and tools designed to help businesses stand out in the crowd are becoming more and more sophisticated. It used to be a big deal when a website launched. Nowadays, sites are launching every minute. Why should people choose to visit your site over the site of any one of your competitors? And how far are you willing to go to get them there? Do you want to get them there at all?

"The best thing a promotion can do is generate a database that can be used for future marketing efforts," advises Kenneth Hein, Senior Editor for *iMarketing News*. "Promotions used to be about driving lots of traffic to a site. Increasingly, they are now about getting people to register or sign up." According to Hein, conversion rates from databases collected during promotional efforts are much higher than traditional conversion rates, "because the member has already raised his or her hand and indicated an interest." Hein continues, "Sweepstakes and contest destination sites are increasingly popular among consumers." Why? "People like to win," Hein explains. "It doesn't take that long to enter. I have iWon.com as my home page. Why not?"

According to Media Metrix, sweepstakes-style websites are well represented as some of the most popular newcomers on the Web. For example, in August 2000, the most popular new sites were:

Fastfreefun.com, with 1.96 million unique visitors (owned by Excite).

Uproarlotto.com, with 1.26 million unique visitors.

Winmesweeps.com, with 882,000 unique visitors (owned by Microsoft).

Bridgestone-Firestone.com, the auto-products site providing breaking news on the auto tire recall.

While this may seem like ancient history by the time you read this, at the time of writing the fact that contest sites were clear winners over the latest news headlines is a sure indication of their popularity.

Some marketers do question the efficacy of sweepstakes and promotions to meet marketing goals. After all, there is no sense in spending money to pursue an audience that has no long-term interest in your business, product, or service. Well-executed promotions should focus equally on the incentive and the desired end result—potential new customers.

Whatever your point of view, the numbers are large. CBS bet $70 million in ad promotion to launch iWon.com (http://www.iwon.com), a consumer search, content, and services portal where every click adds points and entries to daily, weekly, and monthly sweepstakes. The big payoff? A cool $10 million rewarded to one lucky winner on April 15 (tax day) each year. As a result, iWon.com, a latecomer to the search engine market, consistently ranks in the top 20 sites visited monthly, according to PC Data Online.

The Promotion Professional's Bag of Tricks

So, what kind of promotion, event, or attraction is right for you? Just as there are many potential reasons for running promotions, there are many types of promotions that you can run.

What will your target audience respond to best? Let's review some of the most common promotional tactics.

Contests

The proliferation of contests on the Web is almost mind-boggling. It could well be that web surfers have become bored with ad banners and are searching for alternative mindless entertainment. Clickthrough rates on ad banners have been steadily declining over the past few years, as the novelty of clicking on a 468 x 60 rectangle has worn off. Perhaps contests fill that void. Technically, a contest requires the user to answer a series of questions or demonstrate some type of skill in order to enter.

American Airlines built on the *Who Wants To Be a Millionaire?* trend by creating a contest that offered a million frequent-flyer miles as a prize. Visitors answered a series of questions about AA.com services, and then typed in their personal information to enter. This type of contest builds awareness of American Airlines services to a targeted audience by design, as only those who would want a million frequent-flyer miles would bother to enter.

Yahoo! introduced its Fusion Marketing service—an integrated set of sales and marketing solutions that web marketers can use to tap into the huge Yahoo! audience—by also offering a Who Wants To Be a Millionaire? hook, this time offering a million dollars in advertising on the Yahoo! network to the web agency that created the best advertising campaign on behalf of a client. Again, this contest introduced the Yahoo! Fusion service to the very market that will use it—web agencies.

TIP *ZD Net's Yahoo Internet Life Y-Life Daily* (http://www.zdnet.com/yil/content/depts/freebies/freebies.html) **features a daily round up of freebies, bargains, and contests, which is a great way to track promotional trends.**

These contests were extremely effective at targeting their audience while offering a large enough incentive to get a critical mass to enter. Note that the contests and the prizes relate directly to the core business. Whether you offer a million frequent-flyer miles or a million rose petals, there's something to be said for prequalifying your audience through a contest channel.

Sites can also use contests to engage their visitors. For example, American Movie Classics (http://www.amc.com) holds clever contests related to classic American movies. Imagine the fun of the Psycho Scream Off. The best screamer won a trip to the Bates Motel at Universal Studios in Hollywood plus a week in Los Angeles. Screaming must be a popular AMC activity; to celebrate Halloween the site held a Haunted Backlot Scream Contest.

Sweepstakes

Unlike contests, sweepstakes require no skill or special knowledge to enter; contestants simply sign up and hope. Many companies will create and execute a sweepstakes for you. Since the audience tends to be less targeted, a successful sweepstakes promotion will go for the largest number of participants. ePrize (http://www.eprize.net) is one such company. The company's home page presents a straightforward yet amusing theory:

> Give your customers a reason to visit your site—bribe 'em. Statistics show online sweepstakes are an easy way to increase traffic to your site and get valuable information on your customers. And with ePrize, you can have a sweepstakes with minimal effort, because we do all the work!

That theory is backed by hard data. "Marketers can drive a specific act through the use of the sweepstakes, which is a traditional direct marketing tactic," explains Tony Laxa Jr., VP of Marketing and Strategic Alliances at ePrize. "By putting the sweepstakes online, it becomes even more effective. With this call to action, our clients experience from 50 percent to 500 percent increases across all marketing tactics—from banner ad clickthrough rates to email responses." ePrize offers a turnkey sweepstakes program designed to drive traffic to each client's site and to help each client build a permission-based marketing program. Every 90 days, ePrize offers a sweepstakes solution to businesses that includes everything from design and administration to a $50,000 prize. This prize money—and the opportunity to win—is pooled across multiple client sites, each of whom run their own private label sweepstakes administered by ePrize.

"This way, companies can offer the chance to win a significant prize at a fraction of the cost of running their own sweepstakes," says Laxa. "Every 90 days, we have a two-part drawing—first to choose the winning site, and then to choose the winning participant from that site." Participating sites may choose to offer $50,000 cash, or a product equivalent (see Figure 7.1).

One client, an auto manufacturer, gathered 450,000 new names and demographic information in 60 days by offering the opportunity to win a lease on a new car. With a simple "click here to win" button on the home page, this auto manufacturer generated 650,000 user visits to the contest page. Nearly 70 percent of entrants took the time to share their contact information, the make of their cars, the date their lease expired, and

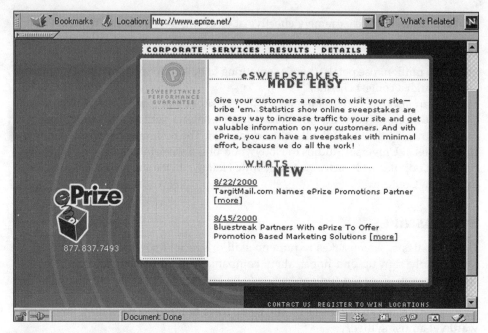

Figure 7.1   ePrize develops and administers online sweepstakes that allow clients to offer their users a chance to win directly from the client's site.

other critical information. As a side note, less than 10 percent visited the Rules and Regulations page to investigate how this information would be used, which speaks to their willingness to share information in exchange for perceived value, such as the opportunity to win a lease on a new car.

Another client, a jewelry retailer, offered a six-carat diamond ring to site visitors over the course of six weeks. This sweepstakes, which was picked up by media for its PR value, resulted in a 500 percent increase in site traffic and a 700 percent increase in prospect acquisitions. The newly acquired database of users is now being filtered and used to market to a qualified audience via email at a fraction of the cost of traditional advertising. You can learn more about effective online direct marketing techniques in Chapter 8, "Direct Marketing and Sales Support."

Other companies will conduct a sweepstakes for you on their site. Rather than offering the sweepstakes on your own site, this type of company will run your sweepstakes on their own *sweepstakes portal*. Webstakes.com is one such company.

TIP   If you are hosting your own promotion, drive enough traffic to the promotion site in order to make it successful. Prepare a significant, outbound, highly targeted campaign that heralds your promotion. Otherwise, you'll have the best darn promotion no one ever heard of.

At Webstakes.com, the participant registers once; if he or she participates in future promotions, entry is expedited simply by entering an email address. This technique keeps the barrier of participation low.

During the registration process, the visitor provides information on his or her interests. As a result, Webstakes.com can deliver highly targeted audiences to companies running promotions through its network. Visitors are able to get free coupons, free trial offers, and other deals on items and brands of interest because Webstakes.com structures promotions within channels, which succinctly defines each target audience. For example, sports-minded surfers visiting the site will naturally want to travel through the sports channels. Likewise, sports marketers will be interested only in the sports-minded surfer. They have the ability to find each other within this channel.

There is a well-rounded mix of different industries, or channels, represented at Web-Stakes.com: sports, technology, business, entertainment, music, family, travel, and leisure. The site offers different prizes, depending on what area a visitor is in. For instance, the family channel might be giving away educational software or a home entertainment system, while the business channel would give away Zip drives or Palm Pilots. Each channel has multiple sponsors. Webstakes.com continually builds its audience with online advertising and by sending promotional emails to the huge opt-in list it has built up over the years. Site owners would choose this type of solution to tap into the large number of participants a sweepstakes portal generates, thus building brand awareness and creating introductions to potential prospects.

TIP **Many people don't have the time to commit to playing a game of skill or answering lengthy questionnaires. They don't want the amount of involvement a contest demands.**

The Web is full of sweepstakes junkies. In fact, entire websites are devoted to finding and promoting up-to-the-minute sweepstakes offerings. Sweepstakes work well for brand building and traffic driving, especially if the prize is compelling. However, a large percentage of the participants will simply enter the sweepstakes and leave the site, never to return. Unless, of course, they happen to win.

Strategic Discounts

Let's say you're trying to attract the type of person who may be wary of the one in a zillion chance of winning. If you were Amazon.com, you could have an ongoing promotion where you offered a $10 discount on every visitor's first purchase, or that offered a $10 discount on a future purchase for each new member registration.

If you were going to buy a book anyway, it's a good chance that this type of ongoing online promotion would be just enough to lure you into buying from Amazon.com instead of Borders.com. In fact, it may be enough of an incentive for you to buy from Amazon online rather than the bookstore down the street. In this case, you have to appeal to the practical side of people's natures. After all, that's why so many people are on the Internet in the first place: for the value they can extract from it.

TIP **Have two promotions that you alternate from one month to the next. For instance, one month you could offer $10 off all books in stock. The next month, you could offer a $10 reward to every current customer who brought a new customer to the site, or free shipping on every purchase. Each time you toggle from one to the other, be sure you herald the new attraction in paid advertising, in email newsletters, and in press releases.**

Ongoing cash incentives of this type are very effective at generating an actual sale at the point of interest. Ideally, these types of promotions will convert a visitor into a customer, and thus begin a long-term relationship. Online retailers of all kinds have entered a bidding war when it comes to attracting customers, especially during the holiday season. It's important that your business is strategically organized so that you immediately begin a positive relationship with new customers, rather than relying upon repeated financial incentives to keep your customers from switching to the competition. After all, you must consider the lifetime value of your customers, which is discussed in Chapter 8, "Direct Marketing and Sales Support." If you must consistently pay them to shop with you, this is not the making of a profitable business.

Coupons

People love a bargain, no question. Bargain hunters can develop some serious online shopping habits. There are websites that cater to such value seekers, such as H.O.T! Coupons (http://www.hotcoupons.com), which will notify you when there are coupons available in the categories you like. CoolSavings (http://www.coolsavings .com) is another such site (see Figure 7.2), and many more are piling on the bandwagon. Some will even accompany you as you surf, such as Dash (http://www .dash.com). As you browse the Web and see products of interest, Dash will busily search its database of participating merchant offers to see if anyone has a coupon related to your interest. These incentivized coupons are delivered at the point of interest to encourage an immediate sale.

Figure 7.2 Coupons are a big attraction on the Web.

CoolSavings is a registered trademark of coolsavings.com, Inc.

Whether you're printing the coupons yourself for download from your site, or joining the ever-growing number of coupon networks, you are saving money over the costs of real-world promotion. You do not have to print the coupons, mail them, and hope that some small percentage of recipients of that direct marketing campaign will actually respond. Some coupon networks even provide real-time feedback so that you can adjust your incentives quickly, according to audience reaction, rather than waiting weeks or even months for the results of a traditional direct mail campaign.

Coupons offer enormous benefits to online marketers. Assuming you have a product or service to sell, your coupons can be:

- Positioned to appear at the point of research or point of purchase.

- Easy to track, especially if online redemption is required, as you can track from point of acceptance through to actual sale.

- Targeted to previous consumer behavior or interests, so that offers can be personalized, or in the case of a network like Dash, consumers looking at your competitors' products can be enticed to switch brands with an offer they can't refuse.

Email as a Promotional Tool

I can't stress enough how important it is for you to develop an email database when planning an Internet promotion. Virtually all Net marketers, myself included, speak of its importance. Perhaps the biggest mistake marketers make is to go to the effort and expense of planning a campaign to drive people to their site, only to let those people get away, quite possibly never to return.

According to eMarketer's October 2000 *eMail Marketing Report:*

Email marketing offers the promise of low costs, rapid response and higher click - through and conversion rates. . .Marketers report clickthrough rates for email ads between 5 percent and 22 percent. This compares to less than 1 percent on average for banner ads.

Once a site visitor has shared his or her email address with you, that visitor has turned into a prospect. That prospect can be marketed to long after your promotion has ended. As such, email is one of the most powerful ways to establish a marketing relationship with site visitors, and is thereafter one of the most effective ways to promote to both prospects and customers.

While I have always touted the simplicity and ubiquity of simple text email, even those times are a-changing. Enhanced (or HTML-formatted) email is becoming more and more popular as a greater number of people upgrade their email and browser programs, most of which now support HTML-formatted email. This means you can send banners, graphics, contests, polls, and even entire web pages by email (see Figure 7.3). It delivers more sizzle, since its colorful graphics can allow for a brighter display of what you have to offer. It also lets you click over directly to a site from your email program.

Many large email service providers offer both simple and enhanced email solutions. If you choose to make your outbound messages available to your subscribers in the

Figure 7.3 Cooking.com's interactive HTML-formatted email serves up everything from recipes to books to products.

enhanced format, try to keep the file size down by going easy on the graphics. If they are too heavy, the email document will be the size of a web page, 30K or more, and will take as long to come in as it would to download on the Net. You know how people hate to wait, so don't import the whole World Wide Wait into people's email boxes.

Coauthor Eileen Shulock, an industry veteran with six years of online marketing and e-commerce experience, used the inspiration garnered from the writing of this book to actually create her own website and email newsletter promotional tool. "After six years in new media, I decided it was time to practice what I preach," explains Eileen. "I felt like I was the only person on earth without my own website and email newsletter." As an e-commerce strategist and Managing Editor of *Web Digest For Mar-*

keters, Eileen is in the business of spotting online trends. "I wanted to provide a quick way for people to learn about new business trends on the Web, and also suggest ways to take advantage of those trends," states Eileen. "That type of information was lacking in the market. In exchange for pinpointing online business trends, I wanted to build up my own email list and create a professional platform for myself." Eileen set up a simple website and email newsletter to house her new online brand, and began promoting the newsletter, collecting email addresses, and publishing the biweekly *eTrendWire* (http://www.etrendwire.com). "My overall objective was to establish a quick, easy, and informative way to promote my current and future activities," concludes Eileen. It's much easier to network and expand my professional life with a promotional mechanism in place." These weekly soft touches keep her in the minds of her target audience inexpensively. I refer to this highly targeted tactical approach as "micromarketing."

Rewards, Loyalty, and Incentive Programs

Online rewards, loyalty, and incentive programs are proliferating just as quickly as their naysayers negate their long-term value. According to online research firm NFO, 53 percent of e-consumers were willing to buy more online with some kind of rewards program, and 47 percent would return to a specific e-commerce site if they knew rewards or loyalty incentives were offered. The real-world equivalent of these programs is an airline frequent-flyer mile program. Are you attached to a certain airline because you are accruing frequent-flyer miles? Are you attached to that airline even if your desired flight can be found on another airline for less money or a more direct connection? According to a study by AC Nielsen, many people choose to fly up to 25 percent longer in time and distance just to preserve their loyalty to a certain airline.

It's an interesting theory to explore. Many sites have established their own loyalty or rewards programs, which require membership on the part of the user, who then accrues some type of reward—usually points—for each purchase. Those points can be redeemed at a later date for merchandise or other special benefits, such as free shipping or free offers from other companies. "Loyalty is tricky," comments *iMarketing News* Senior Editor Kenneth Hein, who covers the online promotion and loyalty industry. "People are not loyal to Amazon.com, for example, because of points or rewards. They are loyal because their book or CD arrives in the mail. On the other hand, loyalty and rewards programs are almost a 'have to have' in today's market."

One example of a rewards program is offered by America Online and American Airlines. Called AOL AAdvantage, the program allows customers to earn frequent-flyer miles that can be used for travel products and purchases from program partners, which include TD Waterhouse Group, 1-800-Flowers, and Cooking.com. By collaborating on the program, these companies offer a more useful incentive to customers, and thus potentially create a more profitable program. Would you only buy from 1-800-Flowers if you earned points for each floral purchase made from that company? Maybe, maybe not. But, would you apply some of your frequent-flyer miles to a floral purchase from a partner merchant if it was within your loyalty sphere? Quite possibly. The lesson here is that even the largest of companies are teaming up to offer more choice, and therefore more incentive, to the consumer.

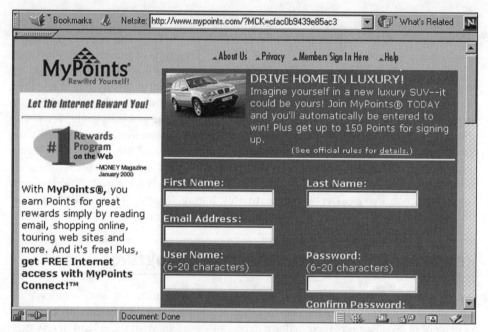

Figure 7.4 MyPoints rewards participants for interacting with member sites.
MyPoints is a registered trademark of MyPoints.com, Inc.

While the technology to build a rewards or loyalty program is relatively easy to acquire, the amount of effort needed to create and maintain a compelling program for your site audience can be a challenge. To the rescue come intermediary incentive programs that aggregate merchants or businesses together to offer network-wide rewards to participants. At MyPoints (http://www.mypoints.com) members pile up points for visiting participating websites, signing up for email newsletters, registering at a site, shopping, or other requested actions. The members do so across any number of MyPoints.com properties, and the more they participate, the more points they accrue. Points can be redeemed for merchandise from the MyPoints.com merchants. Visitors sign up at MyPoints.com according to their interests, and are contacted by MyPoints.com by email on behalf of a merchant with appropriate offers (see Figure 7.4).

Some industry experts argue that dangling a carrot in front of random web surfers is not necessarily the best way to build brand loyalty and repeat traffic. That remains to be seen, but participation in such networks can be a cost-effective way to reach a relatively targeted audience with your promotion.

Chat, Webcasts, and Live Events

They say talk is cheap. It's true. Thanks to the proliferation of chat technology, it's not usually an expensive endeavor to hold a chat online. At the base level, you hold the chat at a place like TalkCity (http://www.talkcity.com), which can set up a section for your company's events and put you on its master schedule. The expensive and/or time-consuming part is promoting the event. You might consider having a weekly or monthly schedule of chats, featuring different speakers. In this way, you can maintain an ongoing promotion that publicizes the schedule as a whole, while also featuring the upcoming events.

I was once a guest on Jill Ellsworth's AOL Marketing Chat, which is held every week. It was a fun thing to take part in, held in one of the AOL auditoriums with other guest speakers on the "stage." The AOL Audience Hall held 300 people. I, as a guest speaker, could talk with other guest speakers and watch the audience members log in and out. I kept wondering, Was it something I said?

> **TIP** When holding a chat event, investigate the options available to you in regard to audience/speaker interactions. In an auditorium setting on AOL, for example, speakers are segregated from the audience. Each "row" of the audience is free to speak among themselves, but you will never see their comments. Questions are filtered to you via moderators. This can work in your favor, but you need to decide on the level of interaction you are looking for with your attendees for these promotional events. Other types of chat do not segregate the speakers from the audience at all, but make it all one big, happy (sometimes rowdy) family, giving it a more intimate feeling.

I noticed the traffic to my site spiked considerably a few days after the chat event. Believe it or not, people actually do pull the archives of these chats and read them. Some people actually prefer to read chats in archive form, since they can then control the read rate, rather than it being dictated by the guest speaker's typing speed, or lack thereof.

The effect of an online event often lives beyond the actual event itself. For example, when the first edition of this book was published, I had the pleasure of participating in an online chat with Janet Attard, founder of AOL's Business Know-How Forum. While in total 60 people wandered in and out of the chat, the event was promoted to the 40,000 members of Attard's forum, and an excerpt from the book was posted in the forum. As a result, more than 200 people subscribed to *Web Digest For Marketers,* which they learned about through these promotional vehicles. The point is that the promotion of an online event may have a bigger impact than the event itself, as many people prefer to take action at their own convenience—whether by reading a transcript or subscribing to a newsletter. I call this a *time shift commitment,* which gives your audience a call to action at their convenience, rather than on your schedule.

If you'd like to know what's happening in which chat rooms around the Web, take a look at Yack (http://www.yack.com), whose online event listings are so popular they are syndicated around the world (see Figure 7.5).

Broadband for the Masses

With all the hype about broadband, streaming media (audio and video) events are becoming more popular. "The business-to-business sector is driving streaming media usage," states Emily Noble Pushman, Sales Manager for iBeam, a global streaming media distribution, application, and webcasting network. "For example, in the finan-

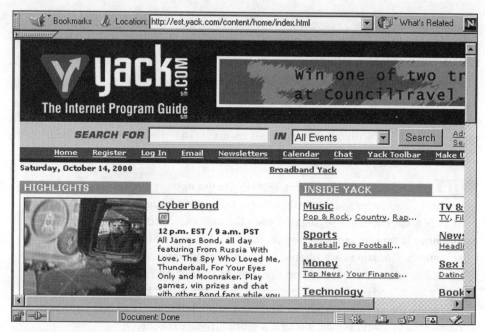

Figure 7.5   Keep up with Internet events at Yack.

cial sector our clients include Dow Jones, Morgan Stanley, and Merrill Lynch." Merrill Lynch hosts a weekly roundtable discussion, which is broadcast to its Intranet and available for all employees to view. "A huge benefit of streaming media is that people don't have to travel to view presentations," continues Pushman. "That translates into a cost and time savings. For example, many of our clients create a password-protected virtual road show to shop their company to investors. That way, CEOs and key company executives are able to present their company without spending all their time traveling." Other clients use streaming media for corporate training or to deliver presentations such as seasonal trend forecasts or analyst reports, which clients or employees can then view at their own convenience.

The use of streaming media in the business-to-business sector makes sense, as these large companies have the infrastructure, technology, and bandwidth to support the creation and consumption of online video productions. "All industries will embrace streaming media," predicts Pushman. "Some will just take longer than others. The key question is—how do you offset the costs?" Pushman sees targeted advertising, commerce, and pay-per-view as three business models that will support the costs of streaming media applications.

Are consumers ready for streaming media? Many companies are banking on it. Use of streaming media in the consumer market ranges from daily news broadcasts by CNBC.com to monthly concerts at Sweet16.com. News and entertainment are two industries ripe for streaming media content (see Figure 7.6). Even the former president has gone the way of webcast. ChannelOne.com produced a broadcast of former president Bill Clinton discussing learning opportunities in the nation's schools. The cynics among us may wonder if the schools were wired enough to view the presentation.

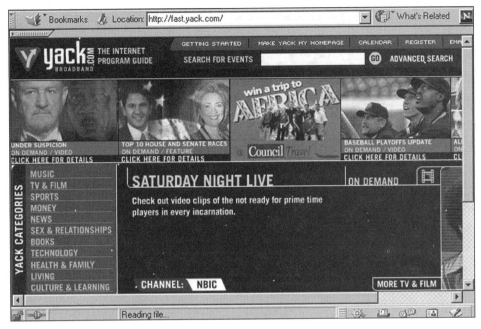

Figure 7.6   Check out Yack's broadband event listings at http://fast.yack.com.

RealPlayer (http://www.real.com) and Windows Media Player (http://www
.microsoft.com/windows/windowsmedia/en/overview/default.asp) are the two
dominant streaming media formats currently used on the Net. Lots of broadcast networks, radio stations, governments, and companies are putting audio components on
their sites. It makes sense. Should you do it? If the content is being used for other purposes, such as promotions, I would say yes. If transmission on the Web is its only purpose or usage, I'd think very hard about it. While RealPlayer and Media Player play
pretty well on a 56k modem, audio streams do take up a significant amount of the
provider's bandwidth, and video streams take up even more. Yes, many users do have
and use the plug-ins out there. But keep in mind that in addition to the server software
you need to push the media stream to them, you may also need to invest in additional
bandwidth if your stream becomes a hit.

Offline to Online and Back Again

Finally, live, real-world events can work in tandem with an online business in a carefully crafted mix. Courtney Pulitzer, founder of Courtney Pulitzer Creations, which
includes Cocktails with Courtney, Courtney Pulitzer's Cyber Scene, and CyberScene
TV, is one example (http://www.pulitzer.com). The company was founded to provide
information about the Internet industry to those within the industry, and to the general
public (see Figure 7.7).

Pulitzer's business began with a weekly email report on the schmoozing, wheel-
ing, dealing social scene in burgeoning Silicon Alley. That column, "The Cyber

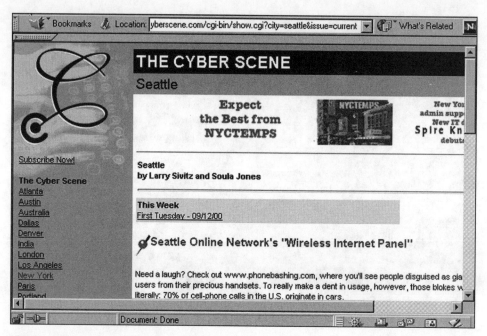

Figure 7.7 From India to Austin, the Cyber Scene, Cocktails with Courtney, and CyberScene TV track the pulse of the Internet industry.
© 2000 Courtney Pulitzer Creations.

Scene," led to an international business that combines the Internet, real-world events, and television.

"To me, promotion is not about technology," explains Pulitzer. "Technology is merely the means to create one-to-one interaction." Pulitzer's newsletter, with an email base of 50,000, tracks the people, companies, and culture in wired cities around the world. Pulitzer's internationally coveted Cocktails with Courtney events actually began as a means for her to gather all her friends together in one space. "The cocktail series was a shooting star," says Pulitzer. "I never expected it. But logically, if you think about who your audience is, how you can reach them, and why they will respond, you are on your way to success." She continues, "I think of myself as a vacuum cleaner salesman. With my email promotions and products, I am knocking on people's doors and going into their homes. It's intrusive. I realize that I am making a personal call and aim to always be respectful of people's lives."

By leveraging three mediums to bring people and companies together, Pulitzer's company is widely recognized as a groundbreaking resource for both tracking the competition and facilitating new relationships and new business ventures.

Viral or Affinity Marketing

One of the best ways to promote your product, service, or site is to get your audience to do it for you. Viral marketing (or *affinity* marketing, as some have renamed it, not wanting to create a virus scare) is the term used to describe the concept of giving your site visitors or email recipients a nudge, or even a tool, to pass along your message. At its simplest, viral marketing means that you include a "Please pass this along to a friend" blurb on every email newsletter you send out. Or you ask your site visitors to "Send this page/article to a friend," and provide the mechanism to do so.

However, praise for the concept of viral marketing has spread like, well, a virus. Word-of-mouth referrals from friends or colleagues are going to be taken much more seriously than even your most carefully crafted advertising campaign. And each visitor or referral can tell at least one friend, or hopefully even more, helping you spread the word while keeping costs down.

Viral marketing tools have sprung up all over the Web. The following are some examples.

Digital postcards. Your visitor sends a digital postcard from your site to a friend. The friend gets a notice from you to pick up his or her postcard. The friend is required to go to your site to pick up the card. The friend is then encouraged to send a card themselves. Entire businesses, such as BlueMountainArts.com (http://www.bluemoutainarts.com), have been built on this premise. Other companies, such as Bloomingdales.com (http://www.bloomingdales.com), provide digital postcards as a powerful marketing tool (see Figure 7.8).

Software pass-alongs. If you are a user of AIM (AOL Instant Messenger), you can immediately grasp how this technology exploded onto the Internet scene. AIM allows for instant, real-time chat, using the proprietary AIM software, which you must install on your computer. After installation, you choose a nickname,

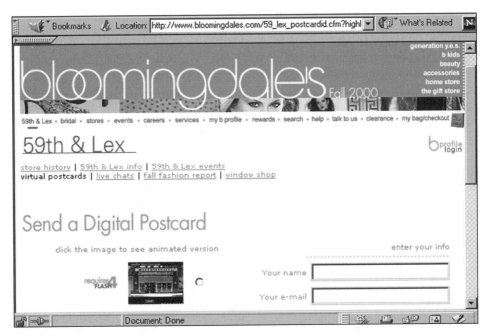

Figure 7.8 Sophisticated digital postcards encourage site visitors to tell others about Bloomingdales.com.

and then add other AIM members that you want to talk to into your Buddy List. If your friend or colleague is not an AIM user, you use the convenient Invite a Friend feature to send an email and request that he or she install AIM so that you can chat with him or her all day long. Originally beloved by teens and other frequent chatters, AIM has quietly become a required means of communication within many companies. "Every new employee is required on day one with the company to install AIM, create a nickname, and inform the team as to how they can be reached," says Cheryl Brinker, Vice President of Human Resources for Knowledge Strategies Group (http://www.kstrat.com). "We communicate all day long by AIM, whether one-to-one or in group chats. Email is no longer fast enough. We need instant communication and answers to get things done."

Affinity marketing is such a powerful concept that major players have stepped into the market to focus on creating mechanisms for marketers to send visual branded messages and content online. Gizmoz Inc. (http://www.gizmoz.com) is backed by heavy hitters such as John Sculley, Chase Capital Partners, Polaris Venture Capital, and AOL Investments. The company's goal is to become the "Net's most effective relationship marketing solution." Gizmoz are interactive, rich media *smart envelopes* created by the marketer using Gizmoz's proprietary authoring tool, the Gizmoz Maker. They can carry 2D or 3D animated objects, photos, text, video, and audio. They do not require plug-ins or downloads for viewing and interaction as they are actually embedded within the email message itself (or they can be copied from a website). Those who create Gizmoz, such as marketers who wish to post a Gizmo to their site, or send a Gizmo to an email list, use these interactive modules to intrigue their audience with interesting, interactive content. The objective is to create such a fabulous experience that the recipient is compelled to pass along the Gizmo to others. Marketers have thus achieved four things:

- A relationship has been established with the recipient, who enjoys the experience and perhaps even looks forward to future dialogue.

- The recipient has been encouraged to pass along the Gizmo, therefore increasing the marketer's targeted audience base.

- Gizmoz are trackable viral marketing programs, so that marketers can definitively measure the effectiveness of their efforts and continuously strive to improve their results.

- A Gizmo is viewed on the Web in real time, allowing the marketer to update the information on an ongoing basis. Those who have chosen to save Gizmoz to their desktops are alerted with visual and audio clues when the Gizmo has been updated, thus prompting return visits.

A word to the wise: Viral marketing needs to be carefully handled to be successful. Anything that hints of manipulation or a thinly disguised advertising message will be rejected by your audience, and may actually backfire. Viral marketing at its best occurs spontaneously, or is an essential component of your product or service offering. However, by understanding how viral marketing works and how it can be measured, you can strategically consider how to successfully add viral marketing components to your site and promotional campaigns.

The Promotional Checklist

Early Netpreneur and Internet pioneer David Rae, who founded and then sold some of the Web's most successful gaming sites, advises marketers to have a distinct set of goals for each promotion.

"It's not enough to go to a prospective sponsor with a simple advertising or promotional idea," Rae explains. There are normally five elements in a promotional campaign:

Database creation. Creating a means for visitors to the site to leave information about themselves for future email marketing and promotional campaigns can be accomplished by an email newsletter sign-up in combination with a special promotion.

Advertising. Advertising the promotion or event with advertising networks is an efficient means of attracting a large audience, which is often a key requirement of a sponsored promotion.

Promotion. The promotion itself needs to be well planned, targeted, and compelling. It's no longer enough to offer what thousands of other sites are offering. A creative promotion rises above the noise level to attract the most participants.

Event coordination. Frequently, an online or real-world event can be held in conjunction with the promotion, or be part of the promotion itself.

Public relations. It never hurts to send out a press release or make a few media calls about your promotion. Again, a creative promotion with an unusual twist may catch the ear of an editor or journalist, who will help you spread the word with a media mention.

TIP When creating your email newsletter sign-up or promotional entry form, think about the information that is most essential for you to learn about your visitor. Balance your need for information with an understanding that the more you ask for, the less likely it is that someone will sign up, or opt in. Is there information that will be helpful to you in addition to an email address, such as the specific industry or employment of the visitor? Also, is there information that is required to notify the entrant if they have won a prize? Generally, phone numbers are an acceptable request in those circumstances.

Who, How, Where, What, and When to Promote

In the first edition of this book, Rae predicted a move from advertising to promotions, which has indeed been the case. It's more fun for both the sponsor and audience alike. Rae explained:

In the past, we've given away Ford Explorers, dungeon crawls through the most ghastly dungeons in Europe, and one grand prize that sent a winner to combat flight training school in a Mig over the Arizona desert. I don't know that the size of the prize is as relevant as how tightly it fits with the topic matter and the target audience's predilections. The promotions that work best are narrow and deep, highly tuned and highly targeted. If the prize attracts too wide of an audience, you'll get people you don't necessarily want. Sometimes, even if you do want them, there are other media that will deliver those numbers at a lower cost, like television.

One of the advantages of online promotions is that, in reality, many promotions are created just weeks prior to their actual launch. These instant attractions aren't easily promoted in print because it takes too long to coordinate the creation and purchase of a print advertisement. Online, a promotion begins working as soon as you post it to a site or email it.

In addition, it is far more effective to continuously hit a tightly defined core group rather than a diffuse audience every so often. If you do in fact focus on a tightly defined audience, the viewer will more likely perceive you as being interesting, instead of getting fed up with your campaign. We've all experienced the phenomenon of being turned off by a repetitive ad. At first, those little talking Budweiser frogs may have seemed innovative, but after seeing them eight times during the Superbowl, a viewer can get annoyed, due to what the advertising industry refers to as "wear out." Hence the move from frogs to iguanas to ferrets, which does make for a long-lasting and amusing campaign. If you're going to cater to a tightly defined niche many times, be especially aware when a campaign turns from positive reinforcement into constant annoyance.

Promotions for Professional Services

Sounds like an oxymoron? Not really. I do it myself. Every year, I stage an event to market my business. In the spring, I promote "The Best of Larry Chase's *Web Digest For Marketers*," which is picked up by industry press as an informational event summarizing the best sites of the past year. Over the years, I've harvested numerous clients whom I can directly track back to those promotions. Similarly, when Morgan Stanley puts up a white paper on Internet commerce or Internet advertising, that too can be considered a promotion, or an event. It's usually referred to as a loss leader instead, but it has the same fundamental approaches in place. All loss leaders, at heart, are really just promotions.

The idea of offering free access to one's database is used often on the Net. Hoover's Online (http://www.hoovers.com) usually costs $29.95 a month. It has run free-month promotions in *Web Digest For Marketers*, and other places, in order to raise its profile and get more people to subscribe. In fact, it's a common practice for a database to go live for free at first, with a clear understanding that it will become a subscription service thereafter.

Just the idea that something you currently get for free will eventually become a paid service often serves as a strong incentive for people to go and see what value is being offered. Many industry research firms use this technique by offering free reports that encourage readers to become regular subscribers.

Other firms utilize technology to create intriguing promotions to attract new clients. International law firm Morrison and Foerster LLP (http://www.mofo.com) launched MoFo Talk Radio so that clients and potential clients could hear Morrison and Foerster attorneys from around the world discuss legal and business issues facing participants in the Internet economy. Web commerce provider SpaceWorks, Inc. has created a series of free business-to-business *webinars* (Web seminars) to help build its brand and generate sales leads (http://www.spaceworks.com/events/spaceworks_webinars.asp). Each month the company produces one-hour webcasts featuring special guest speakers. Topics have included "Buyers On Board: Bringing Your Business Customers Online" and "Selecting the Right B2B E-Commerce Solution: A Maytag Case Study."

Creative Promotions

New and innovative ways to lure you into one site over another are always being developed and tested. New York-based company Promotions.com (http://www .promotions.com) provides a service that allows marketers to add promotional tools to their email marketing campaigns. Entitled Private Label PromoMail, marketers can essentially rent the promotion they think would best entice customers to their sites or respond to other desired calls to action. The service offers 18 prepackaged promotions, including sweepstakes and instant win games, as well as customized programs. The benefit of this service is that the marketer does not have to coerce his or her technology team to create and test mechanism after mechanism to conduct promotions. Promotions.com, an opt-in email promotion provider with a database of more than 6 million subscribers, simply repackaged their existing infrastructure and technology to allow marketers to create entire promotional programs customized to their needs. The payment structure is similar to renting an email list for an email promotion—links to promotional activities such as sweepstakes are an add-on to the targeted mailing.

You position yourself as a smart player if you make technology do the bidding for you. Your promotions should always flow naturally out of your products or service. Your options range from straight discounts to free gift with purchase or free shipping promotions, from charity donations to sweepstakes. Columbiahouse.com chose to partner with Elton John to promote his "Greatest Hits" concert at Madison Square Garden in New York City in late 2000. The deal? Columbiahouse.com made 1,000 preferred-seating tickets available online only for its members, and also hosted several sweepstakes with prizes such as a trip to New York to attend the concert and meet John, and a baby grand piano autographed by the star.

TIP Consumers may view a free gift in a more positive light than a financial discount, depending upon the brand positioning of the company.

Online garden site MySEASONS (http://www.myseasons.com) launched its site in January 2000 with zero people in its database. The company was able to accumulate 250,000 names in nine months by giving away seeds. Yes, seeds. Seeds that were obviously of interest to the target audience—gardeners. In addition, the site ran a sweepstakes to win a trip to Holland, mecca of gardening fanatics around the world (see Figure 7.9).

The database drive began with a Free Seeds campaign. The site ran 20 million-plus impressions across 20 sites and newsletters from March 17 to March 30. The offer was

Figure 7.9   A free seeds giveaway sprouted a 250,000-member database for MySEASONS.

for a free pack of seeds for users who registered at the site. Of those who clicked on the banners and were taken to a registration microsite, 17.5 percent filled out the form. In addition, more than 25 percent of recipients of various email messages went on to register at the site. A follow-up email campaign that offered 20 percent to 50 percent off items at the site yielded a 9.55 percent clickthrough rate.

From July 7 to September 15, the company's free trip offer took its data collection efforts to a new level. It ran more than 50 million impressions on 17 sites and newsletters, which resulted in an addition of 200,000 names to the database—an increase of 395 percent.

Once the site's database was planted with interested consumers, MySEASONS unleashed two one-day sales called Plant Now and the Greenhouse Sale. The latter campaign netted one week's worth of sales in one business day.

Another great promotion is the Guess the Wreck monthly contest, hosted by the Hudson Valley Auto Appraisers (HVAA) (http://www.hvaa.com/guessthe.htm). It's the home of the "only auto damage appraisal contest on the Internet." You can win a $50 U.S. Savings Bond by estimating the cost of damage to a pictured car on its site. To help you out, HVAA gives hints and a list of parts that were needed to fix the actual car (see Figure 7.10).

All of these examples point out that whether you're big or small, you don't have to spend a fortune on your promotions, but you do have to spend some time making sure they match your product's attributes and your audience's tastes and desires. The concept for your promotion should be so good your competition will say, "I wish I'd thought of that first!"

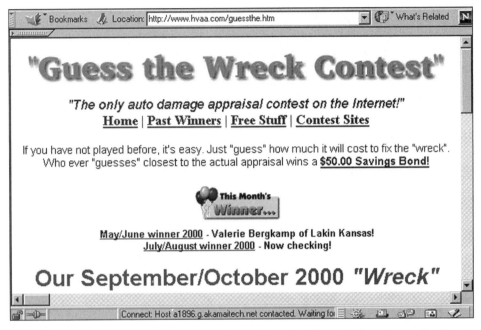

Figure 7.10 How much did it cost to fix this car? Get it right and win at Guess the Wreck.

Spreading the Word

A key component of any successful promotion is driving enough traffic to the promotion to make it successful. The demands inherent to driving a large amount of traffic to a site are one of the reasons that many site owners choose to participate in promotion networks such as Webstakes.com, or rewards networks such as MyPoints.com, rather than hosting such promotions themselves. The lesson of the successful promotions mentioned in this chapter is this: Prepare a significant, outbound, highly targeted campaign that heralds your promotion.

How can you drive traffic to your site in an efficient and cost-effective manner? One answer: by taking advantage of search engines. Optimizing your site in order to achieve a high ranking on the major search engines is one of the most cost-effective investments of time and money that you can make to promote your site and your business.

Here's how it works. Search engines utilize proprietary technology to crawl through your site and read, or *index*, your site pages, as described in Chapter 3, "Mining the Internet for All It's Worth." The search engine reads the specially formatted source code (called metatags), as well as the text on your site's pages, to figure out what your site is about. If the metatags and text on your site refer quite frequently to "windows" and "washing," for example, the search engine will figure that your site has something to do with window washing. When the spider crawls back home and indexes your site's pages in its massive database of all the sites out there on the Web, your site will be on call whenever someone enters the search terms "window washing" in the search engine. Sound simple? It should be, but it is often much more complex. Because 90 percent of web surfers go through a search engine at some point during an average online experience, every single company in the world wants to show up as number one under the keyword(s) of their choice. Unfortunately, with over a billion pages or more on the Web, not every company can show up as number one, or number thirty, or even number seven hundred and thirty-two. And what good does it do to show up as company number seven hundred and thirty-two? Not much. Hence the intense industry focus, angst, and technology devoted to improving your search engine ranking.

So what can you do?

- Absorb all there is to know about search engine optimization and register your site and interior pages of your site yourself with the major search engines, and keep track of it as best you can.
- Hire someone to handle search engine registration for you.
- Utilize one of the free or fee-based software programs on the Web to generate metatags for your site and to submit your site to search engines.

All three of these options are potential paths for you. As Internet marketers with some years of experience and a certain degree of fascination with search engine machinations and their impact on site traffic, we can offer our insight to help you evaluate your choices.

Optimize Yourself

Unfortunately, every search engine has different requirements and rules when it comes to submitting sites. If the art of search engine submission is one that you want to learn, then more power to you. However, if you do need to concentrate on your core business, you should be aware that keeping up with search engine news and changes is a very time-consuming task. Entire businesses and websites are devoted to it. Will those with the biggest budget win? Not necessarily. Search engine specialist Danny Sullivan, publisher of Search Engine Watch (http://www.searchenhinewatch.com), advises, "I think ultimately those with the best content will win, and especially those who freely link to other content, rather than trying to prevent users from leaving their sites."

Outsource Your Optimization

There are companies that specialize in search engine optimization. The fees that these companies charge can range from hundreds to thousands of dollars. If choosing this route, it is essential to find a company or person who personally supervises the submission of your site according to the rules of each individual search engine. Some scam artists will flood a search engine with submissions on your behalf, hoping to score a higher ranking. Search engine personnel do not like this, and it doesn't matter if an intermediary did this on your behalf—your site will suffer the repercussions, which could include a ban for life from that search engine.

Go for the Gold

There are many free services that you can use to automatically submit your site to search engines. So that you may intelligently assess these free services, we decided to review a top-of-the-line, fee-based search engine optimization product that will show you what the gold standard is all about.

WebPosition Gold is a search engine optimization product that will drive traffic to your site by increasing your site's visibility to search engines. *Web Digest For Marketers* was able to work with this product firsthand, and can attest to the power of this program. What WebPosition Gold does is a multistep process designed to create the best possible scenario for every page in your site, for each individual search engine. It works like this:

- The *Page Critic* will analyze your existing web pages and give advice on how to improve them for each search engine's needs.

- The *Page Generator* generates HTML pages designed to rank near the top of the search results, customized for each individual search engine according to its preferences. Users can pick the search engines of interest, and add any search engine they want to the target list. For example, if Yahoo! likes to see web pages with a 25-word site description and 20 metatags, your web page will be built for Yahoo! according to those exact specifications.

- The *Upload Manager* gathers and tracks your newly generated pages.

- The *Submitter* submits your pages to the major search engines automatically.

- The *Scheduler* helps create a schedule for page submission according to search engine preferences.

- The *Reporter* goes out and looks at the search engines, then creates a report on each search engine for each keyword you are targeting to show where you rank.

- The *Traffic Analyzer* tracks the number of visitors to your site, where they came from, and what keywords they used to find you.

WDFM is in the process of optimizing every single page of its site, including every single issue of *Web Digest For Marketers* published over the last five years, for a target list of 15 search engines and 5 keywords. The results thus far? "WDFM is number one on AltaVista under the keyword 'Web marketer'," states Richard Witt, WDFM's producer. "Our goal is to submit every single review ever published by WDFM, which numbers in the tens of thousands, as a separate page to each search engine. . .if I live that long."

WebPosition Gold is priced at $499, and a limited version with less functionality is available for $149. The beauty of the product is that it checks search engine requirements daily, and updates the software every time you log on. Therefore, you are generating pages based on up-to-the-minute requirements without having to monitor each search engine yourself. The tracking and reporting features allow you to monitor your progress and make adjustments as needed. Chad Sterns, WebPosition Gold's Director of Support, advises, "Don't bite off more than you can chew. The software is very powerful. People have a tendency to try to tackle too many keywords at once. Come up with a list of keywords and rank them in order of importance. Start off with the top five, establish a foothold, get a good position on some engines, and then you can spread out and deal with the rest of the search engines and more keywords. It's a lot less frustrating than trying to tackle the whole world in one shot."

The Promotional Chain Gang

There is a strategy to ensuring a promotion's success. First, you need to create the promotional mindset. Where are your site visitors likely to best respond to a promotion? It may be on the home page of your site, but then again, it may not. It may be within a highly targeted and timely email. It may be on a product page of an e-commerce site, where a coupon or discount could provide the first time buyer with the incentive to make a purchase. Once you have lured your participant to take action—to sign up for a newsletter or enter a sweepstakes, for example—don't stop! The visitor has already spent a few seconds or a minute to take advantage of your offer. Chances are they will spend a few seconds more to share additional information or respond to a second or even third offer. We call this the "promotional chain gang."

For example, entice your site visitors on your home page to enter a sweepstakes to win a large prize. Users are already in the promotional state of mind when filling out the form to enter the sweepstakes. On the next screen, instead of a huge page with the words "thank you" floating around in space (more on that in a moment), ask the participant to share five email addresses of their friends or colleagues whom they would like to invite to participate in the contest. Whether or not the participant chooses do to so, invite him or her to sign up for your email newsletter. Finally, thank the participant and offer a special promotion, redeemable right at that moment, for a product or service.

While this may sound tedious and intrusive, it actually only takes a few seconds to go through the entire process, and the user can choose to opt out at any time. What have you gained? A contest participant, potentially the names of five new possible participants, a newsletter subscriber, and a potential sale. Frequently, online promotions are not designed to take advantage of the interested participant. With careful design and attention to your objectives, a promotion can be expanded to meet several goals at once, thereby making it even more cost-effective.

TIP Don't forget about *thank you page* marketing! So many sites simply thank the user for participating or signing up for a newsletter in tiny little words on an enormous white page. Frequently, it's even difficult to figure out what to do next! The thank you page is a perfect place to present an offer in front of a prequalified target. You might direct the user back to a feature that highlights the day's sales or special events. You might ask the user if he or she wants to sign up for additional newsletters or other communications. You can also easily provide a list of magazines or products that might be of interest, and earn a commission if the user opts to subscribe or buy a product.

Finally, to ensure the most successful promotions, don't forget the basics:

Timing. Mondays and Fridays are bad days to launch promotions or send email. Everyone is overloaded and in delete mode. Plan your promotions for mid-week. Also consider holidays or other especially busy times of your target audience. If you are marketing to mothers online, for example, the end of the school year is not a good time to capture their attention. Reach them in September, after their kids have gone back to school and they are ready to pay attention to your message.

Frequency. Should you throw your entire promotional budget into one big attention-getter, or ongoing smallies? Unless you have a multimillion dollar budget, like CBS and its $70 million promotional budget for iWon.com, we recommend frequent, targeted, and deep promotions. Your goal is to stay at the front of your audience's mind while attracting new customers. If you spend all your money at once, you might spend the rest of the year wondering how on earth you are going to build your business. Technology changes quickly. Save room for the next brilliant promotional idea that will hit the Web three months down the road.

Objectives. Make sure to hit as many of your core objectives as you can with each promotion. Use each promotion to build your database, extend your brand, get press, and establish new relationships. Above all, be sure that your site is optimized to capture all the needed information, to entice the visitor, to encourage repeat traffic, and to support your promotional program—before you start any promotional activity. This will ensure that you get the most return from the money spent on promotional activities.

At the beginning of this chapter, I noted that things haven't changed all that much since the time of Thomas Edison's letter to my great-grandfather, discussing the promotion of his "musical telephone." It's true. Use your gut instincts. Human nature hasn't really changed. The difference between then and now is that there are computers and wires serving as conduits between you and the audience, whereas back then it was face-to-face. People still spark to a bargain, inspiration, greed, fear, and the other handful of primal traits with which we're endowed. Make it fun for the participants, and you are well on your way to success.

Finally, ask yourself the following question, Would I myself be attracted to this offer? If the answer is no, go back to the drawing board. If the answer is yes, first do a *disaster check* by testing it on some other people. Then, give it your best shot. Good luck . . .your chance to hit the jackpot is coming up next!

Resource Center

Promotion Tools

PromotionBase   http://www.promotionbase.com

PromotionBase is part of the SitePoint network, an integrated network of sites which together form a central location for information, tools, and resources for Internet-focused businesses and web developers. Because promotion starts at home, or on your home page, to be exact, PromotionBase is highly focused on search engine strategies and resources (consider the other promotional tips and techniques as a bonus). Online tools help you create metatags, submit your site to search engines, check your HTML, and validate links. Rather than wandering all over the Web to find the best free individual tools to add polls or recommendation buttons to your site, see where you rank in search engines, etc., this site compiles them all in a fresh steaming link pile of the latest and greatest.

KeywordCount.com   http://www.keywordcount.com

Keywordcount.com is an online, real-time keyword frequency analysis web service. Using this service, you can compare your keyword frequency against that of other sites. This is helpful when comparing ranking positions from search engine queries. Many services tell you *who* ranks above you—this service offers a way to find out *why*. Once you've seen the keyword landscape, you can also learn how to build your site's copy/content to combat the abusive search engine strategies (of others), such as multiple doorway pages, keyword stuffing, and more. Reports are delivered by email, and best of all, they are free!

NetMechanic   http://www.netmechanic.com

Founded in 1996 by a team of web professionals, NetMechanic has become the largest independent provider of free and low-cost site maintenance tools. The HTML Tool Box scans your site's pages and lets you know if there are misspelled words or broken links; ServerCheck will monitor your web server 24/7; Search Engine Starter will submit your site for free to 12 search engines, and also offers a fee-based ongoing search engine submission service; Search Engine Power Pack will optimize your pages for search engines; GIFBot will compress your graphics, and a free newsletter will keep you up-to-date on the latest in web techniques.

SiteOwner   http://www.siteowner.com

SiteOwner offers free review of metatags, free site submissions to search engines, a site spell check, a ranking report to see where you stand on search engines, and a means to find out what sites are linking to you, to judge your link popularity. The site also provides a daily email full of tips on how to drive traffic to your site.

HTML Metatag Generator   http://kresch.com/metatags/

Having trouble creating your own metatags? This easy-to-use form will create them for you, with all the proper coding intact, in seconds. A great tool brought to you by FreeWebmasterTools.com, which is an invaluable guide to free site promotion and optimization tools.

Contests and Sweepstakes

Web Magnet   http://www.webmagnet.com

Web Magnet is an Internet publicity provider that specializes in promoting websites through contests, directory listings, press releases, and advertising. Web Magnet looks at contests all day long, and it knows a good one when it sees it. Thus, Web Magnet created its value-added Best Contests on the Web and Best Sweepstakes Awards features, which both rate on a four-star system based on criteria such as graphics, concept, prize value, and ease of entry. This site is a good first stop for inspiration and guidance when planning your own online contest. While there, be sure to check out Ideas For You, which is an excellent 25-page primer on how to promote your site.

Contest World   http://www.contestworld.com

It's all contests, all the time. Find the newest, the most popular, or the ones that are about to expire, in addition to a categorical outline of contests around the Web. You can also search by keyword, and corresponding contests will be summarized for your review, which is a good way to quickly scope out what competitors are offering. This site promises the most complete, updated guide to contests worldwide, so if you're feeling lucky, surf on over.

About.com's Contest Guide   http://contests.about.com

Everything that you wanted to know about contests is organized here by guide Tom Stamatson. While the site is geared toward consumers, there is abundant information about new contest trends, new companies in the marketplace, what people want to win, and resources and newsletters galore.

Promotional Products

HALO   http://www.halo.com

At HALO (formerly StarBelly) not only can you create and order promotional items online, but you can also build your own virtual store chock full of your own company-branded merchandise, linked to your own website. Start a trend! If your site visitors are hankering for a T-shirt, coffee mug, baseball cap, or tiara with your logo on it, fulfill their wishes with your very own merchandise. It's a great opportunity to expand brand awareness and have a little fun at the same time.

EPromos   http://www.epromos.com

The Internet offers a more efficient way for businesses to purchase custom-imprinted specialty items. Since many businesses know exactly what they want, ePromos decided to provide an online solution. Products can be selected online, and company graphics are uploaded to ePromos. The product is then virtually presented to the business for approval, graphic intact, in an eProof. This innovative solution allows everyone to see and approve promotional products in far less time than it would take in the real world.

Promotion Resources

PPA Promotion Clinic   http://www.ppa.org/promotion-clinic

The Promotion Clinic is the brainchild of the Promotional Products Association International, a trade association for the promotions industry. The main PPA site is designed to highlight the industry and educate and advise visitors on how to find resources for successful promotional programs. In keeping with the promotional theme, the Promotion Clinic provides immediate therapy and cures for marketing and motivational needs based upon a doctor-hospital interface. Depending upon the severity of your needs, you may simply require an outpatient consultation, a house call, or a quick visit to the ER. Here's a bit of nonmedical advice: wade past the interface, because within lies very valuable information, from case studies to tips of the week. It could be just what the doctor ordered to jump-start your business.

Promo Magazine   http://www.promomagazine.com

Despite the popularity and value of sales promotion, a good online magazine devoted to the topic is difficult to find. *Promo,* brought to us by Media Central, is an excellent resource for promotional marketing information. Topics include news and trends analysis surrounding alternative media, cause-related promotions, couponing, sports promotion, games, contests, sweepstakes, in-store marketing, interactive promotions, sampling, and more. Equally valuable are featured resources such as the *2000 Annual Report of the Promotion Industry,* which literally brings facts and figures together, and the top promotional agencies highlighted in the Promo 100.

PromoMart   http://promomart.com

Need some inspiration for your next promotional campaign? Then you'll want to drop by PromoMart. This site offers a database of case studies searchable by type of promotion (product introduction, convention, recognition, etc.), target audience, or industry (insurance, advertising, or healthcare, for example). Visitors can also browse through catalogs of promotional products, create products online, find a local consultant, read *IMPRINT* magazine, or check out an events calendar for happenings in the promotional industry.

Direct Marketing and Sales Support

Whether you know it or not, you're a direct marketer. Every time you ask for a sale, a job, a signed contract, or to start a new relationship, you are seeking a response. Direct marketing (DM) always includes a call to action. Since the Internet is interactive, that call to action can be answered in seconds or minutes, rather than in weeks or months, as is the case in traditional DM. Understanding and adopting classic DM practices is critical to mounting a successful marketing campaign on the Net. Knowing where traditional DM stops—and where the new practices begin—will be your edge.

In this chapter, you'll learn how traditional DM disciplines are similar to those of the Net, as well as how they are different. Case histories will show you online DM practices that aren't even possible in traditional direct marketing. You'll receive valuable insight into the following areas:

- Key principles of traditional DM
- How traditional DM is like online marketing
- How traditional DM is not like online marketing
- Advantages of online DM
- The art of the invitation
- Succinct sales copy
- Permission marketing
- How to run an email list
- The impact of personalization

- Online DM tactics
- Keyword buys
- Benefits of traffic analysis
- Supporting offline DM efforts

How Net Marketing Is Like Traditional DM

Some of the best Internet marketing books aren't Internet marketing books at all, but rather classic direct marketing books. Understanding and applying some of the key principles of traditional direct marketing to your online efforts will save you time and money, will help you better assess your results, and will steer you in the right direction as you work to constantly improve your call to action. These principles are not necessarily practiced by all Internet marketers, since many of them do not come from traditional marketing backgrounds. Memorize the following principles and use them to your advantage:

- Direct marketing is a business of numbers. It is measurable—and numbers do not lie.

- Translating your numbers into standard DM measurements makes it very easy to analyze the success (or lack thereof) of your online marketing efforts.

- Direct marketing includes a call to action, or an offer, in order to encourage a response.

- Your numbers will be very reliable. You send out x offers, and you get y responses. Your success is—at the most basic level—measured by the number of responses generated by your offer.

- Direct marketing allows you to target your offer to a very specific audience, and to personalize your message down to the individual level.

- The more targeted, or prequalified, the audience, the more you can afford to spend to reach them, because your chances of soliciting a response are better. If you are marketing to a less than ideally targeted audience, you will get a lower response rate. Therefore, spend less to reach them.

- You will also get a better response rate from customers; that is, those who know you and have already done business with you. It makes sense to spend more to retain their loyalty as well.

- Direct marketing is easy and inexpensive to test, in a continual effort to refine your offer for the best response.

TIP According to eMarketer, "Current consensus among marketing and advertising professionals is that effective online advertising is migrating away from branding and toward targeted direct response messages. According to DoubleClick, 90 percent of the billions of ads served through its banner ad network are response driven, and only 10 percent are pure branding in nature."

Because return on investment (ROI) can be so effectively measured online, direct marketers are perfectly suited for the interactive medium. Employment opportunities in the direct marketing field are increasing at almost four times the growth of the overall U.S. job market, according to the Direct Marketing Association. Of all media, the Internet is expected to see the greatest growth in direct marketing-related jobs, with an estimated 36.3 percent annual growth rate from 2000 to 2005. DMA president H. Robert Wientzen says the evolution in technology is helping to drive growth of the direct marketing industry: "Direct marketing is no longer unseen in the U.S. economy. Its ability to deliver accountability and build relationships with customers has made it a winner as we move from the Information Age to the Digital Age."

DM Metrics

The classic rule of direct marketing is the 40-40-20 rule, which says that the success of your direct marketing effort depends upon:

40 percent: Reaching the right audience.

40 percent: Creating the right offer.

20 percent: Making it attractive with the right creative graphics, formatting, and so on.

Direct marketing, as stated earlier, is a business of numbers. These numbers are very easy to calculate and analyze. You will be concerned with:

Number of potential customers contacted. This may be measured in impressions, unique visitors, or other ways, which we will explore further in this chapter.

Number of responses returned. Depending upon your call to action, this can represent the number of sales made, email sign-ups to your newsletter, or other desired responses.

Cost of the campaign or effort. How much it costs, including the cost of renting an email list, the cost for the time spent writing the copy, or your management time, for example.

Cost per response. This is how much it cost you to gain a new customer, subscriber, or lead.

TIP Direct marketers also use a technique known as *RFM analysis* to establish metrics at the customer level. R equals *Recency*, or how recently the customer has purchased from you. F equals *Frequency*, or how often the customer purchases from you. M equals *Monetary*, which means how much money the customer spends with you. RFM analysis can help you identify your most valuable customers, pinpoint areas where you can encourage customers to purchase more frequently and to spend more, and help you establish what is known as the "lifetime value of the customer," or how much that customer will spend with your business over the length of his or her relationship with you. Multiply lifetime values times the number of customers you have, and you have determined the approximate total revenues for your business. How can you improve those numbers? Savvy direct marketing will help.

Let's compare two possible scenarios, and you will quickly see the value of online marketing utilizing direct marketing principles.

Scenario #1: Snail mail offer for personal Larry Chase website review priced at $500 to 30,000 WDFM subscribers.

 # Contacted = 30,000

 # Responses = 300 (a modest 1 percent response rate)

Cost of Campaign = $15,500 (assuming $.50 per letter, including postage, plus a modest $500 to create and manage the campaign)

Cost per response = $51.66 per customer, thereby realizing a return of $448.34 per customer on each $500 review

Not too shabby, right? That's why direct marketing has thrived for so many years. Now let's put those numbers to the Internet test.

Scenario #2: Email offer for personal Larry Chase website review priced at $500 to 30,000 WDFM subscribers.

 # Contacted = 30,000

 # Responses = 300 (a modest 1 percent response rate)

Cost of Campaign = $200 (one hour of management time to write and send the offer)

Cost per response = $.66 (66 cents) per customer, thereby realizing a return of $499.34 per customer on each $500 review

Wow! Quite a difference.

DM Internet Style

Clearly, email marketing—and most forms of Internet direct marketing—offer enormous advantages to the business owner. Of course, not everyone has a database of 30,000 plus to email. You may incur costs to rent an email list of potential customers. That expenditure will obviously cause your cost per response figure to rise.

Throughout this book we have encouraged you to develop your own email newsletter so that customers and potential customers can sign up and receive information of value from you. This is where the time and effort spent developing and nurturing an email list really pays off. As long as you continue to provide value to your mailing list, you also have your own test market, or petri dish, to contact with special offers, incentives, and other enticements. Not only can this list turn into a profit center for you, but it will also serve as practice for any other online marketing efforts you pursue where you do spend money to reach a targeted audience. You will have perfected your offer to such a degree that your response rates are bound to be much better, and therefore your efforts more profitable, than that of others who have not invested the time and effort into refining their direct marketing approach.

To gain that expertise, it's also very important to understand how online marketing is different from traditional direct marketing.

Lower Cost per Acquisition

As we have demonstrated above, it can be far less expensive to acquire a customer on the Internet than it is to do so by traditional methods. Online, you can bring down the cost to convert a prospect into a customer because you don't have the costs of producing a DM mail package, postage, handling, and backend fulfillment for the initial promotion. In DM speak, this is known as *the cost of acquisition.*

As our previous example illustrates, if I want to sell $500 website reviews via direct mail, my cost per acquisition would be $51.66. In contrast, the same offer sent by email had a cost per acquisition of 66 cents. That $50 difference could go directly to my bottom line, or I might choose to leverage that savings by spending a little to create an even more attractive offer, such as offering a free copy of this book with each review.

Immediate Response and Flexibility

When creating a traditional direct marketing campaign, be it an advertisement in a magazine with a toll-free call-to-action number, or a snail-mailed solicitation, the time from implementation to actual results can be weeks or even months. The Internet erases that wait. Results can literally be delivered overnight.

What if you don't get results? Well, you will know that fact immediately as well, which means that you can immediately apply your learnings to your next campaign. You can, as direct marketers do, test and test again to find the best results—and implement your new strategies in record time. Traditional DM'ers call this *split copy testing*, a traditional practice in which you send out three or more test packages and see which copy draws best. This copy can be in the form of an offer, a sales letter, or any other direct marketing copy. Here's one way to take the traditional practice and apply it online.

First, come up with two or three offers for your product or service. Then make some banner ads that tout this offer and set up advertising to place them on other sites that draw the types of people you're looking for. Need a free banner in a hurry? Head to http://www.coder.com/creations/banner/ where you can create banners online in minutes (see Figure 8.1). Simply type in your copy, select a font, select the finished banner size and color schemes, then submit. Voilà, you have a banner ad to place on the website of your choice. Experiment, as graphics typically attract more attention than text-only banners. Put call-to-action words in your banners. Words like Click Here, Enter. . ., or Click Now usually increase clickthroughs.

Okay, now you've got three offers running to see which *pulls* best. There are three ways to know which offer is doing what:

- Set up a unique web address on your site to which each banner will point (in other words, a separate web page within your site). Then, you simply compare which address has the most traffic.

- Use your site traffic logs, which detail where the visitors to your site are coming from, to see if your banner ad placements are sending traffic your way.

- The simplest way to track which offer pulled in a prospect is to simply ask the prospects themselves, if you're planning on having them fill out a form at your site.

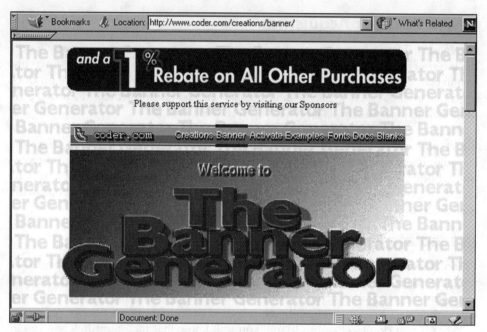

Figure 8.1 Create a free banner ad in minutes at the Banner Generator.
© 2000 Prescient Code Solutions.

The Internet also gives you the opportunity to adjust your offer or creativity during the course of a campaign. If, for example, you are running a banner ad with a sales offer across a number of sites, and that banner ad is not performing well, you can change the ad to try to improve your response rates. This type of flexibility is unknown in the real world—imagine calling back a million issues of *Forbes* because the printed advertisement that you ran was not delivering the desired results! I don't think so.

Tangible Brand Loyalty

According to Digital Idea, which surveyed 16,000 online consumers in August 2000, companies versed in direct marketing in the offline world are outperforming retail giants such as Sears, Target, and Kmart in terms of online loyalty. Loyalty is a subset of retention—a basic DM metric. How loyal your customers are translates directly into your retention rate, and the lifetime value of each customer. According to Digital Idea, the companies leading in online consumer loyalty were those with real-world expertise in aggressively reaching out to the customer, such as QVC, Victoria's Secret, Chadwick's, Lands' End, and L.L. Bean.

The Web offers many ways to tangibly measure the loyalty of your customers, and to encourage them to spend more time with your brand. This concept is called *stickiness,* or how much time your customer spends at your site and how often they come back. Many sites encourage stickiness by creating retention programs, membership programs, aggressive outbound email marketing campaigns, customer profiles, and more. These tactics will increasingly serve as a way to measure and quantify brand loyalty, as the more a customer has invested with you in terms of personal information, membership points, or other special treatment, the less likely that customer is to go elsewhere to do business. It's also much more cost-effective to reach that customer with reminders and special offers so as to increasingly encourage the customer to spend more and shop more frequently. Bottom line: more profits for you.

The Art of the Invitation

A print brochure is pushed out to the recipient through the mail, but you must pull or lure people into your site. In other words, you're asking them to make the effort to visit you. Simply putting your web address on all your collateral pieces, sales materials, and advertising will help those who want more information about you when they see the web address. But, perhaps they're not quite yet in the buying cycle for what you have to sell. You must entice them in by offering them something of value. The first call to action is to ask them to visit the site. There are three basic lures that will pull people to your site:

- Financial incentive
- Valuable information
- Utility

Thousands of sites point to *Web Digest For Marketers,* while only a few hundred point to its parent, *Chase Online Marketing Strategies.* Why? Because WDFM offers more information through its reviews of marketing sites. It offers financial incentive with specials posted for Net marketers, and it offers utility with the CPM calculators or other handy products. So even if people aren't looking for my seminars, training, or consulting at that moment, they come to the site, sign up for the weekly newsletter, and thereby enter into my *sphere of influence.* When they do need the services I vend, they naturally think of me and then get in touch because I am not at all bashful about reminding them of the other services I offer in each and every issue of WDFM. I firmly believe my readers find the sales copy useful not only to inform them of other things I do, but to tell them where I'm coming from. It tells them why I'm doing this newsletter in the first place. Too many times, I will go to a site, find useful information provided, and not know why that provider is doing it—which immediately makes me suspicious. Don't let this happen to you.

You should give thought to what your constituency will find useful. Very often, it's something you already have in-house. In fact, WDFM originally was made for internal purposes, so we could stay on top of what was going on out there. When I realized we needed valuable, updated information to draw people to my site, I posted the newsletter on the Web. Thereafter, I made it available for free via email. The list grows by hundreds of subscribers per week. Last year, 60 percent of my income came from readers of WDFM who requested professional services.

TIP When you figure out what your loss leader is, promote it in all online and offline materials. This is a come-on to get you into the store or website. Bloomingdale's may sell you a canvas bag at below cost to get you in the store, where you then buy a sweater for $185. This is where the store will make back the loss and then some.

Although the content of WDFM is easily converted into print (its reviews have been syndicated to *Advertising Age* and *Business Marketing Magazine*), the searchable archives of thousands of site reviews are not. This is where the Web excels and differs from traditional DM. If you are a marketer, you'll soon find reason to search the WDFM archives for sites of interest. You and I have begun a relationship, you will come back, and you will probably sign up for my newsletter (if you haven't already). My lure has worked. When you surf the Web for good examples of these lures, examine carefully how these companies try to convert you from a passerby into an ongoing relationship. Some do it seamlessly, while some drop the ball and don't do it at all. Make sure you do it well.

Prospecting and Acquisition

Fishing for new potential business is extremely cost-effective on the Net if you do it right. I regularly run acquisition programs for my WDFM online newsletter. For about $245, I garnered 1,200 new subscribers. Here's how I did it.

Many people who read WDFM buy and sell advertising. The unit of measure they use to compare one ad buy over another is cost per thousand, or CPM. I decided to feature and promote CPM calculators (as a computer program) that the surfer could use on the WDFM site (see Figure 8.2). A programmer friend of mine wrote the scripts in a half-hour and didn't charge me for them. In fact, Matt Lederman didn't even want his name associated with it because it was such a simple program! Therefore, there were no costs involved to create the initial attraction. I then put out a press release announc-

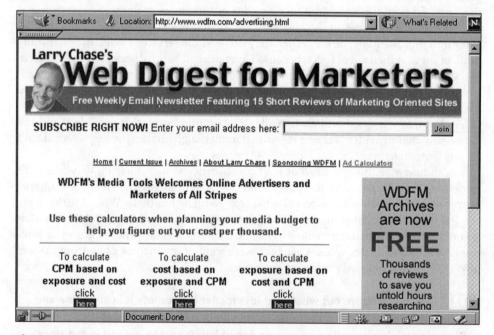

Figure 8.2 Using computer code that I got for free, I attracted 1,200 new subscribers with CPM calculators.

ing the calculators available at the WDFM site. It was picked up by Reuters and a host of other wire services, which brought people to my site by the tens of thousands. They used the calculators, and many signed up for WDFM thereafter. I have since received a great deal of business from those people who joined the list back then and have later called on me to consult, speak, or provide content for them. How do I know that? Because I asked them where they heard of WDFM in the subscription registration form. The point is, you don't have to spend a fortune to acquire prospects that can later be converted to profits.

The lessons here were twofold: Keep it simple and focused. The CPM calculators were nothing more than simple multiplication and division functions. A $1.00 hand-held calculator can do these functions and much more. However, people like single-function tools. People have toasters despite the fact they can toast their bread in the oven.

The CPM calculators had an affinity with the core product of WDFM, which in turn has an affinity with my customer base. I call this *hypothesis marketing*. If you like the CPM calculator, then you'll like WDFM. If you like WDFM, then I want to know you.

Copy for the Net

The best traditional DM copy has every sentence supporting or leading to a sale. It's similar on the Net, but I believe that the attention span of the average Net surfer is actually getting shorter, as we become more and more inundated with email and offers and banners and bells and whistles. Therefore, I recommend that you get to the point fast.

Ad banners are nothing more than *outer envelopes* with a teaser piece of copy. In the same way I want you to click on my banner and come to my site, I want you to read my outer envelope and see what's inside. There are people who look at banner ads as a vehicle for brand advertising. I disagree with this. A banner with your logo on it is use-less, the same way an envelope with nothing inside is useless. Your banner ads should have a call to action, a tease, or an out-and-out offer. I see banners as a component to a DM campaign, just like an outer envelope.

Let's say you've got a 12-panel brochure. It's not safe to say that every recipient of your brochure is going to start with the first panel. It may fall out of the envelope and reveal the back panel first. The brochure could unfold, or the reader could open it up and start in the middle. Because it's uncertain where the reader will start reading, copy points are often repeated in a brochure.

The very same is true for a website. Don't assume that everyone who visits your site begins with your home page. Search engines are very apt to show your sub pages before your home page. Why? Your secondary layers usually have more words on them. The search engine figures those pages with more words on them are more important and rates them higher. Therefore, surfers are coming in from your side doors, which can be confirmed in your log files. This means that there should be key pieces of information about you and your product on every single web page on your site, since probably only your competitor or your best friend looks at every single page.

Dr. Ralph Wilson, publisher of *Web Marketing Today* (http://www.wilsonweb.com), pointed out that I should offer my free subscription to *Web Digest For Marketers* on every single page of the WDFM site, as well as the parent company, *Chase Online Marketing Strategies*. This is what he does for his *Web Marketing Today* newsletter. He was absolutely right. My subscription rate increased 15 percent after doing so. Additionally, my contact and call-to-action information is automatically added in whenever we create a new page for the site.

Your copy style should be succinct, like your brochure copy. It should inevitably lead to a point. If it doesn't, you will confuse and bore the visitor and ultimately lose him or her. Your copy should ask for the sale or some call to action, which is something I notice many websites aren't good at. If your product or service is a considered purchase, then the copy should resemble that of a sales letter, which educates and informs as it sells. Keep in mind that the longer the copy is, the more apt someone is to print it out. In this case, you've just switched your medium from online to offline, which is not necessarily a bad thing, since the customer has made the switch himself without any added cost to you up front. Having said all this, I will now say there are distinct ways in which your online copy should differ from traditional DM copy.

Online versus Offline Tone

Advertisers call it tonality. Publishers call it the voice, while software designers call it look and feel. Whatever you call it, there are differences in the ways you present your wares online versus offline.

Generally, people online like:

- Quick bursts of information, rather than a sea of text.
- Quick-loading information, rather than large, time-consuming graphics.
- The ability to choose to seek more information, if desired, through clearly identified links or resources. (There are products that need extensive explanation, such as cars, insurance, and travel, which are considered purchase items that require deep information—research, comparisons—to aid in making an educated decision. In these cases, you want to be sure to give the prospect everything he or she wants to assist in the purchase decision.)

TIP In deep information copy, use a David Ogilvy practice of planting an offer far into the text. If the reader responds to the buried offer, you probably have a well-qualified lead on your hands, since he or she got that far into your copy. In addition, by planting the larger pages further in, you will save surfing customers much time if they don't want to look at such detailed pages until later in their buying cycle.

While cyberspace is endless and it costs relatively little to put up more copy, that doesn't always mean you should. People like you when you respect their time. We all receive too much email, and according to Jupiter Communications, we're going to be receiving about 40 times more of it in the coming years. So email (and web) copy, with or without the fancy schmancy graphics, has a lot of competition. This is one reason it has to be short, yet engaging enough to convey true value, if you seek to sell something right from the email in box.

Too many people think of the Net as only being the Web, or that online DM is only done through email. The truth is, the best campaigns are circulatory systems that encompass many online and offline media. My favorite current example is JR Tobacco (http://www.JRCIGARS.com). I first came across their charming store on Wall Street Court in New York City. It's an oval building from the mid to late 1800s. It was originally the Cocoa Exchange. I bought some cigars there at a very decent price. Later, I got their content-rich print catalog. I bought more cigars then from their 800 number, where they asked me for my email address. I gave it to them. They send me weekly offers. I actually responded to one, causing me to purchase more products on their site. That was the first email that actually caused me to buy something!

You seldom see well-written DM copy online, or offline for that matter. What follows is an example of engaging, frank, and to-the-point copy for a cigar's introduction. Notice how it brings you right into the pricing process and gives you an insider perspective, while simultaneously setting up permission to discount the cigar without diminishing the product itself, and if anything, building up its image. The writer of this copy is quite a character by the name of Lew Rothman. He's the CEO of JR Cigar, and he is interviewed in Chapter 6, "Retail: Setting Up Shop on the Net." His copy reads as follows:

> One of the World's largest manufacturers will be coming out with the Mantequilla (pronounced Monta-key-uh) brand at this summer's Retail Tobacco Distributors Convention in San Antonio.
>
> Mantequilla is Spanish for Butter. This is a quality handmade Nicaraguan cigar that will retail for 3 dollars or so (depending on size) at tobacconists everywhere. The Mantequilla cigars feature a double fermented Ecuador Sumatra wrapper and a blend of Nicaraguan, Dominican, and Honduran long filler tobaccos.
>
> Objectively, the manufacturer would love to get everyone in "cigarland" talking about their new cigar BEFORE this convention which is actually the premier event at which to introduce a new product to the industry. So we came up with a great idea:
>
> We needed a "box office smash" to really popularize our weekly E-Mail Special, and they needed a way to get 5 or 10,000 people to try their new cigar. The incentive for both of us is really advertising, not profit. . .and. . .anytime you can put together a deal where the manufacturer and the retailer are both happy selling something for nothing, it follows that the consumer is gonna get the deal of a lifetime.
>
> The following offer will be valid until the close of business Thursday, May 4th.
>
> Thereafter, the Mantequilla brand will not be available until sometime this summer.
>
> For THIS WEEK ONLY: any size box of 20 MANTEQUILLA CIGARS*: $19.95.

Permission Marketing

The practice of contacting potential customers who have either explicitly or implicitly indicated an interest in receiving information from you is known as *permission marketing*. These customers may have given their explicit permission for you to contact them by signing up for your email newsletter, for example. Or they may have implicitly given permission for companies such as yours to contact them by signing to receive information on sailing, for example, at a sports e-commerce site. That sports e-commerce site may rent the names of its customers with an interest in sailing to you, the sailboat manufacturer. Those customers have implicitly given their permission to hear from you, as your product or service is likely to be of interest.

TIP   **In a report by the Direct Marketing Association, entitled "State of the Interactive eCommerce Marketing Industry," 86 percent of the respondents expect that interactive media will increase their revenues over the next three years. Frequently used consumer email, or a permission marketing program, was seen as their "most effective" promotional tool.**

Email is called the *killer app* of Internet marketing. Why? Consider the following facts gleaned from eMarketer's October 2000 *Email Marketing Report*:

Email is already used much more frequently than traditional mail. Over 394 billion email messages were delivered in the United States in 1999. This compares to 202 billion pieces of mail delivered by the United States Postal Service. Email volume in the United States grew to 563 billion in 2000, an increase of over 66 percent.

By 2003, permission email will account for 226.7 billion email messages, or 21.9 percent of total emails sent. Permission email volume in 2000 accounted for 12 percent of total email volume, an increase of 60 percent over 1999.

By 2003, Americans will receive an average of 31 permission emails per week. This number includes those from companies/websites with whom they have relationships, opt-in lists, sponsored newsletters, and discussion groups.

The share of permission email volume will shift considerably; by 2003, in-house lists will account for 45 percent of all permission emails sent. In 1999, a full 83.5 percent (33.6 billion) of the 40.2 billion permission emails received were from, or generated by, sponsored newsletters and discussion lists. Another 15 percent (6 billion) were promotional and CRM messages sent by companies to their in-house lists. The remaining 1.5 percent (603 million) were generated from third-party opt-in lists.

Total email marketing spending in the United States exceeded $1 billion in 2000. By year-end 2003, U.S. businesses will spend $4.6 billion, including $2.2 billion in email advertising expenditures.

Email advertising will grow from 5 percent of web advertising dollars in 1999 to 13 percent in 2003. Email advertising revenue includes dollars spent to sponsor or buy advertising space in an independently-published email newsletter or discussion list; to rent lists from an opt-in marketing network or email list aggregator; to send marketing messages to third-party customer/in-house email lists by renting the list or co-marketing with the list owner; and for the delivery of unsolicited commercial bulk email, a.k.a. spam.

Nearly two-thirds of dollars spent on email in 1999 was for retention. Focus on email marketing has shifted from customer acquisition to customer retention, because, given high acquisition costs, etailers are closely scrutinizing how to retain customers through relationship management once they have roped them in as buyers. Not only do in-house lists generate better response than lists purchased from third parties; but they are less expensive, are more cost-effective, and offer significantly higher ROI.

Personalized email will be commonplace by 2001. The shift from traditional demographic segmentation to more sophisticated personalization, as offered by companies like Responsys.com (see Figure 8.3), will make email marketing increasingly powerful. With retention email, a company can use the information it has collected about its customers and prospects to reduce the costs of customer support, create follow-on sales, and build lifetime relationships with customers. Marketers hope that highly personalized email content and product offerings will counter the email response erosion most expect due to the overwhelming popularity of email marketing. In 1998, just over 7 percent of email marketers used some form of limited personalization. By the year 2003, nearly 90 percent of all email marketers will be employing personalization to some degree or another.

Mailing List Rental

Renting or leasing lists offline is a time-honored practice and industry in DM. You lease a list from a list broker or publisher, get the names printed on labels, and send out your mailing. An implicit permission email marketing approach is the rental of opt-in email lists.

Figure 8.3   Email direct marketing is the expertise of Responsys.com.
© 2000 Responsys.com, Inc.

According to eMarketer's October 2000 *Email Marketing Report*, opt-in email list provider YesMail's Top 10 email list categories are:

1. Music
2. Entertainment
3. Internet
4. Computer Software
5. Computer Hardware
6. Sports and Recreation
7. Travel and Leisure
8. Shopping
9. Electronics
10. Games

Because of their highly targeted nature, opt-in consumer email list prices typically range from $150 CPM (cost per thousand) to $300 CPM. Opt-in services usually send the message on behalf of the marketer, without providing them with the customer email addresses. Response rates to opt-in list can go as high as 15 percent, depending upon the offer, although it is prudent to plan for a traditional DM response rate of approximately 2 percent.

With access to over 25 million opt-in names, 24/7 Mail is one of the leading permission-based email list providers. Marketers can choose from 260 categories to target their marketing messages. Using 24/7 Mail, a typical opt-in email program can be executed within 48 hours, at an average cost of $14,500. The same program using direct mail, in comparison, would typically cost $27,500 and would take six to ten weeks to execute.

Mailing List Costs

If you do decide to rent an email list to promote an offer or drive traffic to your site, be prepared to take advantage of that expenditure and that traffic by having your own email mailing list ready and waiting for interested subscribers to sign on up.

If your list is just beginning, you can run a one-way mailing list right out of your mail program, bringing the cost of distribution down to nearly zero. Making a mailing list that goes out to dozens or hundreds of people isn't hard at all and varies from one email program to the next.

Here's how it works for basic email programs: Have a file that holds all the email addresses of the people who have requested to receive your mailings. Put a comma and a space after each address. When you are ready to send your mail out, simply copy all of the email addresses from the document where you keep them and paste them into the "Bcc:" field and then send. Most basic email programs will even allow you to keep all of those email addresses parked in a special place within the program itself. You give that list a name, such as "MailList," and when you're ready to send your newsletter, just put "maillist" in the "Bcc:" field and the program will know to grab all the addresses you've previously set up and send your newsletter to each and every one of them. I suggest buying an email program that does this, such as Eudora from Qual-comm. This feature alone is a time-saver for you.

Short of running the list from your email program, the least expensive way to go is to use a free mailing list server such as Majordomo or LISTSERV. You can either have a techie install it and maintain it on your server (usually it is now included as part of your web server software), or simply pay a local provider that already has it installed. At the time of writing, you can run a list of 1,000 people for around $20. You can also run email lists from sites such as eGroups for free—if you are willing to carry one of their advertisements on each email message. I urge you to set up an email list using a professional technical email provider rather than a web-based community service, although many do opt to pay eGroups $4.95 a month for the ad-free version of their list-host service and run their professional communications from there. It's simple and easy, but so are the LISTSERV-provided services, which can be completely branded under your name and sent from your domain. For a complete reference of other Major-domo lists, you can check out List-Business.com's list of list-hosting services at http://list-business.com/list-service-providers/. By the way, it isn't necessary to use a local provider.

Larger lists require more sophisticated LISTSERV technology. I currently use Spark-LIST (http://www.sparklist.com), which provides great value quite inexpensively (see Figure 8.4).

As a means of comparison, it costs me around $85 a month to send WDFM to 30,000+ subscribers once a week. The WDFM Managing Editor accesses the list man-

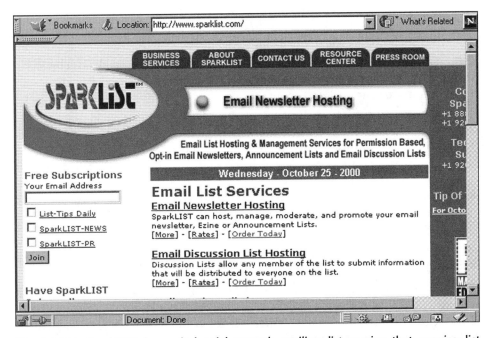

Figure 8.4 SparkLIST is an industrial-strength mailing list service that marries list management with database functionality.

SparkLIST is a trademark of SparkLIST.com Corporation.

agement tools at the SparkLIST website. Amenities include the ability to schedule mailings in advance and a complete audit trail for every mail transaction. I have found SparkLIST's automatic filtering feature, which weeds out dead email addresses, to be particularly useful.

In addition to great service, SparkLIST also offers a daily email newsletter called *List-Tips Daily* filled with email newsletter tips and techniques. Subscription instructions can be found at http://www.sparklist.com.

Mailing List Management

Clean your lists! People's email addresses tend to be much more transient than physical addresses. It is easier to move from one provider to another than from one home to another. Also, people's email addresses change when their jobs change. Cleaning your list will help you in three ways:

- You'll receive far fewer *bounce-backs* from email addresses that no longer exist.

- If you are selling ad space on an email list that boasts 10,000 people, but in reality only has 6,500 active addresses, it will negatively skew the ad response results that your advertiser is looking for. Traditional direct marketers look for a 2 percent response (plus or minus, based on the list and the product category). Online responses often tend to be lower, but there is no cost of production or distribution, which more than compensates for lower response rates on online mailing lists. If you quote your audience at 10,000, when actually it is 6,500, it will further depress the response rate. You want to be sure you're selling a quality product that delivers exactly what you are promising. Both you and the advertiser will come out stronger in the long run. The cleanliness of your list is also a good selling point.

- You will be seen as being a good Netizen for not taking up bandwidth by sending email to nonexistent addresses, which will only bounce back from their old accounts to your mailbox—more clutter.

You can attempt to revive your dead email addresses with an email management service. Try ActiveNames (http://www.activenames.com), the "Internet's email change of address" service. Similar to the USPS national change-of-address (NCOA), this nifty service enables businesses to turn "undeliverable email" into customers again. Users register with ActiveNames in order to have change of address notifications sent to anyone who emails to an old address. Users gain an easy way to manage multiple email communications, while businesses have an opportunity to find lost customers or prospects.

Mailing List Advertising

One of the least expensive ways to reach a highly segmented audience is to simply sponsor a mailing or discussion list that's already out there. There are two basic kinds of lists. One-way lists just go in one direction; for example, WDFM goes from me to 30,000+ people. Therefore, each subscriber can only receive from me and can't add comments to my newsletter.

Two-way lists are discussion lists. Discussion lists themselves come in two varieties: moderated and unmoderated. On a moderated list, the postings are moderated by a list

ASCII

ASCII stands for American Standard Code for Information Interchange. ASCII is simple, unformatted text (nothing but hard returns show up) that can be read on any computer platform. These days, much email is still in ASCII text. It's ugly, but ubiquitous.

manager (for content), and the group is often limited by voting in new members, rather than an open subscription (where anybody could join). An unmoderated list is an anything-goes proposition. I think of mailing list discussion groups as extremely segmented talk radio, where many only listen (online, it's called *lurking*) while a smaller percentage of people speak. Since you want the environment to be somewhat controlled, you'll more than likely want to run your discussion group as a moderated list.

If you're interested in seeing a moderated discussion list specifically for the marketing niche, I recommend Online Advertising Discussion List at http://www.o-a.com (see Figure 8.5).

Advertising on one-way or two-way lists is what I often recommend to clients because it's one of the most cost-effective uses of an ad budget. You reach a no-waste audience with practically no production costs since the message is usually in ASCII text. Since this medium is such a bargain, you can afford to make a really enticing offer to this crowd. Try it, you'll like it. For very little money, you can win the hearts and minds of these list devotees for what must seem like nickels compared to what brand budgets normally run.

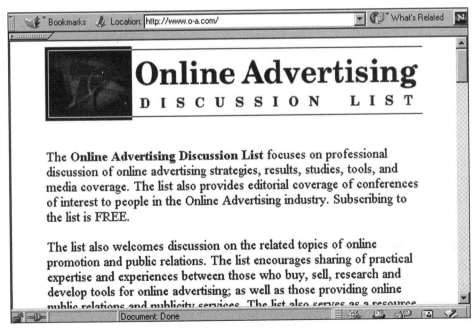

Figure 8.5 Online Advertising Discussion List is one of the most popular and active online discussion lists about online marketing.

© 2000 The Tenagra Corporation (http://www.tenagra.com).

> **TIP** Use someone else's list to run promotions (assuming that list accepts advertising). Set up one of the pages on your site to receive visitors who see your offer in one of these mailing or discussion lists. By lurking in the list, you'll gain a pretty good idea of what will make this group move to action. Then, buy some ad space and make the offer that is available on your site. When they come in, make sure you attempt to convert them to an ongoing relationship somehow. Offer to update them on points of interest you can provide them via email. You won't get nearly all of them, but that's okay.

The following thought may occur to you: Hey, why should I pay for an advertisement, when I can simply post to the list for free, with my ad copy or offer being the focus of the message? Do not do this! This will be seen by the other members of the discussion list as being entirely self-serving and an abuse of the forum. What you can do is have a signature file that gives your URL and other information, as sort of an addendum to your message (see Chapter 4, "http://007: Spying on Your Competitors and Yourself," for more on sig files). This is another good reason to use a sophisticated email package, as it allows you to automatically append your signature information, without having to key it in each and every time. My sig file always includes the free offer to WDFM and points to a site featuring a free chapter of *Essential Business Tactics for the Net.*

The message you post should provide information, observation, a response to someone else's posting, or an honest question. Having said that, it is not entirely inappropriate to inform that discussion list about a timely posting of something truly valuable to that list that is found on your site. This is especially true when someone else on your list asks where he or she might find such information. I know what you're thinking: "Hey, I'll get a friend to ask, 'Where can I find this information?' Then I'll be the hero by saying, 'Lo and behold, it's on my site!!'" Yes, people do this from time to time, but you'll find that discussion list members will pick up on this pattern if you repeat it and they will not think too highly of you. Don't risk your long-term reputation for such fleeting games.

If an existing newsletter or discussion list matches your topic or audience, join it. See how much, or if any, advertising is on it. See who's advertising and what they're saying. Note how many ads there are in an issue and observe whether that number remains constant over a few issues. Just like any other medium, this will give you an idea as to the strength of the advertising rate card, or the price list a media outlet uses to charge for advertising exposure. If there aren't many ads, you might be able to strike a better deal. You might also see if the list owner is amenable to barter. If he or she is loaded with paying advertisers, the answer will probably be no.

Add Some Ads to Your Mailing List

If you start or have a mailing list with unsold ad spaces on it, check out List Exchange at http://www.listex.com. There you can swap ad avails with other lists of similar ilk. In this way, you can help each other build your respective audiences. This bootstrapping method simultaneously builds audience and gives the appearance of having a larger advertising base. That's important when the next advertiser comes around with money.

Make sure your sponsor's ad gets results so she or he returns to advertise in your online newsletter or mailing list again. Give the ad away at first, if you have to, until it works, and be sure to agree that your sponsor will write a testimonial about how effective the ad was on your list. This and other testimonials will help convince future prospective advertisers that your newsletter or mailing list is worthy of their budgets. What if the offers within these ads don't get a satisfying response? Like any good direct marketer, you must test, test, test, and never stop testing. You may find that certain types of products or services pull better on your list than others. This will help you direct your sales focus when attempting to sell advertising space. There's no reason to go after advertisers who will only wind up frustrated and not advertise with you again.

Be creative as you consider how to develop your own permission marketing program. Improved technology has made it increasingly easy and inexpensive to incorporate innovative marketing strategies into your site, your email, and your business. Some to consider are:

Topical email newsletter. A valuable one-way newsletter (such as WDFM) reinforces the brand, serves as a sales platform for related projects and products, and serves as a revenue center by selling ads of interest to subscribers to advertisers.

Discussion list. A discussion list is a two-way forum for you to communicate with your vendors, your colleagues, or other types of community who would enjoy discussing topics of shared interest. One example is I-Sales, an online discussion list for professionals in the Internet sales arena. Hosted by AudetteMedia (http://www.audettemedia.com), the list brands the company as an industry player and also generates ad revenues.

Corporate email newsletter. A corporate email newsletter is designed to keep your clients, vendors, or customers aware of what your company is doing, products or services that you have added to your assortment, industry mentions, and news about special events.

Educational email newsletter. Educational email newsletters are written to provide tips and techniques for using your products, to suggest complementary products, or to provide advice on how to use your company's products or services can help your customers improve their businesses.

Reminder service/scheduled alerts. Alerts can be replenishment programs, gift reminders tied into a simple online calendar interface, or notices of sales or new product arrivals at your site.

The more personal and valuable the service or information you provide, the more successful you will be.

How Personalization Will Revolutionize DM

It is less expensive to retain a customer than to acquire a new customer. Customers who have ordered from you or in some way transacted with you are familiar with your company and your products or services. They have visited your site and it's possible to

> **MAILBOT**
>
> *Mailbot* comes from two words, *mail* and *bot*, where *bot* is short for *robot*. A mailbot is a piece of mail automatically sent out upon request. It may be sent right away, or scheduled to go out days, weeks, or months later, as a reminder message. Mailbots are also used as confirmation notices. Sometimes called *replybots*, these messages can tell you that your order or email has been received and will be acted upon on a certain date.

know where they went and what they looked at. They are likely to open an email from you, especially if they have requested it. They are also likely to participate in programs that you create for them to encourage their loyalty. If employed correctly, the Net can be very good at keeping existing customers satisfied.

Amazon.com has done a phenomenal job of creating customer loyalty. A key component of their marketing strategy has been the development of *one-to-one relationships* with each and every one of their customers. Interested in the latest Internet marketing books? Sign up at the site and you will be informed by email whenever a new Internet marketing book is available. Now, we all know that Jeff Bezos himself is not sitting down and writing this personalized email to you. But do you really care that it was a mailbot that performed this service? No, because it is the value that this service brings to you that counts, and that keeps you coming back to Amazon.com.

What you may not know is that, by identifying yourself both explicitly as a customer who is interested in Internet marketing books, and implicitly as an Amazon.com surfer who also takes a peek at the latest in serial killer thrillers, your site experience is being personalized for you. NetPerceptions (http://www.netperceptions.com) and other online personalization companies are dedicated to creating and maintaining personal information tracking, which enables companies like Amazon.com to show you the promotions, advertisements, products, and even entire layouts of their sites that are likely to be of most interest to you. Personalization technologies can do everything from recommend to a customer what he or she would like to buy next, based on past behavior or information stored on personal preferences, to reminding a customer when a spouse's birthday is coming up and offering web links or other information concerning gifts or cards for the day. Personalization technology is discussed in more detail in Chapter 6, "Retail: Setting Up Shop on the Net."

This use of technology is excellent DM thinking, but also says something about these companies and how they think and do business. These services serve double duty as a DM and branding tool, since they leave customers with a good impression and motivate them to come back and do business in the future.

The Customer Is in Control

The growing use of personalization technology underscores the fundamental shift the Internet has wrought upon business today—the customer is in control. "Years ago I looked at the Internet and saw it as inherently a DM medium. I predicted that DM would own the Net. I was wrong," states Ken Magill, the piquant executive editor of *iMarketing News*. "Direct marketers have a chip on their shoulder the size of Montana."

That doesn't mean that DM fundamentals won't apply, but, according to Magill, "The Internet needs a balance between direct marketers and 'creative types.' Direct marketers are used to being the smartest people in the room. The danger in that is that you stop listening." He continues, "As an industry, we need to look, listen, and react to the market. Neither the numbers-focused direct marketers nor the warm and fuzzy relationship-builders are doing it right—they are failing to empathize with the customer and realize that the customer is in control."

Magill observes, "The Internet is not a passive medium. Most people go on the Net with a task in mind. Direct marketers need to understand that you are interrupting this task. What does this mean?"

Magill advises that direct marketers consider a two- or three-step prospecting technique, as follows:

1. Get new email address.

2. Follow up.

3. Close sale.

"That doesn't mean that I'll get your email address and work you for a year to generate a $50 sale," Magill states. "I'm not a big believer in 'relationships' as applied to direct marketing. Marketers need to see numbers associated with their efforts. Spending $250 to acquire a customer who will spend $100 over his or her lifetime with you doesn't make sense. That's where agencies and creative types go wrong. They need direct marketing metrics. It's an arithmetic problem."

On the subject of one-to-one relationships, Magill has the following to say, "A retailer that I buy from online is not my friend. We may interact, because direct marketing is most effective as a dialogue. But I don't want a relationship. If we have a relationship, it's a precarious one based on mutual exploitation."

Direct Marketing on the Web

The most effective websites are ones that successfully fill a highly defined niche. Sounds just like direct marketing, right? These sites will help you reach a highly defined target audience with your offer online, using a variety of techniques.

Affinity Marketing

Utilizing affinity marketing techniques, you can partner with sites that you, your product, or your service have some affinity with. American Airlines, Avis, and Hilton Hotels are considered affinity sites since they all have something in common; namely, people who travel.

There are three basic ways that these affinity partnerships work:

Engage in an equal barter with another site. This is when no money changes hands. You point to each other's sites, delivering about equal value.

You pay for links. You need them a lot more than they need you, and you are willing to pay for it. This is paid advertising or sponsorship.

They include you in a resource center of links containing sites like yours. No reciprocal link is necessary.

How do you find these sites? For starters, you can do a search to see what turns up. Remember to do this from a few different search engines, as no two cover the exact same territory on the Web.

Ad Networks

You can always run some banner advertising on sites of interest to you to find new customers. You might also want to buy across several different sites in order to capture a particular audience. Ad networks are set up to help you make these buys. The first and best known of these networks is DoubleClick (http://doubleclick.com), which will sell you a batch of impressions targeted to meet your specific audience. The more highly targeted the audience, the higher the cost per thousand, just like in any other medium. Individual sites, rich with demographic data gathered with the cooperation of the users, are doing this segmentation as well. For example, *The New York Times* can specifically deliver your ad to a targeted audience of women aged 18–34 who read books and make more than $50,000 annually. Most individual sites don't have this depth of information from their users because they didn't ask for it up front, or didn't feel the user would part with that information in exchange for access to the site. Asking for this sort of marketing information is a barrier for the user and often gives him or her pause to consider if he or she really wants to give that information away. The NYT made good use of this concept from the very beginning—a free subscription to the NYT online was well worth the effort required to answer a few demographic questions.

Internet Audience Metrics

We all know that many people are online, and the numbers are growing every day. However, knowing how many people are online or how they are accessing the Web is only the tip of the iceberg in terms of audience analysis. Media Metrix, an Internet audience measurement firm specializing in developing sophisticated measurement analysis, is one example of the kind of firm that helps shape marketing and business decisions (see Figure 8.6). How does it work?

The Media Metrix Meter is installed on the operating systems of home and work computers of more than 100,000 panelists worldwide. Each panelist is characterized as to age, gender, household size and composition, income, education level, geographic location, and so on. The Media Metrix Meter records all of the individual's computer activity, online and offline, and relays it back to Media Metrix servers in real time. This enables Media Metrix to measure audience usage of not only the Web, but also of other online services such as AOL, email usage, and software and hardware ownership and

---

IMPRESSIONS

An *impression* represents the viewing of an ad by the surfer. Impressions are a much more realistic measurement to use than hits. One person visiting a single web page can account for 10 hits, but only one impression. Beware of any site that attempts to sell you on the inflated number of hits it gets.

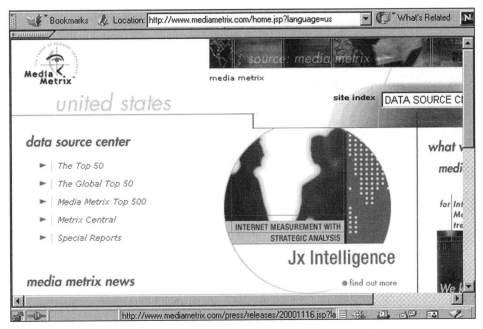

Figure 8.6   Media Metrix provides Internet audience measurement data.
© 2000 Jupiter Media Metrix, Inc.

usage—and this allows Media Metrix to then link user behavior with the demographic characteristics of its panelists.

Another division, Media Metrix AdRelevance, specializes in the automated retrieval and delivery of online advertising data. More than 200,000 unique ads are captured monthly and classified into the AdRelevance database, which then informs subscribers as to advertising trends and where, when, how, and how much the competition is advertising on the Internet.

For example, with Media Metrix's Internet audience research, *ad buyers* and *advertising agencies* can:

■ Maximize ad buys by targeting unduplicated online audiences

■ Get a complete breakdown of websites' user demographics and track demographic changes over time

■ Make effective ad buys by identifying top performing sites per category

■ Analyze entire industries and trends by tracking audience usage and advertising activity

With AdRelevance's online advertising research, *ad buyers* and *advertising agencies* can:

■ Compare their ad buys with competitors' ad buys

■ Leverage media purchasing power with insider knowledge of a site's ad inventory by advertiser

- Evaluate the competitive landscape with the knowledge of which products are being advertised where, when, and how aggressively, and with what messaging

With Media Metrix's Internet audience research, *website owners* can:

- Refine advertising and marketing strategy by pinpointing how well their advertising and promotion drives traffic to their site
- Effectively target their campaigns by identifying traffic usage patterns across demographic categories
- Capture audiences from competitors by identifying and targeting the sites their audience visits before visiting the competitor's site
- Compare growth rate of visitorship/audience (and effectiveness of underlying strategy) relative to that of their competitors' growth rates

With AdRelevance's online advertising research, *website owners* can:

- Increase sales opportunities by identifying top and new advertisers every week
- Get detailed insight into advertisers' strategies before the sales call
- Benchmark advertising sales against key competitors to make sure they are getting a fair share of the ad dollars spent

All of this information is a powerful business tool for all sectors of the market. For example, the financial community uses this information to identify high-growth partners for portfolio companies, complete business plan analyses, and to anticipate quarterly report findings by comparing ad revenue trends with Internet stock performance.

Search Engines from a DM Perspective

Earlier in this chapter, we mentioned that DM online differs significantly from DM offline because you must draw or lure people into your site, rather than pushing a brochure or catalog to them through the mail. One of the most effective ways to lure people to your site is to intercept them at the point where they are making their surfing decision—on a search engine.

Keyword Buys

As you can imagine, it's important to know what search terms people are going to use when looking for a company like yours. You can actually buy a word from just about any search engine—a word that will bring up your ad each time the word is searched for in the engine. This is known as a keyword buy. I was one of the first ones to do this a few years ago, so I got terrific deals for my clients until media buyers caught on. Here's how it worked for one of my first clients, Autobytel.com.

Along with the volume of impressions we bought at InfoSeek (now Go.com), I asked to have some keywords thrown in for added value. Back then, they didn't charge because no one understood the value. We got hold of some very valuable category words like "car," "auto," "travel," and "minivan." When people searched on those words, they got a banner from Autobytel.com at the top, along with their search results. The clickthrough rate for the banner ad campaign went from an average of 2 percent to 15 percent and higher.

Today, Go.com—and all search engines—charge a premium for these words. In other words, for every 1,000 times the word "weather" is used and your ad appears, you pay the negotiated CPM, which depends upon popularity and availability. Some words are less popular than others and you may be able to get a price break. The major words in the major categories are worth more than words in less frequented categories. You'll probably get the word "lobster" or "scuba" for less than you'd pay for "mutual fund." I suggest you pick a few words you're interested in buying and enter them into a search engine again and again to see how many times your competition's ad comes up and how many times a randomly selected ad comes up.

As an alternative to premium keyword-buy sponsorships, Google's innovative AdWords program lets you manage your own account and ad text, with a minimum buy starting at just $50 (http://www.google.com/ads/). AdWords is a great program for advertisers with limited budgets, and for those interested in trying out keyword-based ads before making a larger buy. AdWords ads appear on the right side of a search results page. The Jeeves Text Sponsorship Network, which can be found at http://sponsor.directhit.com, also offers a creative approach to low-cost, targeted advertising—advertisers select and bid for keywords, indicating the top dollar they are willing to spend. The top bidder wins, and that company's ad is served whenever someone enters that search word or phrase.

In contrast, the randomly selected ad runs in what's called *general rotation*. This arrangement is similar to what traditional media charge for premium placements. You spend less money on ad space if you allow the newspaper or TV/radio station to stick the ad in where it fits most easily. This is called *run of station* or *run of paper*. Online it's called *run of network*, or general rotation, where someone who is looking up "pterodactyl" might get the Hotel Discount banner on the search engine.

If you find these general rotation ads running more often than not on the words you're interested in, it may mean the search engine has a large inventory of exposures available for this keyword, and not many people have bought it yet. That's important information to have when negotiating the price.

Observing Search Engine Habits

Sit with other people in front of a search engine and ask them individually to look for something in your category. It's a good idea to do this with people both inside and outside your industry. Note which words they use most. This will not only tell you what words you might want to buy from the search engine, it will also tell you how to write the metatag code on your site so your firm comes up higher in the search results (see Chapter 4, "http://007: Spying on Your Competitors and Yourself," for more information on how to do this). While you're watching people do searches in your category, you may see them tiring after 20, 30, or 40 sites found by that search engine. So what good is it if you're 432 in the listings? Not much.

Often the search engine visits your site and dumps a certain percentage of your site into its database. Since it only has so much room, it may take only the first 25 words of your site and actually show those words when showing the surfer the results of what it's found. Make sure those 25 words telegraph a message to the reader of that search showing why they should visit you. Make it compelling from the user's point of view. In other words, make it so compelling that even you would click on it.

One way to find out where you stand with the search engines is by using a tool such as PositionAgent (http://www.positionagent.com). You give it a search word and it enters it in a few different search engines and comes back and tells you where your ranking is in each. It offers a subscription service for improving your search rankings as well (see Figure 8.7).

Power Tracking

In comparison to such free or low-cost tools, we can also give you an insider's view of one of the Web's most powerful traffic analysis tools—WebTrends.

WebTrends offers more than half a dozen sophisticated analysis and reporting solutions for all sizes of organizations. "A few years ago when the Internet in general was in its infancy, it was really webmasters who were using our products," says Jeff Seacrist, Product Marketing Manager at WebTrends. "They were seeking insight into how many visitors were coming to their sites, whether or not their links were working, and making sure that bandwidth was being utilized efficiently."

The times have changed. "Over the past few years, more and more people throughout the organization are interested in gaining more information about their visitors and how visitors behave," continues Seacrist. "Based on the behavior of people on your site, you can learn so much about them. It's like a traditional retailer watching

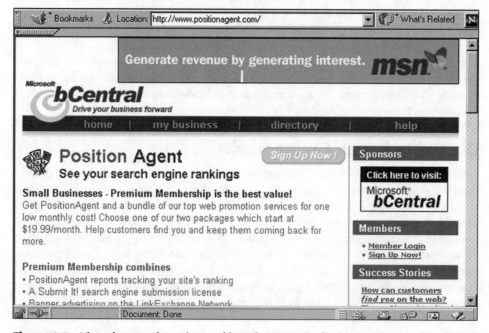

Figure 8.7 View the search engine rankings for your site by keyword on 10 top search engines with PositionAgent.

how people move throughout a store. Online, any site can understand what visitors are interested in, who those visitors are, and can use that information to help convert them into a customer and make them a happy loyal customer."

WebTrends provides both products and services to help businesses get the information they need to make informed decisions based on what is going on in their sites. WebTrends Live is unique in that it is a web-based service that site owners subscribe to, as opposed to a software product. With WebTrends Live, subscribers are able to analyze web traffic reports in real time. Hundreds of reports are available, including visitors, page views, ad campaign tracking, revenue analysis, top paths, content group reporting, and even wireless access usage patterns. "WebTrends Live is attractive to small businesses because it is an ASP solution," explains Seacrist. "The amount of involvement to get it up and running is minimized, businesses can pay as they go, and they can get a lot of stats without an up-front investment." The fee-based versions of WebTrends Live (Enterprise and eCommerce) range from under $40 a month (for up to 25,000 page views) to several thousand dollars a month, based on the number of page views per month. The site owner selects the pages to be tracked and places an invisible image tag on those pages, which reports the individual page activity to WebTrends Live. The site owner then accesses all resulting reports on the WebTrends site.

For those of you who want a free version, the scaled-down Personal Edition is a single site solution that requires only that a small (visible) button is placed on the pages to be tracked.

Another WebTrends solution, CommerceTrends, differs from WebTrends Live in that site owners are using the product to build a full transactional database of what visitors are doing on their site. This database can be used to go back and do more in-depth analysis, and to datamine in all sorts of ways. "This is our Visitor Relationship Management solution," explains Seacrist. "The VRM is essentially a platform that can help a company understand its customers. By being able to correlate back to the behavior of visitors at your site, and the behavior of people who purchase at your site, you can understand how to convert more of your visitors to customers." The VRM is based on open architecture, so that users can integrate any personalization or CRM service on top of the VRM platform to create a closed-loop system. Typically, integration costs range from $50,000 to $100,000 for the CommerceTrends product.

For example, site owners can look at where people are coming from to get to their site, how they are moving through the site, and at what point they are leaving the site. "As a marketer, I think reverse path analysis is one of the most interesting things to look at," says Seacrist. "It's one thing to say where people go. It's quite another to be able to identify ending point and then figure out how the customers that purchase got there. Did it take them 15 clicks to get to your order page? To be able to streamline how people get to your desired end result is important."

WebTrends products also offer campaign analysis, which helps increase marketing effectiveness and ROI by determining how many customers came to your site from an ad (whether banner, email, or print, through the use of distinct landing pages), and to what depth they traveled. "You as business manager can define what a qualified visitor would be," states Seacrist. "In our own case, we think people who download trial versions of our software are qualified leads. The number of visitors matters, but we can also assign value to different types of visitors and behaviors, and then to different types of messaging. What message brings more qualified visitors, what message brings more revenues—not just the copy, but the site, the words and the path that visitors use to get to the end point?"

To demonstrate just how much information can be gleaned from the Commerce-Trends product, WebTrends ran a text advertisement in WDFM and then tracked performance metrics for our review. In this specific campaign, the offer was to download a free report entitled "10 Reports Every eMarketer Lives For" from the WebTrends site. Figure 8.8 shows what percentage of the visitors who responded to the ad actually fulfilled the call to action. According to eMarketing Manager John Simpson, "The fully-qualified column tells me that 41 percent of the respondents completed the registration form and downloaded the guide, which is a very high conversion rate" (see Figure 8.8).

In addition, Simpson assigned a revenue forecast to the various types of leads generated by this campaign based upon qualification level. By extrapolating potential revenues, the ROI of the advertising campaign can easily be established and compared to other marketing efforts.

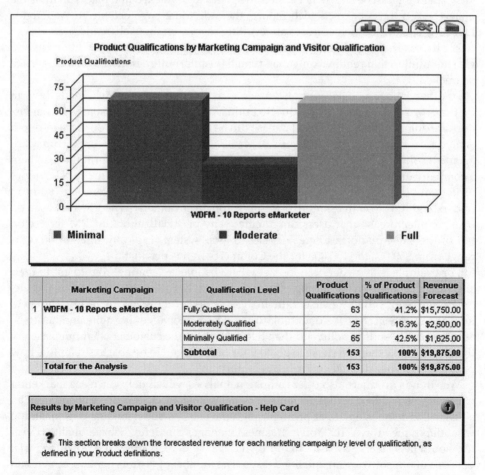

	Marketing Campaign	Qualification Level	Product Qualifications	% of Product Qualifications	Revenue Forecast
1	**WDFM - 10 Reports eMarketer**	Fully Qualified	63	41.2%	$15,750.00
		Moderately Qualified	25	16.3%	$2,500.00
		Minimally Qualified	65	42.5%	$1,625.00
		Subtotal	**153**	**100%**	**$19,875.00**
	Total for the Analysis		**153**	**100%**	**$19,875.00**

Results by Marketing Campaign and Visitor Qualification - Help Card

? This section breaks down the forecasted revenue for each marketing campaign by level of qualification, as defined in your Product definitions.

Figure 8.8 CommerceTrends Report: 41 percent of WebTrends ad respondents fulfilled the call to action.

Finally, Simpson took a look at the top downloads by the visitors who responded to the campaign (see Figure 8.9). "The value here is that I can see that in addition to visitors downloading the free report I was promoting, they are also sticking around at our site and downloading a product brochure and other white papers," Simpson explains. "Both downloads are signs that the potential customer is digesting additional information about the products and services my company offers. That's valuable insight."

By the time you read this, WebTrends will have added an eMarketing Server product to give site owners the ability to send targeted email campaigns to customers based on the behavior they have exhibited on site. "eMarketing Server was designed to help people leverage the benefits of the VRM platform in order to better segment their customers and send targeted campaigns to better meet their needs," explains Colleen Kerry, Director of Product Marketing for WebTrends. "We're merging the *what*—what they are interested in when they come to your site, your customer's needs, behavior, and preferences—with the *who*—the standard age and demographic information. Combining the demographic with the needs and preferences allows businesses to cre-

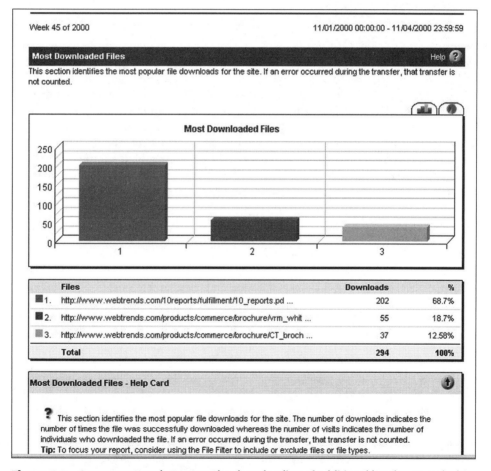

Figure 8.9 CommerceTrends Report: The downloading of additional brochures and white papers indicates the level of prospect interest.

ate much more effective campaigns. The real power in targeting your customer is not just who they are and where they live, but also identifying their needs and preferences." Kerry concludes, "You cannot have that without the clickstream analysis. Traditional traffic analysis falls short of providing the behavioral data. Now behavioral data can be integrated into your marketing campaigns."

For the small business, WebTrends Log Analyzer, priced at $500, provides a wealth of information to site owners about where customers are coming from and what they are doing on the site. This solution evaluates web server log files from a single server. The resulting information can help site owners optimize how they are spending money to bring customers to their site, and it can help them optimize their site for a more user-friendly experience. The Professional version includes alerting, monitoring of server uptime, and link analysis, so site owners will not just measure traffic, but also manage site uptime and bandwidth utilization.

Online Direct Marketing Supporting Offline DM Efforts

One of the richest areas for you to explore is how to have one medium, such as the Web, assist other mediums, such as direct mail or print advertising. Because the Net is such a quick and cheap test bed for what pulls and what doesn't, you should consider using it not only for online campaigns, but for offline efforts as well. Testing print offers takes months of preparation and handling, not to mention significant expenses. In certain categories, you can get a quick response on what offers may or may not work for print mail pieces. This will not be as scientific as an offline mailing list you can buy, because you won't be sure of the authenticity of the respondents online, unless you prescreen them via telemarketing or some other channel. But it can give you an indication of which test packages to use and commit to when putting print offers together. The package that tests best will become your control package. I caution you here. Your mileage will vary depending upon your category, audience, and quality of sample on the Net. Proceed with open eyes. Then be sure to write an article about it so you can get additional mileage out of the experience.

As you can imagine, there are a whole range of ways the Net can be used to help traditional direct marketers work smarter, faster, and cheaper. For one, you can get your traditional mailing lists cleaned up online. MAILnet (http://www.listcleanup.com) is one such example (see Figure 8.10). MAILnet offers a wide range of list-processing services directly through its site, using an online upload of ASCII-delimited text database

---

CONTROL PACKAGES

A *control package* is a classic direct-marketing practice. You create multiple offers for the same product. You run them separately and track which offer *pulls* better. Whichever one wins then becomes the control package. This control package is the one you use in the field and try to beat in the future by creating an even better control package for your next gambit.

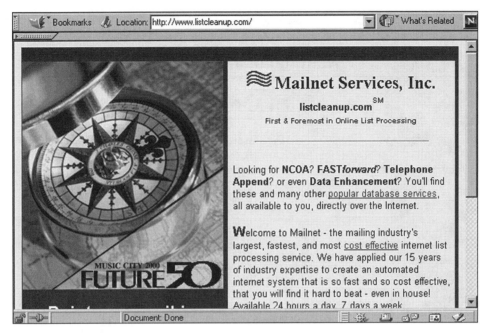

Figure 8.10   Listcleanup.com will take your mailing list to the cleaners!
© Mailnet Services, Inc.

files. List owners can merge/purge, update addresses, and have files CASS (Coding Accuracy Support Standard)-certified to take advantage of postal discounts through bar coding. MAILnet will return updated files in as little as three hours.

Even in the age of email, direct mail (or snail mail) remains a viable and necessary marketing tool. You can explore examples of vintage campaigns, such as a 1941 mail order journal by Paul Muchnick. Who knows? You might get some good ideas for your offline as well as online direct marketing efforts (see Figure 8.11).

Catalogs and the Net

For presenting a wide array of products, there's nothing quite like the Internet, for better and for worse. You can't put enticing, high-resolution pictures in front of visitors without having them spend at least a little bit of time waiting, but you can do other things that print doesn't do as well, providing yet another way online direct marketing can support offline direct marketing efforts.

You can have a dynamic catalog, which deletes an item when you run out of it. This way, no one calls your 800 number (at your expense), only to be told that the item is out of stock. If you have a product that consists of a number of components or peripherals, you can use what's known as a configurator, which adjusts the price of a configuration based on the different components you assemble. Dell Computer uses this tool on its site (http://www.dell.com). A prospective buyer puts in the monitor size, amount of RAM, speed of the processor, and so forth that he or she wants, and the configurator spits out the price of that configuration. If it's too much money for the user, he or she simply tries a smaller monitor, a slower CPU (central processing unit; that is, the com-

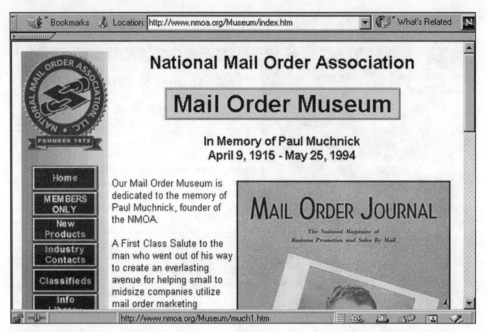

Figure 8.11 For inspiration, visit the Mail Order Museum's collection of classic DM campaigns.

© National Mail Order Association.

puter's engine), or a less-expensive monitor, and the configurator gives the prospect the slimmed-down price for the slimmed-down computer system. That's much cheaper than having a telephone representative take the time on the 800 number to figure out all of the variables to close the sale. For an even more complex example of this, take a look at 3Com's Network Designer at http://www.3com.com, where you can design a whole network for your office this way.

Even if the user doesn't buy the product online, the cataloger has saved a bundle by not having to send the paper catalog to that person, usually. You may have to ship loads of catalogs to potential customers before they even buy, if they ever do at all! When you stop to calculate the cost of sending multiple catalogs to someone who may or may not buy something, you've got incredible savings. Remember, the person who visits your online catalog is already near or in the buying cycle for your product. Why else would he or she be there?

However, many web companies now see a real need to reach their customers where they live. They're taking what they have learned online and closely integrating it with real-world activities to reach customers anytime, anywhere, anyhow. Most etailers with catalogs, such as Bloomingdale's, J. Crew, or Chadwick's, feature easy ordering by catalog stock keeping unit (SKU) right on the home page of their sites. Some etailers are even working backwards, creating mail order catalogs for what were originally pure web-based etailing businesses. One example is Red Envelope, which created a print catalog to expand its market from online to offline.

TIP If you're going to put your catalog online, do your homework first. Go to http://www.buyersindex.com, where you'll find over 19,000 catalog links, and a search engine to help you locate the ones relevant to you. Learn from those who came before you. What are they doing right? What are they doing wrong? What can you do better? I urge you to also look at a few catalogs that aren't in your category. You can probably learn from them and be the first to migrate some of those practices into your business. This can give you an edge over your competitor, at least for a while.

Online Direct Marketing: A Threat or an Opportunity?

It's both. Over time, some percentage of the business that's being handled by traditional DM will migrate to the online world. Historically, new media do partially cannibalize their predecessors. A good example is how computers found a new sales outlet by offering to sell to the consumer right from the magazine or newspaper page. This ultimately took sales away from computer stores. If you feel threatened by this, I suggest you consider the options you have: You can either cannibalize your own market share, or have a competitor do it for you. When this cannibalization will occur depends on the industry you're in, although almost all industries are feeling the impact. Who thought that the Internet would change the automotive industry? Now there are models of cars that are available only over the Web. Consumers can create their custom-built cars online, or they can utilize technology to haggle for the best used car price.

To a direct marketer, in my estimation, the opportunities far outweigh the drawbacks. You can open up new markets, some of which you aren't even aware of yet. You can better serve your existing customer base with loyalty and customer retention programs, including personalization. You can better serve yourself by reducing the costs of DM programs, increasing speed to market of materials and products, and lowering your overhead.

In short, if you're a direct marketer, you're going to be doing business online sooner or later, so it might as well be sooner. Embrace this medium. Marvel at its potential, and know it's limited only by your keen imagination as a direct marketer.

Resource Center

Research

NetGenesis E-Metrics   http://www.netgen.com/emetrics/index.shtml

Do words like abandonment, acquisition, and attrition strike terror into your web marketing soul? The enterprising duo from Net Genesis surveyed web managers from the top sites and discovered that everyone knows that they are sitting on a mountain of invaluable data, but no one has the time or tools to do anything about it. The solution? A handful of free formulas to calculate how well things are going on your site with regard to site navigation, product interest, and promotional success. To analyze your metrics, visit the site and download the white paper.

WebConnect's Site Price Index   http://www.sitepriceindex.com

Sponsored by WebConnect, a leading ad placement service that targets, places, and tracks advertising from impression to click to sale, WebConnect's industry benchmark Site Price Index (SPI) allows Internet advertisers to accurately measure the cost of banner advertisements on the Internet. Updated six times a year, SPI reports the cost of placing banner advertisements on as many as 140 sites, segmented into categories including Children's, Computing, Business Executive, and Women's sites.

Abraham.com   http://www.abraham.com

Marketing and direct mail guru Jay Abraham's site is jam-packed with advice on growing your business using direct mail and Jay's proven marketing techniques. In classic DM style, Mr. Abraham succinctly explains why he does it: "The information we add each month will be worth hundreds, possibly thousands, of dollars if it were to be sold . . .I've been very successful in my advising work. Now I'm moving from selling information and advice to owning pieces of the businesses I counsel. I'm becoming a partner in opportunity venture funds and sophisticated investment groups." Bookmark this one.

Tools

ELetter   http://www.eletter.com

ELetter is the one-stop shop that fully web-automates the entire process of creating, producing, and delivering a mass mailing effort. Simply upload your mailing list (ELetter will verify all addresses), upload your creative, and pay for postage. Voilà! Your mailing is completely produced and distributed. If you need help developing a mailing list, creating a DM letter, or even budgeting for postage, do not despair—ELetter has partners ranging from online mailing list generators to print houses to the USPS.

MAILnet Services   http://www.listcleanup.com

Send your list to the cleaners! MAILnet offers a free CASS (Coding Accuracy Support Standard) cleanup process for first-time users (up to 50,000 addresses). CASS is a process that standardizes addresses and assigns ZIP+4 to ensure the highest number of deliverable addresses possible. Simply upload your ASCII-delimited text database files. List owners can merge/purge, update addresses, and have files CASS-certified to take advantage of postal discounts through bar coding. MAILnet will return updated files in as little as three hours. While there, check out the cost comparison calculators and other tools that will help you make the best use of direct mail list rentals—which are also available at the site via a number of list rental partners, including MyProspects .com and AccuLeads.

Customer Retention

Customers.com   http://www.customers.com

Customers.com is in its fifteenth printing since its publication by Crown Business in November 1998, with more than 225,000 copies currently in print. At this site, author Patricia Seybold and the Patricia Seybold Group extend learnings on how to create positive, interactive relationships with customers that extend their lifetime value and create ROI for your business. Lots of freebies, including a Customers.com handbook, an industry discussion forum, and a bimonthly email newsletter. Treat your customers well—you'll have them for quite some time. You hope.

Ad Networks

SmartAge Media Buyer   http://www.smartage.com

SmartAge is an interesting company that provides Internet-based tools and services to small businesses by aggregating its members to gain bulk-purchasing power. Using the Media Buyer tool, even the smallest of businesses can pool with other SmartAge members and place targeted advertising across major ad networks like DoubleClick and SmartClicks. Other tools, such as AdValues, offer discounted inventory on major sites like Excite and TalkCity. Ongoing results of all campaigns are tracked, analyzed, and managed at the SmartAge Corner Office. The ability to seamlessly purchase banner or email advertising and to track and analyze the results in real time, as you can here, is an idea whose time has come for even the SoHo business owner.

Impower   http://www.impower.com

Developed as a division of American List Counsel, Impower is a team of direct marketing experts, schooled in the established principles of targeted response, who have made the bold move of applying their expertise to the Internet marketing industry. In addition to permission email marketing, Impower has introduced TransAct!—a true transaction-based, direct response Internet network. TransAct! provides advertising space for marketers on network member sites on a cost-per-action model.

Reference

American List Council's Knowledge Center   http://www.amlist.com/ALCWEB/alcweb .nsf/wknowledgehome/home

Many thanks to American List Council, a full-service mailing list and database broker, manager and compiler, for creating an industry resource. The Knowledge Center is a must-bookmark reference for anyone in direct marketing. Here you will find Industry FAQs, a glossary of industry terms, articles and interviews; and if you can't find what you are looking for, click on the Ask the Expert section, email your question, and you'll receive an email response within two business days.

MyProspects   **http://www.myprospects.com**

In addition to providing a very slick service that allows customers to create very specific lists from well-known databases—in seconds—this site offers an excellent tutorial for those new to direct marketing. While many list rental sites leap right into DM-speak, the uninitiated will find the clean, easy-to-follow explanations here to be very helpful. It's as easy as 1-2-3.

Permission Marketing

Responsys   **http://www.responsys.com**

According to Responsys, mass marketing is history. We respect that. Responsys is a premier online permission marketing email management system with capabilities that are leading the industry in terms of campaign management and tracking techniques. One of its greatest strengths is that the philosophy of the solution has clearly been created by some very smart, marketing-oriented brains.

24/7 Mail   **http://www.247media.com/mail/index.html**

With the acquisition of Exactis.com, 24/7 Media has positioned itself as a leading provider of permission-based precision email marketing and communications distribution solutions. End-to-end solutions include: list acquisition and administration, ad sales and serving, subscription management, advanced list maintenance, customer service, 24/7 account management, web-based reporting, rich media formats, a guarantee of uninterrupted service, and more—InformMessaging, for email newsletters; AccountMessaging, for email account communications and confirmations; and TargetMessaging, for email campaigns.

Media

DM News   **http://www.dmnews.com**

DM, DM everywhere. . .from international to interactive, B2B to catalog, list news to postal affairs, this site is the hot bed of direct marketing news. Daily news headlines—whether at the site or via the free email version of *DMNews Daily*—cover the latest DM happenings, a feat that the excellent DM News print publication can only strive to keep up with, albeit in a somewhat more manageable format.

***DIRECT* Magazine**   **http://www.directmag.com**

DIRECT magazine offers DM industry news and analysis, including plenty of columns and advice on everything from list rentals to one-to-one marketing. A member of the MarketingClick Network, owned by Primedia, the site integrates nicely with related companies *Folio* magazine, *Promo* magazine, Bacon's, and more. Be sure to sign up for *DIRECT Newsline*, a daily email newsletter that will deliver the latest site offerings to your email box.

MediaCentral   http://www.mediacentral.com

Cowles New Media's MediaCentral site is an exhaustive guide to direct marketing, advertising and promotion, broadcast, cable, print and interactive media, and media technology. In addition to providing news and commentary, MediaCentral's links to media, agencies, e-zines, critical URLs, and money-making picks bring the best of the Web's media-related sites to your fingertips.

Catalogs

Catalog Age   http://www.catalogagemag.com

Remember when e-commerce was going to make the printed catalog obsolete? How obscure, how very arcane, to send printed pictures on a piece of paper—and through the mail, at that. Catalogs have done very nicely for themselves as direct marketing vehicles for quite some time, and catalog pros do have some insights to share. They do so quite freely at this site, which has done an excellent job of melding print and pixels. In addition to articles and resources that highlight the universal lessons catalog DM can lend, the site focuses on the interactive market with The iMerchant 40 (a list of the top 40 catalog-based e-commerce sites online), numerous white papers and countless articles covering topics such as converting browsers to buyers, and whether or not to add live customer service to your site. With more and more online merchants adding a printed catalog to their marketing efforts, this site should be a frequent visit.

Associations

The Direct Marketing Association   http://www.the-dma.org

Results of a recent Direct Marketing Association (DMA) study found that web marketers considered emails to their existing customers and to site visitors to be one of the most effective promotional tools. The same study (excerpted at the site) indicated that direct and interactive marketing companies are well informed about consumers' privacy concerns, and, therefore, place greater emphasis on targeted email communications. According to the study, *The DMA's State of the Interactive eCommerce Marketing Industry*, 79 percent of web marketers reported using in-house email lists, of which the majority (88 percent) noted that they maintain their email lists in-house. In addition, nearly three-quarters (75 percent) of DMA members and nonmembers revealed that they do not rent permission-based email lists. What else is the DM industry up to? Visit the site of the leading direct marketing industry association to find out.

AIM   http://www.interactivehq.com

AIM, the Association for Interactive Media, is an independent subsidiary of the Direct Marketing Association. In addition to all the great things this association does for our industry, AIM meetings are industry insider schmooze-fests. If you can't make it to their Dinner & A Deal networking events, you can make it to the site. There, you must sign up for one or more of their free weekly email newsletters—*Who's News, Research Update, Internet Politics,* and the *AIM/DMA Scheduler.*

The XXIII John Caples International Awards   http://www/caples.com

John Caples wrote *Tested Advertising Methods* (Prentice Hall, 1998), the bible of the direct response biz. That industry honors him by naming its coveted direct marketing awards program after him. Led by David Moore, President and CEO of 24/7 Media, the John Caples International Awards honors excellence in the creative solution of direct marketing problems.

Mailing List Rental

Marketing Information Network   http://www/miniokc.com

mIn is the direct marketing industry's most comprehensive resource for mailing list, email list, alternative and interactive media rates and information. mIn contains over 30,000 of the most complete direct marketing advertising media rate and data cards. Using the mIn DataCard Title Search, you can search over 30,000 active data card titles. Subscribers to mIn can locate and evaluate highly targeted mail lists, package insert programs, card decks, or sites that accept interactive advertising. It's a leading online list research tool.

Edith Roman Online   http://www.edithroman.com

List broker and manager Edith Roman offers a search engine with access to over 30,000 mailing lists worldwide. And direct marketers won't want to miss Edith Roman's set of freebie calculators: one figures the ROI on a mailing, one helps determine how many pieces to send out, and another computes the benefits of an NCOA (National Change of Address) update on your list.

9

Public Relations, the Internet Way

"The Internet is the golden age of public relations," says veteran public relations man Dan Janal, author of *Dan Janal's Guide to Marketing on the Internet* (John Wiley & Sons, 2000). PR and the Internet have a very basic core value in common: information, both its creation and transmission. With so many media outlets and opinion mongers online, coupled with the technology to quickly transmit a message literally at our fingertips, the Internet can easily be visualized as a blizzard of information exchanges.

In this chapter, you will learn how to leverage your public relations efforts using the Internet. Get ready to explore:

- How to build effective media relationships
- The art of the pitch
- Interaction do's and don'ts
- Targeting your PR program
- Creating news the media can use
- Attention-grabbing copy
- Point-to-point PR
- Online media centers
- Event public relations

- Where and how to post your PR
- How to find out what they're saying about you

What PR Is—and Isn't

To fully leverage the power of public relations, you must first understand exactly what public relations is—and what it is not. As PR industry veteran Jack O'Dwyer, publisher of *O'Dwyer's PR Daily* (see Figure 9.1), explains:

> Thirteen of the fourteen top PR firms have been bought out by advertising agencies. Advertising agencies despise PR. They don't want to deal with PR firms, they want to deal directly with the unwashed, naïve public. They don't want us coming between them and their prey. So ad agencies have come up with a new paradigm for their PR divisions. They've taken a personal relationship and depersonalized it. They've turned PR into a one-way, mass, long-distance, impersonal and cheap system borne on the backs of naïve young college graduates who know nothing about their clients. They've taken away expense accounts and turned PR into sales promotion, email, and telemarketing. An ad agency's number one interest in PR is making money.

Daniel J. Edelman, venerable founder of Edelman Public Relations Worldwide, echoed this sentiment upon his induction into the Arthur Page Hall of Fame. In a speech entitled "Rediscovering the Meaning of Public Relations," Edelman said, "It is,

Figure 9.1 *O'Dwyer's PR Daily* is an essential resource for PR gurus.
© J. R. O'Dwyer Co., Inc., New York.

in my view, an unfortunate accident of business history that public relations firms were acquired by advertising agencies. I wish it had never happened. We're a separate discipline. . .I am aware that to many corporate executives, public relations has become synonymous with publicity—even press agentry, flackery, or more recently 'spin'."

So what exactly is public relations? As the name implies, public relations is about developing and maintaining beneficial, two-way relationships with the people who can put your company in front of the public. In most cases, these people are members of the media. The allure of PR is the chance for a *third-party endorsement* of your product or business in a public medium by a respected journalist, reporter, or editor. What is said about your company in the media has enormous impact. Creating good relationships with the media so that your company can be positively portrayed in a public forum—and so that you can glean information in return from these industry insiders—is what public relations is all about.

Relationships 101: How to Build Relationships with the Media

Weber Shandwick International is one PR firm that believes in building personal relationships with the media (see Figure 9.2). "A press release blast is one component of a PR campaign, but it generally doesn't get picked up," explains Brooke Schulz, Account Executive for several Sharp Electronics product lines, venture capital firm Arts

Figure 9.2 Weber Shandwick International focuses on "building the best reputations in the world."

Alliance, and Internet start-up MaxManager. "It's not personalized. To build a relationship, you must make your news personalized. Keep up with columns, read newspapers and magazines, and if you see something that relates to your client, fire off an email that day to the reporter, along with a press release, and say, 'I read your story, and I don't know if you are aware of my client, but this is something that might be of interest to you.' That's where relationship building starts."

It takes work, but consider the personalization of your company or product news as an investment that will reap lifelong rewards. Schulz continues, "Once you have a relationship with a reporter, they will actually call you when they are doing a story. That doesn't always happen, but if you go about building a relationship properly, if you know the products, if you can get the interview with a key person in a timely manner, then reporters trust you. That's the relationship."

Can business owners establish media relationships without the services of a six-figure PR firm? "Good PR firms are your story broker," Jack O'Dwyer advises. "They weed out all the junk and present good stories, which helps the reporter, who is inundated with information. They act as editor for the reporter. If you go out bragging about yourself, nobody believes you." That is why top-tier PR firms and the power brokers in the PR industry earn such hefty fees. They have spent a lifetime building relationships and building trust, and they have established a track record for delivering timely, insightful, and exclusive information to reporters and analysts.

On the other hand, many members of the media like to hear directly from the source (the business owner) rather than a PR shill. If you can present yourself as a helpful resource to the media, odds are you have a better chance for PR success than the newly employed college graduate whose information sharing boils down to a scripted telemarketing outline. You know your product and your business, you know your industry, you can share exclusive information and insider stories, and you can learn the lure of the newsworthy and the art of the pitch. Let's begin.

Protocols for Interaction with Journalists

Before exploring the *what* of your relationships, let's discuss *how* you will go about developing them. First of all, by actually respecting your potential media contacts, you will immediately distinguish yourself from the masses. Here's a day in the life of Larry Chase.

Put Your PR Life in My Shoes

Before you or someone on your behalf starts contacting the press, think about your target audience—the journalist or editor. I want to share with you what it's like being the Publisher and Executive Editor of *Web Digest For Marketers*.

Every day this office is struck by a blizzard of press releases through every imaginable medium: email, fax, snail mail, Federal Express, even by messenger. And, oh yes, by phone. Many times people call just after sending an email press release to see if I have received it and read it. This just isn't a reasonable expectation. First of all, I have other things to do besides read each individual email the moment I receive it. Secondly, for every site reviewed in WDFM, at least six are rejected. I'd say about one in fifty come from a press release. Why? Most press releases offer my publication and the reader nothing at all, because they are written from the subject's point of view. Some software is coming out of beta, or there's yet another automotive site launched, calling itself the category leader. The trash can is strategically placed under the fax tray for easy access. Any press releases full of hype or self-congratulatory statements find their way into that round file quickly.

The phone rings countless times during the day with chipper voices on the other end who do not bother to announce themselves, but simply ask for Irene. They actually mean Eileen Shulock (Managing Editor of WDFM and coauthor of this book). They have asked for Mr. Shulock, Isaac, and Darlene. I ask them nicely who they are, and they often respond with their first name. I start to lose patience at this point because they are wasting my time. "Sharon," replied one, typically, last week. "Sharon from. . .?" I inquired. "Sharon from Minnesota," she chirped back.

Publishers, editors, and journalists are almost always on deadlines. I find it best, when calling to pitch a story about WDFM to another editor, to ask if they are on deadline and if there is a better time to talk. I give them the angle in 20 seconds, if they want it right away. One can hear the tension drain away when they realize that you understand their predicament and respect their time by being succinct. This resonates with the time branding concept discussed in Chapter 5, "Your Brand Image and the Internet." You get a reputation for using their time well. It's at once courteous, respectful, and focused. People don't like it when you beat around the bush. Get to the point!

Jack O'Dwyer is right. It does seem like PR has turned into telemarketing. Time was, you cultivated relationships with members of the press. Truth be told, that is still what works today.

How would you respond if you had a publication and got cold calls daily where the caller often doesn't know the name of the publication? If they do know, I then ask if they've read it. Invariably they say, "Me? Personally, no." As opposed to their impersonal selves who read WDFM religiously? Since they haven't read WDFM, they don't know it's made up of mercifully short reviews of marketing-oriented sites. So that their pitch asking me to run a long piece on their client or conduct an in-depth interview actually lies well outside the editorial guidelines of the publication.

I pointed out this basic tenant of PR to one such caller. She said she agreed and gave a full-on apology for not having done her research. Her forthright honesty touched me, and we wound up running a review on a different client she had that fit into our editorial nicely.

> **TIP** Entrepreneurs and venture capitalists understand the concept of the "elevator pitch." You have 30 seconds or less to convey your concept, product, or story idea. The same is true when pitching the media. At BPlans.com (http://www.bplans.com), you can use the free MiniPlan online tool to condense your idea into a quick pitch.

Interaction Do's and Don'ts

In general, the more you respect the people who are *the media*, the more likely they are to value your contact. Always:

- Figure out who you want to talk to or email—by name—and get his or her name and role correct.

■ Be clear, whether by phone or by email, about who you are and your subject matter—immediately.

■ Share all forms of contact information—your name, URL, email address, phone number, fax number, beeper, etc.—on all forms of correspondence.

■ Have all the facts at your fingertips.

■ Follow up with information if requested, faster than immediately.

■ Deliver information in the format preferred by the journalist—by email, phone, fax, etc. Determine preferences during your initial exchange.

■ Ask the journalist if you can add him or her to your email list or other method of ongoing correspondence.

■ Learn the golden rule of media contact, as shared by veteran journalist Stacy Albin, who has written for publications from *The New York Times* to Voter.com, "Yes means yes. Everything else means no. If you do not get a yes, dismiss it and move on, or ask why not and move on. But move on."

Even if you have the greatest product or the most newsworthy story on the market, if you are a pain to deal with, your business will not get the attention it deserves. Here's what *not* to do:

■ Do not play cute mind games on the phone to try to reach the person you want to speak with.

■ If you want to be taken seriously, do not create misleading, mysterious, or hyperbolic subject lines or "From" addresses in an email. It's annoying, and it casts doubt upon anything further that you have to say.

■ Unless expressly asked to do so, do not send press releases, software downloads, video clips, etc. as attachments. Not only are we all leery of viruses delivered by attachment, but sending a large file may hold up a reporter who is on deadline. As the file comes in ever so slowly, the journalist or publisher is seething, cursing you out, and vowing never to give you any publicity ever.

■ Do not jeopardize a reporter's deadline or credibility by not following up on a request, or by not delivering an interview or other information as promised.

■ Do not follow up emails or faxes to reporters with phone calls asking if your information has been received. If the reporter wants to talk to you, you will hear from him or her.

■ Do not send a blast email message that lists all 172 of your media contact email addresses in the recipient line. Every single reporter will assume that someone else will cover the story, and all will resent you for sharing their email addresses.

TIP For more tips and perspective from the source, read "The Care and Feeding of the Press," which can be found at http://www.netpress.org/careandfeeding.html. This no-holds-barred article was written by members of the Internet Press Guild to share their frustrations and suggestions with the press-seeking public.

How to Get Noticed In a Cluttered Environment

As the publisher of *Web Digest For Marketers,* I get scores of press releases that simply say in the header: "New Website Launches." So what? Why should I care about this or the blizzard of other similarly positioned pitches I get daily? Getting above this din is key to reaching your audience. The second emphasis should be getting that audience to your site. How do you do this? Focus. Focus on your core audience and the core message to deliver to that audience. I want to see a reason to care about your company right in the header of the email message or press release. Your website, as well as your PR campaign to promote it, has to be focused and deep.

Instead of blasting releases, both online and offline, across the globe, I advise clients to spend their money more adroitly. It's better to identify one audience, thus being a mile deep and a half-inch wide, than the other way around. A tightly targeted program that hits your constituencies again and again over a series of weeks and months will be a better use of your budget, whether you're a small business or a multinational firm. Consider not only your audience, but also the valuable time of those receiving your message. Why should you bother an editor at *Vanity Fair* about a software upgrade? This editor will employ the minimal amount of energy to dispose of your efforts. Put yourself in your receiver's shoes; you'd do the same.

You may say, "It's so effortless to send email to everyone. Why not just let those who are not interested discard the messages that are 'off-topic' for them, and hit the rest who might be interested?" It's a fair question. Some people do just that. If you're on a shoestring budget, that may be all you can do, as targeting does take time and money. However, if you aim well-thought-out messages to the right people, who happen to need such information now or in the near future, you've got a better chance at getting press. In short, give them news they can use. For every one person who reads your unsolicited emailed press release, you might be alienating a hundred, or even a thousand, other people who otherwise may have given your site a good review or favorable press coverage.

Create Value with Newsworthy Ideas

One of the keys to building good relationships with the media and to getting noticed is to create value. One of the best ways to create value is to pitch customized story ideas, rather than sharing general information about the mere existence of your company, product, or service. Your target press list may include news editors, features editors, and technology editors, who will all consider your company or product from different angles. Very few writers will want to devote an entire article to the life and times of your company. (If they do, you have hit the jackpot!) Many stories tend to focus on a concept or trend that highlights one (or usually more) companies or people. Your goal is to be one of those expert opinions or cited products or companies featured within the context of the story. As explained by journalist Stacy Albin, "Freelance writers and staff editors need to constantly come up with ideas for stories. The more ideas you have, the more valuable you are as a contact."

Ellen Ullman, the Technology Editor at *Working Woman* magazine, receives hundreds of press releases a day. Her advice? "Tell me why I should be interested in your information. Don't just send me a press release. Put it in perspective. There's a big difference between pitching a concept or idea and simply reiterating your press release. Make it meaningful. Half of what I get pitched every day are solutions in search of a problem." How would she prefer to receive information? "Just like in the old days, in an ideal world I would have relationships with people who have clients that fit into what I'm looking for," she says. "We would have conversations, and we could talk through things. They would check in with me every few weeks, in an informal relationship. They could call me and say, 'What are you working on? I have something that could help you.'" The lesson? Don't let technology remove personal interaction from your press relationships.

TIP　Become a resource for journalists. Email them information relevant to their beat. Don't overdo it by sending them these snippets too often. Respect your own time as well, and don't spend hours trolling the Web for gifts for them.

That's not to say that press releases and announcement blasts aren't valuable—they do keep your company in the minds of the media, even if they simply scan your message. However, if your goal is to build relationships within a specific industry or niche market, the time spent to customize your information to make it newsworthy and idea-provoking for each specific outlet—and each specific contact—will yield far greater results.

Shaping the News

How do you lure the media to cover your company with a newsworthy twist? Here are some suggestions:

Religiously follow your trade publications and industry-focused media coverage. Know what the media is covering and shape your information to their specific needs.

Anticipate trends. You know your industry—what do you think is an important issue? Pitch it to your reporter contacts. Become a source of news, not a seeker of space.

Ask reporters what stories they are working on, or seek out the editorial calendars of publications. Then shape your stories or even schedule new service or product launches in time for appropriate media coverage.

Use your networking time wisely. Spend time writing your own articles or recapping speaking engagements and sharing that information. It's much easier to catch someone's attention when you say, "It occurred to me last week when I spoke at PC Expo that you might be interested to hear what the audience had to say about this topic."

If you want the media to consider your site as a news source, keep it up to date and stocked with interesting information. Reporters may prefer to surf for information, and your attention to timely updates is crucial.

Place an easily located calendar of events, speaking engagements, or other timely happenings on your site. By giving reporters advance notice of upcoming activities, you may spark an idea—or your information may fit into a story in the works that you don't even know about.

Share your contacts. If you are speaking with a reporter about a certain subject, and can refer someone else, by all means do so. The reporter will do the same for you.

Create an email announcement list and encourage visitors to subscribe to it from your home page. Then send out emails that keep everyone aware of what you are doing.

TIP Want to know what the media is working on? By using EdCals.com (http://www.edcals.com), you can receive editorial calendars and updates by email for over 120,000 publications and other media outlets (see Figure 9.3).

Be Honest and Informative

The art of the pitch, in writing, comes down to a well-written, informative, and alluring press release or other written communication. You always want to help the individual get what he or she wants in the fastest manner possible. Forcing a person to read

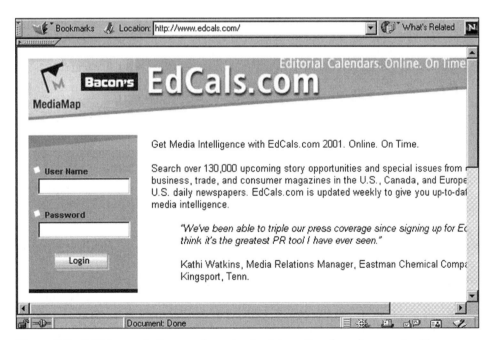

Figure 9.3 EdCals.com is the search engine for international media opportunities.
© 2000–2001 MediaMap, Inc. All rights reserved.

through self-aggrandizing statements and bombast in a press release is tantamount to enticing visitors to your site, only to make them suffer through too many clicks to reach the main attraction. It feels manipulative. So get to the point. "What I would love for PR people to do is just summarize. Give me a paragraph or a couple of sentences about what it is and why it matters," advises Ellen Ullman.

Be very clear about your special benefits from the subject line on down through your entire message. Also be aware of industry jargon, and do try to avoid using it. Reporters receive dozens of communications each day, and every single one promises to be the "Integrated Solution to Multichannel Synergies," or some other equally irritating and nonspecific hype.

So annoying is this tendency for public relations jargon speak that entire sites have been devoted to the subject. The "Decline and Fall of Public Relations" is chronicled by computer publishing newsletter *Softletter* at http://softletter.com/prreport.html. If you would like to review the latest jargon on the media hit list, visit the viciously hilarious site The Buzz Saw, found at http://www.buzzkiller.net/buzzsaw.html, where the world's most annoying buzzwords are displayed, defined and commented upon by the media. If your press release contains a record-setting number of buzzwords, you may find it posted at the site for all to see in the Rogue's Gallery—which is not exactly the kind of press you are seeking.

News Hooks, Cyberbait, and Outrageousness

News hooks make your public relations efforts newsworthy. Assuming you've got your highly targeted audience in mind, get to work on designing something that appeals to them. Previously, the mere introduction of a new site was a news hook in itself. In the early days of the Web, when the GE Plastics catalog went online, it made the NBC Evening News on television.

These days, you need something more dynamic to get the attention of increasingly skeptical journalists and their audiences. Make your message something newsworthy. IBM is a master of the dramatic news story. IBM's Deep Blue chess match was a fantastic news hook. The site was a huge success. Some chess fanatics probably got online for the first time just to get to that page. The fact that IBM put up real-time reporting on the match said a great deal to people who never actually saw the site, but certainly heard about it in traditional media venues offline. This spin-off effect is often greater than the online event itself.

How do you outdo Deep Blue? Try bright red. When DeskDemon.com (a U.K.-based online resource for office management tools and information) was ready to launch its site, the accompanying PR campaign took outrageousness to the limit. The company sent scantily clad men wearing skimpy red shorts and devil's horns to the offices of online and offline magazine journalists to distribute energy drinks and press releases. The predominantly female media executives responded very well to this tactic (an example of knowing your audience!). As a result, the company received nationwide broadcast and print media coverage.

Whatever you conceive of should flow naturally out of your product or service. "If you're going to show a man upside down in an ad to get someone's attention, you'd better make sure you're selling zipper pockets," said Bill Bernbach, the creative genius behind the ad agency Doyle Dane Bernbach. DDB was famous for breaking the rigid rules of advertising in the 1950s, 1960s, and 1970s. When I worked there, I learned to make a left turn, when everyone else in the marketplace was making a right turn. In short, you have to be different to get above the clutter, especially if you're a small company. Even if conducting a mediocre public relations campaign, big companies with big budgets will get attention by sheer repetition. When you're a small company with a small budget, you may only have one exposure, so it had better be good.

> **TIP** Being first may well get you some news attention. Even if it's not in the general press, it may get in the business press, or your trade industry press. As for coming in second? Well, who was the second guy to cross the Atlantic? Don't know? That's the point. Be the first in order to gain recognition and coverage.

Writing for the Internet

Newswire services and journalists use the inverted pyramid style of writing, which puts the most important facts first. All that follows is supporting copy to fill in the details. News stories are written in this way because it is never known where exactly the story will be cut off by an editor, or by a page turn. Advertising copy is written the same way: few words, big ideas. You should write this way as well.

Online, your variable is the attention span of your readers. If you don't dish up the core information right away, you're not apt to keep them. If you do get their attention, they'll stay with you only as long as it suits them. They are in the driver's seat. Therefore, every line of copy you write must either inform, entertain, intrigue, or give some financial or emotional incentive, if you are going to keep their attention.

When I was a wee sprout, I remember reading *Life* magazine ... the whole magazine, including the ads and the copy to those ads. You really got your money's worth back then. There weren't six gazillion websites, 9,000 cable channels, teeming hordes of magazines on the newsstand, email, video games, and other sundry media to compete for our attention. Today you're not just competing with other sites, you're competing with every form of media out there and vice versa. We live in the Information Age.

Put in this perspective, it's not too hard to understand why people aren't bowled over by a press release announcing the latest in revolutionary vaporware, or overjoyed to view a website where the first thing they see is a 30-second soundbite from a CEO that takes two minutes to download. That sounds like a short amount of time, but realize that in two minutes, you can make a pot of coffee, read the front section of a newspaper, or boil an egg. They would probably be pleased, however, to see a CEO's provocative speech (or even better, short quotes) in quick-loading text format, or to read a release directly addressing a flaw in that company's product and how it can be remedied.

A Sample Press Release

The following is an actual press release I wrote several years ago that drew tens of thousands of people to my site. Note that I poked fun at my own site, while delivering useful information. Also, note the keywords at the top, which will be explained in the following section, *Writing Press Releases for the New Ways People Consume Information.*

KEYWORDS: ADVERTISING, INTERNET, MARKETING, MEDIA, WEB, NEWS, ONLINE, ADVERTISER, NET
Contact information:
Larry Chase/President Chase Online Marketing Strategies
847A Second Avenue, Suite 332
New York, NY 10017
email: larry@chaseonline.com
http://www.chaseonline.com
VOICE +01 (212) 876-1096
FAX: +01 (212) 876-1098

Head: Mind-Numbingly Simple Website Helps Marketers Calculate Media Buys.

New York: Larry Chase, Publisher of Web Digest For Marketers at http://www.wdfm.com, introduces WDFM's Online Media Tools. The new area debuts by featuring three calculators that help advertisers figure out their cost per thousand, that common denominator that sets the tone for media negotiations. These CPM calculators are specifically at http://www.wdfm.com/advertising.

"While these tools deliver high value utility, the technology behind them is not at all breakthrough; in fact, it's rather elementary," Chase observed. "That scripting was so basic the programmer, Matt Lederman, pleaded with me not to credit him publicly," Chase concluded.

Larry Chase's Web Digest For Marketers is the original Net marketing publication that is currently read by over 70,000 readers. Since subscriptions were made free six months ago, WDFM's readership grew by thousands virtually overnight. In addition, over 50,000 people now read highlights of WDFM in Net Marketing, a monthly publication sent to all subscribers of Business Marketing magazine, as well as the high-tech crowd reading Ad Age. Chase is fond of saying ". . .more people read Web Digest For Marketers offline than online."

WDFM is a bi-weekly summary of the latest marketing-oriented websites, from Chase Online Marketing Strategies. The analogy that Chase insists on using is that of a three-legged stool, whereby one leg represents Publishing (as in WDFM), the second leg is Consulting in Online Marketing, and the third leg is Seminars. In fact, Mr. Chase will be giving seminars in New York and Holland this Fall on six different aspects of Net Marketing. Chase's favorite seminar of the week is, "How to Sell Your Net Project to Upper Management." Others include examinations of the Net from financial, retail, and sales perspectives.

Chase says, "Employing technology that is easily accessible to millions for practical purposes is the thread that runs through good web marketing sites, each in their respective niche." Chase neatly refers back to his plain vanilla CPM calculators when he says, "These calculators are very handy for people who buy media. Those are the sort of people who would want a free subscription to WDFM. And anyone who subscribes to WDFM is someone we want to know ourselves."

This release worked very well for me for a number of reasons. Note that I was not hyping *Web Digest For Marketers* itself, but rather a few unique (and mind-numbingly simple) tools that were actually helpful to many in my target market. I did not plan to revolutionize the industry, but I did plan to drive traffic to my site by creating something relatively unique and useful. Any mention of my Online Media Tools (and there were many) explained them in the context of my business. No one would have covered WDFM if I'd trumpeted, "Another successful issue published!" Instead, I gave the media something to talk about, in a humorous way.

Writing Press Releases for the New Ways People Consume Information

Notice the keywords at the top of the press release just shown. They are there more for automatic filtering agents than for humans. Many people prefer to have their news delivered to them based upon predefined keywords, using news filters as discussed in Chapter 3, "Mining the Internet for All It's Worth." This includes the media. Journalists may request to receive only those press releases that contain predetermined keywords in the subject line or the first paragraph. Many services also let you rate the importance of each keyword on a scale of 1 to 10. The more often these keywords are used in a press release or news story, the more likely the recipient is to see that story. Additionally, some services rate the importance of these keywords based on how soon they appear in a story or press release. It's for this reason that I put the keywords at the top of a press release and not at the bottom. Be aware of automated filtering and how to cater to it.

Don't be afraid to use unusual words in the header or body of the text that make your copy stand out. Don't be obvious about it, nor should you assume a "go-to-the-dictionary-and-look-it-up attitude," either. I was told later by some reporters and editors that they picked up the story because the whimsical header popped out at them amidst all the other self-serving headlines.

When putting your URL in the message, always start it with "http://" rather than just "www.xyz.com." Your press release is apt to be read in someone's email program. That program is likely to make that URL (one that begins http://) a "live link." This means that the user can actually click on the address within the mail message and be transported into his or her web browser program and over to your site. Whatever you do, do not simply use "yourname.com," without an email or web prefix. People are easily confused about Internet addressing conventions. Many still don't know the difference between an email address and a web address. We have all needed to learn this new language. Help your customers by not confusing them as they learn their way around.

Formula: In all your press releases and PR info sent to the public, use "http://www.xyz.com." for web addresses and myname@xyz.com for email addresses.

TIP For an excellent primer on press release writing, read "The 10 Elements of an Effective Press Release," found at http://netpreneur.org/news/prmachine/pr/default.html. Each of the 10 elements listed links to a more complete explanation, to sample press releases, and to other resources that can help you build an effective release strategy.

Point-to-Point PR

If the content of your PR effort is of sufficient value to your target audience, they may request that you send it to them directly via email, in a method called *point-to-point PR*.

TIP If you put an offer on your site to send information, or update visitors via email, tell them exactly what to expect. Be honest! I recently signed up for an online newsletter that does indeed include information and update notices, but the information is almost always self-serving press releases. I occasionally notice nuggets of useful information buried in the content. However, I seriously doubt people are going to take the time to ferret out the useful from the useless—and the end user is left with a negative feeling about the integrity and merit of that company as a resource.

I worked with a company called Cushman Wakefield, which is one of the largest commercial real estate firms in the United States. In fact, it is so large that it has a department solely devoted to producing quarterly information and trends on commercial real estate values in major markets. An abstract of this information is first released to the *Wall Street Journal*, where it is then published. This is a good example of getting more mileage out of information you already have. Cushman Wakefield further repurposes this data by making charts and trends available on its own site. This information was previously available for a fee, but CW decided to offer it for free, in order to extend its public relations effort. In Chapter 6, "Retail: Setting Up Shop on the Net," you saw how this PR tactic, often referred to as a *loss leader*, can have an impact on building inbound leads.

John Kremer, consultant and author of *1001 Ways to Market Your Book*, offers a weekly email tip sheet full of book marketing ideas (sign up at http://www .bookmarket.com). Within that newsletter, he mentions his other services and products. Thousands of people, myself included, request the newsletter. Kremer is very savvy about the amount of information he puts into each newsletter. He doesn't overdo it. Unfortunately, many senders of such newsletters often go on forever, pontificating and expounding extensively on whatever is on their minds that week. People don't necessarily want that. Less is usually more in the medium of email text.

I was faced with the same choice when I started my newsletter. A number of people advised I do a "Larry Speaks" type publication. I felt a greater number of people would pay more and immediate attention to the coverage of websites, which is something that is timely and newsworthy. This is especially true of the many journalists, always on a deadline, who want a quick scan of what's going on out there with new business-oriented sites. As a consequence, nearly every national magazine, newspaper, and network has someone in its operation who subscribes to *Web Digest For Marketers.* Those journalists, editors, producers, and other media professionals wind up needing quotes on Internet stories at one time or another. When they do, my name will be on the top of their lists, since they see my name and service every week. I'm providing them with a commodity they can well appreciate: well-edited information that might help them do their jobs. This process has to build good relations.

EMAIL BANNERS

Email banners are ads in email newsletters. They have the approximate shape of an ad banner found on the Web. Since many email users prefer to receive text email (as opposed to HTML formatted email content), the space is taken up with a few lines of sales text copy. Ads are often set off from the surrounding content with equal signs or asterisks above and below the sales message.

TIP Less is more. If you're going to send out an email newsletter, keep it short, or at least keep each module short. Remember: You can always point them to your site for the complete story. In fact, it's always a good idea to remind your readers to visit your site for even more valuable information.

For the first year and a half of publishing WDFM, I was very leery of putting commercial messages in the newsletter. I then started working soft-sell copy into the introduction. Nobody said anything, nor did I receive unsubscribe requests because of it. After that, I put in a special offers section. Again, no one minded. In fact, it proved to be successful at drawing qualified leads for those who had offers for my audience. After a while, I put a few email banners in as well. Instead of balking, people responded to the ads themselves. As a consequence, WDFM, originally geared as a PR tool, has converted from a cost center to a profit center for me.

TIP If you advertise in your press relations effort, clearly differentiate between editorial and advertising.

It's important to keep in mind that I built *Web Digest For Marketers* up to a certain point before I introduced commercial content. Whether you're going to promote yourself or another firm, readers are going to have to feel strongly enough about the content not to mind, and even to embrace, the commercial messages. If they do mind, they'll unsubscribe and *flame* you, because they will feel you pulled a *bait-and-switch* on them. Bait-and-switch is a sneaky and self-defeating promotional tool whereby you lure people in by offering them something of value, then switch them off to another offer that they didn't bargain for, of lesser or no value. If you accept money from advertisers and they don't get sufficient results, then you've lost credibility on that side of the quotient as well. Having said all that, if you are providing quality content to a sizable audience, it may be worth your while to test advertising. Take a segment of the mailing list and

FLAMES

Flames are nasty emails sent by someone who really doesn't like what you did. When this happens on email discussion lists or bulletin boards in great numbers, it's referred to as a "flame war." Provoking or participating in these is a pure waste of time, though they can be entertaining to observe.

run a different introduction that's slightly more commercial, and see what kind of reaction you get.

If you moderate a two-way discussion list, it's often understood by those who participate that the moderator (that's you) needs to subsidize the running of the list with sponsors. As moderator, you might filter out unnecessary messages, edit messages, create or help create a FAQ, and help nudge topics back on track as well. Of course, it's important to make your advertising policies clear when you start the list, or to announce new policies if you already have a list going that isn't currently accepting advertisers. I go so far as to ask my readers to make the effort to read and respond to the ads and offers; I tell them that by doing so, it helps WDFM, which in turn helps them.

If you're successful in getting advertisers to underwrite your content, you've effectively gotten out from under the costs of your own email public relations program. In fact, it may very well turn out to be a profit center for you.

> **TIP**   When providing point-to-point email information service, don't overdo it. The point is that there are more than 1 or even 100 ways to get your PR efforts to your target audience. Traditional news outlets used to be the only game in town. Now they're only one of many. With so many people getting their news from so many different sources, public relations opportunities are nearly endless.

Creating a Media Center

With so many public relations opportunities at your disposal, it makes sense to consolidate all of your efforts so that they can be easily accessed from your site. It's amazing how few companies create a media-friendly site. By creating a media center, you make it easy for the media to find relevant information about you, your company, and your products. If you have been reaching out to the media through relationship-building, informative press releases, and potentially a regular email newsletter, do take the final step and bring all of your press relations elements together. Your proactive actions keep you first in mind with the media. As a result, the next time they are on a deadline and writing a story at 3 A.M., they just might visit your site (as you've suggested they do in all of your communications) for a quote, a product shot, or your latest news. Make it easy and informative.

Your media center should be prominently linked from your home page. It should not require registration to access. (Although many companies like to know who is accessing their press information, the registration step will deter a reporter on deadline.) It should also include:

- All essential company contact information
- All essential press contact information (especially if you use a PR firm)
- Executive biographies and photographs
- A downloadable company logo
- Your company history and industry relevance
- Archived press releases, email newsletters, or other point-to-point PR efforts

Figure 9.4 Procter & Gamble's online News section is very media-friendly.

- A calendar of upcoming special events, speaking engagements, product launches, and other activities
- A list of partners, clients, and strategic alliances

Depending upon your business, you may also include full details of product or service offerings, case studies, reports or white papers, publications, books or other materials that provide an overall perspective on your industry, and a downloadable press kit. A great example of a simple yet extraordinarily useful media center worth emulating was created by Procter & Gamble (http://www.pg.com). The P&G News section contains essential information about the company, including a stock ticker, very clearly organized and current press releases, executive bios in PDF format, and even a photo gallery where journalists can download high resolution brand logos suitable for printing (see Figure 9.4).

What Good PR Can Do

Is it worth all this time and effort to truly learn how to work with the media? Absolutely. "We've been blessed with millions and millions and millions of dollars of free advertising, thanks to the media," notes Mark Beckloff, cofounder of Three Dog Bakery, an all-natural dog treat retailer and wholesaler whose success has led to worldwide distribution, a thriving catalog business, television shows, and book deals. For this ten-year-old company, the media rush started when a reporter was passing through Kansas City and saw a mention of the store in a local alternative newspaper. Beckloff, who was working behind the counter, became worried when he saw a stranger in the store taking notes, as their biggest fear was that someone with deep pockets would get inspired and rip off their great idea. Much to his surprise, the man introduced himself as a reporter from the *Wall Street Journal*. "He said to me, 'You have to promise me something,'" Beckloff recalls. "'I want to write a story about you and it will break on Thursday. You can't talk to any reporters before then.'" He agreed, he jokes, "Because it's not like they were lined up down the block." But soon they were. The *Wall Street Journal* story quickly led to an article in *Entrepreneur* magazine, which then led to Oprah Winfrey's show. Since then, the company has been featured in *People* magazine, the *New York Times*, the *LA Times*, the *Boston Globe*, *Forbes*, and hundreds of other publications. Plus they've appeared on the *Today Show*, *Late Night with Conan O'Brien*, CNN, the BBC, PBS, and eighteen 30-minute specials aired on the Food Network.

Needless to say, the company has enjoyed great success as a result of such favorable publicity. As a matter of fact, the cofounders decided to hire a president several years ago to run the company, so that they could focus on building brand awareness. "We have a unique concept," Beckloff explains. "And the media likes that they always talk directly to the founders. No one knows our story better than we do." In addition, having good relationships with reporters and editors means that "we have established open communication with the media." He continues, "A reporter will call us, and we can turn a simple quote request into the main story." Ironically, after years of explaining that there was no big New York PR firm behind it, the company recently hired a big New York PR firm to work with it on the promotion of its third book. "The benefit of a PR firm is that they can do the balancing act for you," Beckloff explains. "If you are going to be on the *Today* show, you're not going to get on *CBS Morning*. The PR firm helps us balance our stories and pitches so that we don't lose opportunities with the bigger press outlets." The company's story is aptly noted on the site, where Three Dog Bakery credits word-of-mouth and the press as being "man's best friend" (see Figure 9.5).

Figure 9.5   Three Dog Bakery's international press coverage is a PR success story.

Event Public Relations

Of course, not all your PR efforts need to be information-based. You can hold an online event and publicize that fact.

Very often, web chats and other events are staged so that statements can be made and then reported on in press releases. A few dozen or hundred people may have seen or heard the actual event, yet millions may wind up reading about it in a newspaper, hearing about it on a TV news broadcast, or seeing it in some online venue. This is a very clever tactic.

TIP When staging an online event for press purposes, you'll want to notify search engines. Most search engines will pay more attention to your event if the web address is configured in a certain way. For instance, search engines will pay less attention to a site whose address is http://www.webgrrls.com/ events/jan/index.html, and pay more attention to http://event.webgrrls.com. This extra addition of the Webgrrls domain name is called a *subdomain name*. Setting up a subdomain name requires techie skills, but may well be worth it in the long run. You may consider setting up one subdomain name and holding different timely events there, rather than setting up a new name for every event.

Webgrrls, an international organization for women in new media, holds a yearly event that garners enormous press interest. The event, International Webgrrls Day, is held on October 22 by dozens of chapters around the world. The chapters hook up using different forms of technology as they become available. "At first we all used IRC chat at designated times so that chapters could talk to one another," explains coauthor Eileen Shulock, former director of the international organization and volunteer director of the New York City chapter. "Then we graduated to CUseeMe and had dozens of chapters waving at one another from events around the world. We've used webcasts, and hope to incorporate video conferencing into our next event." The unique nature of the event—uniting women in new media around the world using the latest in Internet technology—is a press magnet.

Kodak has implemented a unique way of using the Web to share information with the press. Kodak has actually held press briefings and conferences on its site. This is similar to what you would see on television, and is cost-effective for both the company and the publisher alike. This practice of online press events will become more wide-spread as conferencing technology becomes more ubiquitous in our society and more available for easy use on the Web.

Time and cost savings will be the main force to propel this practice into more common usage. Think about it: Journalists are always on a deadline. It's a pretty attractive proposition to get instant, firsthand information without having to travel across the country or across town. They won't even have to leave their own desks! In addition, journalists will also have the transcript available in text format, which makes it much easier to cut and paste quotes, rather than transcribing them. This efficient use of time and resources will be a boon to trade journalists, who are already overwhelmed with press releases and conferences, as well as researching various products for their respective industries.

Chrysler uses the Net in an interesting way for press relations as well. It has a secured, restricted area to distribute high-resolution photographs of its upcoming models. Again, this saves the journalist and his or her publication much time in not having to send the pictures via overnight carrier, as well as being able to put those digital images directly into the publishing production line. Chrysler doesn't want to make these pictures available to the general public because they might be *embargoed* and not available to the public at the time they're made available to the press. Embargoed is a news term that tells the media outlet not to release a story until the specified time. This is often used with the release of government statistics, such as inflation and unemployment figures. The wire services deliver these stories early so local news operations can incorporate the story into newscasts, which are then broadcast at or after the release time.

Where and How to Post Your PR

Everyone has his or her own ideas about how and where to post public relations announcements and press releases. Though some of it may be hype, there are a few gems of information learned over the years that you can put to use.

What's New and Search Engines

You have some options as to how to go about distributing your PR efforts. One is posting to What's New sites and search engines. For my money, there are about 10 that are worth your time and a few hundred more that are going to have less of a payoff. You can also use a one-size-fits-all posting engine that will do it for you automatically. In this category, I recommend SubmitIt! (http://www.submit-it.com), which is as good as any and better than most. It's great if you're on a limited budget. The downside is that each search engine you post to is a little different. Some ask for 25-word descriptions, while others let you go up to 50 words and beyond. You have to use the lowest common denominator approach on the keywords and categories chosen. Some search engines have 6 categories, while others have 8 or 10. Plus, the search engines are always changing their submission requirements. In other words, it's a moving target. Other than SubmitIt!, you can look at other services that do similar things (some free, some not) at Yahoo!'s list of posting engines at http://dir.yahoo.com/Computers_and_Internet/Internet/World_Wide_Web/Site_Announcement_and_Promotion/Search_Engine_Placement_Improvement/. To learn more about effective search engine submissions, see Chapter 7, "Online Events, Promotions, and Attractions."

Human Posting

Another option is using human posters. If you have the budget, nothing beats a human, because humans can make intuitive decisions. A robot can't. It's as simple as that. Eric Ward's NetPOST (http://www.netpost.com) is the most established and

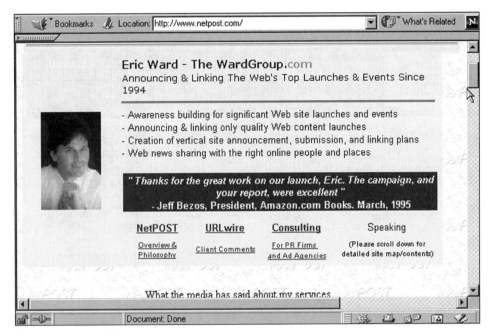

Figure 9.6 NetPOST is manned by a human, not a robot.

respected in this field, in my opinion (see Figure 9.6). You might also train someone in-house at your business to do this on a regular basis, if you have the manpower to do so. TimeWarner found it more cost-effective to have me train its people to submit updates to the search engines than to pay me month by month to do it for them.

TIP Visit NetPOST's site and you'll find detailed articles on when to use robots for posting and when to use humans.

Usenet Newsgroups, Bulletin Boards, and Online Lists

Posting your URL to Usenet newsgroups, online bulletin boards, or discussion lists, such as those hosted by Topica at (http://www.topica.com) (see Figure 9.7), is yet another option. This type of posting must be done by a human. The appropriate discussion groups or lists must be located, monitored, and judged as to whether it is sensible to post an announcement there. Things to look for in any discussion list or bulletin board are:

- How many members are on the list?
- How active is the list?
- Do other firms post useful messages to the group?
- How long are those messages?

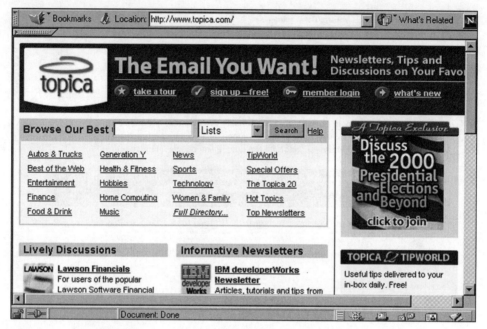

Figure 9.7   Topica hosts tens of thousands of email discussion lists.

■ Are they purely informational, or is there some commercial flavor to them?

■ Look for the Frequently Asked Questions (FAQ) file associated with the news-group; this will often answer questions you have on the subject. Do not post blind questions to the group before you read its FAQ first.

■ Who moderates the group, and what is their email address (in case you want to ask questions after reviewing the FAQ)?

■ How often can you reasonably post without being intrusive?

It's important to note that email lists come in two varieties: one-way and two-way lists. Both show up in your email box. A one-way mailing list goes from one to many. Two-way lists are discussion lists comprised of members who reply to each other in a rolling discussion over time. If the topic is consistently close to your information, I suggest you join and participate in the list. See how the conversation is flowing before barging into a discussion right off. Make an effort to contribute valuable information to the discussion once you have introduced yourself, and your PR information, as well. There's more than one reason to join a discussion list. You'll probably learn something from other constituents of this list. It's also an excellent place to network. Who knows, your next job or client may come from a contact on that list! To find email lists that are suited to your topics, visit EzineCentral's database at http://www.ezinecentral.com (see Figure 9.8). Then contact each zine's manager/editor/publisher to see what you need to do in order to submit your press release.

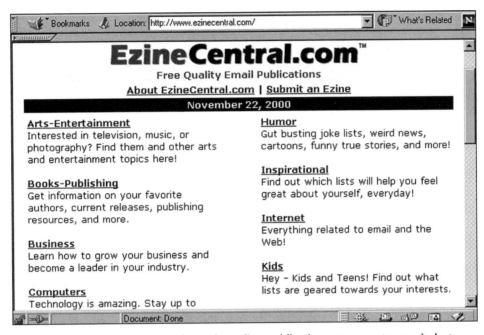

Figure 9.8 Look at EzineCentral.com for online publications germane to your industry. EzineCentral.com is a trademark of List-Universe.com Corporation.

Targeting the Media

There are two paths to travel when specifically targeting members of the press. I suggest you take them both: general targeting through press release distribution services, and the creation of your own targeted press list.

Two offline circuits to distribute your press releases are the traditional PR circuits, such as PR Newswire and Business Wire. It is just as important (and sometimes more so) to use these circuits, especially with all the media attention the Web now garners, in order to be seen and noticed.

TIP Instead of buying a national circuit for $500 or so, save money by buying a city circuit, which costs around $160 for New York City at the time of writing. Smaller cities usually cost less. This is a nifty technique to stretch your budget.

The other option is online circuits. For $250 at the time of writing, Internet News Bureau (http://www.newsbureau.com) will distribute your press release to over 2,300 sources (see Figure 9.9). It limits the number of press releases it sends out, so that journalists and editors aren't inundated with releases from the same source, thus diluting the impact of each release. I use several approaches to target the media: Eric Ward's company for certain high-end placements, Internet News Bureau to cover the lion's share of online news efforts, the offline PR Newswire to make sure I'm getting the traditional press, and my own personal media relationships cultivated over the years.

Figure 9.9 Internet News Bureau is an efficient and inexpensive way to distribute press releases online.

There are many other ways to target and build your media list.

Press Flash (http://www.pressflash.com). As an online distributor of real-world press releases, the company will send your media communication to the personal fax machines of more than 1,100 journalists who cover Internet-related stories. All releases are personally addressed to the editor by name.

IMEDIAFAX (http://www.imediafax.com). This site enables you to create your own press list from its impressive database of journalists, and then you can fax your release only to those journalists who fit your criteria. Prices start at as little as 25 cents a fax (see Figure 9.10).

MediaMap (http://www.mediamap.com). Provides information about publications and the journalists who write for and edit them to PR professionals, which helps them to target their pitches more effectively. Previously out of the budget for many, MediaMap now offers a web-based directory that can be accessed for approximately $200/month at the time of writing.

Newstream.com (http://www.newstream.com). Designed for the twenty-first century newsroom, this site delivers multimedia news to journalists as provided by corporations and PR agencies. The service incorporates text press releases plus photos, graphics, video, and/or audio intended for media publication.

MediaInfo (http://www.mediainfo.com). MediaInfo offers an extensive set of media links including associations, city guides, magazines, newspapers, radio

Figure 9.10   IMEDIAFAX is an Internet-to-media fax news distribution service.

and television stations, syndicates, and news services, for those who would like to create their own media list.

MediaFinder (http://www.mediafinder.com). MediaFinder offers a comprehensive database of more than 100,000 North American print media searchable by type, subject, area, frequency, and circulation.

Trolling the Net for Information about Your Own Company

A good PR effort requires that you not only send out information, but also take in information about your company. After all, people may be talking about you out there, as discussed in Chapter 3, "Mining the Internet for All It's Worth." The old adage of "I don't care what they say as long as they spell my name right" isn't at all true on the Net. Remember the Intel debacle surrounding the computational errors of its then newly released Pentium processor? If Intel had been monitoring the Net more closely, it could have contained the problem and controlled it. However, the longer Intel stayed quiet about it, the more people talked. This made the situation increasingly worse, until it made headline news, even though the original problem was a small one that would have affected few people.

Where should you start looking? The Usenet newsgroups are a good place to start, and for that purpose I recommend Deja and Langenberg.com.

Deja has a comprehensive, searchable collection of Usenet group discussions at http://www.deja.com/=km/usenet. Usenet groups are organized by topic, by city, by industry, and so on; they are almost infinite in number. Deja doesn't have all groups, but it has an incredible collection. I also recommend Langenberg.com (http://www .newsgroups.langenberg.com), where you can search multiple newsgroups, discussion lists, and technical forums. Be careful to narrow your search! There could be literally thousands of mentions in all those newsgroups over the last few years (and some newsgroups have been archived for more than a decade). By searching for myself, I once found out that Larry Chase was the name of an evil character on Dark Shadows! I also found seven other real Larry Chases on the Net. As a result, I immediately registered the domain larrychase.com.

You can also find out what people think about your company, products, and services from public opinion and rating sites such as Epinions.com, at http://www .epinions.com (see Figure 9.11), where real customers are invited to post real opinions. Don't be surprised at what you might find! Disgruntled consumer groups have even formed anti-PR sites to complain about particular firms with whom they have issues. Wal-Mart, Ford, and a number of regional telecommunications companies have been targeted by such sites. History is repeating itself here. Back in the 1960s, hippies and yippies learned how to manipulate the media in order to get press attention for their cause by staging events that the cameras would record and later broadcast. This is the twenty-first-century version of that, Internet style.

Here again, the press picks up on the mouse that roared by covering the controversies and fanning the flames, which turns some poor corporate PR person's job into a nightmare. What do you do? Sometimes nothing. Maybe it will go away, if the complaints are unwarranted. But if the claims have validity, you should consider

Figure 9.11 Find out what the world thinks about you at Epinions.com.

approaching the people responsible for the complaints and opening up a dialog. This has worked in a number of situations, and has actually turned into good PR for some firms, showing that they will indeed listen.

Too busy to keep tabs on your company's online public opinion rating? There are also services that will troll for you on a monthly retainer. You can think of these services as electronic clipping services. They're very effective, since it's their core business.

One such service is eWatch (http://www.ewatch.com). It will monitor top web content sites, Usenet discussion groups, Internet newsgroups, and discussion lists, and even online services such as CompuServe or America Online's forums to let you know when the grapevine is buzzing. All you do is provide keywords and, in the case of web watching, the URLs you want monitored. Each day, eWatch will send you a summary report via email or fax of the day's gossip, news, and site changes. The nice thing about the eWatch service is that, unlike other web alerts, it allows you to specify items, words, or sections of a site to monitor for change, so you don't waste your time rushing back to a site to see that the only change is the background color. At the time of writing, a yearly subscription to an individual coverage category is $3,600, while a year of complete monitoring costs $16,200.

What have we learned? In this many-to-many medium, companies large and small need to devise a PR program that is unique, informative, frequent, and focused, as well as responsive, if they are to cut through the clutter in order to leave a positive, lasting impression upon a highly defined target audience. Public relations professionals are having a field day on the Internet because PR campaigns share something vital in common with the Internet: information. Learn to leverage the Internet to share your information, and the world is yours.

Resource Center

Pillars of PR

NetPOST   http://www.netpost.com

Meet industry veteran Eric Ward, the online PR guy who helped launch Amazon.com. He is one of the foremost experts on promoting site launches and web events. His service, URLWire, is one of the original human-delivered press release sources that posts email and web-based alerts announcing only the higher end new web launches, events, and happenings. Eric's NetPOST service offers content-driven vertical URL submissions and link-popularity improvement based on a site's subject, features, mission, and goals. At the site, you'll also find links to interviews and coverage of Eric's services in the press.

O'Dwyer's PR Daily   http://www.odwyerpr.com

J.R. O'Dwyer is an industry icon. His print *Directory of PR Firms* is now in its thirty-first edition, so the man knows the ins and outs of the industry. His PR Daily site has excellent content, including listings for PR books, upcoming events, job listings, 1,122 PR services, 550 PR firms, and more. Check out the current articles and archives for more.

Janal.com   http://www.janal.com

What do Napster, the San Francisco Giants, and the Beijing Pandas have in common? They've all inspired Dan Janal to write on Internet marketing ... and he has eight books to prove it. Originally one of the PR team members that launched America Online more than 18 years ago, Dan Janal speaks professionally and is also a regular contributor to eFuse.com, NetObjects's friendly place to learn how to build and market a better site. Dan's site has over 26 PR and marketing articles that offer even the most seasoned PR professional food for thought. Eat 'em up.

CompuServe's PR & Marketing Forum   http://forums.compuserve.com

This "old as the Web itself" PR & Marketing special interest group, originally available only on CompuServe, is now available on the Web for free. The forum is filled with ideas, opinion, controversy, and many PR pros willing to share their expertise. It's a wonderful resource for both information and experts in the field.

PR Etiquette

The Care and Feeding of the Press   http://www.netpress.org/careandfeeding.html

Ms. Manners meets PR. Like it or not, PR professionals and the press need each other. Discover the journalists' side of the story through this tutorial by the Internet Press Guild on how to take care of Internet journalists. Compiled by IPG's Esther Schindler "to save our sanity" and to "enhance our ability to work together," you'll learn to never send unsolicited email attachments to a journalist, and that if you must use PowerPoint to get across your message, limit it to five slides. And for heaven's sake, never follow up an email to a reporter with a phone call asking if she received the email. Amen.

Public Relations Tips and Tricks   http://www.tipsandtricks.com

Before you step out in front of the press, learn how to make all the right moves. Nels Henderson, a public relations consultant, offers PR tips and tricks at his site, including PR 101, advice on damage control, press conferences, and even what to wear for a press interview.

PR Copywriting

The Buzz Saw   http://www.buzzkiller.net/buzzsaw.html

Tired of all the e-whatever buzzwords surrounding the "new economy"? If so—and if you're a PR professional with high-tech clients—visit this site and learn how not to write your next press release. You'll find a full listing of tired, empty buzzwords and phrases that we can all do without, along with a request to help kill some "buzz larvae" such as "vortal" and "dot-conomy" before they get dangerous. Also check out the PR

Technique 101 section, wherein they "hang the foul hides of the worst of a bad lot." Not for the meek or humor-impaired.

The Slot   http://www.theslot.com

What is a "slot"? "In the old days, most copy desks were horseshoe-shaped. Rank-and-file editors—'rim men'—sat around the outside, while the guy in charge sat in the 'slot' so he could reach all the rim guys when he needed to hand out stories to work on." So states Bill Walsh, Business Desk Copy Chief at the *Washington Post* and author of *Lapsing into a Comma*, who is reaching out online with a spot for copy editors. Solve one mystery of life by clicking the "What Exactly Is a Copy Editor?" and check out the Sharp Points section with lots of advice on "how to write in da English."

The 10 Elements of an Effective Press Release   http://netpreneur.org/news/prmachine/
pr/default.html

Just when you think you have it straight, there's more advice on how to build a press release that gets noticed. In this case, it's good advice. Krista L. Mohr, President of MarketInk, suggests ways to capture the reader's attention with a headline, the importance of including a customer and/or analyst quote if possible in your release, and the most up-to-date press release formatting rules. Check it out.

EditPros   http://www.editpros.com

How well are you communicating? Take the Great Grammar Quiz to find out. If you fail, EditPros may be your answer. EditPros will prepare effective written communications for you to supplement your own efforts. Browse the online newsletter and tutorial for writing tips and techniques, or simply access the business news email directory of magazines and newspapers to do some communicating of your own.

PR Research

MediaCentral   http://www.mediacentral.com

Chock full of news, features, and commentary for media and marketing professionals, MediaCentral also has 19 categories of free PR how-to articles, including incentive programs and Customer Relationship Management (CRM). Have a news tip or company announcement relating to the media industry? Submit it free. You'll also find a link to MarketingClick, MediaCentral's sister site, where you can submit items of interest to marketing professionals.

Delahaye Medialink   http://delahaye.com

Companies seeking to improve their reputations, plan and evaluate their communications programs, and sharpen their competitive edge can learn from Delahaye Medialink's 36 years of experience. The site's most interesting feature is *The Gauge*, the online newsletter with loads of insight into worldwide communications research. You'll find articles such as "Internet Attitudes and Usage" (more online Americans trust news on the Web than that in newspapers), and some on how to roll out a measurement program, and a full archive of articles.

Press Release Services

PRWeb   http://www.prweb.com

This is a free press release distribution service that distributes your news through the Web and email. Add and edit your release online, and await the thumbs-up of PRWeb's editorial staff, who approve all press releases to cut down on the spam monster. You can also search the PR Web Press Release Database, which contains thousands of business press releases that have been released online within the past 90 days, organized by industry.

Internet News Bureau   http://www.newsbureau.com

Another of the industry pillars of release writing and distribution, Internet News Bureau offers services for both businesses and journalists. Order your press release services online so that as many as 4,500 journalists will know you and yours exist. Journalists can sign up to receive web-related news tips via the Global List, or join one of INB's Targeted Modules to receive news tips on a specific topic or industry. You'll also find media relations tips, info on how to monitor media coverage yourself, and more.

IMEDIAFAX   http://www.imediafax.com

A slick Internet-to-media fax news distribution service, IMEDIAFAX allows you to customize your own target lists and fax press releases anywhere in the world 24 hours a day for 25 cents a page. Select from over 11,000 magazines, 1,500 daily newspapers, 5,700 weekly newspapers, 400 news services and syndicates, 1,300 broadcast TV stations, 1,800 broadcast TV shows, 1,200 cable TV stations, 1,050 cable TV shows, 6,200 AM and FM radio stations, and more than 2,700 radio talk shows.

PRNewsWire   http://www.prnewswire.com

If you're a journalist looking for immediate news from corporations worldwide concerning media, business, the financial community and the individual investor, check out PRNewsWire. Since the news works both ways, PR professionals can also take advantage of PRNewsWire's cutting-edge wire, fax, satellite, and Internet network, capable of pinpoint or mass distribution of news releases and photos to the media, financial community, and consumers worldwide.

Business Wire   http://www.bizwire.com

Want to distribute your news with photos and graphics? Get Business Wire on the line. On the Web since 1995, this company has honed its Smart News Release technology to allow members to embed photos, graphics, logos, and spreadsheets into text news releases—for not much more than what you'd be charged for distributing a plain text press release. We've had great success with this service, experiencing improved click-through rates and lots more attention. Extra bonus: it also includes hyperlinks to your visuals from the thousands of other services that carry Business Wire news. Each release is posted to BizWire.com and is searchable for two years.

PR Contacts

InternetWeek Online   http://www.internetwk
                                          .com/PR/default.html

InternetWeek wants to make it easy for the PR professional to get his/her company/
client heard above the roar. The Rules of Engagement site spells out in very certain
terms how to pitch reporters and editors so your news gets through the door. Want to
raise your profile among the IW editorial staff? Send only news on how companies are
transforming their business through Internet technologies; 215,000 IT and business
managers read *InternetWeek,* and the IW editors are keen on gleaning only the info that
their readership seeks. Click the Beat link toward the top of the page for the rundown
of who covers which technology beat. And remember to keep those emails short!

EdCals.com   http://www.edcals.com

EdCals.com, from MediaMap and Bacon's, is a subscription-based service that offers
editorial calendars for more than 120,000 upcoming stories and special issues from
nearly every leading U.S. magazine and newspaper (both print and web editions).
Search thousands of continuously updated editorial calendars for results that include
editor contact, publication profile, theme issues, special inserts, closing dates, and
complete contact info. We took EdCals for a free test drive. These people are serious.
Where else can you drill down and find the editorial calendar to such publications as
Cheese Market News? Take it for a spin yourself.

AJR NewsLink   http://ajr.newslink.org

AJR NewsLink, a joint venture between *American Journalism Review* magazine and
NewsLink Associates, is one of the Web's most comprehensive news resources. Visit to
try out nearly 20,000 free media links, articles, online columns, and special reports.
You'll also find *American Journalism Review* magazine online. It has a collection of most-
linked-to news sites in the United States by type, which includes newspapers, magazines, radio, and TV link information.

MediaMap   http://www.mediamap.com

Best known for its premier collection of media profiles and public relations software,
MediaMap connects public relations and media professionals with accurate, timely
information. Interested in industry gossip? Read the *Liquid Media* newsletter, with
quotes, notes, and news from industry insiders, such as "Anchor Gumble makes a
fumble." You'll also find the *Web PR* weekly newsletter, which will keep you up-to-
date with the latest in online media. Cruise the resource links, PR white papers, job listings, and trade show info.

PR Resources

Publicity.com   http://www.publicity.com

Publicity in all its forms is the focus of this online magazine, which doubles as a showcase for Media Relations, Inc., a Minneapolis-based public relations firm. You'll find

plenty here on how to get publicity and how to use it, plus success stories, insider tips, industry news, special Internet information, and how to avoid (or handle) public relations disasters. There's something to be said for learning from professionals who are willing to share their unique insights.

Public Relations Society of America (PRSA)   http://www.prsa.org

PRSA does a nice job of serving its members and informing the public at this site. Publicly accessible resources such as PRSA's *Tactics* newsletter provide visitors with good information about developing and managing media campaigns. A searchable member résumé database allows visitors to mine the organization for potential employees. Those on the other side of the employment equation may want to take a look at *Tactics*'s classified advertising section for career opportunities. Drilling further into the site yields a wealth of information in specific areas of practice, such as technology, environment, association work, and others. And, knowing that all this fabulous information has motivated you to join, PRSA has conveniently provided an online membership application form.

Essential Tips for Surviving the Dot-Com Fallout

Presumably, you are about to close this book. What have you learned? What will you remember a week from now and a year from now? What follows are 13 tips to keep in mind at all times. They will serve you well. You may even want to rip this page out and tape it to the wall as a constant reminder of how to stay buoyant in these choppy, exciting waters known as the Internet.

Exponential effect. Try to do everything for at least two reasons. My free email newsletter, *Web Digest For Marketers* (http://wdfm.com), is a branding tool, is syndicated, generates revenue from advertising, and provides information to its audience.

Contiguous cannibalism. One man's core business is another's loss leader. Don't let it happen to you. See if you should employ something yourself.

Don't be a mile wide and a half-inch deep. Focus on a few complementary areas. Spread your risk, but not too far; otherwise, your efforts become too diffused.

Be a category creeper. Look for interesting practices from categories next to and far afield of your industry. Be the first to migrate them into your category.

Borrow your customer's shoes. Live in them all the time, not just in front of the screen when surfing your site. Would you click on your own banners? Your link in the search engines? Why, or why not?

Complementary lines of business. Have a few lines of business that complement each other. For example, I have my publishing line of business by way of this book and my *Web Digest For Marketers* (WDFM) email newsletter that bring business to my consulting and seminar lines of business. Eileen's contributions as author and managing editor of WDFM bring an additional level of expertise to her role as an online marketing and e-commerce strategist. It also works the other way around.

Be your own worst critic. Not only with your interface, but with your Net marketing plans, as well as everything else. Try to punch holes in your own arguments, suspicions, and strategies. If they don't spring leaks, you've got a better chance at making it.

Creative cognition. The challenge today is in making the new technology do your bidding, or twisting it in an unintended way to suit your own purposes. Instead of rigidly saying, "Here's the product, where is the marketing and selling channel?" stay open to, "Here's an interesting channel that already exists. What do I have that can easily be configured for this valuable channel already in place?"

You will be seen as Net savvy, which will only add to the luster of your brand, be it personal or company-wide.

Market to yourself. Be aware of your own thoughts and feelings while surfing the Net. Apply those firsthand impressions when marketing to others. If you don't like home pages that take 30 seconds to come in, it's a good bet that your target audience won't either. The term for this is "Pulse Universe." Take your own pulse and imagine that the rest of humanity might not be that terribly different.

Don't market to yourself. Know when to stop talking to yourself. Most websites make perfect sense to those inside the goldfish bowl known as your company, while outsiders look in and wonder exactly what it is you are trying to communicate. Watch closely the reactions of your target audience as they surf your site. See if they get what you are trying to say. If not, it's time to redesign. Note what search phrases they use when using search engines. They just might be different from what you use or imagine.

Redefine problems as opportunities. Look for solutions to problems you didn't know you had.

Keep your crap detectors set on high. My father used to say, "Believe nothing of what you hear and about half of what you see and you should be okay." That's about right when it comes to filtering through all of the smoke and mirrors in the PR wars of the Internet. We've all seen deals come together and fly apart literally overnight.

Look for the business model. When you look at someone's business model or website, ask yourself how these people make money. If the answer isn't obvious, beware.

Afterword

"The dance instructor saves the best steps for himself." My mother, granddaughter to Edmund Gerson, to whom Thomas Edison wrote the letter pictured in the front of this book, told me this when I was but a mere tyke. Coauthor Eileen Shulock and I did not take her advice with regard to the content of this book. We held nothing back when sharing the best of what we know. But then, why should we? When it comes to the Internet, there are new dance steps to be learned and mastered every day. All the early adopters, including your coauthors, gravitated to the Internet early on, using the awe of learning as the driving force.

Our advice to you is to approach and embrace the Net with that same keen sense of awe, knowing that at every turn you will learn more about your relationship to the Internet. To us, that is one exciting prospect. We sincerely hope you share and harness that enthusiasm. Each person's relationship to the Internet, each company's relationship to the Internet, is special and different from that of any other individual or enterprise. It is the ultimate in mass customization. That is why small and large companies alike ask me to help them define their relationship to the Internet. There is no one finite definition of that relationship for any company, but rather a series of options. Fleshing out those options, along with their trade-offs, is what I do for a living when not writing books or columns, or conducting seminars. I invite you to visit my site (http://LarryChase.com) to learn more about what my firm does. If you have questions thereafter, get in touch either by email or by phone.

Larry Chase
Email: me@larrychase.com
Phone: 212-876-1096

Eileen Shulock
Email: eileens@wdfm.com

Index

3